AIM FOR THE HEART

AIM FOR THE HEART

THE FILMS OF
CLINT EASTWOOD

Howard Hughes

I.B.TAURIS

LONDON · NEW YORK

Reprinted in 2010 by I.B.Tauris & Co Ltd
6 Salem Road, London W2 4BU
175 Fifth Avenue, New York NY 10010
www.ibtauris.com

Distributed in the United States and Canada Exclusively by Palgrave Macmillan
175 Fifth Avenue, New York NY 10010

First Published in 2009 by I.B.Tauris & Co Ltd
Copyright © 2009 Howard Hughes

ISBN: 978 1 84511 902 7

A full CIP record for this book is available from the British Library
A full CIP record is available from the Library of Congress

Library of Congress Catalog Card Number: available

Printed and bound in India by Replika Press Pvt. Ltd.

For Clara

CONTENTS

List of Figures ix

Preface: Aim for the Art xiii

Acknowledgements xvii

Universal Casting: The Early Films xix

Ridin' Easy: Rawhide xxv

Part One: The Westerns

1. *A Fistful of Dollars* (1964) 3
2. *For a Few Dollars More* (1965) 8
3. *The Good, the Bad and the Ugly* (1966) 10
4. *Hang 'Em High* (1968) 16
5. *Two Mules for Sister Sara* (1970) 21
6. *Joe Kidd* (1972) 25
7. *High Plains Drifter* (1973) 27
8. *The Outlaw Josey Wales* (1976) 31
9. *Pale Rider* (1985) 35
10. *Unforgiven* (1992) 38

Part Two: The Cops

1. *Coogan's Bluff* (1968) 45
2. *Dirty Harry* (1971) 49
3. *Magnum Force* (1973) 53
4. *The Enforcer* (1976) 58
5. *The Gauntlet* (1977) 62
6. *Sudden Impact* (1983) 65
7. *Tightrope* (1984) 69
8. *City Heat* (1984) 72
9. *The Dead Pool* (1988) 75
10. *The Rookie* (1990) 78
11. *In the Line of Fire* (1993) 79
12. *A Perfect World* (1993) 83

Part Three: The Lovers

1. *The Witches* (1967) 89
2. *Paint Your Wagon* (1969) 91
3. *The Beguiled* (1971) 95
4. *Play Misty for Me* (1971) 101

5.   *Breezy* (1973)   105
6.   *The Bridges of Madison County* (1995)   108

Part Four: The Comedies

1.   *Every Which Way But Loose* (1978)   117
2.   *Bronco Billy* (1980)   121
3.   *Any Which Way You Can* (1980)   125
4.   *Pink Cadillac* (1989)   129

Part Five: The Dramas

1.   *Honkytonk Man* (1982)   135
2.   *Bird* (1988)   138
3.   *White Hunter Black Heart* (1990)   143
4.   *Midnight in the Garden of Good and Evil* (1997)   147
5.   *Space Cowboys* (2000)   149
6.   *Mystic River* (2003)   152
7.   *Million Dollar Baby* (2004)   155

Part Six: The Thrillers

1.   *Thunderbolt and Lightfoot* (1974)   165
2.   *The Eiger Sanction* (1975)   170
3.   *Escape from Alcatraz* (1979)   174
4.   *Absolute Power* (1996)   178
5.   *True Crime* (1999)   180
6.   *Blood Work* (2002)   183

Part Seven: The War Movies

1.   *Where Eagles Dare* (1968)   191
2.   *Kelly's Heroes* (1970)   194
3.   *Firefox* (1982)   196
4.   *Heartbreak Ridge* (1986)   200
5.   *Flags of Our Fathers* (2006)/*Letters from Iwo Jima* (2006)   202

Epilogue   209
Eastwood Filmography   215
Bibliography and Sources   237
Index   241

FIGURES

0.1 'The Man With No Name', the hero of Sergio Leone's 'Dollars Trilogy';
    Clint Eastwood on location in Almeria, Spain in *For a Few
    Dollars More* (1965)   xiii

0.2 War Hero: As Lieutenant Morris Schaeffer, an OSS assassin,
    Clint Eastwood strikes a Dirty Harry-like pose in the WWII
    adventure *Where Eagles Dare* (1968).   xv

0.3 Stranded in Apache country, Keith Williams (Clint Eastwood) watches
    Sergeant Matt Blake (Scott Brady) tend Teresa Santos
    (Margia Dean) in *Ambush at Cimarron Pass* (1958).   xxiii

0.4 Rowdy Yates, Wishbone and Gil Favor take a break on their way to
    Sedalia; Clint Eastwood, Paul Brinegar and Eric Fleming hit the
    trail to TV fame in *Rawhide*.   xxviii

1.1 Spaghetti Westerns: Bounty hunters 'The Man With No Name' and
    Colonel Douglas Mortimer in *For a Few Dollars More* (1965);
    Clint Eastwood and Lee Van Cleef on location in Los Albaricoques,
    Almeria.   4

1.2 'The Man With No Name is Back!': original poster for the 1967
    US release of Sergio Leone's *For a Few Dollars More* (1965).   11

1.3 'Sorry Shorty': Tuco the Ugly gets the drop on Blondy in the desert;
    Clint Eastwood in the Spanish dunes for *The Good, the Bad and
    the Ugly* (1966).   13

1.4 Clint Eastwood, in costume as Jed Cooper, on set with director Ted Post
    during the making of their 1968 revenge western, *Hang 'Em High*.   17

1.5 Original advertising for United Artists' release of *Hang 'Em High* featuring
    Clint Eastwood, his trademark cigar and the six-man Fort Grant scaffold. 20

1.6 Wounded Hogan uses Sister Sara as a tripod for target practice;
    Clint Eastwood and Shirley MacLaine on location in Mexico for
    Two Mules for Sister Sara (1970).   23

1.7 'Sierra Torride': Spanish poster for *Two Mules for Sister Sara* retitles the
    film *Torrid Sierra*.   24

1.8 *Lo Straniero Senza Nome*: Clint Eastwood stars as the vengeful 'Stranger
    With No Name' in this classic Italian artwork for *High Plains
    Drifter* (1973).   29

1.9 'An Army of One': A Colt Walker in each fist, Josey cries vengeance on
    the pursuing Redlegs in this US one-sheet poster for *The Outlaw
    Josey Wales* (1976).   33

1.10 Once a gunfighter, now a pig farmer, William Munny loads his pistol to
    kill for cash one last time; director-star Clint Eastwood's Oscar
    winning *Unforgiven* (1992).   40

2.1   *L'Uomo Dalla Cravatta Di Cuoio*: Clint Eastwood plays cowboy cop Walt Coogan, 'The Man With the Leather Tie', in Don Siegel's urban crime thriller; Italian poster for *Coogan's Bluff* (1968).   47

2.2   The iconic Golden Gate Bridge stretches across San Francisco Bay, a timeless, recurrent backdrop to Clint Eastwood's 'Dirty Harry' series.   50

2.3   'Did he fire six?': Dirty Harry Callahan bursts onto the scene in Don Siegel's classic *Dirty Harry* (1971).   54

2.4   Harry Francis Callahan, the last hope for law and order in San Francisco: An arresting US one-sheet poster for a 'Dirty Harry' double bill, featuring *Dirty Harry* (1971) and Ted Post's ultraviolent *Magnum Force* (1973).   55

2.5   *The Enforcer* (1976): Harry's up against terrorists in this second sequel to *Dirty Harry*, but his methods remain the same.   60

2.6   Locke and Load: This US lobby card from *The Gauntlet* (1977) depicts Eastwood and Sondra Locke on the run from police and mobsters in this R-rated action adventure.   64

2.7   *Sudden Impact* (1983) gave Clint Eastwood his most famous line: 'Go ahead, make my day'.   67

2.8   The only onscreen teaming of buddies Burt Reynolds and Clint Eastwood was the gangster movie *City Heat* (1984), where they played PI Mike Murphy and cop Lieutenant Joe Speer.   73

2.9   Frank Horrigan (Clint Eastwood) puts himself *In the Line of Fire*, in Wolfgang Petersen's 1993 thriller.   82

3.1   Two scenes from *For a Few Dollars More*; the scene as it appeared in the finished film, with 'The Man With No Name' perusing a Wanted poster and in an alternative take, Mary the hotelier (Mara Krup) seduces the stranger.   90

3.2   'The Musical Goldmine of '69': The unlikely vocal trio of Lee Marvin, Jean Seberg and Clint Eastwood hit paydirt in *Paint Your Wagon* (1969).   93

3.3   Passion Play: The cover of this rare UK reissue of Thomas Cullinan's *The Beguiled* depicts wounded Corporal John McBurney (Clint Eastwood) arriving at the gates of the Farnsworth Seminary for Young Ladies.   97

3.4   'Games for two are more fun': Solitaire-playing McBurney encounters temptress Carol in the leafy arbour, but who is *The Beguiled?*; Jo Ann Harris and Clint Eastwood in Don Siegel's gothic tale of the unexpected.   99

3.5   Deadly Obsession: Evelyn Draper arrives unannounced at Dave Garver's pad; Clint Eastwood and Jessica Walter in the psycho-thriller *Play Misty for Me* (1971).   103

3.6   'Making Pictures': Robert Kincaid snaps Francesca Johnson at Roseman Bridge; Clint Eastwood and Meryl Street on location in Iowa in *The Bridges of Madison County* (1995).   110

4.1   'Beers to You': Barroom buddies Clyde and Philo enjoy a cool brew; Manis and Clint Eastwood in the hit comedy *Every Which Way You Can* (1978).   118

4.2 'It'll Knock You Out': *Every Which Way But Loose's* sequel *Any Which Way You Can* (1980) reprised the Philo and Clyde partnership to great success.   126

5.1 Jazz Man: Clint Eastwood directs Forest Whitaker as altoist Charlie Parker, the 'Yardbird', in jazz biopic *Bird* (1988), Eastwood's best film of the eighties.   140

5.2 Out in Africa, director-star Clint Eastwood plays 'John Wilson', a thinly disguised John Huston, who is loaded for elephant in *White Hunter Black Heart* (1990).   145

5.3 To the Bone: Glacial artwork promoting *Million Dollar Baby* (2004); left to right: Frankie Dunn (Clint Eastwood), Maggie Fitzgerald (Hilary Swank) and 'Scrap Iron' Dupris (Morgan Freeman).   157

5.4 Clint Eastwood behind the camera on *Million Dollar Baby* (2004), which won him his second Best Director Oscar.   159

6.1 Crazy Preacher: John 'The Thunderbolt' Doherty travels incognito in an unlikely disguise; Clint Eastwood smiles in *Thunderbolt and Lightfoot* (1974).   166

6.2 'They have exactly seven minutes to get rich quick':US one-sheet Style 'A' poster promoting *Thunderbolt and Lightfoot* (1974), starring Clint Eastwood and Jeff Bridges as the bank robbing title duo.   169

6.3 'His lifeline held by the assassin he hunted': US one-sheet poster advertising Clint Eastwood's cliffhanging thriller *The Eiger Sanction* (1975).   173

6.4 'All The Bad Eggs': A mugshot of Frank Lee Morris, otherwise known as AZ 1441, in this US lobby card promoting *Escape from Alcatraz* (1979).   176

6.5 'The Rock': The bleak Maximum Security prison known as America's Devil's Island on Alcatraz in San Francisco Bay was used as the setting for *Escape from Alcatraz* (1979) and the climax of *The Enforcer* (1976).   177

7.1 Easy Rider: Lieutenant Morris Schaeffer attempts a great escape in *Where Eagles Dare* (1968); Clint Eastwood, on location in the Austrian village of Lofer, is filmed in close-up by a cameraman positioned in the sidecar.   192

7.2 'We Could Be Heroes': Kelly leads his mercenary troops on a treasure hunt through France in *Kelly's Heroes* (1970); Clint Eastwood on location in Yugoslavia.   195

7.3 *ABC Film Review* (price: 5 pence) celebrates the UK release of *Kelly's Heroes*, *Paint Your Wagon* and *The Beguiled* in November 1971 with cover star Clint Eastwood.   197

7.4 'His Job ... Steal It!': French poster advertising *Firefox* (1982), with Clint Eastwood as ace pilot Mitchell Gant.   199

7.5 The commander directs his troops: Clint Eastwood on manoeuvres during the filming of *Flags of Our Fathers* (2006).   204

8.1 The Beguiler: Clint Eastwood (in costume as Corporal John McBurney) behind the camera on Don Siegel's *The Beguiled* (1971), prior to starting work on his directorial debut, *Play Misty for Me* (1971).   213

PREFACE: AIM FOR THE ART

Clint Eastwood is one of the most popular film stars of all time, whose films continue to find and entertain an audience. Throughout his five-decade acting career, Eastwood remains best known on screen for two action icons: the laconic spaghetti western hero 'The Man with No Name' and the last hope for law enforcement in San Francisco, Inspector 'Dirty' Harry Francis Callahan. Both are influential Eastwood creations – hard man action heroes, whose appeal transcends generation and gender. Eastwood is the cold killer with the soft, soft voice, who made killing sexy.

Eastwood the actor has had an extraordinarily varied career, and critics and fans look for clues to the 'real person' in his films. Is he the tough guy, monosyllabic and ruthless with a macabre sense of humour, from *The Good, the Bad and the Ugly* and *Dirty Harry*? Or the windswept, poetry-quoting romantic of *The Beguiled* and *Play Misty for Me*? Perhaps he's the freewheelin', beer-swiggin', barroom buddy from his comedies with Clyde the Orang-utan. Or maybe he's the motivating idealist of *Million Dollar Baby*, the flawed, wracked hero of *Unforgiven*, or the hopeless romantic, regretful of lost love, in *The Bridges of Madison County*. Whoever he is, there is something about the screen Eastwood which has been riveting audiences for almost 50 years.

Eastwood's style is a rather underplayed form of acting, in which the brooding intensity of Brando meets the vulnerability of James Dean. His screen roles

0.1 'The Man With No Name', the hero of Sergio Leone's 'Dollars Trilogy'; Clint Eastwood on location in Almeria, Spain in *For a Few Dollars More* (1965). Author's collection.

thrive on silence and menace for effect, even when he's the good guy, which gives his heroes added edge. He is also graceful on screen, for someone of his stature (he's six-feet-four-inches tall), and though his face is often immobile, impervious, a granite mask, his eyes tell all – a 'look' from Eastwood can convey many emotions and this technique is something performers can't learn in acting class. Eastwood is not a stage actor, he never has been – it's impossible to imagine him in a theatrical production – but the camera loves him and his appeal radiates from the screen. As Eastwood himself noted, 'Everybody has to play characters that suit them ... Olivier would have looked ridiculous with a poncho and pistol'.

In the second of his famous 'Dirty Harry' cop thrillers, *Magnum Force*, Eastwood notes, 'A man's got to know his limitations'. Since joining Universal-International as an actor on contract in 1954, Eastwood's acting career complements the cinema of his lifetime, beginning with his early days in B-movie bit parts and a role in a popular TV western series, *Rawhide*, where he initially made his mark. He's made Italian 'spaghetti' westerns, American imitations of spaghetti westerns, classic American westerns, a British *Boy's Own* war movie, a US 'GI's on a mission' movie, a war-vet movie, a boxing movie, a horror-thriller, a science fiction adventure, a musical, a Cold War thriller, an Italian 'arthouse' flick, a tear-jerking weepy, a gothic melodrama, cop thrillers, Depression-era dramas, rural Americana comedies, biographical dramas and James Bond espionage thrillers. This is a very broad range of films, even though he has been pigeonholed for years as an 'action hero' above all else.

Eastwood's screen heroes have always stood tall, both physically and morally. Like William Munny in *Unforgiven*, Eastwood's screen heroes have 'killed just about everything that walked or crawled at one time or another', and he's 'always been lucky when it comes to killing folks'. His most consistent victims, dispatched to oblivion, have been Mexican bandidos, German soldiers and myriad members of San Francisco's criminal fraternity, including bank robbers, serial killers and terrorists. Unlike the indestructible action stars who lurched in his wake, like Stallone and Schwarzenegger, Eastwood rarely takes on his adversaries with the help of machine guns, rockets and heavy artillery, disintegrating them like confetti. There's usually no problem Eastwood can't solve with a well-aimed bullet from his pistol.

Despite his close associations with westerns, Eastwood has hardly been prolific by the genre's standards, starring in only 10 period westerns in his 50-year career so far. John Wayne made nine in 1934 alone and had made 40 westerns before he hit the big time with *Stagecoach* (1939). Wayne appeared in over 80 westerns during his long career. But of Eastwood's 10, he has made five that can be counted among the genre's best: the 'Dollars' trilogy (*A Fistful of Dollars*, *For a Few Dollars More* and *The Good, the Bad and the Ugly*), *The Outlaw Josey Wales* and *Unforgiven*. Even more financially successful are the films where Eastwood has played a police officer. The five-film 'Dirty Harry' back catalogue still keeps earning for Warner Bros, while the 'Dollars' trilogy has been re-released, repackaged and re-mastered many times since its first appearance on home video in the 1980s. Eastwood's back catalogue is one of the most lucrative in the history of cinema.

0.2 War Hero: As Lieutenant Morris Schaeffer, an OSS assassin, Clint Eastwood strikes a Dirty Harry-like pose in the WWII adventure *Where Eagles Dare* (1968). Image courtesy Kevin Wilkinson Collection.

Since the early 1970s, there has been another Eastwood – the successful producer-director, with his own Malpaso production company. Malpaso is Spanish for 'bad step' or 'wrong move', and is also a creek in his hometown of Carmel-by-the-Sea. His first directorial assignment, on *Play Misty for Me*, saw him cast himself as a late-night radio DJ, and he has directed himself many times since. The films he has directed, but not appeared in, include a little-seen love story (*Breezy*), a jazz biography (*Bird*), and powerful dramas tackling troubling subject matter, including *Mystic River* and the uncompromising war film *Letters from Iwo Jima*, two of his finest achievements behind the camera. Another line from *Magnum Force* sums up his eclectic, prolific directorial career: 'I'm afraid you've misjudged me'. Perpetually the outsider in Hollywood, his talent and achievements were finally acknowledged with a brace of Best Director Oscars, for *Unforgiven* (1992) and *Million Dollar Baby* (2004), both of which also won Best Picture Academy Awards.

Eastwood's screen legacy has delivered several 'Clintessential' Eastwood moments – an action scene, a quirky exchange of dialogue, a gag or an emotional tug, which remind audiences they are watching a star. They include his 'My mule don't like people laughing' speech from *A Fistful of Dollars*, when facing a bullying welcoming committee in San Miguel. *Dirty Harry*'s 'Do you feel lucky, punk?', when cop Harry Callahan asks a wounded bank robber if he can count up to six. The pool room fight from *Coogan's Bluff*, the final three-way duel in the graveyard in *The Good, the Bad and the Ugly* and running *The Gauntlet* of the Phoenix Police Department in a fortified bus are some of his action highlights. 'Right turn Clyde' from *Any Which Way You Can*, when Clyde the Orang-utan's punch sends bikers toppling, spoofed his tough guy image. In *The Outlaw Josey Wales,* Eastwood warns a bounty hunter that, 'Dying ain't much of a living, boy', before being forced to shoot him dead. The parting of the lovers in the rain in *The Bridges of Madison County* and the death of boxer Maggie in *Million Dollar Baby* are two of his finest, most moving onscreen moments. And, of course, his most famous proposal, 'Go ahead, make my day', from *Sudden Impact* has caught on as a catchphrase worldwide.

Many of Eastwood's best films, including *The Beguiled, Play Misty for Me, The Bridges of Madison County* and *Million Dollar Baby*, deal with affairs of the heart and obsession. Eastwood's portrayal of a film director based on John Huston was called *White Hunter Black Heart*, while in the transplant thriller *Blood Work*, the heart of the story is the heart itself. In the western *A Fistful of Dollars*, Eastwood's first starring role, he famously taunted villain Ramon Rojo to, 'Aim for the heart', knowing that his iron-plated breastplate would stop Ramon's bullets. Eastwood the filmmaker always aims for the emotional heart of the story, and his talent and craft ensures that the heartbeat of his cinema endures even today.

ACKNOWLEDGEMENTS

I would like to thank Philippa Brewster, my editor at I.B.Tauris, for initialising *Aim for the Heart*, and for her great ideas throughout its writing. Thanks also to Jayne Hill, Paul Davighi and Stuart Weir at I.B.Tauris and to Rohini Krishnan at Newgen Imaging Systems for their hard work on this project. Thanks to Mike Coppack, whose knowledge of films and music has again proved invaluable, especially on modern cinema and its stars. Thanks also to Tom Betts, the editor of Euro-western fanzine *Westerns All'Italiana*, whose contributions on Eastwood's westerns, in particular the 'Dollars' films and key episodes of the *Rawhide* TV series, prove again he is one of the most knowledgeable experts on the genre. Thanks also to jazz expert David Weaver, for providing recordings of Charlie 'Yardbird' Parker and biographical information on various key jazz players of the bebop scene.

Many of the posters and lobby cards have been kindly provided by Ian Caunce, from his collection: most are extremely rare, often from foreign promotional campaigns, and I thank Ian for allowing me to reprint them here. Many of the stills were provided by Kevin Wilkinson from his archive of memorabilia. Like Ian, he's unearthed some really rare material – thanks for allowing me to print them. The remainder of the stills, posters, novelisation tie-ins and magazine covers are from my own collection.

Thanks too to Andy Hanratty, who again worked on the restoration of these images, in particular a creased and faded copy of *ABC Film Review* from November 1971. He's done a fine job, as always, and also located rare Eastwood film appearances and soundtrack albums. The images of the Golden Gate Bridge and Alcatraz Island, San Francisco Bay, were taken by photographer Sonya-Jayne Stewart – thanks for allowing me to reprint them here.

Thanks also to Belinda and Chris Skinner, Christopher Frayling, Alex Cox, Alex and Isabel Coe, Mike Oak and Tracey Mansell, Bob Bell, Philip French, William Connolly, Dave Worrall, Lionel Woodman, Rene Hogguer, Ann Jackson, Paul Duncan, Rhian Coppack, Frankie Holmes, Simon Hawkins, Nicki and John Cosgrove, Roger and Chris Brown, Peter Jones, Gareth Jones, and the staff of Chester Library, in particular the member of staff who managed to track down a rare copy of Thomas Cullinan's *The Beguiled*.

I must also thank my parents: my mother, Carol, who again helped proofing the manuscripts, and my father, John, who suggested *Aim for the Heart* as the title for this book.

And finally thank you to Clara, who has helped with the research (particularly on the films based on literary adaptations) and proofing. Without her help, encouragement and support, *Aim for the Heart* would probably have aimed but missed.

UNIVERSAL CASTING: THE EARLY FILMS

Clinton Eastwood Jnr was born on 31 May 1930 in Piedmont, California. Until 1940 his family was constantly on the move across California, wherever his father Clinton Snr found work, with Ruth, his mother, looking after Clinton Jnr and his younger sister Jeanne (born on 18 January 1934). Eastwood's childhood and education were unremarkable, and when he graduated he drifted into various odd jobs – as a lifeguard, in a paper mill and pumping gas. He had no clear idea of what he wanted to do and was eventually drafted into the army for a stint of Military Service in 1950. There he became a lifesaving instructor, rising to the rank of corporal at Ford Ord on the Monterey Peninsular. Released from service in spring 1951, he worked as a lifeguard in Seattle and then moved to Los Angeles to begin college. He was by now courting Margaret Neville Johnson, called Maggie, and they were married on 19 December 1953. He enrolled on a business course at Los Angeles City College, but through friends became interested in acting and eventually ended up on the talent programme at Universal-International, as one of many stars hoping to shine.

Eastwood began his film career at Universal-International in April 1954, on a contract that earned him $75 a week. This was at a time when the studio system was breaking down and TV was beginning to affect cinema grosses – there were more channels to fill and many more opportunities on TV. But his regular income as a film actor at Universal, usually on B-movie science fiction 'creature features' or westerns, was worth his perseverance. These early films offer fans the enjoyable though often frustrating game of 'Spot the Clint'.

Eastwood's film debut was an uncredited bit part in Jack Arnold's *Revenge of the Creature* (1955). It was the first of two sequels to the 3-D *Creature from the Black Lagoon* (1954), starring the scaly, finned deep-sea monster Gill-Man. Eastwood had one scene as a laboratory technician, opposite ichthyologist hero John Agar. Eastwood explains that there should be four rats in the cage, but one seems to have ended up inside a cat. As Agar looks on, Eastwood then puts his hand in his lab coat pocket and discovers the fourth one; 'How'd he get in there?' Eastwood asks, bemused. Eastwood's next film saw him cast opposite Francis the Talking Mule (voiced by Chill Wills) in Arthur Lubin's *Francis in the Navy* (1955) as rating Jonesy, one of Donald O'Connor's sidekicks, in a tale of mistaken identities. O'Connor played both Lieutenant Peter Sterling and ne're-do-well Slicker Donovan, and Eastwood received $300 a week, for four week's work.

In *Lady Godiva* (1955 – *Lady Godiva of Coventry* in the UK), a costume adventure also directed by Arthur Lubin, Eastwood played the minor role of Albert the Fletcher, a Saxon bowman. In his opening scene he offers an excuse for his poor marksmanship ('The sun was in my eyes') and is later thrown into a Norman prison. Albert is sprung from jail and becomes a rebel. Decked out in helmet and gauntlets early in the film, Eastwood looks uncomfortable; his later medieval Robin Hood-like outfit (shirt and jerkin) suits him much better. Eastwood acquits himself well, wielding a broadsword with gusto and even gets to ride into a battle scene, screech to a halt and shout, 'A column of soldiers approaching!' though his voice is obviously dubbed by someone else.

Jack Arnold's *Tarantula* (1955) for Universal-International was one of several 'giant creatures on the rampage' films that crawled out in the wake of *Them!* (1954), a giant ant movie. Eric Jacobs, a biologist, is discovered in the Arizona desert suffering from acromegaly, caused when the 'pituitary gland goes haywire'. In a secluded laboratory, Professor Deemer (Leo G. Carroll) has been testing his powerful 'non-organic food concentrate', injecting animals with a 'Nutrient Type 3Y', resulting in massive and incredible growth spurts in white rats, guinea pigs, rabbits and tarantula. Jacobs, Deemer's assistant, has injected himself with the serum, inducing acromegaly. Desert Rock doctor Matt Hastings (John Agar) has his suspicions and investigates. During a fire at the laboratory, the tarantula escapes, but continues to grow. Soon it is felling telegraph poles and power pylons, flipping pickups and eating cattle, locals and anything else that crosses its path, with the town of Desert Rock next on the menu. As the spider approaches the town, the locals call Sands Air Base for backup. Cue Clint, dispatched as squadron leader of the jet fighters, to deep-fry the arachnid with rocket attack and napalm. Eastwood appears in four cockpit shots, heavily disguised with a flying helmet, tilted visor and breathing apparatus, issuing crackly radio orders. He tells his three co-pilots to 'Fire two rockets on this first pass', then 'Here goes', followed by, 'Dropping napalm, follow in order' and finally, 'Dump 'em all', as their cargo incinerates the creature in a fireball inferno. Agar's love interest is beautiful Mara Corday, as Stephanie 'Steve' Clayton; she would later play small roles in four Eastwood films, beginning with *The Gauntlet* (1977). Leo G. Carroll is excellent as the furtive scientist, who is accidentally injected with the nutrient, resulting in contorted facial disfigurement. Shot in the Lucerne Valley, California, near Dead Man's Point (which features as 'Devil's Rock'), *Tarantula*'s 'special photography' effects, staged by Clifford Stine, are way above average, with the lumbering, hairy-legged title-star ominously stalking through barren Arizona. Equally memorable is Deemer's fantastical lab, with white rats, guinea pigs and rabbits rapidly outgrowing their cages, while the massive tarantula's legs squeakily scrape at the glass imprisoning it. *Tarantula* is easily the best, most successful film Eastwood appeared in during his time at Universal.

In *Never Say Goodbye* (1956), Eastwood played laboratory technician Will opposite Rock Hudson, as Dr Michael Parker. In the lab Will tells Parker that there is a phone call for him, wishes Parker 'good luck' with a forthcoming speech and is instructed to study some X-rays 'when they're dry'. Eastwood uses his own voice here in yet another minor role. *Away All Boats* (1956), directed by Joseph Pevney, starred Jeff Chandler in a WWII Pacific war drama set aboard an attack transporter, the *Belinda*. Eastwood appears towards the climax, as a medic who tends wounded Chandler (Eastwood's voice is dubbed by someone else).

Star in the Dust (1956) again headlined versatile John Agar, this time as Sheriff Bill Jordan. A *High Noon* imitator, *Star* saw Jordan facing two warring factions, the cattlemen and the farmers, in the town of Gunlock. The cattlemen have hired professional killer Sam Hall (Richard Boone) to murder any farmers found north of Coffin Creek. Jordon has apprehended Hall and plans to hang him at sundown. The film follows the action from dawn to sunset, as Hall and his allies try to engineer his escape, and Jordon deals with various problems, including his fiancée Ellen (Mamie Van Doren). *Star* was filmed over 12 days with Eastwood required for only one of them. His contribution to his first western is a single scene. Six minutes into the film, Jordon is walking past a team of joiners constructing the gallows, when ranch hand Tom (Eastwood) moseys along and engages the tense sheriff in conversation. Tom says that at the Bella Vista casino, 'They're giving 5–3 Hall won't hang'. '8–3', corrects Jordon. 'How would you bet, if you were a betting man?' Tom ventures. 'Judge Reb ordered Hall hanged at sundown today. That's when he'll hang'. 'If you say so, sheriff', says Tom, before moseying off the screen, smiling, doing everything possible in this minuscule role to prolong his screen time and get noticed. Eastwood used his own voice here. At key points during *Star* the 'Music Man' (Terry Gilkyson) sings the 'Ballad of Sam Hall', which has the same tune, though different lyrics, as the song Eastwood drunkenly sings as Shirley MacLaine removes an arrow from his shoulder in *Two Mules for Sister Sara*, 14 years later.

After six films Universal decided to drop Eastwood's contract in October 1955. The same studio executive fired Eastwood and his friend and fellow contract player Burt Reynolds on the same day. The exec said that Eastwood had a chipped tooth and his Adam's apple was too prominent, and told Reynolds that he couldn't act. Whether this criticism was taken to heart by Eastwood is not known, but in his three spaghetti westerns, his first films as a star, he hardly ever smiled so as not to show his teeth and wore a black neckerchief which concealed his Adam's apple.

Now a free agent, Eastwood was cast by Lubin in RKO's *The First Travelling Saleslady* (1956). He is billed sixth on the cast list as 'Featuring Clint Eastwood'. The film stars Ginger Rogers as Rose Gillray, a New York corset designer in dire financial straits. She decides that, to strike a blow for the emancipation of women in the America of 1897 and to pay off her debtors, she will become a travelling saleslady for the Carter Steel Company, peddling barbed wire to cattlemen in the Far West. She takes her corset model Molly Wade (Carol Channing) along and the pair fall foul of Joel Kingdom (James Arness), a Texan cattleman who opposes the use of barbed wire.

Romance brings young Eastwood onto the scene as Jack Rice, Molly's intermittent love interest, a lieutenant recruiting for the US Volunteer Cavalry (Roosevelt's 'Rough Riders') in a Kansas City hotel lobby. Molly, on the lookout for a romantic entanglement, catches sight of him and swoons, 'Do you like girls?' 'Yes ma'am, I do'. 'Well I'm a girl'; 'You sure are', says a sheepish Rice. Later Jack gallops into the town of Spur Ridge and frees the Spur Ridge sheriff, then rides to Kingdom's ranch to save Rose and Molly. He proposes (off-screen) and is present in the courtroom finale, affording Eastwood more screen time and a couple of close-ups. Molly and Jack are finally glimpsed fleetingly in the dénouement, kissing awkwardly before running away together, hand in hand. For this prominent supporting role, Eastwood received $750. *Saleslady* is a vaudevillian depiction of the west, with extravagant, colourful costumes and an accent on romance. Mae West was the original choice for Rose, but Rogers was eventually cast. This is Broadway star Channing's film debut. An acquired taste, her barnstorming, giraffe-like showbiz style, goofy face and klutzy double-takes surprisingly provide the film with its most entertaining moments. As *Leonard Maltin's 2001 Movie and Video Guide* notes, 'Carol and Clint make one of the oddest couples in screen history'. As the lanky, tongue-tied lover boy, Eastwood rather overdoes the twitchy 'gee-shucks' amiability, but his blinking, grinning performance earned him his first positive review. A *Hollywood Reporter* article of 28 June 1955 glowed, 'Clint Eastwood is very attractive as Carol Channing's beau'.

After this early career highlight, Eastwood was back down the bill, playing pilots in *Escapade in Japan* (1957) and *Lafayette Escadrille* (1958 – *Hell Bent for Glory* in the UK). He's hardly on screen in either effort. In the first, another Lubin-helmed feature, he plays a US Air Force rescue squadron pilot codenamed 'Dumbo One' who scrambles to save a stricken passenger airliner in the Pacific. His dialogue is brief and to the point: 'Pilot to radio operator...let me know as soon as you get 'em in the scope will you?' and when asked by the airline pilot, 'Have you got radar lock yet?', Eastwood answers, 'No, you're too far out', though at least he uses his own voice. In *Lafayette*, directed by William Wellman, he was George Moseley, a US WWI ace in the French flying squad of the title.

For TV showings and video releases of these movies, Eastwood's name is often shunted up the billing, but in the B-western *Ambush at Cimarron Pass* (1958), produced by Regal Film and directed by Jodie Copeland for Twentieth Century-Fox, he was the bona fide co-star. Eastwood was billed after Scott Brady and Margia Dean, and received $750 for the eight-day shoot, with location filming in the San Fernando Valley. Brady received $25,000.

In *Ambush at Cimarron Pass*, the remains of a 7th Cavalry patrol are riding to Fort Waverly through Apache country, escorting gunrunner Corbin (Baynes Barron) and his stock of 36 Henry repeating rifles. The squad consists of scout Henry (William Vaughn), Corporal Schwitzer (Ken Mayer), privates Zach (John Maier), Lasky (Keith Richards) and Nathan (John Merrick), and their commander, tough sergeant Matt Blake (Brady). En route they encounter a party of ex-Confederates, who are driving their cattle from Texas but have been ambushed and have lost their herd. Led by Captain Sam Prescott (Frank Gerstle), they are Johnny Willows (Dirk London), Judge Stanfield (Irving Bacon), Cobb (Desmond Slattery) and Keith Williams (Eastwood). Hothead Williams in particular hates Yankees, following the death of his mother and sister at the hands of the Unionists. Low on food and water, the groups decide to travel together. They are joined by a Mexican woman, Teresa Santos (Margia Dean), the only survivor of a massacre at the Santos Ranch. Things soon worsen when Cobb is tortured and killed, and their horses are run off by Apaches. The party continues on foot. During the trek Williams tangles with Blake and the party gets whittled down by the ever-stalking Apaches. Reaching Cimarron Pass, they are ambushed by Apache riders and Corbin tries to escape, knifing Judge Stanfield, but is killed by his Apache friends. Blake leads an attack on the Apache camp, stampeding the horses and routing the Indians. Johnny Willows is killed, but the survivors soldier on towards Fort Waverly, until exhausted they can go no further. They burn the guns, which enables them to make it to Waverly.

Set in 1867, *Ambush* is a standard monochrome B-western, more violent than most. Budgetary constraints are obvious, with Copeland unable to afford wranglers and horses for the entire shoot, so the cavalry's animals are run off early in the story. He was also short of Indians and was going to deploy about 40 warriors, whom he would make to look like 400, but with Brady's huge fee, the production was crippled. As Eastwood recalled, Copeland amended his plans: 'I'll make those four Indians look like 40'. For the finale at Cimarron Pass they did manage to muster a dozen Apaches on horseback, but for most of the film the warriors appear in twos and threes, dogging the party from afar. The plot helpfully explains this: the Apaches, armed with inferior weaponry, are wary of the new Henry repeaters. The

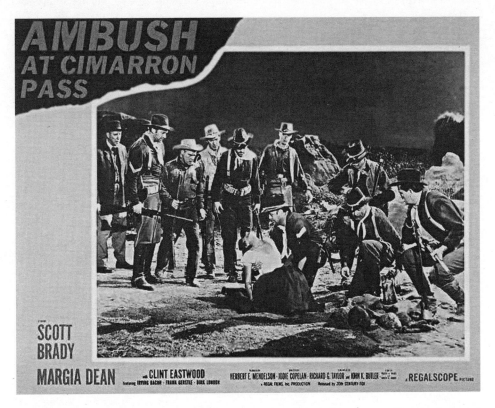

0.3 Stranded in Apache country, Keith Williams (Clint Eastwood, standing background middle) watches Sergeant Matt Blake (Scott Brady) tend Teresa Santos (Margia Dean) in *Ambush at Cimarron Pass* (1958); this is card No 4 of a set of 8 US lobby cards – their equivalents are called FOH (front-of-house) stills in the UK. Courtesy Ian Caunce Collection.

film's uneven cinematography, in black and white 'Regalscope', aided Copeland in his endeavours. It was so bright during the daylight scenes that, Eastwood remembered, 'you needed sunglasses to look at the screen', and that the photography was so dark in the night-time scenes that actors were barely discernible. Cannily, Copeland had his Apaches attack at night.

In *Ambush*, Eastwood was onscreen for almost the entire film – with such a small cast, someone had to be. Fervent Reb Keith Williams is Eastwood's best cinema performance of the fifties. He has a couple of good lines and handles himself well in the action scenes: a production that couldn't afford horses certainly couldn't stretch to stuntmen. Williams also has a mild romantic liaison with Teresa, inviting her back to Texas with him, but she eventually falls for Blake. Most significantly, Eastwood is given the curtain line. As the stack of rifles burns, the party moans that they've lugged them 100 miles for nothing. 'No, not for nothing', says Williams, 'Sometimes you gotta lose before you finally win'.

Despite a dearth of horses and Indians, the film is an entertaining western. On set, Brady, often sporting a heavy hangover, reputedly upset everyone with his foul language. Dirk London as Johnny Willows holds a cigar or cigarette between his teeth for the entire film, something Eastwood perhaps took note of for future reference. All *Ambush*'s night-time interiors were filmed on unconvincing studio sets, but the film's violent action sets it apart from more routine fare. Cobb is tortured to death, gunrunner Corbin is skewered by an Apache war lance, and the party arrives at a waterhole to find it poisoned, their scout's corpse suspended by his feet from poles, his head submerged in the water.

The 73-minute film was released on the bottom half of double bills in 1958. Eastwood and Maggie went to watch it and he was aghast, slumping further down in his seat as the film progressed. He viewed it as the nadir of his career: 'I'm going to quit, I've got to start doing something with my life'. The Valentine's Day 1958 issue of *Variety* said the film 'moves rather well within the limitations of its low budget. Brady is sincere in his approach and quite believable in his performance. Fine portrayals also come from Margia Dean, Frank Gerstle, Clint Eastwood and Dirk London'. Often dismissed as a mess – Eastwood himself called it 'the lousiest western ever made' – *Ambush* is nothing of the sort, but it was to be Eastwood's last film appearance for six years.

RIDIN' EASY: *RAWHIDE*

Between 1956 and 1958, amid scattered film roles, Eastwood also managed to secure some TV work. On *Highway Patrol,* he was a young, leather-jacketed biker. On *Death Valley Days* he was John Lucas, a down-on-his-luck gold prospector who receives 'The Last Letter' (the episode's title). He also appeared in *West Point* (in the skiing episode 'White Fury'), *Navy Log* (as Burns in 'The Lonely Watch'), ABC's *Reader's Digest* (in 'Greatest of the Apaches', a biography of Cochise, where he played a US cavalry officer) and the ever-popular *Wagon Train.*

Most significantly Eastwood had a guest spot in *Maverick,* in the 'Duel at Sundown' episode, again directed by Arthur Lubin. En route to Leadville, ace gambler Bret Maverick (James Garner) arrives in the town of Sundown at the behest of Jed Christiansen (Edgar Buchanan), wheelchair-bound, elderly owner of the Molly-O ranch. Jed wants Bret to court his daughter Carrie (Abby Dalton), who is in love with ne're-do-well gunslinger Red Hardigan (Eastwood). Hardigan has his eye on the Molly-O and refuses to marry Carrie until Jed has passed away. But Carrie finds Bret 'completely resistible' and uses him to make Red jealous. Red is the best shot in the county; 'How big a county is this?' asks Bret nervously. Bret is tracked down by notorious badman John Wesley Hardin ('Never figured he'd find me way down here'), who has a score to settle with him. To everyone's amazement, Bret kills Hardin in a duel and then goes gunning for Red: 'Where's that other big gunslinger? I might as well take care of him while I'm in the mood'. But cowardly Red is nowhere to be seen, leaving Jed happy and Carrie aware of her beau's yellow streak. The duel has been a ruse set up by Bret. 'John Wesley Hardin' is actually Bret's brother Bart (Jack Kelly) and Bret gunned him down using blanks. As Bret and Bart leave town, they run into the real John Wesley Hardin, on his way to Sundown looking for revenge.

With his key role in *Ambush at Cimarron Pass,* this is Eastwood's most promising performance so far. As mean braggart Hardigan, he had plenty of screen time and held his own opposite Garner. Eastwood plays a convincing heavy, smoking a cigar (the first time he would do so onscreen), snarling through his teeth and smiling threats to his love rival. He had already mastered his trademark slow, menacing walk and his stance outside the saloon, standing with his three henchmen, ready to pull his gun – a style that had already begun to hint at his cool-but-tough screen persona. In addition to the action-comedy, Eastwood also gets a couple of love scenes, with Carrie and also with his secret lover, Lily (Linda Lawson). In one scene, Carrie sings, 'Do you remember sweet Betsy from Pike? She crossed the wide prairie with her lover Ike' (the same song Eastwood drunkenly sings in *A Fistful of Dollars*). In the episode's best scene, Doc Baxter (Dan Sherman) demonstrates to Bret what an expert marksman Red is. Outside the Sundown saloon, Doc challenges Red to hit a tin pie plate before it hits the ground. 'Any time you're ready, Doc', says Red, before quick drawing and hitting it four times, sending the plate flying. Later, when Red sees Bret gun down the fake Hardin, he blurts, 'It was an accident – you can't fan a gun and hit anything'.

Fanning the pistol's hammer with the palm of his hand was later the preferred style of shooting for 'The Man with No Name'.

Eastwood's big break came in 1959 when he was cast in the Columbia Broadcasting Systems (CBS) TV series *Rawhide*. Its creator Charles Marquis Warren had produced CBS's *Gunsmoke* for TV, which was one of the first 'adult' western TV shows launched in 1955 (with ABC's *The Life and Legend of Wyatt Earp* and *Cheyenne*). His next idea was a trail drive western series, with two main stars, plus a regular supporting cast, augmented by guest stars. *Rawhide* was clearly influenced by Howard Hawks' cattle drive western *Red River* (1948), starring John Wayne as the tough trail boss, Montgomery Clift as his young 'ramrod' (lieutenant) and Walter Brennan as the irascible old cook. Warren had just directed and executive produced *Cattle Empire* (1958) for Twentieth Century-Fox. Filmed in CinemaScope in Lone Pine, *Empire* starred Joel McCrea as John Cord, who, recently released from prison, agrees to trail boss for a blind rancher, herding 5,000 head of cattle from Hamilton to Fort Clemson. Included in the trail crew were Steve Rains and Rocky Shanan (as drovers Paul Corbo and Dan Quince) and Paul Brinegar (as cook Thomas Jefferson Jeffords). The narrative was straightforward, with magnificent landscape shots of the cattle on the move, punctuated with campfire scenes filmed on studio interiors, a format Warren obviously liked.

Rawhide starred Eric Fleming as trail boss Gil Favor, but a younger actor was needed for the role of ramrod Rowdy Yates. Eastwood auditioned for the role and secured it. The first season was budgeted at $4 million, with Eastwood on $750 per episode, while guest stars pocketed $10,000 per appearance. Each episode ran for 48 minutes (an hour with adverts). The title song 'Rawhide' was by Dimitri Tiomkin, with lyrics by Ned Washington, the same team behind *High Noon*'s 'Do Not Forsake Me Oh My Darlin'' It was sung in whoopin', hollerin' fashion by Frankie Laine in fine whip-cracking style. It proved popular and reached number six in the UK charts in November 1959. In the first episode, an introductory voiceover by Favor explains that the drive is travelling the 1,500 miles from San Antonio, Texas, to the railhead in Sedalia in Missouri. The herd is made up of 3,000 cattle belonging to over 100 owners. This episode established the various characters on the 22-man drover crew. The regular team was Paul Brinegar (from *Cattle Empire*) as Wishbone the cook and James Murdock as Mushy Mushgrove, his 'louse' (assistant). Sheb Wooley appeared as scout Pete Nolan, with Steve Raines and Rocky Shahan as drovers Jim Quince and Joe Scarlet, who ride 'flank' and 'swing' on the herd. Favor himself rides 'point', leading the way.

Rawhide was filmed on sets at MGM Studios and on location at Nogales, Arizona, where the cattle drive, the riding footage and some of the action sequences were lensed – later episodes were shot in Lone Pine, California. All the night-time camp scenes were shot on studio interiors, as were some of the daytime dialogue scenes, and the switch from outdoors to indoors is readily apparent. Though filmed in 1958, the pilot and the first 22-episode series were shown weekly in the US, from January to July 1959. Season two played from September 1959 to June 1960; Season three from

September 1960 to June 1961; Season four ran from September 1961 to May 1962; Season five ran from September 1962 to May 1963; Season six from September 1962 to May 1963; Season seven from September 1964 to May 1965; Season eight from September 1965 until December 1965, with the end of this season made up of reruns until January 1966. With ratings falling for this final season, Fleming left the series and Eastwood became trail boss, augmented with some new characters played by John Ireland, Raymond St Jacques and David Watson. Only 13 of the final 30 episodes had been filmed and Eastwood received $119,000 as compensation.

The pilot was 'Incident of the Tumbleweed Wagon' (in the UK simply titled 'Incident of the Tumbleweed') – most of the episode titles were 'Incidents'. A heavily fortified prison wagon camps near the drovers' bivouac. Its cargo is 'human dynamite' – six murderers, deserters and rustlers, and a woman, Dallas (guest star Terry Moore). The criminals manage to attack their escort, killing the deputy and severely injuring the sheriff. Favor and Rowdy decide to help out and take the wagon to Fort Gregg. The journey is hazardous, with Dallas's husband, machete-wielding outlaw Luke Storm (Val Dufour), and his gang on their trail. Eventually, during a river crossing, the outlaws catch up with them. In a showdown, Luke accidentally kills Dallas before Favor shoots him. This opening episode, actually the ninth filmed, set the tone for the series, with the drovers being drawn into someone else's problem. As Favor puts it, 'Don't go around dipping your bread in another man's bacon grease'. Favor is a man of honour and moral strength, while Rowdy is somewhat inexperienced and naïve. Both learn more about themselves as the series progresses. At the end of each episode, Favor would holler, 'Head 'em up! Move 'em out', driving the cattle off onto the next leg of their journey, and the drovers to their next adventure.

'Incident at Alabaster Plain' – the second episode, actually the third episode chronologically – provided Eastwood with a key prop that he would use later in his career. This episode introduces Favor's crew in voiceover during the intro. Of Rowdy, Favor says, 'New as they come, but he's got the makings'. At a mission run by Father Fabian (guest star Martin Balsam), Rowdy runs into his old friend Charles 'Buzz' Travers (guest star Troy Donahue), who is engaged to the daughter of wealthy rancher Justice Cardin. On the wedding day, Cardin's step-son gunman Ward Mastic (Mark Richman) returns home after many years and breaks up the party, demanding his share of the ranch. In an argument, he beats Cardin to death with his pistol. Rowdy, Buzz and Favor face Mastic and his gang at the mission, and Mastic is killed when he falls from a bell tower. Mastic is a flashy professional gunfighter who owns a Colt .45 decorated with coiled rattlesnakes (in solid silver inlayed in ebony) on the grips. Mastic refers to his weapon as a snake, 'Oiled and packed in leather and faster than anything you'll ever see ... it jumps out and bites a man before he knows what hit him'. After the showdown, Rowdy takes Mastic's pistol for himself, using it in subsequent episodes. Eastwood later used the distinctive snake grips, attached to different pistols, in all three of his Italian westerns with Sergio Leone.

Eastwood's role as Rowdy Yates both helped and hindered his career. He was happy to have regular work and exposure, but he felt typecast. Rowdy was something of a one-dimensional character, always first in line for chow and with half an eye on the ladies. Eastwood christened him 'Idiot of the Plains'. As the series progressed, what was most apparent was Eastwood's complete compatibility with the western setting. What he lacked in dramatic range (which was often the fault of the scripts), Eastwood made up in presence. He was an excellent horseman and was rough and ready in the action sequences. He sported a James Dean-style quiff, and was tall and muscular (he frequently took his shirt off onscreen), which ensured that he soon built up a strong teenage female following. The series was particularly popular in Japan (aired on NET). In March 1962, in addition to doing promotional tours in the US, Fleming, Brinegar and Eastwood travelled to the Far East, where they were mobbed.

One strong feature of *Rawhide* was that the main cast members often had episodes devoted solely to their characters. By far the most interesting episodes are the ones where Rowdy is the focus. These segments, effectively Eastwood solo outings, usually open with Rowdy being sent ahead on an errand. In 'Incident of the Garden of Eden', Rowdy is chosen to buy cattle because the crew, 'can't stand any more of his jokes'. 'Incident of the Day of the Dead' was the first episode of the second season in September 1959. Rowdy, dispatched to collect the mail, gets drunk and loses at poker

0.4 Rowdy Yates, Wishbone and Gil Favor take a break on their way to Sedalia; (left to right) Clint Eastwood, Paul Brinegar and Eric Fleming hit the trail to TV fame in *Rawhide*. Author's collection.

but is bailed out by Mexican contessa Luisa Hadley (Viveca Lindfors). As compensation he must break her wild mustang, 'La Muerta', which he fails to do. The unusual plot and its setting, the Mexican 'Day of the Dead' festival, make this episode the first of several fine showcases for Eastwood. In 'Incident of the Garden of Eden' (aired June 1960), Rowdy rides to buy cattle and finds himself on the ranch of English ex-pat Sir Richard Ashley (Robert Coote) and his daughter Laura Ashley (Debra Paget). Their ranch house is built in the style of a Georgian manor, complete with butler. For dinner Rowdy dresses in formal attire from Bond Street, London, with bow tie and tails, but falls foul of tough foreman Winch (John Ireland – who is in love with Laura) and henchman Crane (Gregory Walcott). This odd episode features an Olde Worlde Englishe Pubbe called the 'Ox Head Inn', where innkeeper Harry Wilkes serves ale to his cockney customers Oliver and 'iggins. In 'Incident of the Reluctant Bridegroom' (from November 1962), Rowdy rides into town to buy supplies, but in an extraordinary set of circumstances, he wakes up after a night in the saloon married to Sheila Delancey (Ruta Lee), the feisty Irish lover of town boss John Landy (Arch Johnson); fortunately, the parson who performed the ceremony is outlaw Sam Weber (Ed Nelson) in disguise, so the union is annulled.

The November 1961 episode 'Incident of the Black Sheep' has become the most famous and sought-after episode of the series. It is the one Sergio Leone viewed as Eastwood's screen-test for the lead role in *A Fistful of Dollars*. Richard Baseheart guested as Tod Stone, a sheepherder en route to Twin Hats, to hook up with his 'Grandpappy' (Will Wright). During a dispute with the drovers, Stone is injured. Favor assigns Rowdy to take Stone to the nearest town to get patched up. Rowdy suffers prejudice in town when he is mistaken for a 'sheepman' and, following a punch-up in a pool hall, ends up in jail. Stone bails him out and each in the course of the journey learns to be more tolerant of the other. When Rowdy learns that the range is infected with anthrax, he warns Stone, an action which could trigger a cattle-sheep war for grazing land.

'Incident of the Running Man' was a highpoint in Eastwood's TV career when screened in May 1961. Rowdy, again sent ahead to buy cattle, is bushwhacked by Deputy Toland (played by Eastwood's friend Robert Donner), who tells Rowdy of a plot to attack nearby Camp Henley. Outlaws have massacred a troop of cavalry at Feather Canyon and are going to infiltrate the post in disguise, wipe out the garrison and sack the territory. But before Toland can verify this story to anyone else, he is shot and Rowdy goes on the run, sought by the outlaws (who know that he's on to their scheme) and by lawman Sheriff McVey (Robert Wilke). In the nearby town of Rawley, the centre of the conspiracy, Rowdy survives various scrapes. With the help of rancher Maddy (Luana Anders), he is able to tip off the troops, who foil the coup. This tension-filled episode has aged very well, with Eastwood the focus of virtually every scene. He rose to the occasion admirably: on the run, he is handcuffed, betrayed, beaten, jailed and hog-tied. He crashes through a window to escape a razor-wielding barber, poses as a mourner at a funeral and hides in an undertaker's hearse to escape, and by the end of the episode he is bloody and bruised.

Eastwood's understated acting was much improved by the 1963–64 season, while Fleming's had become hammier. For this season, the show's three stars (Fleming, Eastwood and Brinegar) were immortalised in the titles as profile busts in silhouette. They were recognisable, bona fide TV stars and Eastwood was now earning about $100,000 a season. For the November 1963 episode entitled 'Incident of the Prophesy', Eastwood was cast alongside scene-stealing Warren Oates, as drover Charlie Waters, nicknamed 'Rabbit', who carries a lucky rabbit's foot. When a bunch from Favor's outfit ride into a sleepy settlement ('All this town needs is flowers and a headstone') and discover the saloon closed, they decide to liven it up with some gunplay. An accidental ricochet kills Judd Horton, the brother of local zealot preacher, Brother William: 'an apostle of the redemptive spirit'. He curses those he thinks responsible: Rabbit and Rowdy. Several unexplained 'accidents' befall Rabbit, after he loses his lucky charm: his horse bolts, a wagon crashes and a cougar attacks him. Rabbit is eventually shot dead (the bullet passing through a Bible in his pocket) – but not before confessing that he went to town to kill Judd deliberately, in revenge for his own wife's murder. The good cast included Harry Dean Stanton and Dan Duryea, as the eerie, harmonica-playing 'prophet'. By this point in the series, Eastwood's close friend and stunt double William 'Bill' Thompkins had joined the regular cast, as gummy drover 'Toothless'.

For 'The Race', the opening episode of the 1964–65 season, the title sequence was altered again, with the three leads now 'legends of the west' bronze sculptures in the style of Frederic Remington – Favor lassos a steer, Rowdy leaps into the saddle and Wishbone lashes the chuck wagon. At Twin Forks, the drovers are exhausted and Favor wants to set off straight away with a herd to Abilene. 'Get yourself another ramrod – I quit', decides Rowdy, but soon afterwards he is offered a drive of his own. He takes up the rancher's offer and recruits his crew, including ramrod Weed (Warren Oates in the third of his four guest starring roles in the series) and Luke (L.Q. Jones). Rowdy even entices Wishbone from Favor's outfit. With typical rash bravado, Rowdy bets that he can beat Favor to the railhead at Abilene and a cattle-driving race ensues. By the end of the episode, Rowdy's brief tenure as trail boss is over – no longer addressed with a respectful 'Mister Yates', he's 'Just plain Rowdy'.

In 'The Enormous Fist', the second episode of the 1964–65 season, one of the guests was Eastwood's future spaghetti western co-star Lee Van Cleef. Early in the episode, Favor is trying to hire drovers during a drought. Braggart Fred Grant (Van Cleef) wants to be hired (to support his wife and three children) but Favor refuses. During a brawl, Favor punches Grant, who is killed when he bangs his head against a cattle pen. Favor looks after Grant's wife, Dolly (Brenda Scott), and her children, including vengeful son Adam (Mark Slade, later of TV's *The High Chaparral*). Van Cleef also appeared in the next *Rawhide* episode 'Piney' as a completely different character – Deck Somers, a part-Indian, who is employed on a robbery because he has exceptional eyesight and hearing. Ed Begley played Piney, a bank robber who assembles a gang (including Deck) to tunnel into a bank. To escape the gang hides out with the cattle drive (Piney is an old friend of Favor's), with the loot hidden in a mattress.

Although Van Cleef and Eastwood share screen time, unfortunately the future co-stars, who became spaghetti western icons, never exchange dialogue.

In its heyday, *Rawhide* was a huge ratings winner. When it was first aired in 1959, *Gunsmoke* was the top-rated TV show, followed by *Wagon Train*, *Have Gun Will Travel* and *The Rifleman*. Other western shows in the top 30 included *Maverick* (No. 6), *Tales of Wells Fargo* (No. 7), *The Life and Legend of Wyatt Earp* (No. 10), plus *Zane Gray Theatre*, *The Texan*, *Wanted: Dead or Alive* (starring Steve McQueen), *Cheyenne*, *Sugarfoot* and *The Lawman*, with *Rawhide* bringing up the rear at number 28. For the 1959–60 season, *Rawhide* rose to 17th place, but by 1960–61, the series' peak, it was 6th. In 1961–62 it was 13th, in 1962–63, 22nd, until it dropped out of the top 30 altogether. By then the golden age of TV westerns had passed, and it was only *Bonanza* (1959–73), *The High Chaparral* (1967–71), *The Virginian* (1962–1971, later *The Man from Shiloh*), *The Big Valley* (1965–69) and *Gunsmoke* (1955–75) which lasted the sixties. Of the late-fifties TV western generation, James Garner, Steve McQueen, Burt Reynolds, Charles Bronson and finally Eastwood made the leap to big screen superstardom. Even by the 1964 season, one thing was apparent: Eastwood was more than ready to carry a star vehicle on his own.

PART ONE
THE WESTERNS

In the early sixties, western films were still locked in a range war for audiences with TV westerns – and losing. What cinema needed was an out-of-towner, a hired gun, a specialist who could turn the tide and entice audiences from their comfy sofas back into theatres, where seats cost money. Their unlikely saviour was an Italian director named Sergio Leone.

Hollywood had counterattacked TV in the late fifties with a series of hugely popular, adult-themed big-screen westerns – including *The Man from Laramie* (1955), *The Searchers* (1956), *The Big Country* (1958) and *Rio Bravo* (1959) – but they were few and far between. By the early sixties some interesting genre one-offs had driven the western into new and interesting territory. Paramount among these was a remake of Akira Kurosawa's Japanese action drama *Seven Samurai* (1955) as *The Magnificent Seven* (1960), which was a massive hit in Italy where the heroes' mercenary adventures struck a chord.

A Fistful of Dollars (1964)

When Sergio Leone cast Clint Eastwood in a trio of westerns, *A Fistful of Dollars* followed by *For a Few Dollars More* (1965) and *The Good, the Bad and the Ugly* (1966), it gave the genre a much needed fuel-injection of style, wit, violence and grit. The 'Dollars' trilogy made Eastwood a stratospheric celebrity climber, from TV star to global success story, and his character 'The Man with No Name' who 'sold lead in exchange for gold' is still probably the most recognisable gunslinger in cinema. Eastwood's hero killed with passion, but no compassion, and was a slender moral cut above the villains he dispatched. 'No Name' was a loner (like perennial western stalwarts Gary Cooper, Alan Ladd and James Stewart) and had no relationships with women and decidedly untrustworthy ones with men. He was just on the side of 'law and order', but only for his own ends – his rewards were a fistful of dollars, a cartload of valuable 'Wanted' corpses or a coffin brimming with stolen gold coins. In an era when image was everything, the trappings of 'The Man with No Name' – the Mexican poncho, the cheroot cigar, the two-days' growth of stubble – were as recognisable and marketable as The Beatles' black suits and mop tops, Barbarella's skimpy space outfits, *raffiné* Holly Golightly's Givenchy, Tiffany diamonds and cigarette holder, and James Bond's tux and tie.

There have been many different versions of how Eastwood came to be cast in *A Fistful of Dollars*. The most accepted one is that in the autumn of 1963 a script called 'Il Magnifico Straniero' ('The Magnificent Stranger') arrived at the William Morris Agency, Eastwood's representatives. Eastwood was hardly the first choice for the lead role of 'Joe the Stranger' – the list of actors who had already been contacted included Henry Fonda, James Coburn, Charles Bronson, Henry Silva, Rory Calhoun and Richard Harrison. The project was to be financed by Italian, West German and

Spanish investors and directed by Leone, then known only for 'sword and sandal' flicks. The film's entire budget was only $200,000 and none of the actors approached would accept the $15,000 offered. Eastwood recognised the verbose, thick manuscript, which resembled a telephone directory and 'wasn't even typed up in regular script form', as a rewrite of *Yojimbo*, a successful 1961 Japanese samurai film directed by Kurosawa, which he'd seen on its American release as *Yojimbo – The Bodyguard*. Eastwood loved Kurosawa's action comedy, masterfully shot in black and white Tohoscope, and though not especially keen on the dialogue rewritten in Leone's adaptation, he accepted the offer and flew to Rome in April 1964, for the $15,000 all-in salary – even though he and Paul Brinegar were making that kind of money in a single engagement as entertainers on the rodeo publicity tours for *Rawhide*.

Interviewed in 1971 for *Photoplay*, Eastwood recalled, 'In *Rawhide* I did get awfully tired of playing the conventional white hat. The hero who kisses old ladies and dogs and was kind to everybody. I decided it was time to be an anti-hero'. Leone had screened 'Incident of the Black Sheep' from *Rawhide*, some sources claim with an eye on casting Eric Fleming, but this seems unlikely as Fleming hardly figures in the story. Leone cast Eastwood, though the hero envisioned by Leone was a far cry from Rowdy Yates. Leone's co-scriptwriter Duccio Tessari had wanted to call the

1.1 Spaghetti Westerns: Bounty hunters 'The Man With No Name' and Colonel Douglas Mortimer in *For a Few Dollars More* (1965); Clint Eastwood and Lee Van Cleef on location in Los Albaricoques, Almeria. Image courtesy Kevin Wilkinson Collection.

protagonist Ringo. The original script called him 'Texas Joe', while the published script (issued in Italy in 1979) calls him Joe, lo Straniero ('Joe the Stranger'), but all UK/US publicity marketed him as 'The Man with No Name'.

Joe arrives by mule in the Mexican border town of San Miguel, where he discovers from cantina owner Silvanito (Pepe Calvo) that the district is controlled by two rival gangs of bandits and smugglers: the Rojos, who deal bootleg liquor, and the Baxters, big gun merchants. The gangs employ hired gunmen and pay in dollars; in Leone's original script, both factions were Mexican (the Rojos and the Morales). 'If you don't mind doing a little killing, you will have no trouble finding someone eager to pay you', Silvanito advises. The stranger sees an opportunity to make a few dollars and exploits the gangs' rivalry, hiring himself as a gunhand to the Rojos. The Rojos' leader, Ramon (Gian Maria Volonte), leads a raid on a Mexican army convoy, stealing their shipment of gold, and tries to make peace with the Baxters. But Joe stirs up trouble, taking payment from both factions. Soon the feud is as fervid as ever, with the gangs shooting it out in a cemetery. Joe helps Marisol (Marianne Koch), a woman who has been blackmailed into living with Ramon as his mistress, to escape, but the subterfuge is discovered and the Rojos capture Joe and beat him up. He escapes and the Rojos search the town, massacring the Baxters, burning them out and shooting them down. Whisked out of town by coffin-maker Piripero (Josef Egger), Joe recovers in a disused mine. When Silvanito is caught bringing supplies to Joe and is tortured, the stranger returns to San Miguel for the last time, killing the Rojos in a duel before unhitching the coffin-maker's mule and riding back into the sierras.

When Eastwood arrived in Rome, he brought his *Rawhide* props (boots, gunbelt, spurs and Cobra-handled Colt), plus a hat, some black drainpipe jeans and a battered sheepskin waistcoat. Leone and costume designer Carlo Simi draped him in a rather unusual addition – a fringed Spanish poncho, essentially a square piece of fabric with a slit for the head, decorated with a series of concentric patterns, including a rope motif, criss-cross lines and geometric Grecian designs. This poncho appears green in some washed-out prints of the film and almost black in Italian prints, but it's actually brown. In the original script, Eastwood's character, a Confederate sergeant called Ray, steals it from a Mexican peon swimming in the Rio Grande. In *Fistful*'s duel scenes, the stranger flicks this poncho over his shoulder to quicken his draw. Eastwood also grew a stubbly beard for the role, possibly inspired by Toshiro Mifune, who played Sanjuro Kuwabatake, the unshaven lead in *Yojimbo*. One key mannerism Eastwood stole from Mifune was his thoughtful chin rubbing. Joe smokes cheroots throughout, even though Eastwood was in reality a non-smoker and the cigar is rarely lit. It is as Joe that he perfected the Clint squint, reputedly caused by the strong Spanish sunlight. The stranger's costume, props and mean demeanour fashioned Eastwood's screen image, which he honed into what became known by critics and fans as spaghetti westerns, Euro-westerns, macaroni westerns, pizza westerns or Western All'Italiana ('Westerns, Italian-style'). After years of being told that he looked 'wrong' for starring roles, that he was too tall, too ungainly, that he didn't look like the popular stars of the day, or that he squinted too much, he found that in this new style western he *was* the look.

Leone shot *Fistful* in Italy and Spain. The budget didn't allow much room for luxury and Eastwood even brought along his own stunt double – Bill Thompkins from *Rawhide*. It is Thompkins as Joe who gallops through the desert in the night-time riding sequences; he also plays the Baxter gunman in the green shirt during the hostage exchange. San Miguel was filmed in 'Golden City', a western set at Hojo De Manzanares (north of Madrid) and the adobe village of Los Albaricoques in Almeria, southern Spain. The interiors of Rojo's residence and its whitewashed walled courtyard were Casa Da Campo, a Madrid museum. The small adobe house where Marisol is imprisoned, currently a hotel called Cortijo El Sotillo, is near San Jose in Almeria, while the Rio Bravo gold ambush was filmed on the River Alberche at Aldea Del Fresno. Filming commenced on Rome interiors in April at Cinecitta studios, moved to Hojo De Manzanares and its environs (for the graveyard shootout and the town scenes) and then wrapped in the Almerian desert.

A notable aspect of *Fistful* is the severe bloody beating Joe the Stranger suffers at the hands of the Rojos in their wine cellar, probably the worst onscreen pummelling Eastwood has taken in his entire career. As Eastwood remembered, 'In the 'Dollars' films, stoic was the word. It was comedy and yet it was played dead straight. The violence tag was hung too tightly around my neck. The fact that they were made by an Italian in Europe had some people going in as edgy as I was when I made them. I personally don't think of them as violent, only perhaps as black humour'. In *Fistful*, Joe is so badly injured (one eye is almost closed) and immobilised that the coffin maker has to sneak him out of town in a casket. This rough treatment reappeared in many of Eastwood's later films and his heroes have had to recover quickly to defeat the villain: a symbolic 'resurrection'.

Fistful contains two quintessential action moments in Eastwood's transformation from clean-cut TV western hero to screen idol. In the first, he guns down four Baxter gunmen hanging around the San Miguel corral, for $100 in Rojo blood money. Having already spooked Joe's mule as a warning, the quartet tells him to leave town. The gang find their threats amusing, but the stranger doesn't: 'My mule don't like people laughing, gets the crazy idea you're laughing at him'. His mood suddenly changes, from amiable cowboy kidding around to lethal killer demanding an apology. Joe flicks his poncho over his shoulder and the tension mounts, until in a flash, guns blaze and four Baxters bite the dust. Having ordered three coffins before the confrontation, Joe corrects his order: 'My mistake…four coffins'. The *Saturday Review* scathingly noted that 'Eastwood…makes full use of his one expression', but the actor's underplayed performance and his delivery marked Eastwood as a new type of action movie star, one for whom understatement and stoicism were trademarks.

In the film's finale, Joe faces Ramon and four of his men in the plaza of San Miguel, near a water tower. The stranger announces his return with two dynamite explosions, which wreath the street in dust, unnerving his opponents: it's a powerful image, with the stranger striding out of the dust cloud. Earlier Ramon has quoted a Mexican proverb to the stranger, claiming that a Colt .45 is inferior to a Winchester rifle. We already know from Ramon's demonstrations of marksmanship that he always aims for the heart. 'Shoot to kill, you better hit the heart', goads the stranger, 'The heart Ramon, aim for the heart, or you'll never stop me'. Ramon fires at Joe repeatedly, hitting him, but each time the stranger gets back to his feet, seemingly supernatural. Eventually, when he's within pistol range, Joe reveals that he's been wearing a sheet of iron strapped to his chest, an armour hidden under his poncho, and there are seven bullet dents in the area of his heart. Real-life professional killer and lawman Jim Miller, known variously as 'Killin' Jim' and 'The Deacon', wore a breastplate during his gunfights. One of the most deadly, not to say indestructible shootists, Killin' Jim survived 14 gun battles.

Fistful's memorable score was composed by Ennio Morricone, a school friend of Leone's. The main theme (or 'titoli') deployed acoustic guitar, bells and whip-cracks backing the melody, voiced by a whistler and an electric guitar (both performed by Alessandro Alessandroni), while I Cantori Moderni ('The Modern Singers') supplied harmonies. This accompanied the pop-art title sequence, deploying rotoscope, an animation process that converts action from the film into garish, comic-strip violence. The titles begin with hypnotic smoke rings, which reveal the galloping hero and ricocheting gunshots herald Eastwood's name onscreen. Elsewhere Morricone used the ominous piano and harmonica of 'Almost Dead' (for the stranger's arrival in town), the cacophonous percussion and trumpet of 'The Chase', the eerie build-up to 'Without Pity' (for the Baxter massacre), and the Mexican trumpet 'Deguello', a funereal Mariachi backed by strings and chorus. Entitled 'A Fistful of Dollars' on soundtrack albums, this was released by RCA as a 45rpm single under the title 'The Man with No Name'. This music and that of Eastwood's later spaghetti westerns were inexorably linked to the actor throughout his career. They became Eastwood's 'theme tunes' and his later films occasionally deployed Morricone-style musical cues as knowing references to his career as 'The Man with No Name'.

Fistful was released in Italy as *Per Un Pugno di Dollari* ('For a Fistful of Dollars') in September 1964, to great word-of-mouth success, eventually becoming the biggest-grossing Italian film of all time up to that point. Italian posters for its premiere trumpeted 'The most recent and sensational western film with the new American idol'. For international release, United Artists dubbed the film *A Fistful of Dollars* (shortened in the animated title sequence to simply *Fistful of Dollars*) and prepared a high-profile publicity campaign ahead of the opening in the US in January 1967. Key art featured Eastwood in his poncho, with the taglines 'He's going to trigger a whole new style in adventure', 'In his own way he is perhaps the most dangerous man who ever lived!' and 'The first motion picture of its kind. It won't be the last!' *Fistful* was rated 'M' in the US and 'X' in the UK, even after it was trimmed for violence; subsequent DVD releases, rated '15', are uncut. In the US, *Fistful* took $4.25 million in 1967 and eventually grossed $14.5 million. Many Italian and Spanish westerns of the sixties and early seventies capitalised on the success of Leone's film, with derivative titles and poncho-clad heroes, including 'Vance Lewis'/Luigi Vanzi's *For a Dollar in the Teeth* (1966 – aka *A Stranger in Town*), starring Tony Anthony as the stranger and Frank Wolff (Leone's original choice for Ramon Rojo) as bandit leader Aguila ('The Eagle'). Eastwood made better films and he also made much more money, but *A Fistful of Dollars* facilitated his leap from TV fame to international superstardom. When, in December 1980, the Museum of Modern Art paid tribute to Eastwood with a one-day retrospective of his films, the works chosen were *Escape from Alcatraz*, *Play Misty for Me*, *Bronco Billy* and *A Fistful of Dollars*.

For a Few Dollars More (1965)

Fistful certainly wasn't the last motion picture of its kind and Eastwood was soon back in Italy and Spain filming a sequel, literally *For a Few Dollars More* – his salary this time was $50,000. As 'the anti-hero to end all anti-heroes' (as *Films and Filming* christened him), Eastwood was again a gunfighter, now a bounty hunter named Manco. The story was based on an original outline by Leone and his brother-in-law Fulvio Morsella, with a screenplay by Leone, Luciano Vincenzoni and an uncredited Sergio Donati.

Manco and Colonel Douglas Mortimer (Lee Van Cleef) are two deadly bounty killers, ridding the American southwest of renegade outlaws and cashing in their rewards. When the territory's most notorious criminal El Indio (Gian Maria Volonte) escapes from prison, the pair teams up to scoop the $10,000 reward offered 'Dead or Alive'. Indio and his cadre of bandidos target the three-ton safe in El Paso, a supposedly impregnable fortress containing almost a million dollars. Working to Mortimer's stratagem, 'one from the outside, one from the inside', Manco infiltrates Indio's gang and tries to sabotage their plan, but Indio is smarter and the gang flees with the loot. The robbers lie low in Agua Caliente, a New Mexican pueblo, where Mortimer also joins the gang and carefully opens the safe without destroying the cash. The bounty killers steal the money and hide it, before being caught and viciously beaten by Indio. Indio releases the gringo gunmen and sets them against his gang in a gun battle, but soon only Indio is left alive, and in a final duel, Mortimer faces Indio and kills him. The colonel reveals that Indio raped his sister, who then killed herself, and that Mortimer has been seeking vengeance ever since. His vendetta complete, the colonel allows Manco to keep the reward.

This time Leone had a larger budget than *Fistful* – $600,000. Leone visited the US in January 1965, re-signing Eastwood (for $50,000), and also hired Lee Van Cleef (for $17,000). Van Cleef was a supporting actor from fifties western, sci-fi and gangster movies; he had guested in two episodes of the 1964–65 season of *Rawhide* but was currently employed as a freelance artist. Leone wanted Henry Fonda, Charles Bronson or Lee Marvin as his colonel, but their unavailability led to Van Cleef's casting – Leone noted: 'His glare makes holes in the screen'. Eastwood received top billing, as the star who would ensure the film's success, even though ex-soldier Colonel Mortimer, 'the best shot in the Carolinas', was the focus for much of the story.

Leone again filmed the interiors at Cinecitta but lensed the majority in Spain: partly near Madrid, but mostly in Almeria, with Eastwood present at most locations. The desolate Spanish deserts, sierras and *ramblas* (dried-up riverbed canyons) took centre stage, as a memorable and breathtaking backdrop. The great riding scenes, filmed in the Almerian sierras, where Manco loses a posse from El Paso, display Eastwood's consummate horsemanship to best advantage; Bill Thomkins didn't double for Eastwood in this sequel. The towns depicted were 'played' by a variety of film sets. White Rocks was a set at Colmenar Viejo, near Madrid; Tucumcari was the San Miguel set at Hojo De Manzanares; a western set at Cinecitta appeared as 'Santa Cruz'. El Paso, the focus for the middle section of the film, was designed and built in grand style by Carlo Simi (who was also the film's costumier) in the desert near Tabernas, Almeria. The whitewashed Spanish village of Los Albaricoques (named 'The Apricots', after its fruit trees) was Agua Caliente, the isolated pueblo which is the setting for the film's last 45 minutes. The ruined, roofless Church of Santa Maria at Turillas was used for Indio's hideout when he breaks out of prison. Las Palmeras, where Manco rendezvous with Indio after the robbery, was El Oasis, a patch of desert with clumps of palm trees, which had been planted during *Lawrence of Arabia* (1962). El Paso still stands in Spain. Now called 'Mini Hollywood', it attracts sunburnt tourists to its 'Wild West' show re-enactments.

The script, which Eastwood and Van Cleef pruned, was tighter than *Fistful* and Leone's visual style began to flourish. This is illustrated by Manco's first appearance in the film. Colonel Mortimer asks the Tucumcari sheriff if he knows the whereabouts of outlaw Red 'Baby' Cavanagh. The lawman answers that a stranger stopped by, also asking after Red. 'I've never seen him before', says the sheriff of the stranger, 'His name is Manco'. Leone cuts to a close-up of Eastwood's trademark rattlesnake gripped pistol, fringed poncho and a leather gauntlet he wears on his gun hand (accompanied by a crash of thunder on the soundtrack), as Eastwood stalks past the camera into White Rocks in the lashing rain. When Eastwood reaches the saloon, he flicks back his poncho, takes a match from his breast pocket and lights a cheroot, as he slowly raises his head – his face has been obscured by the brim of his hat – and reveals his face for the first time (as a thunderclap crashes on the soundtrack). In *For a Few*, Eastwood's hero is more humorous, he even smiles occasionally, and has a great final punchline. As he loads the bandits' corpses into a cart to take back to El Paso, his bounty haul calculations fall short of expectations and he realises he's one villain short. At that moment Manco spins around and shoots outlaw Groggy, who is about to plug him in the back. At the sound of gunfire the colonel shouts, 'Any trouble boy?'; 'No old man', answers Manco, 'Thought I was having trouble with my adding – it's all right now'.

It is Van Cleef's Colonel Mortimer, the Bible-reading 'Reverend', and his tracking of Indio, that drives the film. His vendetta is symbolised by the pair of gold pocket watches (a larger male and smaller female version of the design) in a heart-shaped box. Mortimer's revenge ends the film satisfyingly, with the bandito and 'Il Colonnello' facing each other in a broken ring, marked by a low, crumbling wall and quarried stones – a dusty circle of destiny. Manco, armed with Indio's Volcanic calibre .38 carbine, referees this final confrontation, with the moment the two men draw decided by the carillon of Mortimer's watch – the chiming countdown to life and death.

Ennio Morricone once again provided the distinctive score, with a main theme deploying Jew's harp, flute, whistling, chorus and electric guitars – a 'riding theme' powered along by pounding hoofbeat drums. For duels Morricone created 'La Resa Dei Conti' ('The Settling of Accounts', also called 'Sixty Seconds to What?' or 'Paying off Scores'), with its tinkling watch melody, reverberating Flamenco guitar, blasts of church organ and trumpet: a vocal version was recorded by Maurizio Graf entitled 'An Eye for an Eye' but wasn't used in the film. Eerie feedback scores Indio's gang casing the adobe bank in 'The Watcher Watched', while the side-drums, piano, brass and tolling bell of 'Il Colpo' ('The Raid') accompany them emptying the safe. The delicate guitar and oboe of 'Vice of Killing' bursts into life with galloping snare drums and a heavenly, wordless vocal, as Indio's band speed across the desert with their loot-laden wagon, and as Manco rides alone into unwelcoming Agua Caliente. 'Goodbye Colonel' (sometimes billed as 'Addio Colonnello' or 'Bye Bye Colonel'), with lyrical oboe, strings, carillon and chorus, scored Mortimer's slow ride into the sunset.

For a Few Dollars More was released in Italy as *Per Qualche Dollaro in Piu* in December 1965, to massive and influential success: there was even a parody of the film called *For a Few Dollars Less* (1966). *For a Few Dollars More* was released in the US rated 'M' (later 'R') four months after *Fistful*, to even greater success, initially taking $5 million. Posters featuring Eastwood ('The Man With No Name Is Back') and Van Cleef ('The Man In Black Is Waiting') warned, 'As if one wasn't enough ... as if death needed a double. It's the second motion picture of its kind! It won't be the last'. The UK trailer introduced Volonte and Eastwood as 'the men who excited you so in *For a Fistful of Dollars*'. The superior US trailer, one of Eastwood's best promos, touted: 'Clint Eastwood is The Man with No Name ... Lee Van Cleef is Waiting'. The UK print cut violence, garnering an 'X' certificate, removing, among others, the final explanatory flashback depicting Mortimer's sister's suicide. Even Indio's mad cackling laugh was shortened for US/UK prints, so demonic was his villainy. Critically reviled at the time, *For a Few Dollars More* is one of the most financially profitable Italian westerns ever made, with Eastwood now dubbed 'Il Cigarillo' by his Italian fans.

The Good, the Bad and the Ugly (1966)

Eastwood's next project with Leone, *The Good, the Bad and the Ugly*, would today be called a 'threequel', although in chronological relation to the first two films it's a prequel. In early 1862, Confederate forces led by General Sibley invaded New Mexico from Texas. Amid the confusion, as the war engulfs the Rio Grande, three men have something else on their minds: hired gun Angel Eyes (Lee Van Cleef), Mexican outlaw Tuco Ramirez (Eli Wallach) and his partner, shifty drifter Blondy (Eastwood), are searching for a cashbox containing $200,000 in gold coin buried in a grave marked 'Arch Stanton' in Sad Hill. It is missing following a Union surprise attack on a Confederate payroll wagon destined for the 3rd Cavalry. In Sad Hill, the trio confront each other: Blondy kills Angel Eyes and splits the cash with Tuco, leaving his partner stranded in the middle of nowhere with his hands bound, but $100,000 richer.

1.2 'The Man With No Name is Back!': original poster for the 1967 US release of Sergio Leone's *For a Few Dollars More* (1965). Author's collection.

One scene in *For a Few Dollars More* hints at the central three-way deception of *The Good*. Following the El Paso bank raid, Mortimer and Manco agree to convince Indio to head north, so they can ambush him in Rio Bravo Canyon, but duplicitous Manco suggests to Indio they head south, to the Mexican border. Indio, equally suspicious, rides east, to Agua Caliente, but miraculously Mortimer out-guesses them and arrives there first, telling Manco: 'I just reasoned it out'. The Colonel knew that Manco would ignore their plan and that Indio would second-guess them – 'Since El Paso's out of the question, well here I am'. This elaborate web of trickery and double-cross became the skeletal plot of Leone's third western.

The epic story was written by Leone and Luciano Vincenzoni. Sergio Donati and Age-Scarpelli also worked on the screenplay, which was then translated into English by Mickey Knox. Again working with producer Albert Grimaldi of PEA, Leone had a budget of $1.2 million. This time Eastwood drove a hard bargain: for his role as Blondy 'The Good', he received a quarter of a million dollars (more than the amount the film's cashbox contains), noting, 'I'm probably the highest-paid American actor who ever worked in Italian pictures. Only Mastroianni gets more in Italy. For the first time in my life, I can pick the parts I want to play'. Lee Van Cleef returned to villainy, with his role as Angel Eyes 'The Bad'. Originally called Banjo in the script, then Sentenza during shooting, his name became Angel Eyes during the English dubbing. Eli Wallach, an outlaw in *The Magnificent Seven* (1960) and *How the West Was Won* (1962), played Tuco 'The Ugly'. The remainder of the cast was a rogue's gallery of actors – good, bad and ugly – to play the assorted ruffians and trail trash the heroes encounter. Italian Aldo Giuffre played drunken Unionist captain Clinton who dreams of blowing to smithereens a bridge he's been ordered to take intact. Antonio Molino Rojo portrayed a prison camp commandant with a gangrenous leg, similarly disillusioned with the Union cause. Luigi Pistilli played Tuco's brother, Brother Pablo, a monk tending wounded soldiers at his San Antonio Mission. Mario Brega appeared as brutal Unionist corporal Wallace, at his happiest beating seven shades of grey out of Confederate prisoners of war. Canadian Al Mulock played a one-armed bounty hunter who traps Tuco in a bubble bath but crows too long: 'If you have to shoot – shoot, don't talk', Tuco tells his corpse.

Filming took place between May and July of 1966. That Spanish spring and summer was perfect weather, with solid-blue skies and smoky cloud formations. Interiors were filmed at Elios Studios. Elios' western set was also where the town of Mesilla was filmed, for Tuco's first escape from hanging. His second escape, in Valverde, was shot at the 'El Paso' set in Almeria. The same set was also used for the scene where Tuco robs a gunsmith, when Angel Eyes questions a prostitute in Santa Ana, and when Sibley's Confederate column retreats through Santa Fe. Other New Mexican locations – the Sierra Magdalena and the Sangre De Cristo ('Blood of Christ') Mountains, and white-washed dusty pueblos, ghost towns and farms – were filmed in Almeria. The notorious 90-mile desert, the Jornado Del Muerto (the 'Day's Journey of the Dead Man'), where Tuco tortures blistered Blondy, was filmed at Cabo De Gata. The Union railway depot

1.3 'Sorry Shorty': Tuco the Ugly gets the drop on Blondy in the desert; Clint Eastwood in the Spanish dunes for *The Good, the Bad and the Ugly* (1966). Author's collection.

was La Calahorra Station (on the Almeria-Guadix line) and the San Antonio Mission was Cortijo De Los Frailes ('House of the Brothers'); the mission's interior was filmed at the Monastery of San Pedro de Arlanza, north of Madrid. Battle-torn Peralta was filmed at Colmenar Viejo's western set near Madrid. The scene where Blondy and Tuco first meet was lensed at rocky Manzanares El Real, further north. Most of the Civil War scenes were shot between Madrid and Burgos, in Castilla-León. The entrenched battle between the blue and the grey raged at Covarrubias, on the River Arlanza. Betterville prison camp was built at Carazo and Sad Hill's amphitheatre of the dead, ringed with concentric circles of tombs, was also south of the Arlanza, at Contreras. All three locations were less than 20 kilometres apart, with the prison camp location actually just over the mesa behind Angel Eyes during the final showdown.

Leone's anti-heroic depiction of the American Civil War filled his towns with refugees and troops, while the military hospitals are packed with the bloodied wounded. Outside Valverde's 'Ballroom Music Hall', Angel Eyes questions a Confederate cavalryman who has lost both his legs, calling him a 'Half Soldier'. Betterville Prison Camp had its origins in terrible Federal stockades such as Camp Douglas, Chicago, which lost almost 10 percent of its 3,880 inmates in a single month to dreadful conditions and disease. The film's battle scenes deployed hundreds of extras (played by Spanish soldiers in Civil War period costume) and heavy-duty artillery, including Gatling Guns, Parrott Guns and mortars. The entrenched defence works at Langstone Bridge were also based on archive photos, depicting tiered wicker and sandbagged breastworks, rifle pits, bomb-proof shelters, gun emplacements and the spiky criss-crossed log defences (an anti-cavalry barricade known as 'chevaux-de-frise'). Costume designer Carlo Simi included such details as the Confederate soldiers wearing colour-coded kepis (caps), collars and cuffs, denoting their branch of service: yellow for cavalry, blue for infantry and red for artillery. Leone loved the film's 'big scope'; 'And I liked it, I must say', remembered Eastwood, 'Especially coming from television where you didn't have the opportunity to do that'. As Leone boasted, 'This picture is more accurate than any American western'.

Eastwood's drifting nowhere man is a nomadic con man christened 'Blondy' by Tuco. The Italian print dubs him 'Biondo' (after Eastwood's fair complexion) while the film's novelisation has Mexican Tuco calling him 'Whitey'. His business partnership with Tuco – where he turns the wanted outlaw over to the law and then saves him by shooting through the hanging rope during the execution – provides much humour, as neither trusts the other. Blondy tires of their partnership, reasoning that Tuco will never be worth more than $3,000: 'There's really not too much future with a sawn-off runt like you'. Eventually he cuts loose of Tuco in the desert, 70 miles from Valverde: 'I'll keep the money and you can have the rope'.

In his third Leone outing, Eastwood's performance is confident and effortless. He deploys his full range of 'Man with No Name' mannerisms: the double takes, the squint, mouthing the cigar, the deadpan asides, the long silences and the empty half-smile. Blondy uses a Colt Navy pistol, again fitted with snake grips, and a Henry repeating rifle with a telescopic sight. This time there is more humility and humanity to Eastwood's gunman. Blondy offers a dying Confederate artilleryman a last drag on his cigar. Before Blondy detonates Langstone Bridge, he tells a badly wounded Union officer, 'Take a slug of this capt'n ... keep your ears open'. In one unusual scene, Blondy bides his time in war-torn Peralta by playing with a kitten in his hat. Such compassion, almost tenderness, would be rare in Eastwood's westerns, even in mature works such as *The Outlaw Josey Wales* and *Unforgiven*. During the Battle of Langstone Bridge, as the Union and Confederate forces suicidally attack the bridge under heavy artillery fire, he watches and mutters, 'I've never seen so many men wasted so badly'. But Blondy loots his trademark poncho from the dead Confederate artilleryman and becomes 'The Man with No Name' for the final duel.

Morricone's most famous composition, the film's title music, is cut to an equally memorable title sequence, with colourful tinted stills from the film, explosions and dust. The main theme, a coyote-howling, guitar-twanging, bugle charge, is one of the most famous western themes of all time – its 'Ay-ey-ay-ey-ahhh!' answered 'Wah-wah-wah!' instantly recognisable. Elsewhere, mournful tunes – 'The Fort', 'Marcetta', 'March without Hope' and the ballad 'The Soldier's Story' – score the Civil War devastation. The epic 'The Desert' accompanies Blondy's bubbled agony in the dunes and in 'Ecstasy of Gold', the rolling piano and Edda Dell'Orso's soprano solo soar as Tuco frantically scours Sad Hill. With epic battles and scores of extras, it is ironic that the finale involves only the three antagonists competing for the prize – the contents of the grave marked 'Unknown', the tomb with no name, next to Arch Stanton's, which contains a cashbox. It is one of the most memorable endings to a western and a fitting climax to the 'Dollars' trilogy, as the Good, the Bad and the Ugly shoot it out in the epicentre of the vast graveyard, with Morricone's music 'Il Triello' ('The Trio') thundering on the soundtrack.

For its US release, United Artists considered several different titles for the film – *The Good, the Ugly, the Bad* (a literal translation of the original Italian title, *Il Buono, Il Brutto, Il Cattivo*), *River of Dollars* (a translation of *Un Fiume Di Dollari*, the Italian title of a spaghetti western released in the US by UA as *The Hills Run Red*) and even *The Man With No Name* – before settling on *The Good, the Bad and the Ugly*. Cynical posters announced: 'For Three Men the Civil War Wasn't Hell...It was Practice' and 'This time the jackpot's a cool $200,000'. In equal parts impressive and incompetent, the eventful, epic trailer intoned, 'The Good, the Bad, the Ugly...the blue, the grey, the Civil War...the questions, the answers, the showdown...the reason? The gold!' The US trailer misidentified Tuco as 'The Bad' and Angel Eyes as 'The Ugly', which saddled Van Cleef with the epithet 'Mr Ugly' for his subsequent spaghetti westerns.

Critics were divided on the merits of Leone's third western. On 25 January 1968, the *New York Times,* who called it '*The Burn, the Gouge and the Mangle* (the screen name is simply inappropriate)', said that it 'must be the most expensive, pious and repellent movie in the history of its peculiar genre'. *Variety* noted, 'A curious amalgam of the visually striking, the dramatically feeble and the offensively sadistic'. But most critics agreed that Leone was a talented director with an eye for detail and action. Next to Wallach, Eastwood and Van Cleef were deemed 'expressionless characters with poker faces' as animated as 'a slab of boot leather'. It ran 161 minutes in the US (rated 'M', later 'R'); in the UK, it was cut to 148 minutes (rated 'X'). The original Italian version, which premiered over Christmas 1966, was 171 minutes long and included several extra scenes. In 2003, Eastwood and Wallach, plus Simon Prescott, a Van Cleef voice impersonator (Van Cleef died in 1989), dubbed the missing Italian scenes into English, but in this version the gunshots, cannon fire, explosions and sound effects were altered. The Italian version, which runs 169 minutes on video and has correct sound effects, is the definitive version of the film, while the best English language version runs 156 minutes, still rated '18' on DVD.

A paperback tie-in of *The Good, the Bad and the Ugly* written by Joe Millard was published in 1967. In this version, Tuco doesn't take part in the final duel and Angel Eyes (or Sentenza, as he's known in the book) carries a custom-made pistol with a 14-inch barrel, like Colonel Mortimer. A cover version of Morricone's theme, rearranged and conducted by Hugo Montenegro, was released by RCA Victor on both sides of the Atlantic in 1968 – backed by 'There's Got to Be a Better Way' from *Bandolero!* (1968) in the UK and 'March without Hope' in the US. It went to number one in the UK in November 1968 and peaked at number two in the US. Its success contributed to the film's massive grosses – in the US alone it took over $6 million, putting it inside the 10 most successful westerns of the sixties.

In Italy 'new releases' *El Maladetto Gringo, Il Magnifico Straniero* and *El Gringhero* welded together *Rawhide* episodes ('Incident of the Running Man' and 'The Backshooter'), until an injunction gunned them down. The 'Dollars' films' success in Italy led to the 'spaghetti western' craze, which produced hundreds of films in the next ten years and revitalised, some would say saved, the Italian film industry. Following *The Good*, Eastwood and Leone didn't see each other for years, as their careers diverged on different projects – Eastwood was offered a guest star role in Leone's next film, *Once Upon a Time in the West* (1968), as one of the killers waiting for Charles Bronson in the film's opening scene, but he declined. When Leone was in the US in the early eighties making *Once Upon a Time in America*, Eastwood visited him at his hotel. 'I've often been asked if I could make another film with him', said Leone, 'I always refuse. It is impossible'. They could never have surpassed the Dollars trilogy, especially *The Good, the Bad and the Ugly*, their masterpiece.

Hang 'Em High (1968)

Following his success as the 'Man with No Name', Eastwood said 'Arrivederci Roma' and returned to the US, had a shave and gained a name, as Jed Cooper in *Hang 'Em High*, which straddled the badlands between spaghetti and Hollywood westerns. Eastwood was initially approached to star in the Hollywood western *Mackenna's Gold* (1968), but he turned it down and Gregory Peck eventually took the treasure-hunting role – an adventurer seeking fabled Apache gold in the Canyon Del'Oro. Shot partly in Monument Valley, its plot bore echoes of *The Good* and even featured Eli Wallach in a supporting role.

Though Eastwood had noted during the making of *The Good* that he could pick the parts he wanted to play, on his return to the US he capitalised on the success of the 'Dollars' films by typecasting himself as a Leonesque western hero. With his 'Dollars' earnings and a $119,000 *Rawhide* payoff, Eastwood formed his own production company, Malpaso (named after Malpaso Creek on his land is Monterey), with a view to having a personal stake in his films: this way he would be able to control his own career and the projects he participated in. All of his subsequent westerns were made with Malpaso as co-producer. In collaboration with Leonard Freeman Productions, Malpaso co-produced and financed *Hang 'Em High*, which was released through United Artists. Freeman wrote the script with Mel Goldberg, and Ted Post, who had worked with Eastwood on *Rawhide*, directed the film.

Cooper, an ex-lawman from St Louis, is herding his recently bought cattle through Oklahoma, when he is accused by a posse of stealing the herd from Johansen, a rancher who has since been murdered. The men, led by their employer Captain Wilson (Ed Begley), are Miller, Reno, Stone, Jenkins, Maddow, Tommy, Loomis and Charlie Blackfoot. They lynch Cooper and leave him for dead, but Marshall Dave Bliss (Ben Johnson) finds Cooper, revives him and takes him to Fort Grant, where 'Hangin' Judge Fenton' (Pat Hingle) presides. Acquitted and left with a nasty scar around his neck (which he conceals with a neckerchief), Cooper is convinced by Fenton to become a deputy marshal, which will enable him to take revenge on the men he seeks legally. While on a routine jail pickup, Cooper kills Reno. Then Jenkins turns himself in at Fort Grant and Cooper discovers that the rest of the lynch party are in the town of Red Creek. Cooper arrests Stone, Red Creek's blacksmith, and tracks down Miller, but Wilson, Loomis and

Tommy try to kill Cooper during a public hanging at Fort Grant. Cooper is nursed back to health by widow Rachel Warren (Inger Stevens), who is searching for the men who raped her and killed her husband. On his recovery, Cooper rides out to Wilson's 'Big W' ranch and kills Loomis and Tommy, before discovering that Wilson has hanged himself high, committing suicide. Not convinced that the law always hangs the right people, Cooper negotiates amnesty for Jenkins, who was only a bystander, before riding out after the remaining killers, Maddow and Charlie.

1.4 Clint Eastwood, in costume as Jed Cooper, on set with director Ted Post during the making of their 1968 revenge western, *Hang 'Em High*. Author's collection.

Commencing in June 1967, *Hang 'Em High* had a budget of $1.6 million, of which Eastwood received $400,000, plus 25 percent of the box office. It was filmed on location near Las Cruces in New Mexico – in the Organ Mountains (the posse's pursuit of Miller), the spectacular White Sands dunes (Cooper's trek with three rustlers) and beside the Rio Grande River (Cooper's lynching). Some location footage was shot at the Albertson Ranch in Conejo Valley, California (for Jed and Rachel's picnic). Fort Grant's interiors and exteriors were shot on a town set at Lot Three in MGM Studios.

Hang 'Em High has a rich western cast, blending old hands with up-and-coming talent. The younger cast members included Dennis Hopper and Bruce Dern, two counterculture actors who would go on to make their names in biker movies. Dern honed his screen persona in a series of western roles as a toothy maladjust. Hopper has a startling two-minute cameo as 'The Prophet', a mad zealot ('He's plumb loco') wearing a claw necklace and sackcloth rags, who dies theatrically when shot by sheriff Ben Johnson. Johnson himself had appeared in many John Ford westerns and would enjoy a renaissance in the sixties working for Sam Peckinpah, as would L.Q. Jones, cast here as taggle-haired Loomis. Reliable supporting character actors included Charles McGraw as the sheriff with a 'cardboard jail' and a permanently bad back, Pat Hingle as almighty Judge Fenton and Ed Begley (from *12 Angry Men*) as bad guy Captain Wilson. Eastwood's onscreen lovers were blonde Swedish beauty Inger Stevens as storekeeper Rachel and brassy redhead Arlene Golonka as Jennifer, a prostitute. Roxanne Tunis, Eastwood's lover from *Rawhide* days, appeared briefly as a prostitute in a blue dress amongst the crowd attending a public hanging.

Judge Adam Fenton and the mass hangings at Fort Grant are based on real-life 'Hanging Judge' Isaac Charles Parker and his courthouse on the edge of Indian Territory in Arkansas, which operated from 1870 to 1891. Parker's gallows could accommodate 12, but the most that was carried out simultaneously was six, as depicted in *Hang 'Em High*. Homer Croy's 1952 biography of the judge was called *He Hanged Them High*. Parker's trusted, notorious lord high executioner was George Maledon, photographs of whom show he had all the charm of a reanimated cadaver. James Westerfield, who played a tobacco-chewing criminal hanged by Fenton in *Hang 'Em High*, actually played Parker in the opening Fort Smith scenes of John Wayne's *True Grit* (1969). *Hang 'Em High* is set in 1889, towards the end of Parker's period, and accurately depicts Parker's macabre event hangings, with huge crowds enjoying the hymn singing and the carnivalesque public holiday atmosphere. This scene at MGM was the largest crowd to be filmed in Hollywood since *Gone with the Wind* (1939).

From its opening sequence, where Eastwood appears in cowboy chaps, herding cattle across the Rio Grande, *Hang 'Em High* more closely resembles a TV western than Leone's films, its excessive, bloody moments of violence excepted. Though Eastwood affects a cigar and wears his trademark gunbelt and boots, Jedediah Cooper is not 'The Man with No Name'. *Hang* provides its black-clad deputy marshal with legal justification for his revenge killings. As Fenton tells him, 'You used the law and a badge to heal that scar on your neck'. The *New York Times* noted that the film at least 'had a point, unlike the previous sadomasochistic exercises on foreign prairies where the grizzled Mr Eastwood stalked around in a filthy serape, holster-deep in corpses'. The story bears a passing resemblance to *The Ox-Bow Incident* (1943), one of Eastwood's favourite films, which cast Henry Fonda as a drifter enlisted in a posse that lynches three blameless men for murder. The name Jed Cooper references Hollywood westerns, recalling *High Noon*'s Gary Cooper. In 1966, Vittorio De Sica had introduced Eastwood to the French press during a promotional appearance for *For a Few Dollars More* as 'the new Gary Cooper'. *Hang 'Em High*, the only period western where Eastwood plays a straightforward lawman role, sees the star attempt to don Cooper's mantle onscreen.

Hang 'Em High is a Hollywood attempt at a spaghetti western, but the camera-work is overly lit and devoid of style, the MGM town set looks rather newly built and the film's costumes too clean. Even Dominic Frontiere's score attempts to replicate Morricone's 'Dollars' cues. In fact, when Hugo Montenegro and his Orchestra and Chorus recorded 'Music for the Man with No Name', a tribute album to the 'Dollars' trilogy in 1967, the *Hang 'Em High* theme was tacked on to it. *Variety* famously called the film 'a poor American-made imitation of a poor Italian-made imitation of an American-made western'. But the script is too verbose, especially in Judge Fenton's monologues detailing capital punishment, his moral abhorrence at revenge and the fact that, for some judged men, the only arbiter between Fenton and God is a length of rope. These scenes do give an early insight into the way subsequent Eastwood characters, in particular Harry Callahan, would argue at length with City Hall officialdom. Eastwood is at his best when bluntly confronting the judge's reasoning. When told to go to Hell, Cooper answers, 'I've already been there judge'.

The lynch mob deals its justice in uncompromising fashion, which led to the bloodier, boot-twitching shots of Eastwood being cut for TV screenings. Cooper is dragged across the Rio Grande by the neck, beaten and strung up. When Bliss finds Cooper he is near to death and the bumpy journey to Fort Grant in the mule-drawn tumbleweed prison wagon, essentially an iron cage on wheels, is suitably arduous, with Eastwood at his most dishevelled. Such a vehicle had also been the focus of the first ever episode of *Rawhide*, 'Incident of the Tumbleweed Wagon'. When, in unexpected subplot padding, Cooper is side-tracked into leading a posse pursuing three rustlers it emerges that one of them is lynch mob member Miller. But when the posse deserts him, Cooper must bring the trio in alone. 'You ain't ever gonna get me alive to Fort Grant, boy', sneers Miller, looking at the three-to-one odds. 'Then I'll get you there dead, boy', replies Cooper, through gritted teeth. The thirsty trek across White Sands culminates in a lengthy fistfight between Cooper and Miller, during which Miller's arm is savagely broken by Cooper. Already Eastwood's screen heroes will go to any lengths to see justice done.

Hang 'Em High was released in the US in August 1968, rated 'M'. Posters depicted cigar-smoking Eastwood and the six-man gallows, with the tagline: 'They made two mistakes – they hanged the wrong man and they didn't finish the job', a sensational variation of the subtle moral message of *The Ox-Bow Incident*. It made $6.7 million in

1.5 Original advertising for United Artists' release of *Hang 'Em High* featuring Clint Eastwood, his trademark cigar and the six-man Fort Grant scaffold; Australian daybill, courtesy Ian Caunce Collection.

the US, eventually garnering $11 million. The *New York Post* praised Eastwood: 'His good-looking tranquillity in the midst of life and death issues may really be nothing but the limitation of a strong, silent hero, but it looks good on him'. In the UK, rated 'X' following some cuts, the *Daily Express* joked, 'Eastwood has made his first talking picture', while *Films and Filming* noted that the movie 'has an air of sincere earnestness which the Italian films carefully invert, and so it is far harder to accept its graphic depiction of violence'. Most agreed that this was better than his three spaghetti westerns, a consensus that hasn't stood the test of time.

Two Mules for Sister Sara (1970)

Two Mules for Sister Sara, Eastwood's second film with director Don Siegel following their collaboration on *Coogan's Bluff* (1968), was the closest that an Eastwood film came to resurrecting 'The Man with No Name'. The story was originally written by Budd Boetticher with Robert Mitchum in mind; Boetticher was a director already noted for *The Tall T* (1957), *Ride Lonesome* (1959) and *Comanche Station* (1960). But the script was transformed by Albert Maltz into something that closely resembled a Leone western, made on a $4 million budget and shot on location in Mexico in 65 days with a predominantly Mexican crew. Ennio Morricone even supplied the score.

Elizabeth Taylor had shown Eastwood the *Two Mules* script during the making of *Where Eagles Dare* in London in 1969. Taylor planned to star as nun Sister Sara, with the production lensed in Spain. But Taylor bowed out and Shirley MacLaine was cast instead as feisty Sara. Eastwood received second-billing as Hogan (named Lucy in Boetticher's story); in Italy, Eastwood received top-billing in the retitled version *Gli Avvoltoi hanno Fame* ('The Vultures Are Hungry'). Following the American Civil War, Hogan is drifting south through Mexico towards Chihuahua to meet up with Juarista revolutionaries fighting the French. On the way, he saves Sara from three drunken bandits and she tags along with him and reveals that she's wanted by the French for collecting funds for the revolutionaries. Mercenary Hogan plans to dynamite the French Treasury at Chihuahua, which has a heavily armed garrison, for a fortune in gold and agrees to take Sara with him. Sara knows that the garrison will be drunk on 14 July, celebrating Bastille Day. At the railway depot at San Tevo, they discover an armaments train is due to reinforce the French. Although Hogan is wounded by an arrow in his shoulder during a Yaqui Indian ambush, he and Sara manage to blow up a trestle bridge with dynamite, obliterating the train. They contact Juaristas in the El Gato Negro cantina in Santa Maria and hook up with Colonel Beltran (Manolo Fabregas) and his rebel forces in the hills. But the train attack has alerted the garrison and on the 14th no one is drunk. During a night-time assault on the stronghold, orchestrated through a tunnel from the former Bishop's residence, now a 'cathouse' (whose employees seem to know Sara very well), the Juaristas and Hogan overrun the French and take the treasury.

The action-packed story is set during the French Intervention (1862–67), also the locale for *Vera Cruz* (1954), *Major Dundee* (1965), *The Undefeated* (1969) and

Adios Sabata (1970), though the weaponry on display, including Colt Peacemakers and Winchesters, is too early for the period. Siegel placed Eastwood's gunslinger in the middle of some pyrotechnic action sequences. Hogan demolishes a bridge and fights for 'the cause', participating in the Juarista assault on Chihuahua's 200-strong garrison and artillery. Hogan is in the thick of the action, lighting sticks of dynamite with his cigar, commandeering a Gatling gun and surviving a French bayonet-charge. Trailers called Eastwood a 'one-man suicide squad' and 'Mister Action himself ... a hero for hire'. The blown up supply train and trestle bridge were created, highly convincingly, in miniature by the Mexican special effects crew, while the rebels' attack on Chihuahua commenced with an explosive piñata (usually filled with sweets and treats). Buddy Van Horn, Eastwood's regular stunt double from *Coogan's Bluff* (1968) onwards, supervised the finale's elaborate stunts. Unsurprisingly, Boetticher, who'd conceived the project as a realistic, low-key story, wasn't very impressed with the spaghetti western-style results, calling it 'another Eastwood thing'.

The film's main point of interest is the attempt to cast Eastwood's lonesome 'Man with No Name' opposite a strong female lead – and they don't come much stronger than Shirley MacLaine. A rewrite re-nationalised her from Mexican to Anglo, as MacLaine is fair-skinned and redheaded. The audience knows Sara isn't a nun almost immediately. On the trail she exhibits several bad habits behind Hogan's back: swigging whiskey, swearing and smoking cigar dog-ends. The *Hollywood Reporter* cruelly commented on the obvious plot ending: 'The only one who was surprised when [Sara] became a hooker was Clint Eastwood'. For the demolition of the bridge scene, wounded Hogan gets drunk and slurs a bawdy ballad, while Sara removes the Yaqui arrow from his shoulder. Eastwood maintained that this was the best scene he'd ever played. But *Time* wrote of his performance that he 'looks grizzled, stares into the sun and sneers, but anything more demanding seems beyond his grasp'. Throughout their journey Eastwood rides a horse, while Sara wobbles along behind on a mule (a horse-donkey hybrid) and later a burro (a thoroughbred donkey); MacLaine had trouble staying on the mule, so the burro was written into the story. The film's running joke is that Hogan is as stubborn as her mule (she christens him 'Mr Mule') and thinks he's in control, while Sara craftily always gets her own way. But according to Boetticher, Martin Rackin, the film's producer, admitted in interviews of not knowing 'who the second mule was'.

Two Mules for Sister Sara is one of Eastwood's best post-Leone westerns. The comedy is well played by the two co-stars and Gabriel Figueroa's Panavision photography of a crumbling, unforgiving Mexico ensured it looked splendid. The film was shot around Cuautla and Jantetelco in Morelos from February 1969. The fort and the surrounding settlement of Chihuahua were constructed from scratch in six months. The ruins at Pantitlan and Cauixtla also appeared in the film. *Two Mules* has a special place in Eastwood's post-Leone western filmography as it boasts a Morricone score – not an imitation of a Morricone score, as most of his other non-Italian westerns did – as part of the Clint Eastwood-spaghetti western 'brand'. The

1.6 Wounded Hogan uses Sister Sara as a tripod for target practice; Clint Eastwood and Shirley MacLaine on location in Mexico for *Two Mules for Sister Sara* (1970). Author's collection.

main theme, as Eastwood rides out of a burnished orange Mexican dawn, crossing the plains and fording a river, opens the film in fine style. Morricone orchestrates flute trills, honking 'mule brays' and angelic incantations (intoning 'Lead Us Not into Temptation' sung in Italian), backed by a very unusual off-kilter guitar and strings arrangement. This opening scene was actually shot in two weeks by second unit director Joe Cavalier, with Eastwood and a menagerie of desert and mountain wildlife, including an owl, fish, jackrabbits, snakes, a cougar and a tarantula. Hogan's horse crushes the spider with one of its hooves, the second time Eastwood had exterminated an arachnid onscreen. Morricone also deployed delicate Spanish guitars on the moving 'A Time for Miracles', echoing strings and juddering Flamenco guitars on 'La Cueva' ('The Cave' – used for the trek to Beltran's mountain HQ); there's even a Mariachi Deguello for the firing squad scene at San Tevo. *Two Mules*'s great score, recorded in Rome by Morricone and his Italian orchestra, is one of the film's plusses.

There are also several typically spaghetti western moments, with Sara's rescue the best example. Hogan shoots two of her attackers, but the third (Armando Silvestre) takes her hostage. Hogan lights a stick of dynamite and tosses it from cover behind a rock. It lands at the bandit's feet and he panics and runs, whereupon Hogan coolly shoots him in the back. Hogan saunters down, cuts the fuse and then proceeds to loot the corpses. This is comic book western action, stylised and implausible, and Maltz's script strives for pseudo-religious significance. Sara's beliefs dictate that the Lord will provide on her journey. Hogan indicates to the corpses: 'Three more like them?'; 'He also provided you', she smiles. Hogan looks just like Leone's hero, in waistcoat, hat and neckerchief – he even dons a poncho disguise to spy on the Chihuahua garrison. But it is Sara who wins their battle of wits and in the final scene, Hogan sullenly leads

1.7 'Sierra Torride': Spanish poster for *Two Mules for Sister Sara* retitles the film *Torrid Sierra*. Poster courtesy Ian Caunce Collection.

his packhorse, now loaded with hat boxes and luggage, into the desert, followed by Sara in a gaudy, low-cut red dress, hat and feathers, under a parasol and still riding her mule. Like Eastwood's bounty hunters, Sara has got her man.

In the US, the film was released on 16 June 1970, rated 'M' (later re-rated 'PG') and took $5 million. It was even more successful worldwide; in the UK, it was distributed by Rank, rated 'A'. Posters concentrated on Eastwood's stranger and the Sergio Leone connection, with the tagline: 'The deadliest man alive faces a whole army with 2 guns and a fistful of dynamite!' *Women's Wear Daily* thought of Siegel's film, 'Eastwood acts with greater naturalness than he has in the past', *Variety* said that the stars 'don't generate any chemistry', while the *New York Times* praised their efforts: 'I'm not sure it's a great movie, but it is very good and it stays and grows in the mind the way only movies of exciting narrative intelligence do'. Whatever the critics' opinions, for once they couldn't argue that Eastwood's acting was second to nun.

Joe Kidd (1972)

Following *Dirty Harry* (1971), his biggest box office hit to date, Eastwood's next western was *Joe Kidd* – with him playing the title role. It was directed by John Sturges, who had made several great westerns, including *Bad Day at Black Rock* (1955), *Gunfight at the O.K. Corral* (1957), *The Magnificent Seven* (1960) and *Hour of the Gun* (1967). *Joe Kidd* didn't join that illustrious list.

The film opens with Kidd, an ex-bounty hunter and tracker, languishing in the Sinola jail for poaching on reservation land, disorderly conduct and resisting arrest. Offered a choice between a $10 fine and 10 days in jail, he has taken the latter but is put to work with a broom – literally cleaning up the town. A group of Mexican farmers led by sheepherder Luis Chama (John Saxon) arrives in Sinola. They have been locked in a two-year legal battle with gringo land barons and before escaping proceeds to burn the land deeds at the County Court House. Sheriff Bob Mitchell (Gregory Walcott) leads a posse in pursuit but fails to catch them and Chama becomes a wanted man. Soon afterwards land baron Frank Harlan (Robert Duvall) steps off the train with his 'associates', Lamarr Sims (Don Stroud), Olin Mingo (James Wainwright) and Roy Gannon (Paul Koslo), professional hunters and crack shots, armed with the latest weaponry – high-powered, long-range rifles with telescopic sights. They try to persuade Kidd to scout for them, in a manhunt for Chama; Kidd initially refuses but accepts when his farm is raided by Chama, his horses run off and his foreman Emilio trussed up with barbed wire. Kidd and the hunters head into the sierras, capture Chama's lover, Helen Sanchez (Stella Garcia), and hole up in Arroyo Blanco, Chama's home town. Harlan threatens to execute the local peons if Chama doesn't surrender. Kidd sides with the Mexicans, saves Helen and persuades Chama to return to Sinola to face trial. Back in town, Harlan and the manhunters lie in wait, but Kidd busts the ambush by driving a train though a drugstore, the Cattlemen's Association and into the appropriately named 'Railroad Saloon'. In a shootout Harlan is killed and the posse defeated. Chama turns himself into the custody of Sheriff Mitchell, and Kidd rides off with Helen to await the outcome of the trial.

The screenplay, originally called 'The Sinola Courthouse Raid', then simply 'Sinola', was written by Elmore Leonard, the veteran western writer who had penned the stories on which *3:10 to Yuma*, *The Tall T*, *Hombre* and *Valdez is Coming* were based. The central sheepman-cattleman conflict was a staple of range westerns, including *Rawhide* ('Incident of the Black Sheep'), while *Joe Kidd*'s filming locations are equally familiar – shot in Panavision by Bruce Surtees in November 1971, largely in the Alabama Hills at Lone Pine, California. 'Sinola' was a western town set at Old Tucson, Arizona, from John Wayne's *Rio Bravo* and *El Dorado*, while the Mexican pueblo 'Arroyo Blanco' was constructed in the Inyo National Forestry Park, which featured in Sam Peckinpah's *Ride the High Country* (1962).

Joe Kidd owes a debt to Euro-westerns. With its two warring factions, Eastwood was back in *Fistful of Dollars* country – there's even a bad guy named Ramon. The train climax was borrowed from the West German-Yugoslavian *Winnetou the Warrior* (1963 – also called *Apache Gold*). The wintry sierra setting recalls *The Big Silence* (1967) and Lamarr Simms is armed with an 1896 Mauser 'Broomhandle' machine pistol (also from *Silence*). Lalo Schifrin's too jazzy score is also spaghetti-flavoured, with electric piano, whirring feedback, reverberating electric guitar, rattled percussion and Mariachi trumpets competing on the soundtrack.

Like all Eastwood's westerns, *Joe Kidd* boasts a strong cast. Gregory Walcott is good as the ambling Sinola sheriff, John Saxon is effective as idealistic hero Chama and Robert Duvall is suitably hateful as the land-grabbing villain, who claims, 'I don't have time for court hearings'. Support is provided by Joaquin Martinez as Chama's lieutenant Manolo, Pepe Hern as the padre of the Church of Saint Raschal Bayon and Don Stroud (from *Coogan's Bluff*) as hulking ursine, lank-haired killer Lamarr.

Although not up to the 'Dollars' films, or even *Two Mules*, *Joe Kidd* is saved by Eastwood, though he was ill during filming. His debilitating allergic reaction, originally thought to be to horses, was, in fact, to cats at his hotel. Introduced dressed as a dandy, in tie, starched collar and bowler hat, Eastwood tries not to play Kidd as his supercool stranger, but from the moment he straps on his trademark gunbelt, swaps his bowler for a Stetson and lights up a cheroot, Kidd is awfully familiar. In the shootout, he casts himself as a judge, sitting in his honour's swivel chair as he guns Harlan down: justice is done.

The best moments of the film involve violent action from Eastwood. In jail, Kidd douses Naco, a cellmate and one of Chama's men, in stew and then lays him out with the empty pan. Their subsequent confrontation in the saloon, when Kidd nonchalantly enjoys a pint and blasts Naco through the swinging saloon doors with the barkeeper's shotgun, is Eastwood at his unsubtle best. Such rare moments hint at what could have been, if the narrative hadn't been so aimlessly confused, rushing to the action scenes in fits and starts, with little sense of rhythm or character development. In the UK, Rank distributed *Joe Kidd* (rated 'AA') and it took $5.8 million when it was released stateside in July 1972, rated 'PG'. *New York Post* summed up the film's failings, noting the 'surpassing excellence of western performances by Clint Eastwood, Robert Duvall and John Saxon. In a sense, they are diamonds set in dung'. The *San Francisco Chronicle* called the star 'one of the most limited actors on screen', which is particularly scathing as Eastwood had by now appeared in both *The Beguiled* and *Play Misty for Me*.

High Plains Drifter (1973)

For *High Plains Drifter*, Eastwood's third western for Universal and made immediately after *Joe Kidd*, he took the directorial reins. A stranger (Eastwood) drifts out of the high sierras and arrives in the desert mining town of Lago. He kills three toughs who provoke him and then discovers that he has just eliminated the town's hired protection. Lago harbours a dark secret: their marshal, Jim Duncan, was whipped to death by three outlaws – Stacey Bridges (Geoffrey Lewis) and his cousins, Cole and Dan Carlin (Anthony James and Dan Vadis) – without the townsfolk intervening. Duncan lies hidden in the cemetery in an unmarked grave. The townspeople live in fear of the trio's impending release from territorial prison and try to convince the stranger to protect them. He accepts, on the condition he is given free rein in town and receives a bounty of '$500 an ear'. He appoints Mordicai (Billy Curtis), a dwarf who is mistreated by the town, as sheriff and mayor, and forms the 'City of Lago Volunteers', consisting of the town's cowardly menfolk. The stranger's requests become increasingly excessive, as he plans a homecoming neither the murderers nor Lago will ever forget. He tells the people to set out picnic tables and put up a banner reading 'Welcome Home Boys'. He also orders 200 gallons of red paint, which is used to paint the entire town red, renaming it 'Hell'. With the ambush set, the three outlaws arrive, as the stranger leaves. Bridges and the Carlins run amuck, killing several citizens and torching the town. That night, with the cowering townsfolk hostage in the saloon, the stranger returns, bullwhipping Cole to death, hanging Dan and shooting Bridges, who dies shouting, 'Who are you?' Having exacted retribution on both the town and the outlaws, the stranger rides on. As the stranger leaves, Mordicai is carving Jim Duncan's name into the wooden marker. The marshal can rest in peace at last, now that his brother has avenged his death.

High Plains Drifter, like *Hang 'Em High*, fuses violent action with an interesting subtext. Here the town's social responsibility and hypocritical morality are shown to be a façade. Their only sense of community spirit is the reasoning, 'One hang, we all hang'. *Drifter* is a hybrid of *High Noon* and William S. Hart's silent western *Hell's Hinges* (1916), mixed with elements of the first two 'Dollars' films. The stranger's adversaries, which as in the Leone westerns come in threes, are straight out of the spaghetti west. Billy Curtis, cast as dwarf Mordicai, was no stranger to westerns. He'd played Pat, the hero of the notorious 'all-midget western' *The Terror of Tiny Town* (1938). Eastwood's stranger seems to be helping the town, but at the moment when Gary Cooper's marshal in *High Noon* strides down the Hadleyville street to face Frank Miller's gang, the stranger deserts Lago: the cowardly townsfolk here get everything they deserve. As in *Hell's Hinges*, the hero takes almighty revenge on the town: William S. Hart, as reformed gunman Blaze Tracey, goes 'killin' mad' and torches the town of Hell's Hinges ('a good place to ride wide of') when its iniquity corrupts and kills its new parson.

Though dressed in a long leather range coat, Eastwood's vagabond drifter strongly resembles Joe the Stranger in *Fistful*, especially when dealing with his 'welcoming committee'. The stranger rides into Lago and the townspeople warily eye him in silence. In the saloon, three gunmen (played as bullying slobs by Ron Soble, Scott Walker and Russ McCubbin) pester him with some classic tough talking: 'Flea-bitten range bums don't usually stop in Lago. Life here's a little too quick for them. Maybe you think you're fast enough to keep up with us, huh?' 'I'm faster than you'll ever live to be', cautions the stranger. Across the street, in the barber's for a shave, the stranger is again accosted by the trio. This time their threats result in violence, but in seconds they are dead, plugged with a pistol the stranger has concealed beneath his draped barber's robe. 'What did you say your name was again?' asks Mordicai, striking a match and sparking the stranger's cigar – 'I didn't'.

Based on a screenplay by Ernest Tidyman (the writer of *Shaft* and *The French Connection*) and an uncredited Dean Reisner, *Drifter* is often named by critics as one of the best westerns of the seventies. But like other Eastwood action films of the period, its sexual politics have dated badly. The female roles waste two fine actresses in a simplistic Madonna-whore synergy that was outmoded even in 1972. Verna Bloom was squandered as cardboard Sarah Belding, the virtuous wife of the corrupt hotelier, trapped in an unhappy marriage, who sleeps with the stranger and guesses that he may be related to Jim Duncan. Marianna Hill, as Lago's resident floozy Callie, had already appeared in the Spanish-shot *El Condor* (1970), where her only contribution to the plot was to perform a striptease. In the opening sequence of *Drifter*, she is raped by the stranger in a barn. Rape was a consistent and unpleasant feature of many westerns in the late sixties and early seventies – almost as though it was a matter-of-fact, everyday occurrence out west, or even worse (as here), to inject a little sex into the films. There is no narrative justification for this scene and TV prints often heavily edit it. *Drifter* is the only western of the period that features a hero committing rape and highlights the dark morality of the story.

Drifter was shot on a specially built set designed by Henry Bumstead on the shores of Lake Mono in California, an unusual location chosen by Eastwood because it was 'highly photogenic' – 46 technicians and 10 labourers used 150,000 feet of timber to build 'Lago' (meaning 'lake' in Spanish) in 18 days. The town's clean timbers suited the story's nascent, recently built mining town. The opening and closing desert shots were filmed at Winnemucca Dry Lake, near Reno, Nevada, and the woodland scenes were the Inyo National Forest, California.

The two eerie flashbacks in *Drifter* – one tormenting the stranger, the other Mordicai – resemble *For a Few Dollars More*, even down to the strange soundtrack audio effects. The music was by Dee Barton, who provides a sub-Morricone score that favours electronica (whirrs, whines, echoing voices) augmented with traditional

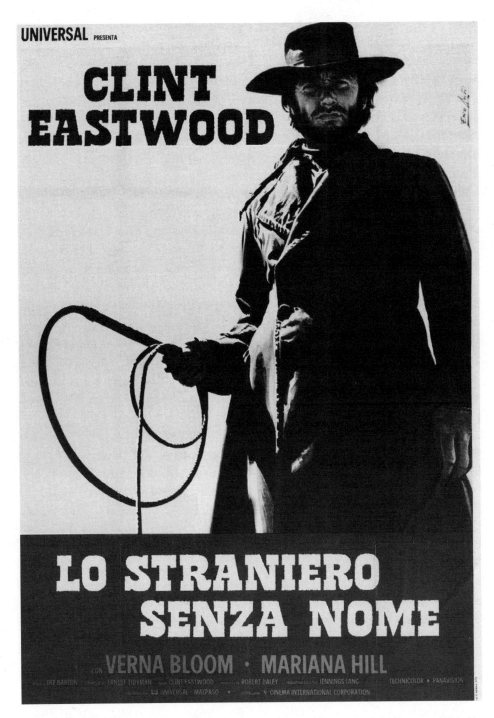

1.8 *Lo Straniero Senza Nome*: Clint Eastwood stars as the vengeful 'Stranger With No Name' in this classic Italian artwork for *High Plains Drifter* (1973). Poster courtesy Ian Caunce Collection.

western guitar and percussion riding cues. The bullwhiplashes in the flashbacks, electronically enhanced, sear into the town's conscience and tear Jim Duncan's flesh, as the townspeople silently watch the three outlaws lash the marshal to death. Only Sarah Belding and Mordicai feel any compulsion to help the lawman, but neither can. The back-story is that Duncan discovers the Lago Mining Company is on government land and must be closed. The mining consortium, Dave Drake, Morgan Allen and Lewis Belding, hires Stacey Bridges and his cousins as 'trouble-shooters', to dispose of the marshal. They are then railroaded and imprisoned for stealing a gold ingot and now want revenge.

Some critics have interpreted *Drifter* as a ghost story, with Eastwood's hero the spectre of Jim Duncan, back from the dead to avenge his own death, but Eastwood said the script made it clear that he was the dead lawman's brother. Nevertheless, Eastwood played on this ambiguity, even having the stranger materialise from the desert heat haze under the titles and then evaporate into the shimmering wasteland at the close. As Mordicai carves the gravestone, he says, 'I never did know your name'. 'Yes you do', answers the stranger, as the camera pans down to the inscription: MARSHAL JIM DUNCAN REST IN PEACE. Dubbed prints of *Drifter*, for example in France and Italy, stressed that Eastwood was Jim Duncan's vengeful sibling. In the flashback depicting Duncan's death, the lawman is played by Eastwood's stunt double, Buddy Van Horn. Thus the town's 'new guardian angel' turns out to be a vengeful exterminating angel. As a hotelier notes: 'Couldn't be worse if the Devil himself had ridden into Lago'.

High Plains Drifter was released in the US in August 1973 but had a hard time convincing critics, especially Judith Crist, who deemed it a 'Middle-American, R-rated substitute for *Deep Throat*' with Eastwood 'God's original gift to the ladies'. Rex Reed in the *New York Daily News* called it 'one of the year's most hysterical comedies ... I've seen better westerns at the Pepsi Cola Saloon at Disneyland'. *Variety* saw, 'pulp magazine mysticism, banal sight gags and spray-on psychedelics'. French critics also sharpened their knives: 'An apology for fascism', thought *La Revue du Cinema*; *Positif* claimed it was, 'a *Mein Kampf* for the west ... back in 1950, not *one* scene, not a single *shot* of this film would have obtained Universal's stamp of approval'. It didn't matter: *High Plains Drifter* took almost $8 million in the US, making it the 11th highest grossing western of the seventies. The action trailer highlighted its spaghetti western roots: 'A drifter came riding out of the west – you know him as Clint Eastwood ... Aim to see it!' Distributed in the UK by CIC, *Drifter* gained an 'X' certificate. Cut TV prints omit most of Callie's rape and much of the graphic gore: the flashback whippings were trimmed and the scene where Morgan Allen has a sharpened stick thrust through his throat was excised. 'Not at all a likeable film, but an impressive one', said the *Observer*, while the *Financial Times* noted: 'The Leone trademarks are all well in evidence: the long, brooding pauses, the low angle camera shots, the percussive score'. John Wayne hated *Drifter* and accused Eastwood of depicting the west coldly and unrealistically, but Eastwood agreed: 'It's just an allegory ... a speculation on what happens when they go ahead and kill the sheriff and somebody comes back and calls the town's conscience to bear. There's always retribution for your deeds'. As Sarah Belding tells the stranger, 'You're a man who makes people afraid and that's dangerous'. 'Well, it's what people know about themselves inside that makes them afraid', he answers. *High Plains Drifter* is Eastwood's most excessive revenge western and the last film in which he would play a spaghetti western 'stranger with no name'. It was also the last time Eastwood wore his trademark gunbelt with its distinctive decorative stitching, which he'd used onscreen in all his westerns since *Rawhide*.

The Outlaw Josey Wales (1976)

Eastwood reinvented his 'Man with No Name' western screen image and emerged from the shadow of Leone with *The Outlaw Josey Wales*. During the American Civil War, Kansas 'Redlegs' (red-gaitered Unionist regulars) commanded by Captain Terrill (Bill McKinney) attack the property of Missouri farmer Josey Wales (Eastwood), burning his house and killing his wife and son. His life laid waste, Wales meets a roving Confederate guerrilla band of border raiders, led by Bloody Bill Anderson, heading up to Kansas to 'set things aright'; 'I'll be comin' with you', decides Wales. With the South crushed, Wales won't admit defeat and becomes 'the last of the hold-outs'. Following a trap in which many of Anderson's men are murdered by Redlegs during an 'amnesty', Wales goes on the run with Jaime, a young soldier. Terrill and Fletcher (John Vernon), Wales's ex-comrade-in-arms, are dispatched to run Wales down. Wounded in the Redleg ambush by Terrill, Jaime soon dies and Wales, now with a price on his head, negotiates the rabid, ravaged post-Civil War mid-west, avoiding or gunning down assorted carrion who smell blood money. Wales heads into the Indian Nations, a glorified reservation for pacified tribes, and meets civilised Lone Watie, a Cherokee chief. When Wales learns that Colonel Joe Shelby plans to gather Confederate stragglers in Mexico, he rides south, with Lone Watie in tow. Wales liberates Navajo Little Moonlight (Geraldine Keams) from a crooked Indian trader and once in Texas also saves settlers Grandma Sarah Turner (Paula Trueman) and her granddaughter-in-law Laura Lee (Sondra Locke) from an attack by Comanchero liquor and gun traders. Grandma's son has been killed in the war and they are travelling to Crooked River, in untamed Comanche territory near the town of Santo Rio, where his farm stands dormant. The party arrives and Wales brokers peace with Comanche chief Ten Bears (Will Sampson), enabling the group to settle on the farm, but Terrill, Fletcher and the Redlegs track him down. In a confrontation, the settlers repulse the Redlegs and Wales kills Terrill. Fletcher acknowledges that Wales is a changed man, allowing his quarry to go free to begin a new life with Laura Lee as a farmer.

The Outlaw Josey Wales was based on *Gone to Texas*, a 1972 novel by Forrest Carter, later republished as *The Rebel Outlaw: Josey Wales*. Eastwood liked the story and saw himself in the lead. It was transformed into a screenplay by Sonia Chernus; Phil Kaufman also worked on the draft and was slated to direct the picture, a

$4 million production for Warner Bros and Malpaso. But Kaufman and Eastwood didn't get along and Kaufman was fired soon after shooting began in September 1975. The filming schedule, now with Eastwood at the helm, ran until November. Kanab Canyon, Utah, was used for the Crooked River Ranch; Ten Bears' camp was also in Utah. Santo Rio was Paria, an actual ghost town in Utah. The dusty, bustling Texan town of Towash, where Wales guns down four Union soldiers, was the western set at Mescal, Arizona. The Civil War and Indian Nations scenes were filmed in Northern California, during the autumn around Oroville, and the Oceola Ferry traverses the Feather River as the Missouri. The Civil War, as featured in the film's blue-tinted title sequence, is battle footage lifted from *Shenandoah* (1965).

Eastwood deployed a well-chosen cast: a sort of 'greatest hits' package of actors he had worked with throughout his career. John Mitchum appeared as a trapper, John Quade as a Comanchero, Woodrow Parfrey as a travelling carpetbagger plying 'Secret Elixir', and William O'Connell played a flippant ferryman who sings 'Battle Hymn of the Republic' and 'Dixie' 'with equal enthusiasm'. Bruce M. Fischer, as another trapper, later appeared in *Escape from Alcatraz* and John Russell, here cast as 'Bloody Bill' Anderson, was villain Stockburn in *Pale Rider*. Doug McGrath, as hunter 'Lige', also went on to appear in *Pale Rider* (as prospector Spider Conway); his cohort, Abe, was played by Len Lesser (from *Kelly's Heroes*). In the 'Lost Lady' saloon in Santo Rio, there were cameos by Matt Clark (a seventies western regular), Royal Dano (a fifties western regular) and Sheb Wooley (from *Rawhide*). Paula Trueman, as Grandma, had appeared in *Paint Your Wagon*. John Vernon (from *Dirty Harry*) played Fletcher, Bill McKinney was 'Redlegs' Terrill, and Sam Bottoms portrayed Jaime. Eastwood's new lover Sondra Locke played Wales's new love Laura Lee, a hippy dreamer who represents the golden summers of youth. This is the first of Eastwood's 'Locke Cycle', the six-film series in which they co-starred. Locke had appeared to great acclaim (and an Oscar nomination) in *The Heart Is a Lonely Hunter* (1968); she had also made an impact in *Reflection of Fear* (1971 – aka *Autumn Child*), playing a boy raised as a girl, which also featured her husband, Gordon Anderson. The real casting coup of *Josey Wales* was the employment of several Native American actors in key roles: Geraldine Keams played Little Moonlight, Will Sampson was Ten Bears and 76-year-old Sioux Chief Dan George (from *Little Big Man*) appeared as Lone Watie, a pacified Cherokee leader dressed in the style of Abraham Lincoln.

Josey Wales, or 'Mr Chain Blue-lightning' (due to his swiftness on the draw), is a baccy-chewing loner with a catchphrase ('I reckon so'). Eastwood noted at the time, *Josey Wales* 'is a saga, a little like *The Good, the Bad and the Ugly*, except that in the Leone film the only character you got to know, somewhat, is the Eli Wallach character. In other words, Josey Wales is a hero, and you see how he gets to where he is – rather than just having a mysterious hero appear on the plains and become involved with other people's plight'. Here Wales loses his wife and son and swears to avenge his family honour. Eastwood's cowboy appears on screen for the first time without his trademark cigar. The idea that such a loner, 'a hard-put and desperate man' on the run and travelling incognito, would find himself with his own little community provides

1.9 'An Army of One': A Colt Walker in each fist, Josey cries vengeance on the pursuing Redlegs in this US one-sheet poster for *The Outlaw Josey Wales* (1976); this artwork was also used on the cover of a reissue of Forrest Carter's source novel. Poster courtesy Ian Caunce Collection.

the film's humorous undertow. Interviewed during the US release of *The Good, the Bad and the Ugly* about the Dollars trilogy, Eastwood observed, 'In the beginning, I was just about alone. Then there were two. And now there are three of us. I'm going to end up in a detachment of cavalry'. *Josey Wales* provides this 'detachment'. 'I don't want nobody belonging to me', says Josey, though he can't shake his surrogate family, who encounter him by accident but stick like glue. Even a mangy hound tags along: 'Well he might as well', spits Wales, 'Hell, everybody else is'.

Like so many Confederate western heroes on the big screen, Josey too sees no end to the war and flees south. Fletcher pleads with Senator Lane, 'Let Wales be, let me be', but the senator wants Wales hounded 'to Kingdom Come'. 'A man like Wales lives by the feud', warns Fletcher. Deaf to Fletcher's reasoning, Lane snaps, 'Hell is where he's headed'; 'He'll be waiting there for us, senator'. Wales is a well-equipped 'walking arsenal', with a pair of heavy-duty .44 calibre Colt Walkers at his belt, a Sharps rifle with a telescopic sight, a Colt Navy, plus a pocket pistol hidden in a shoulder holster. He needs all the help he can get – in the course of his flight he faces and outwits fur trappers, bounty hunters and Union soldiers, in a succession of action scenes. Abe and 'Lige, two backwoodsmen, sidle out of the undergrowth and crow, 'We got the Josey Wales…he's meaner than a rattler and twice as fast'. They're right, of course. Jaime says they should bury their bushwhackers. 'To Hell with them', says Josey, spitting a wad of baccy at Abe's forehead, 'Buzzards gotta eat, same as worms'. At a trading post near the Creek Nation, hunters Al and Yoke capture 'Mister Chain Blue-lightning hisself'. Al tells Wales to unholster his pistols slow, 'Like molasses in wintertime'. Unfortunately, Wales moves like molasses in summertime, twirling his pistols and killing both men. The film's most Leonesque moment occurs when Wales faces four bluecoats on the sidewalk outside the Towash saloon. They itch to draw and he provokes them: 'You gonna pull those pistols, or whistle Dixie?' Later in the desert, he takes on a gang of Comancheros single-handedly, riding on horseback with a pistol in each hand, *True Grit*-style. 'Hell is coming to breakfast', observes Watie, as Wales cunningly rides into pistol range under a white flag. A scene in the 'Lost Lady' saloon in Santo Rio provides the film with its best-remembered exchange. A bounty killer (John Davis Chandler) has tracked Wales south. 'I'm looking for Josey Wales', he says; 'That'd be me', says Wales from the shadows. 'You're wanted Wales'; 'Reckon I'm right popular…you a bounty hunter?' 'Man's gotta do something for a living these days'. 'Dying ain't much of a living, boy', Wales snarls before the inevitable.

Over 30 years later, the film *Josey Wales* most resembles, in tone and narrative, is John Ford's *The Searchers* (1956). *Josey Wales*'s emphatic action scenes, the trek plotline and the majestic Panavision landscape photography by Bruce Surtees give the film an epic sweep befitting Ford. The small-scale, realistic human drama of Eastwood's film provides an intimacy almost completely absent from his earlier westerns, though he stopped short of the book's original resolution, which saw Josey marry Laura Lee. 'Whenever I get to liking someone, they ain't around long', notes Wales. He knows he can never again be a farmer until his ghosts are laid to rest: 'You know there ain't no forgetting'. Having killed Terrill, Wales rides back to Laura Lee, into a beautiful sunrise.

The Outlaw Josey Wales premiered on 26 July 1976 at the Sun Valley Centre, as part of a conference on westerns. 'When you're an outlaw, there's no turning back', intoned the solemn trailer, 'He lives by the gun, he lives by his word and he lives for revenge'. On general release in August, it was rated 'R' in its uncut version but was trimmed for violence and nudity; this new version, which shortened a gratuitous assault by the Comancheros on Laura Lee, was rated 'PG'. Equally cut, it was rated 'AA' in the UK, though DVD prints are now uncut and rated '18'. Carter wrote a sequel, *The Vengeance Trail of Josey Wales*, which was made into a dreadful western by actor-director Michael Parks, under the title *The Return of Josey Wales* (1986).

Time and others named *The Outlaw Josey Wales* in their top ten for 1976, but critics were divided. 'Formula Clint Eastwood slaughter film for regular market', was *Variety*'s view: 'nothing more than a prairie *Death Wish*'. 'Seems like two days', thought Rex Reed of Josey's 'interminable journey', which saw him 'accompanied by a stock company of ferocious hams'. Eastwood himself views the film as one of his personal favourites and it is one of his great accomplishments, as both actor and director. It's now often named by critics in 'all time' western top tens and remains one of Eastwood's most popular films.

Pale Rider (1985)

Almost 10 years after *Josey Wales*, Eastwood returned to the genre with which he had made his name – as the director-star of the mystical *Pale Rider*, at a time when cinemas were western-free zones. 'Pale Rider' was the name of one of Red Stovall's songs in Clancy Carlile's novel *Honkytonk Man*, which was cut from Eastwood's 1982 film version, and there had also been 'Incident of the Pale Rider', episode 136 of the 1962–63 season of *Rawhide*, written by Dean Reisner. The film's screenplay was written by Michael Butler and Dennis Shryack, though it bore more than a passing resemblance to *Shane* (1953), the most popular western of the fifties.

Eastwood's scriptwriters riddled *Pale Rider* with *Shane* homages, whilst also adding a mystical element of revenge, evoking Eastwood's own *High Plains Drifter*, and the snowy setting recalls *The Big Silence*. A community of tin-pan prospectors in Carbon Canyon, California, are fighting hard to keep their stake against C.K. LaHood & Sons – father Coy (Richard Dysart) and his son Josh (Christopher Penn) – hydraulic miners who are 'raping the land' of its gold deposits with the latest, high-pressure machinery. The Preacher (Eastwood) unexpectedly arrives in Carbon Canyon to help the 'tin-panners' and stays at the home of Hull Barret (Michael Moriarty), who lives with his fiancée Sarah Wheeler and her daughter Megan, both of whom proceed to fall in love with the Preacher. When LaHood's thugs are foiled by the resourceful Preacher, Coy sends for the infamous Marshal Stockburn (John Russell) from Yuba City, and his six deputies, to kill the Preacher. The stranger may look like a man of the cloth but is actually an ex-gunslinger and he forces a confrontation with Stockburn, with whom he has an old score to settle – seemingly from beyond the grave.

The Carbon Canyon mining camp of shacks, cabins and tents was filmed in the Sawtooth Mountains, Idaho, during the autumn of 1984 – an often snowbound, always rugged, landscape. The stout town of LaHood, home of the LaHood Mining Corporation, was a specially constructed 12-building set in Sun Valley, Idaho, while Railtown 1897 State Historical Park, Jamestown, California – 'The Movie Railroad' – appeared as LaHood station and provided the prop Sierra Railways locomotive. The bustling town of 'Yuba City' was filmed in the historic buildings of Columbia State Park, California.

Pale Rider's cast included Oscar nominee Carrie Snodgress as Sarah Wheeler and Sydney Penny as her daughter Megan: both of whom fall for the Preacher, despite Megan being only 14. 'Fifteen next month', she says, which hardly makes her advances to the 54-year-old Preacher any more palatable. Their interludes, where she proffers undying love and the Preacher politely turns her down, are the film's most risible. In *Shane*, Megan was little Joey, a boy who adores the gunfighter, but *Pale Rider* introduced a romantic element to the idolatrous relationship. The resolution of the Preacher's liaison with her mother is equally distasteful. By way of 'happy ending', Sarah spends the night with the Preacher: 'This is just so I won't wake up at night for the rest of my life ... wondering'. Her curiosity satisfied, she can rest easy. She's now free to begin her married life with Hull.

Michael Moriarty played Hull, while villainous father-and-son combo the LaHoods were Richard Dysart and Christopher Penn. Eastwood's regular stand-in Wayne Van Horn played a stagecoach driver and executive producer Fritz Manes appeared as a stage rider in Yuba City. For the Preacher's nemesis, Eastwood cast John Russell as Stockburn, the Yuba City marshal. Russell had played chief villain Nathan Burdette in *Rio Bravo* (1959), had appeared as a scar-faced, eye-patched killer 'Patch' in the TV western *Buckskin* (1968) and played the lead in the TV series *Lawman* (1958–62). Gaunt, hawk-faced and moustachioed, Russell closely resembled Lee Van Cleef.

Visually, *Pale Rider* is Eastwood's darkest western, the weather permanently overcast. Eastwood was quoted on set as saying: '90% of my last pictures [*Sudden Impact, City Heat* and *Tightrope*] have been shot at night. Here we'll only have two night shots'. Perhaps, but instead Bruce Surtees (on his last film with Eastwood) lenses several cabin interiors that are equally impenetrable. Surtees deploys little available light, natural or otherwise, which may be authentic, but it's also hard on the eyes, as audiences squinted along with Clint.

When Coy LaHood first meets the Preacher, he notes, 'When I heard a parson had come to town I had an image of a pale, scrawny, Bible-thumping easterner with a linen handkerchief and bad lungs'. 'That's me', says the rugged, six-foot four-inch, fit-as-a-fiddle Preacher. Only the bullet holes in the Preacher's back, the scars of an earlier run-in with Stockburn's men, possibly in a previous life, are a clue to his vendetta. 'To develop the biblical parallels I ended up accentuating the supernatural aspect a bit', said Eastwood. The supernatural element is overt in *Pale Rider* and Lennie Niehaus' score channels *High Plains Drifter*'s. As the Preacher gallops away into the snowy sierras and Megan calls, 'Preacher, we all love you Preacher. I love you. Thank you, goodbye' (a blatant replay of the finale of *Shane*), the ghostly soprano augmenting the main theme recalls Dee Barton's end title cue for *Drifter*.

The villains are typical Eastwood adversaries, outwardly respectable but really profiteers – covetous, exploitative, avaricious and cruel. The LaHoods wash away the landscape with their jetting hydraulic water monitors in their search for gold. In this way, *Pale Rider* has been touted as an ecological western. Over the grave of Megan's pet dog Lindsey, killed by LaHood's men, she prays, 'Please, just one miracle', as the Preacher rides out of the mountains, an answer to her prayer. On his arrival in town, the Preacher intervenes in a miner altercation, when Hull tangles with four of LaHood's men – McGill, Jagou, Tyson and Elam – outside the general store. Grabbing a pickaxe handle, the Preacher soon crumples the opposition, noting, 'There's nothing like a nice piece of hickory'. Later Josh takes giant henchman Club a-visiting, to scare the miners. Club is played by seven-foot two-inch Richard Kiel – 'Jaws' from *The Spy Who Loved Me* (1977) and *Moonraker* (1979). But the Preacher resourcefully dispatches his towering adversary by whacking him in the groin with a sledgehammer. For the finale, the Preacher destroys LaHood's mining operation with dynamite and then takes on Stockburn's men armed with his lever-action, six-shot Remington percussion revolver.

The half-baked script is the simplest western revenge story, told in lacklustre fashion, with little flourish or élan. In *Shane*, the Wyoming cattlemen send to Cheyenne for Jack Wilson (Jack Palance) to clean out the 'nesters'. Instead of a single hired gun, LaHood recruits a less-than-magnificent seven. Coy sends his henchman by train to contact Stockburn (presumably on the '3:10 to Yuba'). The lawman and his robotic deputies, dressed in long leather duster coats like the railroad's hired guns in *Once Upon a Time in the West*, are as crooked as they come. 'They uphold whatever law pays 'em the most', says the Preacher, 'Killing's a way of life'. When asked if he knows Stockburn, the Preacher answers mysteriously: 'I've heard of him'. When Stockburn hears a description of the Preacher – tall, mean and with strange eyes – he hisses, 'Couldn't be, the man I'm thinking about is dead'. For the Preacher, 'It's an old score – it's time to settle it'. Cue one of the slackest, least exciting final showdowns in Eastwood's oeuvre.

When *Pale Rider* galloped into US cinemas in June 1985, poster artwork portrayed a parchment portrait of Eastwood, backed by Stockburn's crew. The tagline was '*Pale Rider*... and hell followed with him', after a quote from Chapter 6, Verse 8 of the Revelation of St. John the Divine, the last book of the New Testament. When the Preacher first arrives in Carbon Canyon riding his dappled grey, Megan reads, 'And I looked, and behold a pale horse: and his name that sat on him was Death, and Hell followed with him'. *Pale Rider*'s trailer optimistically predicted it was 'the next great American western', adding, 'Some called him Preacher, others called him gunfighter'. The music used in the trailer was 'Best Endeavours' by Alan Hawkshaw, a driving, trumpet-led composition known in the UK as the theme to *Channel 4 News*. As usual there was a paperback tie-in and the film was rated 'R' in the US for its violence, '15' in the UK. *Pale Rider* was the first Eastwood movie I saw on general release at my local Odeon and 23 years later my opinion hasn't changed: at 111 minutes, it's still half an hour too long and three shades too dark.

Critics relished the chance to review a western. The *New York Times* raved, 'An entertaining, mystical new western...*Pale Rider* is the first decent western in a very long time', without mentioning it was almost the only western in a very long time. Pauline Kael called it, 'Eastwood's art western', *Playboy* saw, 'A six-gun classic', while *Time* called Eastwood 'an American icon'. Rex Reed in the *New York Post*, often a scathing critic of Eastwood, liked the film but hated the *Shane* references: '*Pale Rider* owes such a nostalgic debt to *Shane* that the similarities, scene by scene, become almost parody'. 'Easily one of the best films of the year', noted *Sneak Previews*, while the *Los Angeles Times* thought the *Shane* references were a 'fond backward glance at a slice of the past'. The film was exhibited even at the Cannes Film Festival. It took over $20 million in the US and is the highest grossing western of the eighties, against scant competition. In 1997, Eastwood launched his own beer 'Pale Rider Ale', with the ad line: 'You Didn't Expect Clint Eastwood to Make a Salad Dressing Did You?' on a western-style playbill poster.

Unforgiven (1992)

Eastwood's next western project had been at Malpaso since 1983 – 'The Cut Whore Killings' screenplay was written by David Webb Peoples in 1976. Inspired by the story's main character, it was retitled 'The William Munny Killings', before it was eventually directed by Eastwood as the $14.4 million production *Unforgiven*. Eastwood knew it was a great script and bided his time, until, aged 61, he felt he was old enough to play the lead – grizzled ex-gunslinger and killer William Munny.

Wyoming, 1880. In the town of Big Whiskey, two ranch hands from the 'Bar T', Davey Bunting and Quick Mike, facially disfigure prostitute Delilah (Anna Thomson) with a Bowie knife. Their lenient sheriff 'Little Bill' Daggett (Gene Hackman) lets them off with a fine. Furious, the other prostitutes, led by Strawberry Alice (Frances Fisher), want justice and put up a $1,000 reward for the men who kill the Bar T boys. The following spring, young gunslinger the Schofield Kid (Jaimz Woolvett) locates William Munny in Hogeman County, Kansas. Once a murderous gunfighter with 'no weak nerve or fear', Munny now lives the quiet life as a struggling pig farmer, raising his children Will and Penny since the death of his 29-year-old wife Claudia Feathers from smallpox three years earlier. With an outbreak of swine fever to deal with, Munny is tempted by the bounty and decides to join Schofield and recruits his old partner Ned Logan (Morgan Freeman). Anyone tempted to try and collect 'the whores' gold' will be humiliated and kicked out of town, as in the case of braggart gunslinger English Bob (Richard Harris). In Greely's saloon in Big Whiskey, Munny is singled out and severely beaten by Daggett. Holed up in a wilderness shack at nearby Lone Pine, Munny recuperates. In a canyon ambush, Munny and his companions manage to shoot Bunting. Logan then loses his nerve and rides for Kansas, while at a stakeout at the 'Bar T', Schofield shoots Quick Mike. When Schofield and Munny receive payment for the killings, they discover that Logan has been captured at Cow Creek by Bar T cowboys and then brutally flogged to death by Daggett. Sending Schofield back with the money for Will and Penny, Munny rides into town to face Daggett and his crooked deputies. In a shootout in Greely's bar, he guns them down and leaves a final stark warning in his wake: 'You better bury Ned right. You better not cut up nor otherwise harm no whores, or I'll come back and kill every one of you sons-of-bitches'.

Eastwood himself played William Munny, his most grittily authentic western portrayal and his tenth western starring role. As in *Pale Rider*, Eastwood played a hero who faces a corrupt sheriff. Munny also rides a grey, like the Preacher, and as in *The Outlaw Josey Wales* and *Pale Rider*, he is a non-smoker. The film deployed a formidable cast as its array of gunfighters, who range from seasoned killers to the cowardly, from the merciless to the spent. Oscar-winner Gene Hackman was cast as sadist Daggett. Hardman Richard Harris, a veteran of such westerns as *A Man Called Horse* (1970), had a great cameo as white-haired, dandyish 'John Bull' gunslinger English Bob, who turns out to be a low-down liar. Canadian Jaimz Woolvett was cast as boastful Schofield Kid, a myopic pistolero. Morgan Freeman was cast as Logan, who comes out of retirement to help Munny but ends up losing both his nerve and his life. Anna Thomson was excellent as facially scarred Delilah. Frances Fisher (Eastwood's then-lover) played madame Strawberry Alice and Saul Rubinek appeared as W.W. Beauchamp, English Bob's myth-making biographer, who realises that the real west seldom resembles dime novel fantasy. *High Plains Drifter*'s Anthony James was vapid saloon-owning pimp Skinny Dubois, while Daggett's deputies and the Bar T boys (ably played by an array of fine supporting talent) are typical skunks and polecats.

Unforgiven was filmed from September to October 1991 on location in Canada, in 52 days. The 'Big Whiskey' set was built at Longview (Alberta, Canada) in 32 days by production designer Henry Bumstead. For this eerie, hellish setting, cinematographer Jack N. Green used mud, lanterns, rain and torchlight to accentuate the maelstrom of violence that engulfs Munny. Swirling sprinklers drenched the set. The 'Northwest Railroad' scenes, depicting English Bob's arrival, were filmed by a separate unit using a narrow-gauge railway locomotive at Red Hills Ranch in Sonora, California. Other Alberta locations included landscapes at Drumheller, Brooks and High River. The creeks, rolling meadows and shimmering cornfields the group traverses on their journey to Big Whiskey are in stark contrast to the town's locale, perched atop a ridge, its barren surroundings reflecting miserable life in the high country. Green's Panavision cinematography invests these landscapes, from sun-drenched cornfields to snowy whiteouts, with painterly magnificence, making this one of Eastwood's best-looking films as director. The music score embellishes this imagery: the gentle arching guitar melody 'Claudia's Theme' was composed by Eastwood, with the piece orchestrated by

1.10 Once a gunfighter, now a pig farmer, William Munny loads his pistol to kill for cash one last time; director-star Clint Eastwood's Oscar winning *Unforgiven* (1992). Author's collection.

composer Lennie Niehaus. The guitar solo was played by Brazilian maestro Laurindo Almeida, with Tommy Johnson the tuba soloist augmenting Niehaus' ebbing, flowing bittersweet symphony.

William Munny is a haunted, emotionally fractured, guilt-wracked gunfighter: no superman, but a human being. We first see him, in silhouette, in a burnished sundown, burying his wife, Claudia Feathers. An introductory scrawl tells us that she was 'a comely young woman and not without prospects', who found herself married to 'a known thief and murderer, a man of notoriously vicious and intemperate disposition'. Claudia 'cured me of drink and wickedness'. Coaxed out of retirement, Munny doesn't immediately revert to drinking and killing but finds that in the end that's all he knows. When he discovers Logan has been maliciously killed by Daggett, he slugs down a bottle of whisky, his mood changing instantly, as the demon liquor takes hold and he's a 'crazy killin' fool' once again. In an early scene, citing *A Fistful of Dollars* and *The Outlaw Josey Wales*, Munny takes his pistol and uses a tea caddy balanced on a log for target practice. But rusty Munny's marksmanship is off and he misses with all six shots. 'Did pa used to kill folks?' Penny asks her brother. Their father, disgruntled, strides back into the house, emerging with a sawn-off shotgun, and proceeds to demolish the tin with a blast of buckshot. With the onset of age, accuracy is relinquished for sheer killing power.

Munny prefers to downplay his past exploits, to the extent of toning down the odds of the shootouts he's survived. But he does acknowledge, 'I've always been lucky when it comes to killing folks'. Munny is also haunted by his victims. Hallucinating in the Big Whiskey saloon, Munny imagines he can see deceased Eagle Hendershot. 'His head was all broken open, you could see inside of it ... worms were coming out'. Later, when Little Bill asks Munny his name, he replies 'William Hendershot'. Following the death of Logan, *Unforgiven* provides the final piece of the puzzle as it develops into a classic Eastwood revenge scenario, with Munny stalking into town, no longer seeking bounty money like 'The Man with No Name', but vengeance.

The film's action can be summarised as two murders, three beatings and a funeral. But in contrast to his earlier, spaghetti-style forays west, *Unforgiven* has Eastwood commenting on screen and real-life violence. The murders of the two Bar T wranglers, Davey Bunting and Quick Mike epitomise Eastwood's queasy attitude to violence in the west. They ambush Davey in a canyon, Logan shooting his horse, which falls and breaks Davey's leg. Logan's nerve fails him, myopic Schofield can't shoot a seven-shot Spencer at distance, and Munny is not used to the weapon, eventually hitting the crawling, whimpering cowboy in the guts after several attempts. There Bunting dies an agonising, oozing death, hunkered in the rocks. Later, Munny and Schofield stake out the Bar T bunkhouse and wait for Mike to use the outside privy. With Mike occupied with his trousers around his ankles, Schofield sneaks up, opens the door and plugs the defenceless man three times. These scenes don't depict two iconic gunfighters meeting in the arena of death, with Mariachi trumpets on the soundtrack. As Schofield tearfully recalls, 'Three shots and he was taking a shit'. It is reality, in contrast to Leone's stylised line-'em-up, shoot-'em-down shooting gallery mythology, the film's equivalent of dime novel fiction. The Schofield Kid notes, 'It don't seem real', and yet it is.

Only in the finale does the confrontation resemble Eastwood's previous westerns, as he quietly enters the thronging saloon and loudly cocks his shotgun. For Eastwood's last western hurrah, he takes his bow in style. Having told Schofield, 'It's a hell of a thing killing a man. You take away all he's got and all he's ever gonna have', Munny heads into town. Despite the heavy odds and the second barrel of his scattergun spluttering a misfire, Munny opens fire with Schofield's pistol. In dime novel argot, coolheaded Munny's gun pours hot lead, and he plugs Daggett and four deputies, hitting five for six shots. Just as Joe the Stranger, Jed Cooper, the High Plains Drifter, Josey Wales and the Preacher experienced, revenge is sweet for William Munny. When the smoke clears, there stands a legend, ensuring Eastwood's western heroes will be unforgotten, unforgiven.

Murky posters depicted Eastwood in his long coat, a pistol concealed behind his back, with no tagline: simply '*Unforgiven*'. Rated 'R' in the US on its release in August 1992, it was '15' in the UK, but some TV prints have edited the language and violence. Trailers aptly noted, 'Some legends will never be forgotten, some wrongs can never be forgiven'. Reviews were fantastic, with the film called 'a profound work of art' (*New York Observer*), 'gripping and haunting' (*New York Daily News*), 'Eastwood's finest hour as a moviemaker' (*Newhouse News Services*) and 'a classic western for the ages' (*Variety*). 'Highly acclaimed' doesn't always mean it's any good, but *Unforgiven* is worthy of all praise. It has as much moving drama as action, and enough great performances for half a dozen features. It's Eastwood's best film as director, one of his finest as an actor and one of the greatest westerns of all time. It rapidly became the highest grossing western, taking over $100 million at the US box office and £4.6 million in the UK. Footage shot on location during *Unforgiven* surfaced in two excellent documentaries: *All on Accounta Pullin' a Trigger* and *Eastwood & Co: Making Unforgiven*, narrated by Hal Holbrook (from *Magnum Force*).

Munny was Eastwood's only western portrayal for which he was nominated for a Best Actor Academy Award, but westerns rarely bore performances worthy of Oscar celebration. The winner of the Best Actor Oscar for 1992 was Al Pacino in *Scent of a Woman*, based on the Italian film *Profumo di Donna* (1974). Luckily, Eastwood was also nominated for Best Director and the film Best Picture, besides six other categories. Joel Cox won for his editing and Hackman deservedly took Best Supporting Actor. In a night of triumph, with his 83-year-old mother Ruth in attendance, Eastwood won Best Director; then Jack Nicholson announced that *Unforgiven* had won Best Picture. 'The Man with No Name' was back and this time his haul was a fistful of Oscars. Perhaps more significantly, Eastwood has also been honoured with a Founders Award at the annual 'Golden Boots' ceremony for screen cowboys at the Beverly Hilton on Saturday, 12 August 2006. He was presented the award by his old friend Burt Reynolds. To modern audiences at least, Eastwood is the most popular western hero, and with John Wayne, an icon of the genre.

PART TWO
THE COPS

Clint Eastwood has played a cop more times than he's played a cowboy. Although a big fan of James Cagney, who famously played crime movie villains in *The Public Enemy* (1931) and *White Heat* (1949), Eastwood drew on iconoclastic fifties heroes, in uncompromising films noirs such as *Kiss Me Deadly* (1955) and *The Big Combo* (1955). Adding the gun fetishism of *Point Blank* (1967), a dislike of bureaucracy that would be cheered by anyone struggling against the red tape of City Hall and a dash of his western heroes, Eastwood reinvented the modern cop as 'Dirty' Harry Callahan, who throughout the seventies and eighties turned the streets of San Francisco into a shooting gallery.

Coogan's Bluff (1968)

Harry Callahan's genesis can be traced to soon after Eastwood returned from Italy. Following four hugely profitable westerns (the 'Dollars' trilogy and *Hang 'Em High*), *Coogan's Bluff* brought his westerner into the modern world rather by fluke. In the original story written by Herman Miller, which was envisioned as a TV movie, Arizona Deputy Sheriff Walt Coogan was a country hick, adrift in the big city of New York on the trail of an escaped murderer. In the film – assembled from versions written by Miller, Roland Kibbee, Jack Laird, Howard Rodman and Dean Reisner, and starring Eastwood – Coogan is a streetwise urban cowboy.

Piute County deputy Coogan is dispatched to extradite killer James Ringerman (Don Stroud) from New York. When Coogan arrives, hippy Ringerman is in Bellevue Hospital, having taken LSD, and can't be moved, but Coogan bluffs his way in and releases the felon. At the airport, Ringerman's girlfriend Linny Raven (Tisha Sterling) has arranged for Ringerman's escape and Coogan is ambushed and knocked out. Coogan is now in hot water with NYPD Detective Lieutenant McElroy (Lee J. Cobb), who takes him off the case. Coogan befriends probation officer Julie Roth (Susan Clark) and discovers Linny's address and tracks her to a hippy disco. Linny says she will take Coogan to Ringerman but instead leads him into an ambush at Pushie's Pool Hall. Badly beaten, Coogan escapes and forces Linny to take him to Ringerman, who is hiding in the Cloisters – a fortress-style building in Tryon Park overlooking the Hudson River. Coogan chases Ringerman through the park until he corners the criminal on a promontory known as Coogan's Bluff. As McElroy arrives, Coogan makes a citizen's arrest.

Coogan's Bluff is Eastwood's first film with director Don Siegel, who became a mentor to Eastwood through their five films as a director-star team. *Coogan's Bluff* was something of a dry run for *Dirty Harry* three years later. Both screenplays were co-written by Reisner, with music provided by Lalo Schifrin. When Coogan receives his next assignment from his superior, Sheriff McCrea (Tom Tully), he is told that if he wants to 'play lonesome boy,' he'll get 'every lousy one-man job that comes along'.

Eastwood's first non-western starring role starts in familiar territory, at the culmination of a three-day desert manhunt. Running Bear, a renegade Navajo murderer, is being tracked through the badlands by Coogan. The lawman, travelling by jeep, is ambushed by the fugitive, but canny Coogan manages to apprehend his man, who has shed his reservation 'white man's clothes' and is now dressed only in a breechclout. 'Put your pants on chief', says Coogan, lighting a cigarette. Eastwood is now a lawman in a modern, albeit still western, world – a stark desert land familiar from the 'Dollars' films (it was filmed in the Mojave Desert, California, subbing for Arizona). Eastwood wears the khaki uniform of a county deputy, with Stetson, shades and gun belt, but the non-smoking actor still puffs cigarettes onscreen, a prop that was an essential part of his screen persona.

Much of *Coogan's Bluff* was filmed on location in New York. Eastwood lands on the roof of the Pan-Am building, as a passenger in a red and white New York Airways Boeing-Vertol Turbocopter, while the 23rd Precinct NYPD police station can be seen as McElroy's headquarters. Coogan and Julie have dinner in the Tavern on the Green. Three sets (the Golden Hotel room, and two hospital rooms) were built in a studio in New York. The night-time street scenes, plus many interiors (including Pushie's Pool Hall) were filmed at Universal Studios on the 'New York Street' set. The 'Pigeon-Toed Orange Peel' discothèque was the *Phantom of the Opera* set filled with 125 extras and 400 hippies. Much use was made of Fort Tryon Park, Manhattan, filmed during the autumn. The scenes featuring Coogan and Julie chatting were filmed on lookout points near the flagpole, while Ringerman hides out in the Cloisters, a medieval-style portcullised fortress, now a museum. For the motorbike chase in Highbridge Park, culminating at Coogan's Bluff itself, Stroud had a stunt double, while Eastwood did most of his own skiddy stunt work on icy paths and lethal steps. Eastwood was a motorcycle enthusiast, and scenes showcasing his riding appear in *Where Eagles Dare*, *Magnum Force* and *The Gauntlet*. The chase finale is the modern equivalent of countless westerns, with the hero in dogged pursuit of the villain on horseback, riding across the dusty prairie. Now the location is an urban park, on two wheels instead of four legs, though 'horsepower' still figures.

Westerns more often transplanted the eastern 'dude' to the 'wild west' – here the situation is reversed. The film also features one of the few occasions when West Coaster Eastwood appeared in an East Coast setting. As soon as he was able to control his filmmaking through Malpaso Productions, Californian Eastwood often tried to film on his own doorstep on the Monterey coastline, or else in San Francisco. Coogan arrives in the big city dressed in brown suit, pointed cowboy boots, Stetson and bootlace tie. Siegel depicts the clash between straight-laced Coogan and New York's nocturnal melting pot of cops, vagrants, hookers, hippies, homosexuals, cab drivers and drug addicts. Coogan is called 'Tex' by McElroy, who notes of Coogan's determination, 'A man's gotta do what a man's gotta do – is that it Wyatt?' Elsewhere he's referred to as 'Mister Cowboy', 'Buffalo Bill' and 'Hoot Gibson'. A jailbird notes: 'Well lookie, lookie, lookie – and they say the west ain't wild any more'. In the same way that Coogan obviously hates hippies, the film equally ridicules other aspects of

2.1 *L'Uomo Dalla Cravatta Di Cuoio*: Clint Eastwood plays cowboy cop Walt Coogan, 'The Man With the Leather Tie', in Don Siegel's urban crime thriller; Italian poster for *Coogan's Bluff* (1968). Poster courtesy Ian Caunce Collection.

New York life that differ from Arizona. To the hippies, country boy Coogan is 'Joe Straight', but when Coogan starts to hunt Ringerman, he quickly adapts to their concrete jungle, putting his 'Poe-lease trainin'' to good use.

Powerhouse Lee J. Cobb portrayed McElroy, an authoritarian figure in the manner of Pat Hingle in *Hang 'Em High*. Don Stroud, who had appeared as a cop in Siegel's New York-set thriller *Madigan* (1968), would go on to appear in subsequent Siegel or Eastwood movies (*Charlie Varrick* and *Joe Kidd*), but 'Jimmy' Ringerman remains his most memorable incarnation, in leather jacket and Lennon shades, his marble face defiant. Pushie, Ringerman's chief cohort, was played by David Doyle, years before he was Bosley in TV's *Charlie's Angels*.

Both Susan Clark and Tisha Sterling gave good performances in *Coogan's Bluff*, but their roles – probation officer and hippy wacko respectively – are cardboard cut-outs deployed to make Eastwood look cool and sexy. 'You're so enigmatic', coos Julie in Fort Tryon Park; 'Enig-what?' squints Eastwood. Other female roles are even sketchier: Millie (Melodie Johnson), who is a down home Arizona gal with a heaving bosom; a hooker (Eve Brent, once Tarzan's screen Jane), who in the Golden Hotel gets a kick up the rear end when she tries to steal Coogan's wallet; and Ringerman's mother Ellen (Betty Field), who is a lush with a cigarette hanging from her mouth. The sexual politics of Eastwood's early action films often stumbles when he attempts to interact with female characters convincingly, as in *Coogan's Bluff*. This is common in the sixties and seventies cinema, particularly action movies, which often cast women as victims.

The violent set pieces and the tension between McElroy and Coogan have helped the film age rather better than might be expected. In 'The Pigeon-Toed Orange Peel', a Technicolor, strobe-lit nightclub 'happening' with a flashing dance floor and wall projections (including a clip of the giant spider from Eastwood's early *Tarantula*), Coogan, cowboy hat and all, picks his way through the grooving counterculture throng. Coogan finds Linny and fellow stoners Omega (Skip Battyn) and Wonderful Digby (Albert Popwell) passing around a spliff. Coogan tries to chat to Linny, but the others interrupt, calling him 'Charlie', 'As in: "Goodbye Charlie"'. Digby pulls a switchblade and Coogan smashes Omega across the head with a bottle, before threatening Digby with the jagged bottleneck: 'I don't like violence', Coogan hisses, 'Mister Wonderful whatever-your-name-is. You better drop that blade, or you won't believe what happens next – even while it's happening'. In probably the best remembered scene in the film, and the finest fistfight in Eastwood's canon, Coogan takes on six toughs in Pushie's Pool Hall, using cues, pool balls and anything else that comes to hand to defend himself. Wayne 'Buddy' Van Horn was employed as Eastwood's stunt double for the first time on *Coogan's Bluff* (he falls off a pool table as 'Coogan' for one shot) and reappeared in that capacity in many of the star's future projects, while Eastwood himself choreographed the scene. These tightly edited action spots, a Siegel trademark, and Eastwood's adept handling of them led the *New York Times* to christen Coogan 'a sort of "Cactus Jim" Bond'.

When it was released in the US in October 1968, Universal advertised *Coogan's Bluff* with taglines reminding audiences of his spaghettis: 'Clint Eastwood gives New York 24 hours … to get out of Town' and 'The Man with No Name takes on a Killer with No Fear on a Man-hunt with No Rules!' Its $3 million success propelled him to fifth place in the top 10 US box office attractions of the year. It also inspired the TV series *McCloud* (1970–77), starring Dennis Weaver in the title role. For *Coogan's* UK release, distributed by Rank, the film was 'X-rated'. Vincent Canby in the *New York Times* noted, 'If James Dean had lived to grow a few inches taller and to attain a lean, graceful, movie middle-age, and if he had been tranquilized beyond all emotion, the result would have been Clint Eastwood. Like some of the most popular movie stars of the past (Alan Ladd, for example), Eastwood doesn't act in motion pictures; he is framed by them'.

Dirty Harry (1971)

Don Siegel's *Dirty Harry* marks the first time Eastwood strapped on a Magnum to play Police Inspector Harry Callahan, the San Francisco cop who plays 'dirty'. Known for his unconventional procedural methods, Callahan is in charge of the Scorpio case: a serial rooftop sniper is whittling down the population of San Francisco, demanding a $100,000 payoff. Having claimed three victims (a young woman, a 10-year-old black boy and a policeman), Scorpio (Andy Robinson) kidnaps Ann Mary Deacon, a 14-year-old girl and buries her alive. Callahan, assigned rookie partner Chico Gonzales (Rene Santoni), agrees to deliver the ransom, now raised to $200,000. Callahan is led around the city, from phone booth to phone booth. At a rendezvous in Mount Davidson Park he manages to wound Scorpio with a switchblade, but Chico is injured. Callahan tracks Scorpio to the Kezar football stadium, where he lives and works. The cop tortures Ann's whereabouts out of Scorpio, but by the time the police reach her, her oxygen has run out. Claiming police brutality, Scorpio walks free but ups the ante: he hijacks a school bus carrying seven children from the Park Street School. In return for their release, he demands a fully fuelled jet waiting for him at Santa Rosa airport and $200,000. Callahan loses patience with his ineffectual superiors and the indecisive mayor and takes on Scorpio himself. He waylays the bus, frees the children and kills Scorpio, before throwing his police badge away in disgust.

The film was based on 'Dead Right', a screenplay by Harry Julian and Rita Fink. Their version pitted Callahan against sniper 'Travis'. The project was originally announced in the Hollywood trade papers in November 1970 as '*Dirty Harry* starring Frank Sinatra and directed by Irvin Kirshner', accompanied by a still from Sinatra's *The Naked Runner* (1967). John Wayne, Robert Mitchum, Steve McQueen and Paul Newman had all passed on the role. But Sinatra injured his hand and Eastwood accepted the role in December 1970. Like *Play Misty for Me*, Eastwood's previous film, *Dirty Harry* saw him locked in a deadly game with a psychopath. Don Siegel was hired as director and the film was a Warner-Malpaso production. Among the cast were John Larch as the chief of police and Harry Guardino as Lieutenant Al Bressler, Eastwood's boss. John Mitchum and Woodrow Parfrey, as Callahan's one-time partner Frank DiGeorgio and Burger Den proprietor Mr Jaffe respectively, both appeared in later Eastwood movies, while Mae Mercer, cast as a murder victim's mother, had appeared as housekeeper Hallie in *The Beguiled*. Andy Robinson, a theatre actor, was cast as Scorpio, after James Caan dropped out and Audie Murphy, Siegel's original choice, was killed in a plane crash.

The script was spruced up by Dean Reisner; John Milius too worked on early drafts, uncredited – part of his payment was a Purdy shotgun. Siegel himself wrote the final shootout at 'Hutchinson Company Crushed Rock', which ended with Scorpio floating dead in the quarry sump. The Finks' story was set in Manhattan, then switched to Seattle, but Eastwood and Siegel shifted it to Eastwood's home turf. This enabled them to use many 'Frisco landmarks, including the abandoned Kezar football stadium (as Scorpio's lair), the Golden Gate Bridge and the San Francisco-Oakland 'Bay Bridge', the Hall of Justice, California Hall (at the corner of Polk and Turk Streets), City Hall (including its splendid rotunda, with pillars, vaulted ceilings and marble staircase), Saint Peter and Paul's Roman Catholic Church opposite Washington Square (in the North Beach area) and the urban Potrero Hill district. Most of these sites are referred to in dialogue or radio traffic during the film. For the finale, Callahan waits for Scorpio on the railway trestle over Sir Francis Drake Boulevard – for authenticity, the cop's leap onto the speeding yellow Deichel Charter Service bus was performed by Eastwood himself (with the children inside the bus for this shot played by midgets). With police helicopters keeping Scorpio off the rooftops

2.2 The iconic Golden Gate Bridge stretches across San Francisco Bay, a timeless, recurrent backdrop to Clint Eastwood's 'Dirty Harry' series. Photograph courtesy Sonya-Jayne Stewart.

by day, much of the action takes place at night, captured by cinematographer Bruce Surtees in darkly lit, *noir vérité* photography. Those wishing to recreate Callahan's phone booth cat-and-mouse trail across San Francisco should start in the South Side Marina (Marina Green East Harbor), take the Muni Metro from Forest Hills Station, getting off at Church and 20th to go to Mission Dolores Park; from there, head for the Aquatic Park (though the disused Fort Mason railway tunnel is now sealed), then up to the towering concrete cross in Mount Davidson Park for a rendezvous with Scorpio.

'Dirty' Harry Callahan is probably Eastwood's most famous screen character and his most lucrative – it is the one he has revisited most often. Harry does his job well, but on his own terms and almost outside the law. A couple of vague allusions to his dead wife, killed by a drunk driver, attempt to provide him with motivation. He stops the robbery of the United Bank of San Francisco during his lunch break, blasting felons as he chews a jumbo hotdog. This shootout, which more closely resembles the O.K. Corral, was filmed on the city street set at Universal Studios. Callahan is the most gunslinger-like of the seventies cop heroes. Callahan goads a man about to jump off California Hall's rooftop into attacking him, curtailing his suicide bid; but when he corners Scorpio in the middle of the floodlit, empty Kezar stadium pitch, he treads on the injured man's leg wound until Scorpio divulges his victim's hiding place (a manhole on highlands near Golden Gate Bridge). Callahan kicks down doors and tortures suspects but is told that all the evidence he has garnered is inadmissible: the criminal's rights have been violated. 'Well I'm all broken up about that man's rights', says the inspector. His methods may be dirty, but at least his conscience is clean.

Dirty Harry provided Eastwood with a highly quotable monologue. During the bank robbery, Harry kills two hoods and wings a third. On the sidewalk, the wounded man's hand edges towards a shotgun; 'Uh-uh', warns Harry, pointing his pistol at the felon, 'I know what you're thinking. Did he fire six shots or only five? Well to tell you the truth, in all this excitement I've kind of lost track myself. But being as this is a .44 Magnum, the most powerful handgun in the world, and would blow your head clean off, you've got to ask yourself one question. Do I feel lucky? Well do you, punk?' The punk prudently doesn't.

One of the most memorable aspects of the film is Lalo Schifrin's intense score. Schifrin had also composed the themes to TV's *Mission Impossible* and the San Francisco-set cop movie *Bullit* (1968). *Dirty Harry*'s catchy, punchy title theme introduces Callahan as he arrives to examine the bikini-clad body of Scorpio's first victim – Sandra Benson (played by Diana Davidson), who is shot in a pool on the sundeck of the Holiday Inn. Callahan then follows the fatal bullet's trajectory to the roof of the Bank of America building, where Scorpio has been positioned; there he finds attached to a television aerial Scorpio's first ransom note addressed 'To the City of San Francisco'. Schifrin's *Dirty Harry* score is jazzy, but not in the way other Eastwood films use the form. Schifrin fuses traditional jazz styles with altogether more hip, urban 'cop music', which became a trademark of the 'Dirty Harrys'. As Scorpio takes aim with his silenced rifle, an echoing female voice (provided by session singer Sally Stevens), whining feedback and staccato percussion add a disturbing edge to his presence, in the compositions 'The Swimming Pool' and 'Scorpio's View'. Flute, strings and electric piano are deployed to equally haunting effect in scenes such as Ann Mary Deacon's exhumation from a manhole ('Dawn Discovery'), or Callahan tossing away his badge at the end titles, a scene Eastwood initially objected to. There is also a profusion of 'real sound': music wafting from car radios ('No More Lies, Girl', with lyrics by Schifrin's wife Donna and sung by Bernard Ito), strip clubs, peep shows, ice-cream vans and burger joints, on tracks such as 'Small World' and 'Go with It'. This music, the city's sonic soundscape, often mingles with distant police sirens, a recurrent aural motif.

Serial killer Scorpio was based on the Zodiac Killer, who terrorised California between December 1968 and October 1969. Zodiac contacted local newspapers and signed his name with a crossed circle 'target' signature – he was never caught. In Robert Graysmith's book, *Zodiac*, the author recounts that on one occasion the killer even threatened to hijack a school bus. Scorpio taunts the police throughout *Dirty Harry*, via notes in the *San Francisco Chronicle*. Callahan was reputedly modelled on Zodiac investigator Inspector Dave Toschi, who was also the inspiration for the police officers in *Bullit* and *Streets of San Francisco*. The same year as *Dirty Harry*, there was a very low-budget, exploitation movie called *The Zodiac Killer* (1971) and Graysmith's book has since been filmed by David Fincher as *Zodiac* (2007).

Dirty Harry's trailer voiceover said, 'This is about a movie about a couple of killers: Harry Callahan and a homicidal maniac – the one with the badge is Harry'. Poster advertising designed by Bill Gold, featuring Eastwood firing his Magnum through shattering glass, included the tagline, 'He doesn't break murder cases, he smashes them'. Seven-foot high cut-out 'standees' of Eastwood, made of cardboard supported by a wooden armature, were produced for display in cinema lobbies. *Dirty Harry* hit US cinemas in December 1971, rated 'R'. It was an 'X' in the UK and distributed by Columbia-EMI-Warner. TV prints have removed much of the profanity and trimmed some of the more violent scenes (for example, when Scorpio removes Callahan's switchblade from his thigh). A novelisation of *Dirty Harry* by Phillip Rock was published in 1977. The book follows an early draft: there is no suicidal rooftop scene, the bank robbery takes place in pouring rain, there are various astrological references to the star sign Scorpio, and Harry doesn't throw his badge away at the end. The book even offers an identity for pseudonymous 'Scorpio': Charles Davis, an escaped mental patient from Springfield, Massachusetts, which somewhat dissipates his air of mystery and menace.

Critics were impressed by the film's action (it even made *Time*'s top 10 for the year) but appalled by its politics, branding it 'fascist'. The film opens with shots of the San Francisco police memorial, commemorating officers killed on duty, accompanied by bells tolling 'O God Our Help in Ages Past'; the memorial's police badge then fades into Scorpio's silenced rifle barrel. Eastwood and Siegel both said that they were unaware of the film's political power, claiming it was just another thriller, but demonstrators outside the 1972 Oscars held placards reading 'Dirty Harry Is a Rotten Pig'. Scorpio wore a CND belt buckle, demonstrating his apparent allegiance to the peace movement and antagonised Callahan throughout with a variety of porcine insults, ranging from 'Hubba, hubba, hubba, pig bastard', to 'You rotten oinker'. In the *New Yorker* Pauline Kael called the film 'a right-wing fantasy', noting, 'fascist medievalism has a fairytale appeal'. But audiences cheered Callahan's exploits and the film became the fifth biggest earner of 1971 in the US, taking $16 million on its initial run, making it Eastwood's biggest hit up to that year. Its earnings have since risen to almost $36 million in the US and it was the film that transformed Eastwood into a superstar in his native country.

Magnum Force (1973)

Although *Dirty Harry* ends with Callahan discarding his badge, Harry was soon back on the force. The first of four sequels appeared in 1973, following two of Eastwood's forays west (*Joe Kidd* and *High Plains Drifter*) and his love story *Breezy*, a commercial flop. The appropriately named *Magnum Force*, directed by *Hang 'Em High*'s Ted Post, was concocted by John Milius (who wrote the screenplay) and then revised by Michael Cimino, a newcomer to the movie industry with ambitions to direct.

The worst mobsters in San Francisco are being slain by an unknown killer with a grudge against the slow, often lenient, judicial system. Labour leader Carmine Ricca is acquitted of murdering Anthony Scarza and his family, but on his way home he's shot dead. Detective Harry Callahan is now working on stakeout duty with Early Smith (Felton Perry), his new partner. Callahan runs into his old friend Charlie McCoy (Mitchell Ryan), who is psychologically disturbed and rails against the judicial system. Callahan also makes the acquaintance of four hotshot rookie motorcycle cops: Davis, Sweet, Astrachan and Grimes, who met in the Special Forces' Airborne Rangers and 'stick together like flypaper'. A mobsters' pool party is shot up and the guests massacred, then a pimp is shot dead in his Eldorado after he has brutally murdered one of his girls. Pretty soon Callahan is reinstated on homicide by Lieutenant Briggs (Hal Holbrook). Briggs thinks it's a gang turf war and puts key crime bosses under surveillance, while Callahan suspects a renegade cop, possibly his old friend McCoy. At the stakeout of hood Lou Guzman, an assassin manages to execute Guzman under the cops' noses, but suspicion is lifted from McCoy: he is murdered when he confronts the killer, who is disguised as a traffic cop. At the police department's annual shooting competition, Davis beats Callahan. Retrieving one of Davis's slugs from the shooting range, he matches it up to the one that killed McCoy. During a dockside raid on crime boss Frank Palancio, Sweet is killed. Callahan tells Briggs his 'killer cops' theory; shortly afterwards Callahan is almost killed by a booby-trapped mailbox. He tries to warn Early, but is too late: his partner is killed in a blast. Briggs is in league with the rookie 'Death Squad'; in a chase through the San Francisco docks, Callahan confronts and kills Briggs and the remaining three cops.

2.3 'Did he fire six?': Dirty Harry Callahan bursts onto the scene in Don Siegel's classic *Dirty Harry* (1971). US three-sheet poster, courtesy Ian Caunce Collection.

2.4 Harry Francis Callahan, the last hope for law and order in San Francisco: An arresting US one-sheet poster for a 'Dirty Harry' double bill, featuring *Dirty Harry* (1971) and Ted Post's ultraviolent *Magnum Force* (1973). Poster courtesy Ian Caunce Collection.

Filming began in April 1973 on location in San Francisco, with cinematographer Frank Stanley capturing California at its most sun-drenched. The *New York Times* liked the 'stunning' cinematography, though Eastwood could only manage 'a frown that suggests tension'. The Potrero district featured in the action, a prostitute murdered by her pimp picks up a taxi outside the Fairmont Hotel; City Hall also reappeared. But there are less recognisable locations this time around – *Magnum Force* could have been set anywhere. Only in the exciting climax in the dockside and on a derelict aircraft carrier does the film make its locations count.

One of the film's big plusses is its supporting cast. Hal Holbrook was suitably shifty as Briggs, Callahan's disingenuous boss, and Felton Perry was suitably nervous as Early, Callahan's new partner. Mitchell Ryan, as loose screw Charlie McCoy, who is 'ready for the rubber gun squad', had appeared in *High Plains Drifter*. John Mitchum reappeared as Frank DiGeorgio – with Callahan the only character carried over from *Dirty Harry*. Officers Davis, Sweet, Astrachan and Grimes, four clean-cut, all-American boys, rookie traffic cops who turn out to be a vigilante death squad, are played by a quartet of young actors: David Soul, Tim Matheson, Kip Niven and Robert Urich. Both Soul and Urich went on to stardom in their own cop TV shows. Soul played Ken 'Hutch' Hutchinson in *Starsky and Hutch* (1975–79), while Urich appeared as Officer Jim Street in *SWAT* (1975–76), as Dan Tanna in *Vega$* (1978–81) and as private eye Spencer in *Spencer: For Hire* (1984–88). Albert Popwell, from *Coogan's Bluff* and *Dirty Harry*, appeared as an ostentatiously dressed, Eldorado-driving pimp straight out of a blaxploitation movie.

It has already been established in *Dirty Harry* that Callahan's partners have a high mortality rate. By the beginning of *Magnum Force*, Callahan is partnering Early Smith, a black officer. There are even glimpses of Callahan's secluded home life in his apartment, where his evening meal is cold hamburgers and beer, and he spends the night with his sexy Asian neighbour Sunny (Adele Yoshioka). But these shadings of Callahan's character and his Sunny intervals are the slightest of brush strokes, and it's the film's grandiose action and bloody violence that remains most memorable.

'Fascist' cop Harry is contrasted here with some real fascists: a 'Death Squad' of killers who execute mobsters beyond the law. The film's original working title was 'Vigilance'. The murders which pepper *Magnum Force* make it the most violent 'Dirty Harry' movie, with many bloody killings and a fair amount of nudity (both aspects have been trimmed for TV airings). The opening killing sees a faceless motorcycle cop shoot Ricca, his driver, his attorney and a bodyguard at point-blank range with a Magnum. At the poolside massacre, a cop tosses a smoke bomb into the swimming pool and then opens up with an automatic rifle. A pimp kills one of his girls, who owes him money, by pouring drain cleaner down her throat in the back of a taxi, and is then shot at close quarters in his pink and yellow *Superfly*-style 'pimp-mobile'. Another hood is executed in his luxurious pad, where he enjoys sexual games with a young, cocaine-snorting couple, which ends with the naked woman smashing through the high-rise apartment's window. Critics wouldn't be able to call Callahan a fascist this time. He looked like a liberal compared to the vigilante, Vietnam vet assassins: clean-cut, kidding-around, all-American boys masking a shocking subculture in the police force. Callahan notes that they 'Sure show a sense of style'. These young men live by the credo 'All our heroes are dead'; it is their job to fight back, reasoning that acquitted criminals must die. 'You of all people should understand that', they tell Callahan. When asked to join them ('Either you're for us or against us'), Callahan is unconvinced: 'I'm afraid you've misjudged me'. Pauline Kael, such a critic of *Dirty Harry*, said that the killer cops were 'explicit versions of what we accused Harry of being; they might be the earlier Harry's disciples, and the new Harry wipes them all out … *Magnum Force* disarms political criticism and still delivers the thrills of brutality'.

Magnum Force's extravagant action, propelled by Lalo Schifrin's funkadelic score, makes Harry's gravel-pit shootout with Scorpio seem a subdued affair. In place of *Dirty Harry*'s hotdog-stand shootout, Callahan here enjoys a burger and foils a hijack at San Francisco International Airport. This may have been inspired by the original ending of *Dirty Harry*, which Siegel vetoed, with Scorpio picked off by a marine sniper at Santa Rosa airport. In *Magnum Force*, noticing a panicky air among the terminal staff, Harry volunteers to board the Sovereign Airways plane being held to ransom by two hijackers. Disguised as a pilot, he taxis the plane down the runway without taking off. 'Excuse me captain', asks a worried-looking co-pilot as they speed along, 'I know this may sound silly, but can you fly?' 'Nope', smiles Callahan, 'Never had a lesson', as he slams on the brakes and then proceeds to neutralise and kill both hijackers. Each of the 'Dirty Harry' sequels would have at least one such 'Clintessential' moment. In the final motorbike chase through the docks, on deck and down into the dark bowels of the rusty, hulking aircraft carrier, Eastwood had the chance to demonstrate his cycling skills, performing much of his own stuntwork. With the three remaining traffic cops outwitted and killed, Callahan is captured by Briggs, who says that he's going to prosecute: 'It'll be my word against yours – and who's going to believe you? You're a killer Harry, a maniac'. But as Briggs drives off, Callahan has managed to re-activate the mailbox bomb and Briggs is blown to smithereens; 'A man's got to know his limitations', smiles Harry.

In terms of straightforward, macho action, *Magnum Force* could be viewed as something of a step back for Eastwood, after his directorial efforts on markedly different material, such as *Play Misty for Me* and *Breezy*. But it was in this way that he was able to finance such gambles: alternating artistic risk with sure-fire hit. The trailer informed audiences: 'Eastwood is back in full force, as Dirty Harry in *Magnum Force*. There are killers on the loose dressed as cops and they always use a Magnum'. *The Hero Cop: Yesterday and Today*, a short 'Making of' documentary, was prepared to publicise the film, comparing policing methods through the ages. At the end of the film's opening titles, accompanied by a punchy, screeching variation by Lalo Schifrin of 'Scorpio's Theme' from *Dirty Harry*, Eastwood aims a pistol at the screen and intones: 'This is a .44 Magnum, the most powerful handgun in the world and it could blow your head clean off. Do you feel lucky?' before the gun goes off, blasting right into the audiences' faces. Bill Gold's key art for the poster also concentrated on the heavy hardware, depicting a cut-out shooting range target and Callahan menacing theatregoers. It was rated 'R' in the US and 'X' in the UK on its release in December 1973. The 1974 novelisation by Mel Valley contained a couple of extra scenes and some odd inconsistencies: Frank DiGeorgio is named Sal DiGeorgio, and Callahan and his wife Bernice are separated – she wasn't killed by a drunk driver.

Because *Dirty Harry* was scrutinised and criticised so intently, subsequent outings would be equally dissected. 'He [Eastwood] makes a wonderful hero, as practically everyone in the country has already noticed', praised the *New York Post*. *Variety* thought the slack film, 'picks its way so carefully that we tire of it as we would tire of watching an uninspired ant negotiate a maze'. But *Magnum Force* appealed to the vigilante in everyone and rapidly became Eastwood's most lucrative film, grossing almost $40 million during 1973's otherwise festive season.

The Enforcer (1976)

Following the artistry of *The Outlaw Josey Wales*, one of his finest, most poetic films, Eastwood returned to the cop genre for one of his most formulaic: *The Enforcer*. No two films of the 'Dirty Harry' series share the same director, which partially accounts for their variable class. *The Enforcer*, or 'Dirty Harry III', is another topical stab at pitting Harry against the killers of today. The film was adapted from the story 'Moving Target' (written by Gail Morgan Hickman and S.W. Schurr) by Dean Reisner and Sterling Silliphant.

Now partnered by Frank DiGeorgio, Callahan finds himself bumped down to the personnel department by his boss, Captain McKay (Bradford Dillman), after he causes $14,379 worth of damage foiling a liquor store hold-up. Meanwhile a militant organisation calling itself the People's Revolutionary Strike Force (PFSF) raid the dockside Hamilton Firearms Works, taking explosives, M16 automatic rifles and M-40 LAWS rockets (Light Anti-tank Weapons Systems, one-shot, lightweight, disposable bazookas). During the raid, DiGeorgio is knifed and killed by their leader, Bobby Maxwell. The police department receives a tape detailing the PRSF's demands: they want $1 million or they'll start 'blowing things up' (the ransom has been inflated since Scorpio's day). Callahan is hurriedly reinstated on homicide and assigned a new partner, freshly promoted Inspector Kate Moore (Tyne Daly). While they attend an autopsy, the police station is bombed. Callahan and Moore chase and capture the culprit, Henry Lee Caldwell, a black militant. His explosives are linked to the wharf theft, but McKay has his own ideas. He thinks a black political group called UHURU, led by Big Ed Mustapha (Albert Popwell), is the culprit and raids its headquarters in the Mission District. UHURU isn't responsible, but for voicing his objections, Callahan is suspended. The PRSF kidnap the mayor of San Francisco and demand $5 million. They hide out on Alcatraz Island in the disused maximum-security prison, but Callahan and Moore storm the island in a fireboat and free the mayor. The revolutionaries are wiped out but not before Maxwell has killed Inspector Moore, who takes a bullet meant for the mayor.

Attempting continuity with *Dirty Harry*, Harry Guardino is back as Lieutenant Al Bressler, here functioning as little more than Callahan's straight man, while John Mitchum's Inspector Frank DiGeorgio is prominently featured; DiGeorgio's demise is Mitchum's big scene. Never as well known as his older brother Robert, Mitchum's appearances in Eastwood's films from *Paint Your* Wagon onwards were his most prominent roles. Tyne Daly – soon to become a household name as Mary Beth Lacey, one half of the popular TV, Emmy Award-winning female cop duo *Cagney and Lacey* – played Harry's new partner, who, like all his sidekicks, has to endure Harry's Neanderthal humour. Bradford Dillman turned in a well-tuned performance as Bradford McKay, Callahan's by-the-book, humourless boss, while DeVeren Bookwalter as Bobby Maxwell, pimp-turned-people's revolutionary hero, is one of the all-time hokey crime film performances.

A bulging blue-eyed psycho so over the top as to be a comic-book parody, Maxwell's Vietnam vet has been kicked out of the army on a 'Section 8' (mental instability) and has recruited a ragged cult of followers. These include Lalo (Michael Cavanaugh), hippies Wanda and Miki (straight out of Charles Manson's murderous sect), slow-witted hicks Tex and Karl and bomber Henry Lee (played by Tim Burrus). This crew, fashioned after the real-life Bay Area 'Symbionese Liberation Army', who made headlines in February 1974 when they kidnapped newspaper heiress Patty Hearst, has members who have as much personality as the cut-out targets Harry riddles on the shooting range, which in essence is what they are. From the finely drawn characterisation of Scorpio, and even *Magnum Force*'s 'Death Squad', Callahan's pathetic opponents this time, with their headbands, army fatigues and misguided cries of 'This is for the people! Right on!' are the thinnest of excuses for political activism. As Pauline Kael noted in the *New Yorker*, '[The Enforcer] sets up a collection of villains so disgustingly cruel and inhuman that Eastwood can spend the rest of the movie killing them with a perfect conscience'. For all their brutality there is a comedic ineptitude to their brand of terrorism. Operating from their conspicuous van with flames on the side and kidnapping the mayor using a 25,000-volt paralysing Taser gun, they're the kind of outfit who might write a return address on a letter bomb.

The title sequence introduces Callahan and DiGeorgio driving across Bay Bridge, accompanied by Jerry Fielding's jazzy cue, which he composed on the heels of *The Outlaw Josey Wales*. This is the only 'Dirty Harry' film not scored by Lalo Schifrin. Callahan spends much of *The Enforcer* railing against bureaucracy, with McKay constantly criticising Callahan's methods: 'I never said to use violence'. 'Well what'd you want me to do?' asks Harry, 'Yell trick or treat at them?' When he's demoted, Callahan tells McKay, 'Personnel? That's for assholes'; 'I was in personnel for 10 years', retaliates McKay, proudly. When the police records office is stalling during a search for vital information, Harry hisses down the phone for them to hurry up: 'You pencil-pushing son of a bitch'. He also has a new, one-word catchphrase, a sarcastic 'Marvellous', and hates the 'stylish' mayor's modern ideas on the police force, which advocate even women being promoted to inspectors. When Callahan airs his views, he's handed a

2.5 *The Enforcer* (1976): Harry's up against terrorists in this second sequel to *Dirty Harry*, but his methods remain the same; US insert publicity, courtesy Ian Caunce Collection.

suspension and hands over his badge to McKay: 'There's a seven-point suppository, Captain'.

The only character Callahan bargains with is UHURU's leader Big Ed Mustapha (originally called Big Ed Mohamid), another guest appearance by Albert Popwell. In the black Mission District, Mustapha agrees to help the cops only if they free one of his men held on a possession charge. When McKay is convinced UHURU (itself based on the African-American militant party The Black Panthers) is behind the terrorist threats, Mustapha is arrested. Later Callahan meets Mustapha again, only this time the cop blackmails him into divulging information: 'You really are a dirty bastard', notes Mustapha; 'The dirtiest', corrects Harry.

In keeping with tradition, bullet-proof Callahan's hapless partners end up in the morgue – in *The Enforcer*, he loses both DiGeorgio and Moore. When Callahan and Moore first meet, Harry is on a personnel panel to decide promotions to inspector. Callahan tries to humiliate her during her oral test, but she gives as good as she gets. When he's reinstated on homicide, McKay spitefully partners him with Moore. 'Oh shit', Callahan comments succinctly on the pairing. His attitude is, 'If she wants to play lumberjack, she's gonna have to learn to handle her end of the log', but he grows to respect her professionalism, and she his. 'Whoever draws you as a partner', Callahan concedes, 'could do a hell of a lot worse'.

The Enforcer also features much rough humour, which was becoming Eastwood's forte. When Callahan is called to a restaurant to help a suspected heart-attack victim, he recognises the culprit as conman 'Freddie the Fainter', whom he promptly ejects from the establishment, to the shock of the staff and diners. Staking out 'Tiffany's Massage and Sauna', Callahan introduces himself as 'Larry Dickman' (in the original script he says 'Bradford McKay'). In the same scene, the tough, moustachioed owner of the joint is named Buchinski, Charles Bronson's real surname. Bronson, another monosyllabic tough-guy, consistently challenged Eastwood's popularity in the yearly box office top 10, especially with his *Death Wish* movies, where vigilantism was something to be cheered.

Billed as 'The Dirtiest Harry of Them All', *The Enforcer* is certainly the daftest and most senselessly violent of the series. Callahan's 'wild-west show' scene here has three hoods hold up the 'La Franchi Liqors' store. They rough Callahan up when he arrives to negotiate and then demand a car to make their escape. DiGeorgio asks what Harry's going to do. 'Give 'em one', Callahan replies, as he wheels his car around and screeches straight through the shop's glass frontage, destroying it in a shower of shelving, liquor and glass, totalling the car, before shooting the would-be robbers. The film was again shot on location in San Francisco. Prominent locations included the Third Street swing bridge in China Basin (used in the mayor's kidnap), San Francisco City Hall, where Callahan and Kate have their pictures taken and receive commendations as publicists for the mayor's new law enforcement programme, and Coit Tower on Telegraph Hill (which Kate deems phallic and christens 'Coit-us interruptus'). Callahan chased Henry Lee across Embarcadero district rooftops, and the actual Alcatraz Island prison was used for the finale when Harry disintegrates Maxwell and a watchtower with a LAWS rocket, with the words, 'You fucking fruit'.

Posters for *The Enforcer* featured Callahan and his Magnum, with Bay Bridge as a backdrop, or firing his pistol through the shattered windshield of his car. It was rated 'R' in the US, 'X' in the UK. The trailer smirked: 'Harry's got a lady partner – this is a first for him', continuing: 'Like every city, San Francisco has its share of crime and violence. San Francisco is the only city with a cop like Dirty Harry'. A 'Making of', *Harry Callahan-Clint Eastwood: Something Special in Films*, depicted the staging of the liquor store hold-up, the rooftop chase and the mayor's kidnap. On its release in December 1976, critics were contemptuous. *Variety* called it a, 'Worn out copy of *Dirty Harry* ... the format seems to be falling apart at the seams. The next project from this particular mold had better shape up or give up', while Rex Reed in the *New York Daily News* laughed: 'Save your money, it'll be on TV by Easter'. *Harvard Lampoon* named Eastwood 'Worst Actor of the Year'. An *Enforcer* novelisation spin-off by Wesley Morgan was published in 1976. Though the book closely follows the screenplay, in a noticeable lapse in consistency Harry's deceased wife is now named Louise. In the wake of the success of the first three 'Dirty Harry' movies, fictional 'Never Before Published or Seen on the Screen' novelisations were issued by Warner Books, starting in 1981 with Dane Hartman's *Duel for Cannons* (and continuing with *Death on the Docks*, *The Long Death* and *The Mexico Kill*), which was dedicated 'to Harry's very spirit: Clint Eastwood and Don Siegel'. The blurb ran, 'The Magnum maverick ... who blows away the rules when the rules get in the way'. He blew away audiences too: *The Enforcer* took $24 million, eventually grossing over $46 million, making it Eastwood's most profitable film up to 1976.

The Gauntlet (1977)

Almost a year after the release of *The Enforcer*, Eastwood unleashed his next release, *The Gauntlet*, an action cop movie that out-dirtied Harry and featured some of the worst marksmanship ever committed to celluloid. Eastwood directed himself as Ben Shockley, a loser detective on the Phoenix police force, who is chosen by boss Blakelock (William Prince) to extradite Gus Mally from Las Vegas: 'A nothing witness for a nothing trial'. On his arrival at Clark County Jail, Shockley discovers that 'Gus' is actually Augustina Mally (Sondra Locke), a smart-mouthed, quick-talking hooker with a graduate degree. She claims that her life is in danger – Shockley initially doesn't believe her, even though he sees that in the 10th race at Santa Anita: 'Mally No Show' is deemed 50–1. On their way to the airport, a car Shockley requests as backup is blown to pieces by a booby trap and they are fired on by mobsters. Hiding out at Mally's house, Shockley calls Phoenix for help, but instead the house is ambushed by police, with Mally and Shockley narrowly escaping with their lives. Hijacking a police car to the Nevada-Arizona border, they avoid another ambush, as more mobsters lie in wait. Someone at the Phoenix police headquarters is tipping off the Vegas Police and the mob: gradually it dawns on Shockley that Mally is telling the truth. She is the key witness in the trial of Angelo DeLucca, a mobster who had once hired her to 'entertain' a member of the Phoenix police force; during the evening, the officer had savagely assaulted her. Shockley realises from her description that her attacker is Blakelock and that Shockley has been chosen, not because he will get the job done, but because of his ineptitude. Shockley hijacks a Phoenix-bound Southwest Trail Lines Greyhound bus in Wickenburg, ejects the passengers and fortifies the cabin with quarter-inch steel, while Mally puts her $5,000 life savings on 'Mally No Show' (now at 100–1). Informing Blakelock of their route, they run the gauntlet of hundreds of Phoenix police officers, who blast away at the bus through town. Finally Shockley, subpoena in hand, delivers Mally to the steps of City Hall; during the face-off, she shoots Blakelock dead.

The Gauntlet is Eastwood's most extravagant cop fantasy – a way-out action movie whose over-the-top pyrotechnics anticipate the ridiculous superheroics of Stallone, Willis and Schwarzenegger. In the course of their dash for Phoenix, Shockley and Mally survive several spectacular action scenes, reportedly costing $1 million – a huge chunk of the $5.5 million budget. Filming took place on location in Las Vegas, Nevada (on the boulevard known as 'The Strip' and at the McCarran International Airport), the Nevada and Arizona deserts, and Phoenix itself. When Shockley and Mally are holed up in her bungalow, the entire Las Vegas police force lay siege, opening fire with automatic weapons and destroying the building, to the extent that the structure is so bullet-ridden (7,000 bullet-hit squibs were used) that it creaks and then collapses. As the cross-country chase accelerates into a mad scramble, resembling Hitchcock's *North by Northwest*, Eastwood-style, Shockley and Mally, on a commandeered Harley Davidson, pause to phone Josephson, his colleague in Phoenix. As Shockley chats in the phone box, a chopper swoops down and a sniper starts shooting at him. This chase sequence is particularly risible, with a shades-wearing Eastwood astride his 'hog', his best girl hanging onto his waist, in a swirling dusty fantasy, as he photogenically outruns the helicopter on long, straight desert roads. The inaccurate sniper on board (played by Malpaso producer Fritz Manes) gives his profession a bad name. His bad day is rounded off when the pilot snags the helicopter on high-voltage power cables, frazzling the chopper and its occupants. The film's most famous scene is 'the gauntlet' of the title, an incredible, effects-laden sequence shot on the streets of Phoenix, where an army of cops loose 8,000 rounds. This time it is Eastwood's hero who hijacks a bus, in a variation on Scorpio's gambit. Shockley drives slowly down the palm tree-lined streets through a hail of bullets, but unfortunately the cops haven't packed any armoured-piercing ammo and don't think to aim at the tyres.

The screenplay was by Michael Butler and Dennis Shryack, though the plot borrows freely from *Coogan's Bluff*, including the transposition of the cop, this time from urban to rural: the deserts of Arizona and Nevada. A novelisation was published by Star, billed as 'A Malpasso (*sic*) production starring Clint Eastwood and Sandra (*sic*) Locke'. The language and violence is even more explicit in the book, which opens with a detailed description of Blakelock's assault of Mally. An in-joke that didn't appear in the film featured Mally telling Shockley, as they leap onto the stolen Harley, 'You're

2.6 Locke and Load: This US lobby card from *The Gauntlet* (1977) depicts Eastwood and Sondra Locke on the run from police and mobsters in this R-rated action adventure. Card No 4, of a set of 8; courtesy Ian Caunce Collection.

one hell of a cop', only to receive the answer, 'Yea, me and Dirty Harry'. In the film, Mally worries, 'D'you know how to drive this thing?' and Shockley assures her: 'It's been a few years…but we'll fake it'.

Throughout the seventies Eastwood recast reliable actors. For *The Gauntlet* he again worked with Pat Hingle (from *Hang 'Em High*) as 'Josie' Josephson, Shockley's ally in the Phoenix police force. Jeff Morris (from *Kelly's Heroes*) appeared as the jail's desk sergeant. Bill McKinney had a cameo as a foul-mouthed, redneck flunky Vegas cop while Dan Vadis (an Eastwood regular) and Roy Jenson (from *Paint Your Wagon*) appeared as bikers. McKinney, Jenson and Vadis would play bikers in Eastwood's two vehicles with Clyde the orang-utan, beginning the following year with *Every Which Way But Loose*. In fact, the genesis of these later comedies can be seen in *The Gauntlet*, during a confrontation between 'The Noblemen', a gang of shambling, hairy bikers, and steely eyed Shockley. Pistol-wielding Shockley sends the gang packing and steals one of their bikes. 'This is our choppers, Charlie!' moans Jenson; 'And this is my gun, Clyde', answers Eastwood.

The Gauntlet is a transitional film in Eastwood's career. There is a strong jazz flavour to Jerry Fielding's score (with jazz solos performed by Art Pepper and Jon Faddis). Shockley is the first of Eastwood's down-at-heel, crumpled cops – low-key, anti-heroic variations on his Dirty Harry persona. *The Gauntlet* also saw the birth of 'Superclint', the indestructible blue-collar *überman*. For the climax in Phoenix, Eastwood wears what would become another of his screen trademarks: a white T-shirt. By 'The End', Eastwood's clothes are torn and bloody, and he resembles Philo, the bare-knuckle boxer of the 'Clyde' films, a man who believes only in beer, brawls and pick-ups – both the four-wheeled and the two-legged varieties. Several critics noted that Shockley was, for Eastwood, a character role, which gives some insight into how limited they viewed his talents to be. Seen today, it's an archetypical tough Eastwood performance.

In a role originally slated for Barbra Streisand, Sondra Locke surprised everyone with gutsy Gus Mally, her best performance opposite Eastwood. Onscreen the pair sometimes lacked chemistry, but in *The Gauntlet* there are several scenes where their off-screen attraction is apparent. Their early scenes mostly consist of their slanging match sparring, as Mally shocks Shockley and chips away at his tough-guy exterior. 'I just do what I'm told', cop Shockley tells Mally; 'Yea? Well so does an imbecile', she scoffs. He's 'a nothing, a nobody, a faded number on a rusty badge'. But their relationship in the latter stages of the story improves, when Mally realises that Shockley is actually a decent man, trying against the odds to do his job and protect her. *Cue* thought Locke showed 'guts and vitality', and *Village Voice* noted that she gave 'the most natural, unaffected performance of the year by any young actress' and, getting carried away with itself, noted that she 'blossoms forth as a young Susan Hayward or Barbara Stanwyck'. Seeing Locke in this period as Eastwood's regular co-star, it's easy to forget that he was still married and this must have been difficult for Maggie, his wife of 24 years. It is hard enough breaking up with someone, or suspecting an affair, without the 'suspected affair' being released nationwide to cinemas. Early in the film, hooker Mally tells Shockley that most of her clients are 'married men, cheating on their wives'. Shortly after this film, Maggie filed for divorce.

The Gauntlet was released in the US for Christmas 1977, rated 'R' for strong language and violence. Judith Crist in the *New York Post* called the film, 'The pits', nothing more than 'a mindless compendium of stale plot and stereotyped characters varnished with foul language and garnished with violence'. Critical opinion mattered little and *The Gauntlet* grossed $17.7 million at the US box office. In the UK, *The Gauntlet* was rated 'X'. TV showings have abridged the language and nudity, though DVD versions in Panavision, rated '18', run uncut at 105 minutes. Probably the most enduring aspect of the film's release is its tremendous artwork, including one of the most sought after Eastwood posters. With the tagline, 'Clint Eastwood is the man in the middle of *The Gauntlet*', it was designed by ex-comic-book illustrator Frank Frazetta in fantasy style, featuring muscled colossus Eastwood, brandishing a pistol, and scantily clad Locke, her clothes teasingly shredded, clinging onto her hero, as they emerge from the smoking wreckage of the bullet-ridden bus.

Sudden Impact (1983)

Whenever there was a major dip in Eastwood's box office takings, he, like the people of San Francisco, would look to Harry Callahan as his saviour. He bounced back from the commercial failure of his personal project *Honkytonk Man* with *Sudden Impact*. It was time for Harry to reload his Magnum and coin a new catchphrase, which became Eastwood's most enduring and might be his epitaph.

Originally written as a revenge vehicle for Sondra Locke by Charles B. Pierce and Earl E. Smith, *Sudden Impact* was adapted by Joseph Stinson into a 'Dirty Harry' vehicle for Eastwood, with Locke in an important but supporting role. Smith had directed Locke as accursed Drusilla in the ultra-weird *The Shadow of Chikara* (1977), a creepy post-Civil War supernatural, diamond-hunt western. Shot in autumnal Arkansas after Locke made *The Gauntlet*, the film also featured John Davis Chandler (from *The Outlaw Josey Wales*) and stock footage battle scenes from *Shenandoah*. *Sudden Impact* would be Locke's last film opposite Eastwood – though he directed her in the 30-minute TV episode *Vanessa in the Garden* (1985) for Steven Spielberg's *Amazing Stories* – and effectively the end of her film career, as their personal relationship fizzled. Their next appearance together would be in court.

In *Sudden Impact*, Callahan's bad publicity begins to embarrass the San Francisco Police Department, so he is sent down the coast to the seaside resort of San Paulo. He is to investigate the death of George Wilburn, born and raised in San Paulo, who has been found in a car overlooking San Francisco Bay, having been shot in the genitals and then through the head. With little help from suspicious San Paulo police chief Lester Jannings (Pat Hingle), Callahan begins to piece together the case, as more San Paulo residents are killed in the same manner – fisherman Kramer is found executed on a beach; storekeeper Tyrone is murdered in his garage. The link between them is the fact that 10 years ago, six locals sexually assaulted sisters Jennifer and Beth Spencer at the seafront fairground; Beth was particularly traumatised and is in a permanent catatonic state in hospital, while Jennifer (Locke) is now an artist whose intense work is 'a howl of anguish'. Callahan becomes involved with Jennifer and figures out that she is responsible for the murders. Ray Parkins, a lesbian who convinced the sisters to attend what they thought was a beach party, is soon shot. The culprits' leader Mick (Paul Drake), with help from local fishmongers the Stagnaro brothers, beats up Callahan and kidnaps Jennifer, taking her back to the scene of the beachside crime. In a shootout in the fairground, Callahan emerges triumphant: his adversaries dead, the cop suppresses evidence, allowing vigilante justice to win out and Jennifer to walk free.

The only film of the series directed by 'Dirty Harry' himself, *Sudden Impact* is a lame addition to the franchise, though a few familiar faces crop up in an attempt to add gravitas. Bradford Dillman returned from *The Enforcer*, not as McKay but as Captain Briggs (Hal Holbrooks's character, killed at the end of *Magnum Force*). To Briggs, Callahan is 'a dinosaur'. To Callahan, Briggs is 'a legend in your own mind'. Even though DiGeorgio is dead, various cops and attorneys replay tiresome 'You're a class act, Harry' routines with the hero. Albert Popwell pops up as Horace King, a fellow inspector on the SFPD, who during the investigation in San Paulo has his throat slit when he is mistaken for Harry. Pat Hingle, an actor afflicted with a

2.7 *Sudden Impact* (1983) gave Clint Eastwood his most famous line: 'Go ahead, make my day'. Author's collection.

permanent wince, was cast as unhelpful Jannings; he is actually protecting his own son, Alby (who is one of the rapists), and is wary of 'Big City Hotshot' Callahan. Fifties B-movie star Mara Corday had appeared in such films as *The Giant Claw* (1957 – opposite a huge buzzard), *Tarantula* (1955 – opposite a giant spider) and *The Black Scorpion* (1959 – opposite an oversized scorpion). She had small roles in several latter-day Eastwood films, including *The Gauntlet* and *The Rookie*. Here she plays Acorn Café waitress Loretta.

It is Loretta who tips Harry off that there is a robbery in progress, in the film's most famous scene. Callahan walks into the café for a coffee, immersed in a newspaper; Loretta pours sugar into his cup, not a spoonful, but a cupful. Outside Callahan samples the brew and promptly spits it out onto the sidewalk. Guessing correctly that Loretta was trying to tell him something, he returns through the back door where he finds four black hoods holding up the café. Callahan confronts them: 'We're not just gonna let you walk out of here'. 'Who's we, sucker?' one asks of lone cop Callahan; 'Smith & Wesson and me', says Harry, drawing his Magnum from inside his sports jacket and opening fire. Three robbers are down when the last one, wounded, grabs

Loretta. As the police arrive outside, Harry points his cocked pistol at the hood, exhorting him to try to kill his hostage and make an escape: 'Go ahead', says Harry, 'Make my day'.

Filmed, like all the previous 'Dirty Harrys', in Panavision, *Sudden Impact* forsakes the usual San Francisco locales for much of the action, setting Jennifer's vendetta and Callahan's investigation in the fictional seaside town of San Paulo. San Francisco locations include the Golden Gate Bridge and the Mark Hopkins international hotel, where Callahan threatens crime lord Threlkis (played by Michael V. Gazzo, star witness Frankie Pentangeli in *The Godfather Part II*), resulting in the old man having a fatal heart attack at his granddaughter's wedding. Other settings include the Bowles/Hopkin Gallery, where Jennifer's angsty 'Dark Visions' exhibition is staged, and Callahan shoots it out with three mobsters and their bullet-proof car at the Embarcadero Ferry Building in the neon-lit port of San Francisco. 'San Paulo' location filming was done in Santa Cruz, south of San Francisco. A key location was the beach boardwalk on stilts, which includes the funfair and amusement park.

The most interesting character in the film is Locke's avenger, Jennifer. Her cover for being in San Paulo is to restore the fairground's vintage carousel for the historical society, but the film's narrative closely resembled *Death Wish* (1974) and revenge-for-rape films such as *Rape Squad* (1974 – starring Jo Ann Harris, from *The Beguiled*), *Lipstick* (1976 – starring the Hemingway sisters, Margaux and Mariel) and the notorious *I Spit on Your Grave* (1978 – also released as *Day of the Woman*). Critics were pleased to see a woman cast in such a prominent revenge role in a mainstream action movie, the film's general tattiness notwithstanding. Some even dubbed the film 'feminist' and Jennifer 'Dirty Harriet', who dished out '.38 calibre vasectomies', as the film tastefully puts it. But the assault itself is depicted exactly as in the exploitation movies mentioned above and is periodically returned to in tacky, unpleasant flashbacks. Her attackers are subhuman scum, and terrible actors, including Paul Drake, as their leader Mick, a graduate of the DeVeren Bookwalter academy of histrionic crime movie loonies. *New York Magazine* compared *Sudden Impact* to films noirs, noting its largely nocturnal setting, where 'sinister thugs emerge from the shadows, or Sondra Locke, blond hair curtaining her face in the style of Veronica Lake, moves into the frame'. At no point does *Sudden Impact* reach the atmospheric, psychological heights of film noir, and Locke is no Lake. Murky, almost impenetrable, cinematography and a hairstyle don't miraculously create noir.

Variety detected a case of ballistic one-upmanship throughout the movie: 'Everyone in the picture carries a firearm, one bigger than the next, and it's safe to say no one feels shy about using them'. It's equally safe to say that Harry Callahan carries the biggest one, the .44 Magnum AutoMag. Callahan is forced to increase his firepower when the hoods pursuing him arrive in heavily armoured, bullet-proof cars. Harry uses it in the fairground, when he appears – wreathed in neon, silhouetted, gun in hand – to save Jennifer. In a replay of the hostage finale that culminated two of the three previous 'Dirty Harrys', he faces Mick, who is holding a rifle to Jennifer's head atop the fairground's rollercoaster gantry. 'Let the girl go, punk – come on, make my day', goads Harry. The cop hits his mark and the villain plummets down, smashing through the roof of the carousel and skewering himself on one of the merry-go-round's unicorn's horns.

For the end titles, Roberta Flack belts out 'This Side of Forever', which is approximately how long it seems to take Callahan to solve the case. The opening lyric, which concerns an injured bird which regains its strength to soar, appears to anticipate Mike's demise: 'Wounded, I fell from the sky'. Lalo Schifrin reprises snatches of the original *Dirty Harry* score, but mostly his cues here have a funkier disco flavour, with brass, synthesisers and turntable 'scratching', a reflection of the shift in popular music since the seventies. Probably the most lamentable addition to the series is the 'comedy' element, which has Callahan teamed with a farting, pissing bulldog named 'Meathead'. The entire population of San Paulo seems to subsist on Budweiser and Coors, the story is as simplistically by-the-numbers as possible and still counts as 'plot', and dangling loose ends are tied up neatly with that multipurpose solve-all: 'ballistics'.

Sudden Impact was filmed in the spring of 1983 and released in the US just in time for Christmas. Critics couldn't fault the film's action and neither could the huge audiences, which earned the film almost $70 million, making it the most commercially successful 'Dirty Harry' film. This triumph is put down largely to astute marketing, as *Sudden Impact* is the worst of the series. Posters promoted the film with the tagline: 'Dirty Harry Is At It Again'. Trailers laboured the 'Go ahead, make my day' line, using it twice in the brief promo, which largely consisted of the excellent Acorn Café scene – so much for the rest of the movie. Republican President Ronald Reagan used the famous line in a taxation speech to Congress in March 1985 and the phrase entered the pantheon of great movie quotes. Eastwood himself complains, 'I must have heard it about 10,000 times', though bumper stickers during his 1986 mayoral campaign threatened, 'Go Ahead – Make Me Mayor'. The *New York Post* thought *Sudden Impact*'s Eastwood looked, 'Leaner and tougher than ever. The man doesn't seem to age. His face is becoming pure granite – and his body sheds bullets like the same stone', but the film was still, 'a whirligig, an explosion, and absolutely senseless'.

Tightrope (1984)

The 'Dirty Harry' films had by now spawned an industry of imitators, with everyone from John Wayne and Charles Bronson, to Burt Reynolds and Eddie Murphy cashing in. The Chicago-set, Chuck Norris vehicle *Code of Silence* (1985) had actually been a possible 'Dirty Harry' scenario and reviewers dubbed Norris 'Dirty Chuckie'. Following the mammoth success of *Sudden Impact*, Eastwood made yet another violent cop thriller, *Tightrope*. Though on the surface a 'killer on the loose' movie, *Tightrope* is quite different from the 'Dirty Harrys'. It is one of the star's darkest films, both in terms of cinematography and subject matter, as Eastwood examines the sinister flip side of his urban cop hero.

New Orleans detective Wes Block (Eastwood), a divorcee with custody of his two young daughters, Amanda and Penny, is investigating a series of murders of Bourbon Street prostitutes: Melanie Silber, has been found strangled, Jamie Corey is discovered drowned in a Jacuzzi, Judy Harper is washed up on the shores of the Mississippi, and lollipop-sucking Becky Jacklin is found dead in a fountain. All the victims are involved in 'unusual or abhorrent sexual activity', especially favouring handcuffed bondage games. At the murder scenes, the police find red fibres, glass fragments and traces of barley residue. Drawn into this twilight world of deviance, Block finds himself implicated in the murders. After visiting one prostitute, he accidentally leaves his tie behind, which later shows up at another murder scene. He leaves his handcuffs after another bondage session and the girl he was with is found murdered soon afterwards. The killer is actually stalking Block and seems to know him well. In the course of the enquiry, Block becomes involved romantically with Beryl Thibodeaux (Genevieve Bujold), a rape councillor, who recognises in Block the effect that investigating such dark worlds is having on his personality. Eventually the barley residue is traced to the local Dixie Brewery, where Leander Rolfe (Marco St John), an ex-cop, works. He has just finished 11 years in Angola State Prison for two rapes and Block was the arresting officer. Rolfe kills Block's babysitter and trusses up Amanda; later he attacks Beryl in her home. She stabs Rolfe with scissors and Block chases the stalker to a railway depot, where during a struggle, Rolfe is run over by a train.

Tightrope is Eastwood's most sexually explicit film, though the nudity is depicted with all the emotion of neon-bathed, badly acted, eighties soft-porn movies. It's a strange choice of film in which to cast your nine-year-old daughter, but that is just what Eastwood did: Alison Eastwood appeared as Amanda Block, Eastwood's screen daughter. Writer-director Richard Tuggle originally set *Tightrope* in San Francisco, but it was switched to New Orleans. Some sources suggest that Eastwood directed several scenes and the star did pay special attention to the family scenes with his daughter. Canadian actress Genevieve Bujold gave an effective performance as rape councillor Beryl and Dan Hedaya (Detective Joe Molinari) was a good foil to Eastwood's cop, as his partner on the investigation, while the sexy actresses cast as the prostitute victims were obviously chosen for their looks rather than their acting ability. In a Malpaso in-joke, the cast list also included First Assistant Director David Valdes appearing as a character called 'Manes' and Unit Production Manager (and Eastwood's regular Malpaso producer) Fritz Manes billed as 'Valdes'.

In *Tightrope,* Eastwood transforms Dirty Harry Callahan into a more human, three-dimensional protagonist. Block juggles his police investigations with raising his two young daughters. He even shows his soft side, through his weakness for stray dogs, of which the family has four. But Block, another of Eastwood's heavy-drinking, haunted characters, is enamoured of sadomasochism too, just like his deviant prey. The kinky cop likes to handcuff his sexual partners; both rape councillor Beryl and Block himself recognise that he and the killer are of the same persuasion – as the French poster asked: 'Flic ou violeur?' ('Cop or rapist?'). In a nightmare, Block images himself to be the masked killer, attacking Beryl in bed. When he visits Dr Yarlofsky, a psychiatrist, she tells him, 'There's a darkness inside all of us, Wes. You, me, the man down the street. Some have it under control, others act it out. The rest of us try to walk the tightrope between the two'. Block finds himself being implicated in the crimes. In one interesting scene, having received a tip-off, he visits Praline's gay bar and is propositioned by a hustler who the killer has arranged to approach the cop. Block turns down the man's advances, saying it's not his thing. 'How do you know if you haven't tried it?' asks the hustler. 'Maybe I have', answers Block.

This carefully established sexual ambiguity is dispersed in the film's weak second half, where *Tightrope* resembles a stalk-and-slash movie. The narrative crosscuts between Block's home life (in bright sunshine) and the neon-lit alleys, fleapits, strip joints, massage parlours and dives, with names such as 'Palace of Pleasure', populated by hookers, dominatrix, pimps, hustlers and Gello wrestlers. The film's opening scene pays homage to the kind of foggy, dimly lit street pursuits of victim by hunter, while Lennie Niehaus's score, his first for Eastwood, is in equal parts 'upbeat jazzy sax' (in keeping with the setting), 'guttertrash sleazy sax' and discordant, nail-biting edginess, for the killer's peculiar nocturnal activities. *Tightrope* was shot in the fall of 1983 in a rainy, shady New Orleans, with virtually no showbiz fanfare and apparently precious little lighting equipment. The action on screen is often so deeply wreathed in shadow as to be an abyss, an odd feature of Bruce Surtees's cinematography for Eastwood.

Tightrope has some genuinely unsettling moments. The killer appears dressed as a clown selling balloons at the Halloween parade, his identity given away to us by the brown tennis shoes with yellow laces which we have associated with the murderer since scene one. He also materialises behind frosted glass at a Jacuzzi or in a Mardi Gras devil mask watching Block and prostitute Judy Harper through a wired cage roof. Later he handcuffs and gags Block's daughter Amanda and leaves babysitter Mrs Holstein's corpse shoved in the oven, with her face grotesquely pressed against the glass door. The mask imagery throughout the film is highly effective, with the Halloween parade masks and the killer's disguises echoing the 'mask' behind which Block hides in everyday life.

For its apparent psychological depth, *Tightrope* is ultimately an empty film. The tension of the early scenes doesn't translate to the night-time finale, where Block resembles Dirty Harry as he first races by car to save Beryl and then chases Rolfe through a graveyard into a railway marshalling yard. Wrestling on the railroad as a freight train approaches, Block clears the tracks at the last moment, with Rolfe's hand still at his throat trying to throttle him. Rolling clear, Block realises that the killer's severed arm is all that is left of the murderer, whose corpse has been dragged off by the undercarriage of the loco.

Tightrope appeared in US cinemas in August 1984 and was a solid commercial success, even with its 'R' rating. Ironically, Alison Eastwood wasn't old enough to be admitted to see the film she had just appeared in. Considering *Tightrope*'s dark subject matter, the trailer predictably played up the action elements with Eastwood again on the trail of a serial killer: 'A Cop on the Edge', ads dubbed him. The *New York*

Daily News wrote, 'Eastwood is simply terrific, his lean and hungry face revealing all the right emotions' and *Time* noted that the film 'offers more intimacy, suspense and atmospheric colour than most of Eastwood's other gumshoe safaris through the urban jungle'. In the UK, the film was rated '18' but released uncut at 114 minutes. It took $48 million at the US box office, promoted by a seedy, red-lit portrait of Eastwood on the posters, with hints at Block's sadomasochistic predilections in the background: a bedstead with handcuffs attached. After such an unexpected departure for the star, audiences were relieved that in Eastwood's next cop film, he only used his handcuffs to apprehend criminals.

City Heat (1984)

If *Tightrope* was a departure for Eastwood, his next film would be that most traditional of crime movies. *City Heat* cast him in the type of gangster film his idol James Cagney turned out so successfully at Warner Bros in the thirties. Kansas City, 1933: Lieutenant Joe Speer (Eastwood) suspects his old partner, ex-cop-turned private eye Mike Murphy (Burt Reynolds) and Murphy's partner Dehl Swift (Richard Roundtree) are mixed up with hoods. Soon afterwards Swift is killed, 'falling' from a fourth storey window, and his lover, nightclub singer Ginny Lee (Irene Cara), a witness, goes into hiding. Swift held ledgers detailing some creative accounting – evidence that would put mobster Leon Coll (Tony Lo Bianco) behind bars forever and promote rival hood Primo Pitt (Rip Torn) to 'Public Enemy Number One'. Swift plans to sell the ledgers to Coll but is killed by Pitt. Pitt kidnaps Murphy's girl, socialite Caroline Howley (Madeline Kahn), forcing Murphy to locate the ledgers. To further complicate matters, Speer is dating Murphy's secretary Addy (Jane Alexander). Murphy receives a letter from Swift, posted before his death, with a ticket for the Majestic Pawn Shop. This yields a key to a locker at the Riverside Athletic boxing club containing the evidence. Ginny is run over when she is chased by Pitt's hoods, and Swift's bookkeeper Aram Strossell is fished out of the river, wired to a cement block. With the ledgers in a suitcase, rigged with dynamite and a grenade, Murphy and Speer track Caroline down to a high-class bordello and free her, killing Pitt along the way. Coll has taken Addy hostage and wants the ledgers in exchange – Murphy hands them over, but as the hood drives away, the booby-trapped case detonates.

Conceived as a knockabout period piece like *The Sting* (1973), *City Heat* began life as a script called 'Kansas City Blues' by Blake Edwards, who was also going to direct it. Eastwood and Reynolds, friends off-screen and a potent box office combination, were cast in the leads, whereupon according to Reynolds, Eastwood and Edwards got along like 'Custer and Geronimo'. Edwards left the project and was so displeased by the rift that he insisted on the pseudonym 'Sam O. Brown' for the story and screenplay credit (Edwards had just finished making *S.O.B*, his Hollywood satire). Actor-turned-director Richard Benjamin took the helm of the film with the working title 'Kansas City Jazz'. The film was set in the gangster era at the tail end of Prohibition; *Gold Diggers of 1933* and the Marx Brothers' *Horse Feathers* are on at the

Roxy Cinema, and a huge poster for Jimmy Cagney's *The Public Enemy* appears in the film's opening scene. On paper it must have looked a sure-fire hit, but it cost $25 million. They couldn't blame Eastwood for the film's huge budget – he bought his own costume for $400 in a Brooks Brothers' sale.

On the first day's filming, in February 1984, during a fistfight in Lou's Diner between Murphy and two repo men, one of the stuntmen hit Reynolds across the head with a real metal chair, instead of a breakaway balsa one, which caused severe damage to his inner ear and affected his balance. His performance suffered throughout the shoot, with bouts of nausea and tinnitus (ringing in the ears), which he numbed with painkiller Percodan. Reynolds, here dressed like Bogart, is a naturally funny actor, with a gift for comedy, but his showing in *City Heat*, dulled by illness and medication, is less than dynamic. Eastwood plays his partner/adversary, a hard-nosed lieutenant with a nice line in sarcasm and long black coats, but lacking finesse and manners. 'I didn't hear you knock', says Murphy, as Speer barges in unannounced; 'What a relief', answers Speer, 'I thought I was going deaf'. Interrogating a mobster, who has been buckshot in his backside, the two pour ether on his wound and then ignite it. But unsubtle humour and their repartee hits rock bottom when they are reduced to calling each other 'Shorty' and 'Ape Face'. Murphy tells Speer that he's going to hit him so hard, 'I'm gonna knock you back into the stone age … where you came from'. For the big finish in the bordello, Murphy appears from one of the role-play rooms in drag

2.8 The only onscreen teaming of buddies Burt Reynolds and Clint Eastwood was the gangster movie *City Heat* (1984), where they played PI Mike Murphy and cop Lieutenant Joe Speer. Image courtesy Ian Caunce Collection.

as Little Red Riding Hood's granny, in a 'Big Bad Wolf' mask. Whether debilitated Reynolds is even behind the mask at this point in the production is not known.

Several action scenes pepper the story, but the convoluted plot and brief romantic interludes (so underwritten they might as well not exist) dispersed any tension the stars' on-screen confrontations may have generated. The diner fistfight opens the film with a bang but is the last time Reynolds is seen in top form. The action scenes follow a pattern, with Speer an observer until roused, and two big shootout set-pieces stand out. In the first, filmed at the New York Street at Universal Studios (the film was made there and at Warners'), rival Pitt and Coll gang members shoot it out with Tommy guns outside Murphy's apartment, with Murphy pinned down. To break the deadlock, Speer strides down the street with a pump-action shotgun and blasts a gasoline-soaked delivery truck. Soon the street resembles a fire-bombed war zone, with a car colliding with a hydrant, sending a geyser into the air – the scene is a Jazz Age take on the foiled bank robbery in *Dirty Harry*. *Variety* noted that Eastwood 'earned whatever he was paid (actually $4 million) just by the way he stalks down a street brandishing a shotgun and showing a nasty look in his eye'. In a later scene, Speer and Murphy arrive at Pitt's 'front', a garage. The duo claims that the building is surrounded by cops, but all that the hoods can see outside are an old man and his dog. Speer says that the old guy is Sergeant Lowskowitz. 'Who's the guy in the dog suit?' asks Murphy; 'That's Connors', deadpans Speer. During the ensuing shootout, Speer and Murphy engage in a contest of singularly male one-upmanship. Murphy draws a long-barrelled pistol, thinking he has bettered Speer's police revolver, but the lieutenant wins, producing a massive, 14-inch-long pistol, resembling the fancy weaponry from Sergio Leone's westerns.

A capable supporting cast is squandered in futile attempts at character development. Richard Roundtree (the superhip *Shaft*) is killed off too early, while Jane Alexander is criminally underused as Murphy's put-upon secretary Addy. Madeline Kahn, one of the best female comic actors of the seventies – from *Blazing Saddles*, *Young Frankenstein* and *The Cheap Detective* – delivers as always. *City Heat*'s rival mobster villains were ably portrayed by perennial menaces Rip Torn and Tony Lo Bianco, while Irene Cara, the talented singer of *Fame* fame, is convincing as nightclub chanteuse Ginny. Also worth noting is the list of actors who were almost cast. Marsha Mason was to play Addy, as was Blake Edward's wife, Julie Andrews, while Kahn's role had been promised to Sondra Locke, then to Clio Goldsmith, who was fired about a week into the production.

Probably the most interesting aspect of *City Heat* was its Jazz Age setting, a locale of particular interest to jazz fan Eastwood. The soundtrack features several period songs, mixed with new compositions, including the title song 'City Heat', written by Cara and Bruce Roberts and sung by Joe Williams. Cara also performed the Gershwins' 'Embraceable You' and Ted Koehler and Harold Arlen's 'Get Happy', while on the soundtrack Eloise Laws sang Koehler and Arlen's 'Between the Devil and the Deep Blue Sea', Rudy Valee crooned Cole Porter's 'Let's Do It' and Al Jarreau sang 'Million Dollar Baby'. Composer Lennie Niehaus also penned 'Montage Blues' – the

pianists are Mike Lang, Pete Jolly and Eastwood himself. The actor can be seen playing at the end of the film, backing Cara.

City Heat, a Christmas 1984 release, fared passably well with both critics and
public. Village Voice stated that Eastwood's second-half performance, when 'he starts
killing people and loosens up a bit', is enjoyable and that 'Burt's a crowd-pleaser,
Clint's a crowd-slayer... it's a Hope and Crosby movie for action freaks: The Road to
Mayhem'. It was rated 'PG' in the US and '15' in the UK, mainly due to two need-
lessly violent scenes: Swift's fall from the fourth storey onto the windshield of a car
and Ginny being run over outside the Roxy. The film took $38 million in the US, a
respectable profit. As the film's poster stated: 'When the hot-shot cop and the wise-
guy detective get together... the heat is on!' Unfortunately, it's not on the screen.

The Dead Pool (1988)

Having returned to the western with Pale Rider (1985) and to war films with
Heartbreak Ridge (1986), the final instalment of the official 'Dirty Harry' series sur-
faced in The Dead Pool. Whereas The Enforcer and Sudden Impact played the action
straight and unintentionally often came off like send-ups of Dirty Harry, The Dead
Pool is deliberately comic-book. It's set in the nocturnal, seedy world of eighties cult
horror movies, heavy metal music videos, sex, drugs and rock 'n' roll, where Harry
finds himself investigating the walking wounded, or rather the living dead, of the
decade of excess.

Callahan and his partner, Lieutenant Al Quan (Evan C. Kim), are called to
investigate the death of rock star Johnny Squares, from an apparent synthetic heroine
OD. Callahan discovers that Squares was on a list known as 'The Dead Pool', a bizarre
tontine. Each 'contestant' chooses eight Bay Area celebrities and whoever has the
most 'R.I.P.'s on their list is the winner. The celebs chosen should be high-risk, who
through their lifestyles or age stand a good chance of dying in the near future. The
sick game is being played among the crew of horror movie Hotel Satan, which is being
directed by Peter Swan (Liam Neeson). Callahan, himself a celebrity since his highly
successful prosecution of mobster Lou Janero, is also on the list. Hassled by the press,
Callahan loses his temper and destroys a TV camera, which brings him into contact
with reporter Samantha Walker (Patricia Clarkson). With further deaths it becomes
clear that someone is trying to implicate Swan in the killings. The killer is revealed
as schizophrenic horror superfan Harlan Rook, who bombarded Swan with death
threats and sought revenge on the director for not commissioning his screenplay.
Rook now works for Swan's security, disguised under the alias 'Ed Butler'. He tries to
blow Callahan up with a remote controlled car but succeeds only in putting Quan in
hospital: Callahan is literally bombproof. Rook kidnaps Samantha, Callahan tracks
them to a dockside film set and in a shootout kills Rook with a harpoon.

While by no means the best of the series, The Dead Pool is a notable improvement
on its predecessor. Written by Durk Pearson and Sandy Shaw, ironically the authors of a
series of Life Extension books, it is parodic and casually violent, but Callahan and Quan

make a good team and, like the villains' lives, it's mercifully short. At only 88 minutes, it's the briefest 'Dirty Harry'. Michael Currie returns from *Sudden Impact* as Donnelly, this time as a captain rather than a lieutenant, a lone familiar face among all-new characters. Michael Goodwin plays Lieutenant Ackerman, Harry's superior. When he and Callahan argue, Harry asks, 'You got any kids, lieutenant?' When he hears not, Harry snaps, 'Lucky for them'. Patricia Clarkson, as Callahan's love interest Samantha (a reporter for Station KWSF, *Channel 8 News*), resembles Sondra Locke. She had debuted the previous year in *The Untouchables*. The film's best performances come from the supporting players. Liam Neeson is effective as the pony-tailed British 'stalk-and-slash' director working on his latest opus – *Hotel Satan* (tagline: 'You check in, you die'). Future star Jim Carrey (billed as 'James Carrey') had a small role in the film, as junkie rock star Johnny Squares. Filming a Swan-directed rock video on the set of *Hotel Satan*, Squares mimes to Guns 'n' Roses' 'Welcome to the Jungle'. The video is an *Exorcist* 'homage', complete with 360° rotating head. The band themselves show up at Squares' funeral: W. Axl Rose, Izzy Stradlin, Duff Rose McKagan, Steven Adler and Slash can be seen among the mourners. When Swan shoots *Hotel Satan* on a pirate ship, Slash, in his distinctive top hat, can be seen firing a harpoon.

Filmed from February to March 1988 in familiar 'Frisco locations, *The Dead Pool* is the only movie of the series not filmed in Panavision. The film's murders resemble those of *Halloween*, *Friday the 13th* and *My Bloody Valentine*, with their prowling, subjective-view camerawork and scenes depicting the killer's preparations. *The Dead Pool* opens with one of the series' trademarks: night-time helicopter shots of the Bay Bridge, Coit Tower and the city. It also features scenes filmed in Washington Square (where a pyromaniac threatens to immolate himself in front of Saint Peter and Paul's Church, used for the stakeout in *Dirty Harry*), the dry-dock (scene of the harpoon climax), Chinatown (where Callahan and Quan foil a restaurant robbery) and San Quentin Prison. The film's most famous scene features Callahan and Quan pursued in their car by a remote-controlled Ferrari, rigged to explode, with Rook operating the model. This scene, an intended send-up of *Bullit*, was even filmed on the same bumpy streets of Potrero Hill.

Harry's partner this time around is kung fu kicking Al Quan, played by Evan C. Kim. Kim had played Loo (a spot-on Bruce Lee imitation) in the 30-minute *Enter the Dragon* spoof 'A Fistful of Yen' in *The Kentucky Fried Movie* (1977). Kim parodied Lee's way with awful dialogue ('This is not a shawade – we need total concentwation' he tells his kung fu pupils) whilst taking on Dr Klahn in his hideout on the 'Isle of Lucy'. In *The Dead Pool*, Callahan foils a stick-up, only this time his partner lends a hand. In the Nam Yeun restaurant, four hoods hold up the diners, one of whom turns out to be Harry. 'You forgot your fortune cookie', hisses Harry, cracking open the biscuit: 'It says, "You're shit out of luck"'. The one member of the gang who manages to evade Harry's bullets is pursued by Quan and subdued with kung fu. Quan knows the dangers of becoming Harry's partner and his grandfather has given him a mystical tattoo, to ward off evil spirits: 'When he heard I was gonna be your partner, he figured I could use all the help I could get'. Quan also has a nice line in subtle humour. At the murder scene of movie critic Molly Fisher (who some reviewers saw as representing Pauline Kael), Quan surveys the bloody mayhem and says, 'On a scale of one to ten ... I think I'd have to rate this one an eight'.

Callahan's liaison with reporter Samantha is the warmest relationship Callahan enjoys in the series. Initially she wants to do an in-depth profile; 'You've had quite a colourful career over the years', she massively understates. Samantha has a scrapbook of cuttings with headlines relating to his past exploits. This is as close to nostalgia as the 'Dirty Harry' series gets, but the cop, true to form, rails against helping a journalist, until he falls for her. This scene shows an interest in the legend of Harry Callahan and his place in history. It would have been disastrous if *Sudden Impact* had turned out to be the series' epitaph.

For the final shootout, Rook thinks he has Callahan trapped on a quay, unarmed. But in a worthy climax to the series, beside a moored tug called 'The Lost Soul', Harry's voice cuts through the bay fog. 'You're out of bullets', gloats Harry, 'and you know what that means – you're shit out of luck', as he emerges from the fog brandishing a harpoon. Firing the huge barb, he skewers Rook to a wall. 'He's hanging out back there', Callahan tells the police as they arrive at the scene. Callahan and Samantha walk away, perhaps to a new life together, with Harry retired and writing the first volume of his eventful memoirs – his Magnum opus.

Released in the US in July 1988, rated 'R', *The Dead Pool* took $37 million. Reviewers were surprised by the quality of the film, with *Variety* noting that Callahan, and the series, can't be killed 'with cannon, mace and chain'. It also perceptively detected, in a film where the hero pins the villain to a shed with a whaling harpoon, that there might be 'a bit of self-mockery with this one'. The trailer made good use of 'Welcome to the Jungle' and resembled a cheap horror movie ad, the type of schlock that Peter Swan might put his name to. In fact, Swan's oeuvre is illustrated with clips from the likes of *It's Alive III*, *Time after Time* and *Cujo*. 'Clint Eastwood is Dirty Harry', said *The Dead Pool*'s trailer's voiceover, 'He's just learned a new game – *The Dead Pool*'. It was released in the UK, rated '18', and in *Film Monthly* David Quinlan announced, 'Good news! This is quite a lively thriller'. With no sign of the series being resurrected, Harry has since been turned into a video game, also called 'Dirty Harry', with Eastwood providing the cop's voice and Gene Hackman as Al Bressler.

Somewhat unexpectedly, *The Dead Pool* contains one of Eastwood's most interesting debates on screen violence. The killer on the loose is inspired by Swan's cinema, blurring the line between 'real' and 'fantasy' violence. Unhinged Rook says of Swan, as he is about to film Samantha's death, *Peeping Tom*-style: 'He stole my nightmares and made them real, so I stole his Dead Pool. I'll play his game and make it real'. 'The Dead Pool is just a harmless game', Swan earlier tells Harry, 'Death and violence – that's why my films make money ... they're an escape'. But screen violence permeates real society, often explicitly. Two hold-up men forced five of their victims to drink 'Drano' after seeing *Magnum Force*, and in the wake of the racially motivated 1974 'Zebra Murders' in San Francisco, graffiti read: 'Dirty Harry, where are you when we need you?' At these moments, fantasy and reality blur. Until *The Bridges of Madison*

County (1995), all Eastwood's biggest grossers had been action movies, despite the star's repeated attempts at calmer, contemplative fare.

The Rookie (1990)

The Rookie looms low in Eastwood's legend and is certainly the worst of his cop movies. Eastwood plays Nick Pulovski, an LA cop in the Grand Theft Auto Squad, on the trail of German crime mastermind Strom (Raul Julia), Strom's lover Liesl (Sonia Braga) and their gang of Mexican car thieves, who run an East LA 'Chop Shop', stealing cars and then re-spraying them with a new identity. During a pursuit of the gang, Pulovski's partner Powell is shot dead. Saddled with David Ackerman (Charlie Sheen), a rookie college boy partner from a privileged background, Pulovski swears revenge, even though he's been taken off the case, now a homicide. Ignoring their superiors, the duo continues to track Strom, bugging him. Eventually, during a casino heist, Strom captures Pulovski and ransoms him for $2 million. Strom receives the money, but Pulovski has already escaped. At San Jose Airport during a shootout, Ackerman kills Liesl and Pulovski avenges Powell, shooting Strom dead on a luggage conveyor. Pulovski is promoted to lieutenant and Ackerman is saddled with a new rookie sidekick, Heather Torres.

Basically *Dirty Harry VI*, or a buddy cops TV movie with slightly better special effects and saltier language, *The Rookie* is one of Eastwood's laziest efforts, as both director and star. The film was shot on location in San Jose, California, mostly at night, with the climax filmed at San Jose International Airport. The bizarre casting sees the two German villains, Strom and Liesl (as played by Julia and Braga), look even more Hispanic than their stereotypical Mexican gang of car wreckers – Braga is Brazilian and Julia Puerto Rican. *The Rookie* trades heavily on past glories and is clearly influenced by the first two *Lethal Weapon* hit comedy thrillers (made in 1987 and 1989). Even Lennie Niehaus's score is below par, with the bossa nova over the end titles sounding like two saxophones and a trumpet having a fight.

The best fun is to be had spotting the references to Eastwood and his movies. A clip from *Tarantula* appears on TV; Pulovski has a collection of motorbikes (including a 69 Norton and 67 TCR Triumph), just like Eastwood; the $2 million ransom recalls *Dirty Harry* and *The Enforcer*; Pulovski provokes a villain by putting a cigar out in his drink (*Hang 'Em High*); Pulovski swears to avenge his partner's death (also *The Enforcer*); Pulovski has always been stuck in the small-time and wants to crack one big case (*The Gauntlet*); and he likes cigars, but never carries a light, so the cigar in his mouth is conveniently rarely lit, like 'The Man with No Name'. After he's wounded Strom in the airport, Ackerman is told by Pulovski, 'Didn't I ever tell you that you should always aim for the heart', only to receive the reply: 'I was aiming for the heart' – a lame reference to *A Fistful of Dollars*.

The Rookie lists a massive stunt crew (87 stunt personnel, plus Bill Young's Precision Driving Team) and their hard work is displayed well on screen; the second unit director was Buddy Van Horn. The opening chase has Pulovski in pursuit of

Strom and his gang, who are driving a transporter loaded with stolen luxury sports cars, which they jettison onto the freeway into Pulovski's path. Pulovski and Ackerman drive a car out of an upper-storey window, just as the building explodes, land on a nearby warehouse roof and then plummet through a skylight. Sheen's motorcycle riding footage compares unfavourably with Eastwood's own onscreen bike work. In a nod to action movie *Road House* (1989), Ackerman loses his cool in 'La Casa Blanca', a Mexican biker bar, and spits ignited tequila at the barman, fire-eater style, and then torches the place, turning it into a bar and grill. Even the climax, with two jets colliding on the runway at San Jose airport, falls flat for its truncation and lack of velocity.

Eastwood's performance as Pulovski is somnambulant. He doesn't seem to care about the material and noticeably comes alive in the scenes when he's talking about motorbikes. He plays an ex-bike racer, now divorced: 'Didn't she like racing?' asks Ackerman; 'No, she loved racing – she just hated me'. For the rest of the film – his clashes with his superior, Lieutenant Ray Garcia (a good performance by Pepe Serna), and his freewheeling, larger-than-life style as he cracks the case – his act doesn't quite gel this time around, though the scene where Pulovski tells suited Ackerman to loosen up and dress hipper ('You look like an old fuck') raises a smile. *The Rookie* also features one of the most distasteful scenes in Eastwood's entire career, when Braga forces him to have sex with her, while he's handcuffed to a chair in the Chop Shop. *The Rookie* is Grade-Z junk – movie fast food, or rather reheated takeaway. Perhaps Eastwood's mind was elsewhere, as his next film was *Unforgiven* (1992).

The Rookie was released at Christmas 1990, to bad reviews and average business (it took almost $22 million). A novelization by Tom Philbin based on Boaz Yakin and Scott Spiegel's screenplay was issued through Warner Books in January 1991. It's bizarrely dedicated to 'all the folks at Karl Ehmer's Quality Meats in Huntington, Long Island, whose turkey sandwiches have always been an inspiration to me'. For release on video in the UK in November 1992, a tie-in competition offered a grand prize of a Harley-Davidson leather jacket, 25 runners-up prizes of a *Rookie* baseball jacket, and a free *Rookie* poster to everyone who entered. There were three easy questions (including 'What is the surname of the character *Dirty Harry*?'), plus a tie-breaker – in no more than 15 words, complete the sentence: 'Clint Eastwood and Charlie Sheen make a great partnership because...'. Viewers of *The Rookie* can no doubt fill in the blanks.

In the Line of Fire (1993)

Following the financial and critical triumph of *Unforgiven*, and no doubt to atone for releasing *The Rookie* on unsuspecting audiences, Eastwood enjoyed another success with the glacial *In the Line of Fire*. The story was written by Jeff Maguire and was produced by Columbia and Castle Rock Entertainment, with no Malpaso involvement. It was directed by Wolfgang Petersen, the German-born director of the acclaimed claustrophobic U-boat drama *Das Boot* (1981 – *The Boat*), originally made for TV, but edited for cinema release.

Eastwood was cast as Frank Horrigan, an agent working for the Secret Service, who on 22 November 1963 had failed to protect President John F. Kennedy in Dallas from murder by persons unknown. Thirty years later, still in the service in Washington DC, Horrigan becomes involved again in an attempt on the current president's life, in the six-week run-up to the 1993 election. Horrigan is telephoned by the cocky assassin, identifying himself as 'Booth', and is engaged in a tactical game of cat-and-mouse, as the secret service agents, including Horrigan's partner Agent Al D'Andrea (Dylan McDermott) and female agent Lilly Raines (Rene Russo), try to out-guess the killer. As the president is lagging 12 points in the opinion polls, his advisors continue with his high-profile campaign trail, departing from Washington Dulles International Airport across the Midwest and culminating in a huge rally in the Bonaventure Hotel in LA. Horrigan and the agents are assigned to the presidential protection squad but Horrigan is on edge. He and D'Andrea pursue every lead, eventually discovering that their prey is Mitch Leary, an ex-CIA 'wetboy' or specialist assassin, and master of disguise. Back in Washington, a chase across rooftops results in the death of D'Andrea. In LA, on the evening of the Bonaventure rally, Horrigan is taken off the detail and sent ahead to San Diego, but en route he figures out Leary's identity – he is present as a guest at the rally posing as James Carney, a presidential-supporting donor. Horrigan rushes back to the hotel and puts himself in the line of fire, taking Leary's bullet (the agent's wearing a bulletproof vest) but is taken hostage by Leary in a glass elevator. In the struggle, the assassin plunges to his death and Horrigan is atoned.

In the Line of Fire was shot on location in late 1992, with the approval and co-operation of the United States Secret Service (USSS). Several Washington DC monuments appear in the film, including the Capitol building, the George Washington Monument needle, the Lincoln Memorial, the oblong Reflecting Pool and the White House. One of Leary's phone calls is traced to Lafayette Park, across the street from the USSS offices, adjacent to Pennsylvania Avenue. Horrigan drinks and plays a piano in the Old Ebbitt Grill. The assassination attempt was filmed at the actual Bonaventure Hotel, LA, with a fake elevator built for the final scenes. The White House interior was an already existing set at Columbia, while the interior of the president's Air Force One jet cost $250,000. Several impressive crowd scenes were created using computer generated imagery. For the Denver rally, an actual rally with then-president Bill Clinton addressing 500 Democrat supporters was digitally altered, adding the film's president (played by Jim Curley, codenamed 'Traveller' by the USSS in the movie) and Horrigan into the shot. In another scene, trickery multiplied 1,500 extras to become 10,000 people lining a motorcade route, cheering the presidential party's black limos and police motorbike escorts. With a budget of $40 million, the film was the most expensive Eastwood had ever appeared in. To add credence to Horrigan's back story, clips of a young Eastwood (some of it seventies Academy Awards footage) were inserted into actual period newsreel, including the arrival of the Kennedy entourage at Love Field Airport, Dallas, in November 1963; Horrigan 'appears' beside Kennedy and is grafted into the background of photographs.

Horrigan is a familiar late-period Eastwood character – a lonely, tarnished hero, wracked by guilt and self-doubt. Horrigan, formerly Kennedy's favourite agent, is divorced (his wife and daughter left when his drinking problem enveloped their lives) and now sits alone in a bar playing a piano. When Horrigan is assigned to the presidential detail, he has trouble keeping pace with the younger agents, wheezing as he jogs alongside the president's limousine. His relationship with Agent Raines in the course of the presidential campaign offers a warmer side to his character and their scenes together are among Eastwood's best romantic moments. Watching her walk away from the steps of the Lincoln Memorial towards the Washington Monument, Horrigan, in a silly little game, muses: 'If she looks back, that means she's interested' – and, of course, she does, making Horrigan smile. When they first meet, their relationship is initially prickly: 'Secretaries get prettier and prettier around here', says Horrigan; 'And the field agents get older and older', Raines counters, as she's introduced as an agent herself. Horrigan explains to her why he never wears shades: 'A good stare can be just as effective as a gun', which seems to be a credo for the star's acting career. Later his account to her of the fateful day in Dallas is movingly effective, as they end the scene standing silently hand-in-hand. Rene Russo had just appeared as Mel Gibson's love interest in *Lethal Weapon 3* (1992). She accepted the role after Sharon Stone had turned it down. Dylan McDermott (later TV's Boston lawyer Bobby Donnell in *The Practice*) was excellent as Horrigan's young partner and John Mahoney (*Frasier*'s father Martin on TV) was equally effective in a well-written role, as Horrigan's understanding boss.

Leary is an interesting character, with John Malkovich excellently cast as the assassin who has 'A Rendezvous with Death', to quote Kennedy's favourite poem. He and Horrigan are two sides of the same coin: the government trained them both – one to protect the president, the other to kill him. Leary's fingerprints are C12, 'classified information', and the CIA and FBI are after him too. Like Scorpio in *Dirty Harry*, Leary is a spectral killer, standing in the shadows, elusive in a crowd – an everyman. Donning a variety of disguises, Leary stays one step ahead of the USSS – he could be a suited businessman and a Scorpio-like hippy. Leary identifies himself on the phone as 'Booth' (actor John Wilkes Booth, Lincoln's assassin). Horrigan asks, 'Why not Oswald?' 'Because Booth had flair and panache', answers Leary.

The meticulous depiction of Leary's preparations recalls *The Day of the Jackal* (1973), which detailed an assassination plot to kill President de Gaulle. Leary, using *New Age Modeller* as an instructional manual, moulds a double-barrelled pistol out of plastic, which he can assemble under the table unnoticed during the presidential dinner. The pistol has no metal parts, so it passes invisibly through security metal detectors, while the two bullets are concealed in his lucky rabbit's foot key ring. Throughout the film he has been carefully constructing a persona: 'James Carney', the head of business Microspan. As a party supporter of the president's bid to stay in office, 'Carney' is invited to the Bonaventure rally – like the Wooden Horse hauled into the doomed walls of Troy – and given a great seat, with a nice clear view of the president.

2.9 Frank Horrigan (Clint Eastwood) puts himself *In the Line of Fire*, in Wolfgang Petersen's 1993 thriller. Image courtesy Kevin Wilkinson Collection.

Intercut with Leary's planning is Horrigan's Special Ops investigation. His routine check on a crank 'wacko' rapidly escalates into a full-blown assassination investigation. Horrigan checks an apartment and finds a wall shrine of newspaper and magazine articles devoted to the John Kennedy assassination and a quote from Sirhan Sirhan (Robert Kennedy's killer): 'They can gas me, but I am famous. I have achieved in one day what it took Robert Kennedy all his life to do'. The agents discover that according to records the room's current tenant 'Joseph McCrawley' died in 1961, aged 11 (another plot detail echoing *The Day of the Jackal*). Leary has chosen

Horrigan as his opponent – a high-profile agent who failed to react quickly enough in 1963. The USSS investigation is punctuated with several memorable set pieces as they almost catch Leary, including a chase through speeding traffic and a foot pursuit across Washington rooftops, culminating in the tense finale: the motorcade snakes through LA as evening falls and Horrigan figures out the final pieces of the puzzle, rushing to avert disaster.

Leary leaves a trail of death, killing a bank employee and her housemate (who almost unmask him), two hunters (just for the hell of it), Wickland (a model maker in Phoenix who identifies Leary from a police identikit) and Horrigan's partner D'Andrea. Horrigan is left dangling off a rooftop parapet, relying on Leary's helping hand to save him from a plunge (Eastwood actually hung off the building for this stunt). D'Andrea's death transforms the narrative into a familiar 'This time it's personal'-type Eastwood vehicle; however, Petersen ensures it's anything but formulaic. The hunt is fuelled by Ennio Morricone's suspenseful music, with weird, wired high-pitched feedback scoring Leary's stalking of Horrigan and the president, warm love themes for Horrigan and Raines's introspection, and grandly orchestrated compositions providing triumphal emotional swells, incorporating trumpet fanfares, piano, syncopated strings and the pan flutes the composer had used so well on *Once Upon a Time in America* (1984) and *Casualties of War* (1989).

Given the film's subject matter, *In the Line of Fire* is the most un-political of political thrillers. Leary isn't a political opponent of the president but rather obsessed with the celebrity – or rather the notoriety – such a crime will furnish. The political setting adds a sense of importance to the story, without actually imbuing it with any political ideology or stance. Eastwood himself has always kept a low political profile. In 1986, he was elected mayor of Carmel and served a two-year term, though he had no interest beyond local politics, unlike actor-turned-president Ronald Reagan.

For the release of *In the Line of Fire* in the US in July 1993, trailers featured the edgy phone conversations between Leary and Horrigan. Leary says that he can see Horrigan 'standing over the grave of another dead president', cut to Eastwood, slamming down the phone, cocking his gun and vowing, 'That's not gonna happen' – a shot that doesn't appear in the finished film. It was rated 'R' in the US for violence and language (much of which has been cut for TV airings) and '15' in the UK (after it was trimmed by eight seconds). Posters warned: 'An assassin on the loose. A president in danger. Only one man stands in his way', and 'This summer, Clint Eastwood is *In the Line of Fire*'. It was even more successful than *Unforgiven*, taking over $102 million in the US and $187 million worldwide, making it Eastwood's top earner up to that point.

A Perfect World (1993)

Eastwood's next film, *A Perfect World*, again cast him as a lawman, Red Garnett, a rural cop, who harks back to Eastwood's Arizona deputy in *Coogan's Bluff*. Texas Ranger Chief Garnett could be Walt Coogan's dad. The story, written by John Lee

Hancock, takes place in 1963 Texas, at a time when John Kennedy is on the campaign trail to Dallas – perhaps *In the Line of Fire*'s Frank Horrigan is not too far away.

On Halloween, Robert 'Butch' Haynes (Kevin Costner) and Terry Pugh (Keith Szarabajka) escape from the maximum security unit in Huntsville, Texas, and go on the run, taking Phillip Perry (TJ Lowther), the eight-year-old son of Jehovah's Witnesses, hostage. A manhunt swings into action, co-ordinated by Garnett. Sally Gerber (Laura Dern), a criminologist with the state prison, is also assigned to the hunt, as is Bobby Lee (Bradley Whitford), a specialist FBI marksman. Garnett's party travel in a mobile home, a state-of-the-art headquarters on wheels, loaned to the operation by the state governor. As the chase progresses at a leisurely pace, Pugh, by far the more violent criminal, quarrels with Haynes, so he shoots Pugh dead in a cornfield. Haynes plans to head for Alaska, where his father lives (he carries an Alaskan postcard from his father in his pocket). During their flight, Haynes and little Phillip become friends. The boy admires the felon, who encourages Phillip to do everything in life that being a Jehovah's Witness forbids him to. The pair rob a store and Phillip steals a Caspar the Friendly Ghost Halloween suit, which he wears. They hide out with a family of farmers, but when fatherly Mack (Wayne Dehart) beats his grandson Cleveland, Haynes, himself a victim of parental abuse, seems about to shoot Mack. Phillip intervenes and shoots Haynes in the stomach. In a final stand-off, on grassland nearby, Garnett, Phillip's mother Gladys (Jennifer Griffin) and the cops negotiate Phillip's release. FBI agent Lee thinks he sees unarmed Haynes reaching for a pistol in his waistband and shoots him dead with a high-powered rifle. Haynes was actually reaching for his Alaskan postcard. Phillip is free, but it's the end of his perfect world.

A Warners-Malpaso co-production directed by Eastwood, *A Perfect World* was filmed on location in the mighty fine countryside of Austin and Central Texas during the spring and summer of 1993. Even though it was shot in Panavision by Jack Green, the cinematography is oddly flat, with a constantly overcast sky in a film that is desperately in need of some heartening sunshine. The 'country and western' atmosphere is enhanced by a selection of rural numbers on the soundtrack. These include two tunes by Bob Wills and his Texas Playboys, 'Sea of Heartbreak' by Don Gibson, the pessimistic classic 'Guess Things Happen That Way' by Johnny Cash and tracks by Willy Nelson, Marty Robbins and Chris Isaak. Unfortunately, the incidental music by Lennie Niehaus is ponderous, with the end theme a mediocre Mantovani mimic. In fact, *A Perfect World* should have been much better all round. The making of the film, conceived as a pairing of Oscar winners Eastwood and Kevin Costner, was troubled. Costner's acting style didn't suit Eastwood's working methods and Costner, a director himself, gave input that slowed down the production.

A Perfect World presents Haynes as an amiable lawbreaker. Scant biographical information informs us that aged only eight he shot a man in a whorehouse where he grew up and that later Garnett sent him to prison, ostensibly to protect Haynes from his abusive father. The two runaways find common ground, in a variation on Stockholm Syndrome, to the extent that when Phillip has the opportunity to escape, he remains with Haynes. Haynes appeals to the boy's sense of adventure, telling him that their car is a 'Twentieth Century time machine', with Haynes the captain and Phillip the navigator. What's behind them is past, what's ahead the future: 'This is the present Phillip, enjoy it while it lasts'. Haynes's nickname is 'Butch', though he tells a family of picnickers he's called 'Edgar Poe'; so Phillip, who has always wanted to fly in a rocket ship, chooses 'Buzz' as an alias for himself. 'Butch 'n' Buzz' become a sort of Bonnie and Clyde duo, a reference made explicit during their robbery of a hick 'Friendly's' general store; their escape, with Haynes ramming two local police cars, closely resembles Bonnie and Clyde's Dustbowl felonies. At a lonely roadside diner, 'Dotties Squat 'n' Gobble', Haynes is seduced by a wanton waitress, but their tryst is interrupted by Phillip. Finally, Haynes threatens to kill a farmer. In this bizarre, uncharacteristic scene, Haynes gaffer tapes the family to their sofa, accompanied by a weird march on the soundtrack. This misjudged musical interlude is Eastwood's bagpipe ditty 'Big Fran's Baby', one of the star's few dud compositions.

Eastwood is hardly on screen and his performance as a 'Hillbilly Sherlock Holmes', in Stetson, shades and badge, is without resonance. Equally, his pairing with Laura Dern, as criminologist Gerber, is almost superfluous to the story. Any expected tension in the chase fails to materialise, as scenes are allowed to play out too long, and Dern and Costner's Texan drawling further distends the drama. The huge silver mobile home converted into a mobile ranger HQ, an 'amazingly futuristic piece of law enforcement equipment' in the governor's words, is an interesting concept. One of the film's few genuinely exciting moments has the vehicle careering through a wood in pursuit of Butch. But *A Perfect World* feels too loose and the chase, lazily drawn out for 133 minutes, has all the pyrotechnics of a snail race.

A Perfect World was rushed into release in the US in November 1993 and, despite some fine notices, fell well short of the grosses of *In the Line of Fire*, taking just over $31 million. It was rated 'PG-13' in the US, '15' in the UK. Costner was top-billed, and this was the first time Eastwood had not been the star since *Two Mules for Sister Sara*. The nostalgic poster key art featured a black and white photo of road buddies Costner and Lowther, with Eastwood's face fading into the background, emulating his hazy presence in the film. The trailer's voiceover sagely intoned: 'In a perfect world, there would be no crime, no fear, no prisons. But sooner or later 'most everyone learns there's no such thing as a perfect world'. For in a perfect world, all law enforcers would have the integrity and patriotism of Frank Horrigan, the adaptability and tenacity of Walt Coogan, and the marksmanship and 'case solved' success rate of Harry Callahan.

PART THREE
THE LOVERS

During his first decade of stardom since *A Fistful of Dollars*, Clint Eastwood was known and loved by audiences primarily as an action hero, with little time for romance. Many of his most popular films, for example *For a Few Dollars More* or *Dirty Harry*, don't feature any significant female roles in the cast – *Kelly's Heroes* has no women in it at all – and his non-action projects were often his most disappointing at the box office. Love scenes for 'The Man with No Name' were filmed during *For a Few Dollars More* and *The Good, the Bad and the Ugly* but were cut before release. Even when Joe saves Marisol in *A Fistful of Dollars*, he doesn't 'get the girl' – she returns to her husband – even if advertising made it appear that Joe and Marisol ended up together. In his action movies, Eastwood occasionally found himself briefly entangled romantically: for example, in *Hang 'Em High*, *Coogan's Bluff* and *The Outlaw Josey Wales*, but Eastwood was rarely involved in conventional screen relationships, as the following films demonstrate.

The Witches (1967)

Between filming *For a Few Dollars More* (1965) and *The Good, the Bad and the Ugly* (1966), Eastwood appeared in another, lesser-known Italian film, *Le Streghe* (*The Witches*). *The Witches* was produced by Dino De Laurentiis to highlight the acting talents of his wife, actress Silvana Mangano, who plays the lead in each of its five stories. It was lensed at Dino De Laurentiis Studios, Rome, from January to March 1966. The five episodes were *The Witch Burned Alive* directed by Luchino Visconti, *Civic Spirit* by Mauro Bolognini, *The Earth Seen from the Moon* by Pier Paolo Pasolini, *The Sicilian Belle* by Franco Rossi and *An Evening Like the Others* by Vittorio De Sica.

Eastwood appeared in the last episode as Charlie, the husband of Giovanna (Mangano), a bored Rome housewife trying to stir her perpetually half-asleep husband into action and avoid being put 'in cobwebs for good'. Amid their mundane chat in their apartment, Giovanna has wild romantic flights of fantasy about Charlie, where they waltz down the street in slow-motion, or he springs acrobatically into bed to make love. Eventually Giovanna imagines herself striding down the street, glamorously dressed, pursued by admirers who fill a football stadium, where she performs a striptease. Charlie climbs a lighting pylon, struggling for Giovanna's attention, before shooting himself with a pistol and plunging to his death.

Eastwood's role in this segment, sometimes referred to in filmographies as *A Night Like Any Other*, is a bizarre change of pace for the newly established action star. Charlie reads out the Rome cinema listings, but his voice is so dull, the list 'sounds like an obituary': the films on exhibition include *The Agony and the Ecstasy*, *Wake Up and Kill*, *The Tenth Victim*, *Operation Moon*, *The Bible* and *A Fistful for Dollars*. Eastwood looks uncomfortable in the fantasy scenes and even more uncomfortable when delivering lines such as, 'We'll make love like two parakeets'. In the end, Charlie, like the

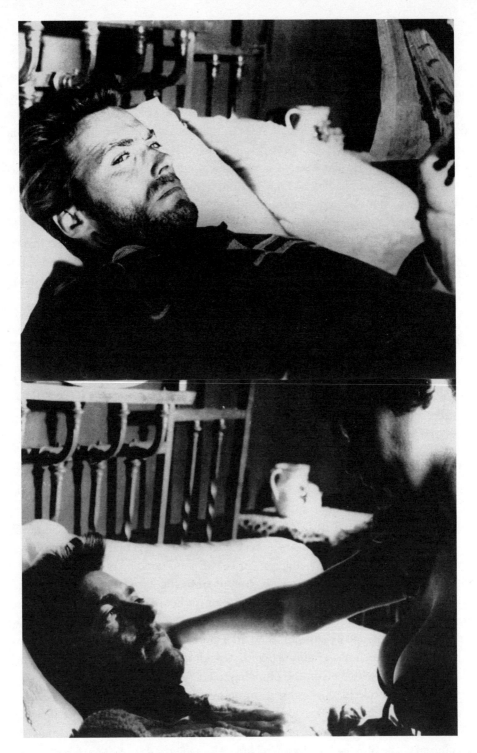

3.1 Two scenes from *For a Few Dollars More*; (top) the scene as it appeared in the finished film, with 'The Man With No Name' perusing a Wanted poster and (bottom) in an alternative take, Mary the hotelier (Mara Krup) seduces the stranger.

audience, nods off to sleep, having recommended a cup of Camomile tea before bed, to curb Giovanna's highly strung ramblings. She hugs him and realises, 'I love you'.

Eastwood noted that *The Witches* 'was a drawing-room thing, half reality, half fantasy', though 'it was good to get my boots off'. During the stadium finale, Eastwood did actually appear as a black-clad cowboy who mows down a dozen of Giovanna's admirers with his six-guns. When *The Witches* was released in Italy in February 1967 in the wake of *The Good, the Bad and the Ugly*'s Christmas success, Italian posters made sure to display Eastwood prominently. Ennio Morricone even co-wrote the jazzy sax lounge score. *An Evening Like the Others* is probably Eastwood's most little-seen performance. Although it was owned by United Artists, it was exhibited in the US in March 1969 to limited 'arthouse' exposure but wasn't released in the UK.

Paint Your Wagon (1969)

Having just appeared in *Where Eagles Dare* (1968), his first starring role without a cowboy hat, Eastwood decided to branch out further. The musical *Paint Your Wagon* is one of Eastwood's most unexpected roles – a singing prospector. Eastwood had crooned in TV variety specials, on junket tours promoting *Rawhide* and in the series itself: most memorably his rendition of 'Beyond the Sun' on stage in a saloon in 'Incident of the Pitchwagon'. In 1961, he cut the 45-rpm single 'Unknown Girl' (with 'For All We Know' on the B-side) on Gothic Records and later 'Get Yourself Another Fool!' (backed with 'For You – For Me – Forevermore') on Crescendo – with Eastwood on the sleeves of both in a homely, chunky-knit sweater. He recorded an LP selection for Cameo Records called *Cowboy Favourites* (1962), his baritone well-suited to the loping clippety-clop rhythm and twanging steel guitar of 'Tumbling Tumbleweeds', 'Sierra Nevada' and 'Don't Fence Me In'. He also recorded a *Rawhide* signature tune called 'Rowdy'. Eastwood even sings briefly in *A Fistful of Dollars*, feigning drunkenness at the Rojos's Mexican spit-roast – 'Do you remember sweet Betsy from Pike? She roamed the world with her lover Ike' – but he'd never appeared in a musical. Written by Alan Jay Lerner and set to tune by Frederick Loewe, *Paint Your Wagon* was a humdinging western musical set in the California Gold Rush. The stage version had been a great success, but sceptics winced when Paramount cast Clint Eastwood and Lee Marvin, two action stars not exactly known for their crooning, as the leads in the film version.

Act One begins with prospector Ben Rumson (Marvin) saving the life of 'Pardner' (Eastwood) from a wagon accident that kills Pardner's brother. During the funeral, Rumson discovers gold on the site and stakes his claim, with Pardner his partner. Soon the tented settlement of 'No Name City' has materialised, packed with gold miners, gamblers and ne'er-do-wells hoping to make a fortune. Into this all-male populace arrives Mormon Jacob Woodling and his two wives. But as a local observes, 'It just ain't equitable man, for you to be having two of something all of us have got none of'. Woodling auctions Elizabeth (Jean Seberg), one of his wives, and Ben buys her. The two are married, but while paranoid Ben is away, hijacking a troupe of

French saloon girls so that the prospectors will stop staring at his wife, Elizabeth and Pardner fall in love. In fact, she claims to love both of them and they decide to live together in a *ménage-à-trois* – 'a happily married triple'.

Act Two begins with the arrival of a Parson in the now-booming timber metropolis of No Name City, who rails against the den of iniquity. When a wagon train marooned in the sierras is rescued, the prim Fenty family is shocked by the marital arrangements at Rumson's. Elizabeth gets 'a bad case of the respectabilities' and kicks Ben out. In the saloon, Ben and Mad Jack Duncan (Ray Walston) hit upon a scheme. They'll dig a series of tunnels under the gambling joints and saloons and harvest the gold dust that has filtered between the floorboards. No Name City is thus destroyed in biblical fashion, as the tunnels collapse, swallowing the town. The gold played out, Rumson moves on with the miners to the next strike, leaving Pardner with Elizabeth.

There were considerable changes made to the stageplay for the film. In the original version, Rumson's daughter Jennifer discovers the gold and the town of 'Rumson' springs up on the spot. Jennifer falls for Mexican prospector Julio Valveras and it is their love affair that is the focus of the story – Pardner doesn't exist. It is not known who introduced the idea of troilism. For the screen version, Lerner cut some songs and added new ones, penning the lyrics while Andre Previn wrote the new music. Original songs that reappeared include 'I'm on My Way', 'I Still See Elisa', the hoedown 'Hand Me Down that Can o' Beans', 'I Talk to the Trees', 'There's a Coach Comin' In', 'Wand'rin' Star' and, probably the best number, the rousing 'They Call the Wind Maria'. The additions, necessitated by the new plot and character of Pardner, were 'The First Thing You Know' (sung by Rumson), 'A Million Miles Away behind the Door' (sung by Elizabeth), 'The Gospel of No Name City' (sung by the Parson), 'Best Things' and 'Gold Fever' (both featuring Pardner).

Eastwood was cast opposite Marvin, who eschewed *The Wild Bunch* to appear for $1 million. Eastwood received $750,000. Julie Andrews and Diana Rigg were prospective Elizabeths, until Jean Seberg was cast in the role. Little wonder that the film's budget soon ballooned from $10 million to an eventual $20 million. Shooting began on location in Oregon, where the tented prospecting camp of 'No Name City' ('Population: Male', reads the welcome sign) was constructed on East Eagle Creek in the Wallowa-Whitman National Forest. The camp looked splendid, incorporating sluices and a huge waterwheel, at a cost of $2.4 million. They built two versions of the set, one using tents, the second in timber, but it was constructed on bedrock. When it came to sinking the entire town for the film's climax, the hydraulics needed for the saloon alone cost $300,000. The closest hotels were 60 miles away in Baker, costing $80,000 a day to ferry cast and crew by air to the secluded set. It was five months of very troubled production. Marvin, like his character, liked a drink. Director Joshua Logan didn't seem to have a clue how to make the film and was almost fired by producer Lerner; the weather was awful, veering from perfect sunshine to rainstorms, mud and eventually snow, which forced the crew back to the Paramount lot to complete filming in October 1969.

3.2 'The Musical Goldmine of '69': The unlikely vocal trio of Lee Marvin, Jean Seberg and Clint Eastwood hit paydirt in *Paint Your Wagon* (1969); US one-sheet poster, courtesy Ian Caunce.

The results reflect the filming conditions. The film often has a rainy, depressing look most unlike a Broadway show. Harve Presnell provides the film's one powerful moment with his moody rendition of 'They Call the Wind Maria': 'Away out here they've got a name, for rain and wind and fire: the rain is Tess, the fire's Joe and they call the wind Maria'. Ray Walston is memorable for all the wrong reasons as Mad Jack, a redheaded renegade who comes on like Yosemite Sam. Alan Dexter has fun as the hellfire Parson, dispensing 'The Gospel of No Name City': 'Sodom was vice and vice versa, you wanna see where the vice is worser?' Seberg's singing voice was dubbed by Rita Gordon, but she still manages, through convincing mime, to make the fragile, sentimental 'A Million Miles Away behind the Door' her own ('I need a threshold I can cross, where I can sit and gather moss, forevermore'). But it was Marvin who surprised everyone, not with the calibre of his vocalising, but its success with the record-buying public. In the Broadway original, as performed by James Barton, 'Wand'rin' Star' is much more tuneful; however, over a loping clippety-clop rhythm and male chorus, Marvin's is an almost sub-sonic bass, as he growls, 'Aaaaah was booorn under a wand'rin' staaaar'.

Eastwood's performance as 'Pardner', actually named Sylvester Newel, isn't as embarrassing as those of his co-stars. *Newsweek* thought Eastwood was 'destroying his taciturn reputation by speaking often and badly, as if the script girl had neglected to give him each succeeding line'. He performed three solo numbers in the film – 'I Still See Elisa', 'I Talk to the Trees' and 'Gold Fever' – and a duet with Marvin, 'Best Things'. His best vocal is 'I Still See Elisa', as he strums a guitar with his arm in a sling ('Her heart was made of holidays, her smile was made of dawn'); he made a fair attempt at 'Gold Fever', a paean to addiction sung in the Grizzly Bear gambling house ('Gold, gold, hooked am I'). Unfortunately, the song everyone remembers is his rendition of 'I Talk to the Trees'. It's not an easy song to carry off under any circumstances ('I talk to the trees, but they don't listen to me'), but he is at least saved by the western setting (he didn't have to don lederhosen or Victorian period dress for his musical excursion) and the melody is lowered in key, to better accommodate his whispery baritone vocal range. 'As to my singing', Eastwood said in *Photoplay*, 'I'll let the public be the judge of that', but he made a point of mentioning, 'It's all our voices, without a lot of tricked up electronics, which is nice'. His soft-focus, wide-open-space romance with Seberg is all flowery shirts, skimmers and strolls through Oregon magnificence – they make a beautiful screen couple but are too small a part of the much bigger and longer picture.

Paint Your Wagon was released in the US in late 1969. Audiences were quite taken with the ill-matched prairie threesome and it took $15 million at the box office, making it Paramount's sixth biggest success of all time, but the huge budget ensured it never made a profit. Critics weren't taken in, with Rex Reed in *Holiday* calling it 'a monument to unparalleled incompetence', which features 'actors who can't dance or sing', but in the midst of all this, Eastwood 'has a casual soft elegance that instantly makes him a friend to the audience', while *Women's Wear Daily* gingerly noted that it was 'overproduced and sometimes a little weird'. The best things Eastwood gained from the experience were a determination to control his own career via his Malpaso production company and meeting several actors who went on to appear in later Eastwood films, including Paula Trueman, William O'Connell and John Mitchum. A Paramount 45 single of 'Wand'rin Star', produced by Tom Mack, went to No.1 in the charts for three weeks in the UK (with Eastwood's conversation with pines on the B-side) in March 1969, while 'They Call the Wind Maria' was popular in the US. After his experiences in Oregon, Eastwood's westerns since have ensured that the only 45's he tackles are of the Colt variety.

The Beguiled (1971)

Based on Thomas Cullinan's 1966 novel, originally published as 'A Painted Devil', *The Beguiled* remains Eastwood's boldest career decision. Following the protracted, noisy, disorganised Yugoslavian location shoot for *Kelly's Heroes* (1970), Eastwood was happy to tackle a small-scale, character-driven story directed by Don Siegel. The action director and the action star teamed up to create a tale of the unexpected, a Gothic melodrama that was the most surprising film of both their careers.

As the Civil War scorches through the Deep South, Union Corporal John McBurney (Eastwood) of the 66th New York Infantry is badly wounded in action. He is found by 12-year-old Amy (Pamela Ferdin), a pupil at the nearby Farnsworth Seminary for Young Ladies. The Confederate-sympathising seminary is run by Martha Farnsworth (Geraldine Page) and her 22-year-old deputy, tutor Edwina Dabney (Elizabeth Hartman). Although McBurney is a Union soldier (a 'Billy Yank' and a 'Bluebelly') and some of the young women think that sheltering an enemy is treason, Martha and Edwina agree that they'll allow McBurney to recuperate in the music room. As he begins to recover, hobbling around on crutches, McBurney sets about beguiling those who can help him: frosty Martha, who will decide his fate, fragile Edwina, vivacious temptress Carol (Jo Ann Harris), even little Amy, who worships 'McB'. He plays on their insecurities, their longings and desires, slyly charming them until one fateful night he must make a choice. Indecisive on the landing, between Martha and Edwina's doors, he's waylaid by Carol. Their noisy lovemaking in the attic awakens Edwina, who in a jealous rage throws McBurney tumbling down the spiral staircase. With McBurney's leg now fractured in three places, Martha decides to prevent the threat of gangrenous infection – they must amputate it. They anaesthetise him with wine and laudanum, and Martha hacksaws through the bone. When McBurney awakens, his apologies for his behaviour are short-lived. He explodes with rage, commandeers a pistol and gets drunk. He exposes Martha to her pupils as a jealous hypocrite (she had an incestuous relationship with her own brother Miles years before) and kills Amy's pet turtle Randolph. Only Edwina stands by him and the women concoct a plan to kill McBurney. Amy will pick poisonous mushrooms which will be served to him that evening. Over dinner, McBurney and Edwina announce they are to go away together to be married, but it is too late: McBurney has eaten the mushrooms and collapses, dead. The young ladies put their sewing skills to good use as they make a shroud for the corpse and set off to bury him in the woods.

In the novel, the school is run by Martha Farnsworth and her sister Harriet and the story is narrated in the first person by each of the tutors and pupils in turn, giving various perspectives of their relationship with the soldier. McBurney is only 20 in the book, while Eastwood turned 40 during the film's making – in the novel, McBurney's fateful meal is served to him on his twenty-first birthday celebration. The novel was transformed into a script called 'Johnny McB' by Albert Maltz, then by Irene Kamp as 'Nest of Sparrows' and finally by Claude Traverse (the film's associate producer). Maltz's draft allowed McBurney to escape the seminary, but both Siegel and Eastwood wanted to retain the novel's downbeat denouement. None of these writers' names appeared on screen: Traverse's work went uncredited, and unhappy with Traverse's dark changes Maltz adopted the pseudonym 'John B. Sherry' and Kamp became 'Grimes Grice'.

Aside from a few Confederate stragglers and Martha's missing brother Miles (seen in flashback), McBurney is the film's only significant male role. Jeanne Moreau, Claire Bloom, Maureen O'Hara and Eleanor Parker were all keen to play headmistress Martha, but acclaimed stage actress Geraldine Page was cast. Elizabeth Hartman played repressed Edwina and Jo Ann Harris was cast as foxy temptress Carol ('I know a lot more than girls my age') and deploys the best purring southern accent. There's no denying that Eastwood had a gift for casting beautiful women in his films during this period. Elfin Harris in *Beguiled*, arty Donna Mills in *Play Misty for Me*, vampish Marianna Hill in *High Plains Drifter*, alluring Adele Yoshioka in *Magnum Force* and future 'Daisy Duke' Catherine Bach in *Thunderbolt and Lightfoot* – not great actresses, but very pretty. Black actress Mae Mercer appeared in *Beguiled* as slave Hallie, the school housekeeper and cook (Hallie is called Matilda, or 'Old Mattie' in the novel, and is considerably older). For the role of 12-year-old Amy, 16-year-old Karen Wyman asked to be considered, before 11-year-old Pamela Ferdin was cast.

Universal wanted the film shot on the 'Southern Mansion' set at the Disney Studios Ranch, but Siegel deemed it unsuitable. Instead he filmed on location over 10 weeks, beginning in April 1970, in Louisiana, at the Belle Helene Plantation, Ashland Estate, on the River Road, south of Baton Rouge. All exteriors and several interiors were shot in this authentic mansion and its grounds, with most interiors recreated by Ted Haworth at Universal Studios. The dank setting – with trees draped in Spanish Moss, an essential feature of any movie set in the 'Deep South' – gives the film a distinctive look, a kind of misty netherworld hidden from the war. Eastwood's 'making of' documentary called *The Beguiled: The Storyteller*, written and produced by Attila De Lado, was the first time that the title 'Directed by Clint Eastwood' appeared onscreen.

The Beguiled is set in the Civil War, circa May 1863, and spans the period when General Ulysses S. Grant's Union forces approached Vicksburg and drove General John C. Pemberton's Confederates back across the Big Black River. The Confederate defeat at the Battle of Champion's Hill (16 May) and the need to secure the road to

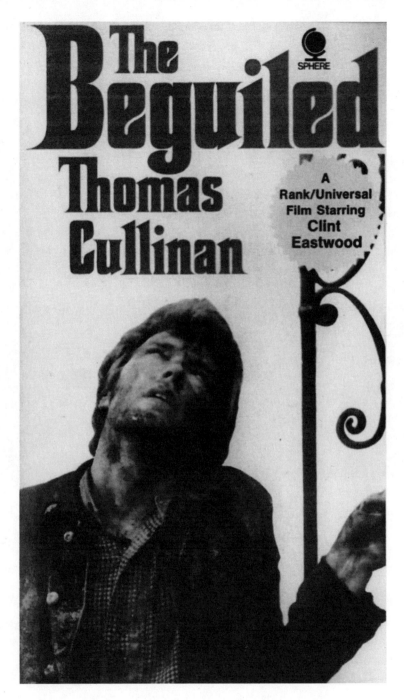

3.3 Passion Play: The cover of this rare UK reissue of Thomas Cullinan's *The Beguiled* depicts wounded Corporal John McBurney (Clint Eastwood) arriving at the gates of the Farnsworth Seminary for Young Ladies. Author's collection.

Vicksburg are mentioned. As in *The Good, the Bad and the Ugly* and *The Outlaw Josey Wales*, the war and its participants are seen in an anti-heroic light. The filthy military prison McBurney would end up in if captured, probably dying of his wounds, would resemble the horrific conditions of the infamous rebel stockade Camp Sumter, Georgia (better known as 'Andersonville'), or Libbey Prison, both of which are mentioned by name in the novel. When McBurney explains to Martha how he was wounded, he says he is a pacifist Quaker medic, while a flashback reveals that he was a infantryman who did his fair share of killing. Later, when Martha begins to entertain the idea of keeping McBurney on to help run the school, he claims, 'I have a great respect for land', but a flashback shows him torching haystacks as part of the Unionists' scorched earth campaign.

The Beguiled opens with authentic sepia-tinted plates by Mathew Brady and Alexander Gardner, the official US Government Civil War photographers. The title sequence also depicts a cavalry charge and artillery under fire, using stills from *Shenandoah* (1965 – an earlier Universal Civil War movie). As the titles end, a whispering a cappella vocalist (actually Eastwood himself) sings the poignant, Civil War period, anti-war ballad 'The Dove':

> *Take warning by me, don't go for a soldier, don't join no army*
> *For the dove she will leave you, the raven will come*
> *And death will come marching at the beat of a drum*
> *Come all you pretty fair maids who walk in the sun*
> *And don't let your young man ever carry a gun.*

With McBurney's death, the ballad is reprised as his shrouded body is readied for entombment, book-ending the story in haunting fashion.

The Beguiled is a complex, multi-layered dream within a dream, full of eerie, strange moments. In the film's opening, Technicolor seeps into the monochrome scene of little Amy gathering mushrooms in a misty, Spanish Moss draped wood, a fairytale setting straight out of a child's storybook. But the mood is quickly shattered by her discovery of McB's blood-soaked boot. Later, schoolgirls skip joyously outside to see McBurney's severed leg disposed of: 'Hallie's going to bury it', they laugh.

Eastwood viewed John McBurney as 'an opportunity to play true emotions and not totally operatic and not lighting cannons with cigars'. In an interview for *Playboy* in 1974, he was still trying to distance himself in the public's eye from 'The Man with No Name': 'My role in *Beguiled* was easier to play than the lone Westerner was. In those Leone films, I had to establish an image for the audience while saying very little. In *Beguiled*, I was dealing with straight, normal emotions from my own standpoint, which were simply those of survival'. With the arrival of McBurney, the power and focus of the school shifts, resulting in social competition between the women. Forgotten by the war, locked away in their 'castle', they compete for McBurney's attention. Pent-up sexual frustrations and fantasies are placed upon him. McBurney exploits this to the hilt and handsome Eastwood is highly convincing in the role. With flowing white shirts and heroic hair, Eastwood resembles the dashing leading man of romantic fiction, refracted through the dark prose of Edgar Allen Poe and Ambrose Bierce.

As director Siegel observed, 'Women are capable of deceit, larceny, murder... any young girl who looks perfectly harmless is capable of murder', though critic Judith Crist called it 'a must for sadists and woman-haters'. Martha covets McBurney for herself,

3.4 'Games for two are more fun': Solitaire-playing McBurney encounters temptress Carol in the leafy arbour, but who is *The Beguiled?*; Jo Ann Harris and Clint Eastwood in Don Siegel's gothic tale of the unexpected. Image courtesy Kevin Wilkinson Collection.

fantasising that she and Edwina share him in a ménage-à-trois. This sacreligeous rev-
erie, complete with tolling bells and church organ on the soundtrack, is photographed
to recall Martha's icon of Christ cradled by Mary following his crucifixion. 'I'll try not
to dictate your personal behaviour', Martha tells McBurney, when she leaves his door
unlocked, but secretly hopes it will be to her he comes. McBurney's decision – which
door, which woman – is one that will change all their lives. Hysterical Edwina hits
him with a candlestick and pushes him down the stairs, shrieking, 'You lying son of a
bitch, you bastard, you filthy lecher: I hope you're dead'. Carol claims that McBurney
forced himself on her, when, in fact, she enticed him into her boudoir (in the novel the
women hold a trial to decide how to deal with McBurney's behaviour, which includes
his alleged theft of $200 and a locket). Martha takes revenge on McBurney, ostensibly
so he won't die 'inch by inch in screaming agony'. McBurney spits, 'Just because I didn't
go to your bed'. 'I should have let you die screaming', reflects Martha.

Hartman's sensitive, childlike demeanour anticipates Sondra Locke's persona in
later Eastwood movies. McBurney appeals to Edwina's romantic notions of love and
asks her if she thinks of herself 'as a sleeping beauty in a castle, waiting for a prince
to free you with a kiss'. She naively believes McBurney could be the man for her, but
she's wary, having witnessed her father's adultery. Panting, sensual Carol has no such
insecurity: cooing into McBurney's ear, whispering, kissing and caressing, making
her very hard to resist. But as Edwina says, 'A hussy is a hussy' and when McBurney
prepares to leave the seminary, it will be Edwina who accompanies him.

Unlike some of Bruce Surtees' later cinematography for Eastwood, often murk-
ily underlit, *The Beguiled* uses light and shade well. Half-lit faces and shadows con-
ceal half-revealed truths – the protagonists' secret desires are suppressed, buried in
the shadows of their pasts, or emotionally masked. The eerie music by Lalo Schifrin
deploys twanging cimbalom and harpsichord opposite lush romantic cues, incorporating melodic piano, flutes and strings, echoing the divergent emotional moods of the
film – seductive amore and destructive hysteria.

Though the only pistol Eastwood brandishes in the film is an antique flintlock,
poster artwork armed him with a Colt six-shooter and the tagline: 'His love ... or his
life'. Other ad copy assured that 'Clint Eastwood has never been in a more frightening
situation' and 'One man ... seven women ... in a strange house'. It was rated 'R' in the
US and 'X' in the UK, when released through Rank in 1971. Critically, the film fared
better than any previous Eastwood movie. *The Times* saw 'a remarkably beguiling
film', and Eastwood's acting for once garnered praise. 'An astonishing, though certainly not great, performance', noted *Motion Picture Exhibitor*. *Hollywood Reporter*
wrote that Eastwood demonstrates 'a greater versatility and range than his best past
work has indicated'. The film was well-received in Europe, especially in France and
Italy. In France, *L'Aurore* observed that if it had been shown at Cannes, 'It would have
rivalled Losey and Visconti'. *Match* said of Siegel, 'After nearly forty films, he ranks
now among the greatest' and *Combat* noted that Eastwood 'is at once charming and
cunning, amoral and pathetic, lustful and naïve'. The 10 March 1971 issue of *Variety*
noted that '*The Beguiled* doesn't come off ... [and] cues audience laughter in all the

wrong places. Period pic doesn't look strong enough to sustain class first run book-ings and would probably perform best with fast playoff'. They were right. Audiences didn't like Eastwood as 'The Man with No Leg' and Universal's marketing campaign backfired, attracting neither the action fans nor an audience receptive to melodra-matic Gothic horror. It limped to gross just over a million dollars, far below even *Coogan's Bluff*, making it Eastwood's first financial failure. Producer Jennings Lang summed it up: 'Maybe a lot of people just don't want to see Clint Eastwood's leg cut off'. But *The Beguiled* is one of Eastwood's great performances – finally proving that he could be convincing onscreen without smoking, squinting or shooting – and is Siegel's personal favourite of all the films he directed.

Play Misty for Me (1971)

After completing *The Beguiled*, Eastwood began work on his feature directorial debut *Play Misty for Me*, the first time he had complete control over a project as producer-director-star. He played the lead, Dave Garver, 'The Big D', a womanising late-night radio disk jockey who plays 'five hours of mellow groove' on the jazz and blues station Radio KRML in Carmel-by-the-Sea on the Monterey Peninsula. During his show he is regularly phoned by an avid fan, who asks him to 'Play "Misty" for me', Erroll Garner's classic disk. At his local bar, The Sardine Factory, he picks up Evelyn Draper (Jessica Walter) and they spend the night together, though it soon becomes appar-ent that Evelyn is his '"Misty" chick' and that she has contrived their meeting. He presumes they have had a 'no strings' one-night-stand, but Evelyn misconstrues their relationship, showing up at his home unannounced and acting as if they're lovers. Matters are further complicated by the return to Carmel of Tobie Williams (Donna Mills), Dave's long-term girlfriend; their relationship was scuppered by his woman-ising and the constant parade of intrusive roommates at her house, affording them little privacy. Dave tries to discourage Evelyn, but her behaviour becomes increas-ingly obsessive, erratic and psychotic. She eventually tries to commit suicide in Dave's bathroom, by slashing her wrists, then in a frenzied attack she wrecks Dave's house and attempts to murder his cleaner, Birdie. With Evelyn committed into psychiatric care, Dave is able to enjoy some time with Tobie, including a visit to the Monterey Jazz Festival. But during one of his broadcasts he receives a call from Evelyn, asking for 'Misty'. She says that through therapy she's recovered and is on her way to Hawaii to start a new job and signs off with a line of poetry – 'Because this maiden she lived with no other thought than to love and be loved by you'. That night she appears unex-pectedly in Dave's bedroom and attempts to kill him with a butcher's knife. Sergeant McCallum (John Larch) tries to jog Dave's memory as to what Evelyn's poetic ref-erence might mean. During Dave's show, McCallum goes to check on Tobie, who is settling in with her new roommate, Annabel. Too late it dawns on Dave that the quote is from Edgar Allen Poe's macabre verse 'Annabel Lee'. Over at Tobie's, Evelyn, or 'Annabel', stabs McCallum to death with a pair of scissors and takes Tobie prisoner. Dave races to Tobie's and is met by manic Evelyn, who attacks him with a carving knife. Badly cut, Dave manages to punch Evelyn, who plummets off the cliffside veranda, dying on the rocks below.

The novelisation of *Play Misty for Me*, published in 1971, was written by Paul J. Gillette 'from the screenplay by Jo Heims and Dean Reisner'. The screenplay had originally featured a prologue with Evelyn in an asylum (which was never filmed) and included many more references to Poe's poetry. Dave is referred to as 'Edgar Allen Garland' (most sources bill him as 'Dave Garland', though he's clearly called 'Dave Garver' throughout the film). Also, Evelyn attempts suicide much earlier in the original screenplay. When the opportunity arose, Eastwood suggested it as a candidate for his directorial debut, even waiving his director's fee to be able to tackle the project.

Budgeted at $950,000, the film was completed by Eastwood for $900,000, and four days under its five-week shooting schedule. Heims' story was originally set in Los Angeles, but Eastwood wanted to save costs by shooting completely on location on his home turf of Carmel-by-the-Sea. 'It was a small story', Eastwood said, 'and lent itself perfectly to being shot on natural sets. Working in authentic and realistic backgrounds in Europe during my years there as an actor has taught me the value of utilising such locations'. Many of the shoreline scenes were filmed in the 200 acres he owned on the Monterey Peninsula, along the beaches dotted with distinctive, mushrooming Monterey Pine trees. Tobie's woodland house – with its cliffside veranda, which appears in the opening and closing moments of the film – was an actual property on Spindrift Road in the Carmel Highlands. Dave drives his black Jaguar convertible (an MG in Heims' story) from the Highlands along the spectacular coast road into Carmel, where the Radio KRML station was situated in the Rancho Shopping Centre ('Home of The Buccaneer', intones Garver, 'The man's boutique'). The Sardine Factory was a restaurant and bar on Cannery Row, Monterey (Johnny Murphy, the barman, was played by Don Siegel, who appeared in two scenes). Dave meets Madge Brenner for lunch at the Windjammer restaurant on Fisherman's Wharf in Monterey. In an in-joke, Brenner is looking to recruit Dave to present a music show, an 'unstructured, loosy-goosy, Monterey Pop, Woodstock kind of thing', for 'Malpaso TV Productions' in San Francisco.

The film took full advantage of the Monterey coastline, its headland and coves, the rolling waves and rock outcrops of Carmel Beach, jagged Point Lobos and Big Sur. The spectacular scenery, often filmed in sweeping helicopter shots, provides an elemental expression of the tempestuous emotional turmoil in the story. In the opening scene, Dave looks down from Tobie's veranda at the waves crashing on the rocks below – the rocks where Evelyn is dashed against in the finale. When Eastwood cuts away from the story, the rugged coastline, battered by the sea, with gulls screeching and waves crashing, recalls Roger Corman's Poe adaptations, such as *Pit and the Pendulum* (1961), *The Raven* and *The Terror* (both 1963) – Monterey Gothics shot in California. *Variety* warned that the film 'suffers from frequent digressions into landscape; the effect ... on pacing is murderous', while other critics noticed that Tobie and Dave get lost in the landscape, with their dialogue scenes often filmed in long shot. These criticisms misinterpret Eastwood's intent because

3.5 Deadly Obsession: Evelyn Draper arrives unannounced at Dave Garver's pad; Clint Eastwood and Jessica Walter in the psycho-thriller *Play Misty for Me* (1971). Image courtesy Kevin Wilkinson Collection.

they chillingly provide an Evelyn's eye-view, as she stalks the couple along the coast.

Eastwood invokes the troubling spirit of Poe. In fact, the opening verse of Poe's 'Annabel Lee' could have been written for the film:

> *It was many and many a year ago, in a kingdom by the sea,*
> *That a maiden there lived whom you may know by the name of Annabel Lee;*
> *And this maiden she lived with no other thought than to love and be loved by me.*

Eastwood also used Roberta Flack's then-unknown song 'The First Time Ever I Saw Your Face', one of the most poetic love songs ever written, as an accompaniment to Dave and Tobie's woodland tryst. It's a song that tells of an ethereal, indestructible love between soul mates:

The first time ever I saw you face, I thought the sun rose in your eyes
And the moon and the stars were the gifts you gave,
To the dark and the endless sky, my love.

Evelyn Draper is a nerve-jangling example of what has since become known as a 'Bunny Boiler'. *Misty* deals with the misinterpretation of love – not just avid fandom, but all-consuming, psychotic destructiveness. Jessica Walter gives an unnerving performance as Evelyn, the jealous psychopath. Ann Guarino in the *New York Daily News* noted that 'Walter is so good as the possessive and obsessive woman that the viewer will want to strangle her'. In the Sardine Factory bar, Murphy and Dave play a board game called 'Cry Bastion', with whisky stoppers and champagne corks. Evelyn, sitting alone at the bar, approaches them, intrigued. During the game, she and Dave start talking and Dave wins the 'game', which is simply a ruse to enable him to chat her up. Evelyn is initially just another in a long line of one-night-stands for Dave, but when she sees Tobie stealing him back, it affects her psychologically. Evelyn is the ultimate groupie who knows everything about the object of her affections. 'You're talking to your number one fan', she tells him, ominously. High-strung and unstable to begin with, Evelyn's unreciprocated love scratches away her thin veneer of sanity – her wired, sudden mood swings and spurts of rage shock Dave. These rapidly escalate from pestering phone calls and unexpected visits, to housebreaking, stalking and murder.

Apparently rid of Evelyn, Dave returns to Tobie, an artist and sculptor. She wears a poncho and is typically the kind of bohemian waifs who appear in many of Eastwood's films. Her portrait of Eastwood/'Garver' on an easel in her house was actually painted by renowned Californian artist Don Heitkotter. Evelyn is Tobie's opposite: calculating, controlling and far from chilled out. When she poses as lodger 'Annabel', she tells Tobie, 'God, you're dumb'. In retribution for Dave shunning her, Evelyn restrains Tobie and cuts her long blonde hair, getting her 'all nice for David'; 'I hope he likes what he sees when he walks in here', Evelyn tells her, 'Because that's what he's taking to Hell with him'.

Unsurprisingly for a film set around a radio station, music features extensively. Despite Evelyn's repeated phone-in requests, Erroll Garner's 'Misty' is heard in its entirety only when the film's end titles roll. At the Monterey Jazz Festival, The Johnny Otis Show and The Cannonball Adderley Quintet (led by sax player Julian 'Cannonball' Adderley) perform numbers. Otis's set, including the classic Bo Diddley shuffle 'Willie and the Hand Jive', was released in 1971 as *Live at Monterey*. Jazzman Dee Barton (a drummer, trombonist and arranger for Stan Kenton) provided the film's jazz and blues score and is also name-checked during Dave's show. The opening scene, with Eastwood (wearing shades at night) driving along the coast in his con-vertible Jag, while Barton's rock 'n' roll number (with fuzzbox guitars, blues piano and punchy sax) blasts out of the radio, is about as self-consciously groovy as a title sequence can be. The actual KRML Jazz and Blues Radio is still going strong. It now broadcasts from new studios in the Eastwood Building in Carmel and can be listened to online at www.krmlradio.com. At the time of writing, its late night presenters include Misty Red and Misty Blonde.

The menacing voiceover during its Hitchcockian trailer noted that *Play Misty for Me* is 'for Clint Eastwood, an invitation to terror. There's no escape in passion...in speed...from terror'. It was advertised as a horror movie: 'The next scream you hear will be your own'. 'Play Misty for Me', intones the voiceover, are 'the most frighten-ing words you'll ever hear'. UK posters for the film (rated X) put out by Rank Film Distributors noted: 'Dave Garland had it made. Top Deejay, success, girls, an idyllic life – until the phone rings, and a husky voice says...*Play Misty for Me* and his night-mare begins!' In the US, the film was rated 'R', for its release in November 1971, a month before *Dirty Harry*. In fact, *Play Misty for Me* is publicised on a cinema hoard-ing included in the bank robbery sequence of *Dirty Harry*. This was deliberate in-joke self-promotion by Eastwood and Siegel, as *Misty* wasn't yet on release when *Dirty Harry* was shot. *Misty* grossed over $5 million on its initial release in the US, while Flack's 'First Time Ever I Saw Your Face' went to the top of the US charts in 1972. Most critics seemed both surprised and impressed by *Play Misty for Me*. *Time* liked it ('A good little scare show'), noting Eastwood's nods to *Psycho* and *Repulsion*. The *New York Times* compared it to *Vertigo* and *Laura*, the *Chicago Sun-Times* thought it was 'the best thriller...in a long time' and Archer Winston in the *New York Post* wrote that the results suggest 'strongly that Clint Eastwood is more than a multitalented actor, producer and gunman'. But Rex Reed called it '*Psycho* in mothballs', which makes up 'in helicopter shots what the movie lacks in plot, motivation and script...To guarantee commercial success [Eastwood] even throws in a nude scene, a visit to the Monterey Jazz Festival, and his best friend is black'. Almost 40 years later, *Misty* stands up remarkably well, despite some terribly dated fashions, with Eastwood's col-ourfully resplendent creations provided by 'Brad Whitney of Carmel'.

Breezy (1973)

Although *Breezy* was originally written as a possible Eastwood vehicle, he decided to stay behind the camera, as director-producer. It was to have been made immediately after *Play Misty for Me*, but Eastwood starred in *High Plains Drifter* instead, a safer box office bet. 'I love acting', said Eastwood in an interview, 'and I mean to continue doing it, but I must admit that the satisfaction of directing goes even deeper'.

Again based on a screenplay by Jo Heims (who also acted as associate producer), *Breezy* is the Los Angeles-set story of a relationship spanning the generations, between Edith Alice Breezerman, called 'Breezy' (Kay Lenz), a 17-year-old hippy musician, and Frank Harmon (William Holden), a 50-something, divorced real estate agent for Masterpiece Properties. Hitching through Laurel Canyon into the San Fernando Valley (known as 'The Valley'), chatterbox Breezy is picked up by Frank. During the journey, they see a dog that has been run over lying at the roadside. Breezy runs away and Frank takes the dog to a vet. Later he notices that Breezy has left her guitar in his car. Frank was dating Betty Tobin (Marj Dusay), who is his own age, but she has now begun a relationship with Charlie Eisen, a lawyer, and they are about to be married. Breezy arrives at Frank's house that night to retrieve her guitar and so begins their relationship. He is cynical, reclusive and miserable – she christens him 'Black Cloud' – while she is optimistic, full of vitality. He is unsure about their relationship but falls for her freewheeling, naive charm, as they enjoy Pacific Ocean beach walks and dinner dates. Slowly Frank changes, losing his world-weary cynicism. He surprises Breezy by taking her to the vet, where she sees that the injured dog has recovered. Breezy names the dog, now their pet, Sir Love-A-Lot. When Frank and Breezy run into his tipsy ex-wife on a date in town, he feels uncomfortable, and later at the cinema they meet more of his friends, who are shocked to see Frank with a girl Breezy's age. Eventually Frank decides their love can never gain social acceptability and Breezy departs, leaving Love-A-Lot as Frank's sole companion. In the middle of the night, Frank is woken by a phone call: there has been a car accident and he's called to the hospital. There he finds Betty, badly injured; her husband of one week has been killed in the accident. This epiphany prompts Frank to take Love-A-Lot to Plummer Park to find Breezy. 'Hello my love', he tells Breezy; 'Hello my life', she answers. 'If we're lucky we might last a year', says Frank. 'A year!' she answers, 'Just think of it Frank, a whole year'.

For the title role, Eastwood was going to cast Jo Ann Harris from *The Beguiled* but instead chose Kay Lenz, a TV actress. During these auditions, Eastwood saw Sondra Locke for the first time, but she was deemed too old for the role. Hollywood star William Holden was cast as Frank. Holden told Eastwood, 'You know something? I've been this guy', to which Eastwood replied, 'I thought so'. *Breezy*'s supporting cast was a good one, made up of largely little-known but gifted actors, mostly from television. Roger C. Carmel was Frank's boozy, out of condition tennis partner, Bob. Marj Dusay was cast as Betty, Frank's one-time lover, now engaged to another. Joan Hotchkis was Frank's boozy ex-wife Paula, who takes one look at Breezy and hisses, 'God you're young'. Holden himself had divorced Brenda Marshall, his wife of 30 years, in 1971. Their son, Scott Holden, appeared briefly in *Breezy* as the vet who patches up Love-A-Lot (the dog was played by 'Earle'). In a harbour-side boutique, as Frank waits for Breezy, a little boy shoots at him with a toy pistol, saying, 'Pow!'; 'Got me partner', says Frank. The little boy is Eastwood's son Kyle, following in his father's gunslinging footsteps. The film that Breezy and Frank go on a date to see is *High Plains Drifter* and as the couple wanders along the promenade, Eastwood himself can be seen leaning on the railings.

Breezy was filmed on location by cinematographer Frank Stanley over five weeks in November and December 1972 in the Encino district of L.A. for $750,000. As befits a film depicting a real estate agent, it features location filming in some spectacular

Los Angeles properties, providing a general sense of Californian high living, especially for Frank's middle-aged spread. Scenes were shot in Laurel Canyon, between Hollywood and 'The Valley', on the Pacific coastline and at a harbour promenade. Although Lenz was inexperienced, she and Holden got along well and Holden noted, 'I'd forgotten what it is like to make pictures this agreeably. I'll work with Clint any time he asks'. The seventies L.A. clothes look dated today and the film is most interesting when viewed as a time capsule of the era, with its parties, health clubs, dinner dates and rich lifestyles. The two protagonists' wardrobes mark them as different people: Frank is a cardigan and slacks man, while 'hippy dippy' Breezy dresses in denim flares, buckskin jacket, tight sweaters and a floppy hat and carries a guitar with 'Breezy' painted on it. His friends are bourgeois, hers are hippies. When asked by a co-worker what a group of scruffy hippies reminds him of, Frank sneers, 'Low tide'.

    Breezy features a sentimental title song, 'Breezy's Song' (lyrics by Marilyn and Alan Bergman, music by Michel Legrand), sung in flowery fashion by Shelby Flint:

> *Morning is a friend of mine, it always plays my song*
> *And any time I ask the wind, it lets me tag along*
> *I read the lessons in the leaves, they've a world of things to tell me*
> *I always keep my pockets filled with pumpkin seeds and thyme*

    Breezy also includes a reprise of the song, as Holden and Lenz walk hand-in-hand along a beach, with massive waves crashing in the background. This is similar in tone to Eastwood's use of Roberta Flack's song in *Play Misty for Me*, but this time the only threat to the lovers' bliss is social rejection. Over the end titles, the simplistic lyrics peer towards the couple's future:

> *Maybe we'll make each other laugh and maybe we will cry*
> *And maybe we'll be each others friend, before we say goodbye*

    Though the song's lyrical content gives a fair indication of *Breezy*'s depiction of romance, the unusual storyline, its adult themes and nudity (Lenz has several topless scenes) are considerably more complex. To avoid being charged with vagrancy, Breezy claims to be Frank's niece; in a boutique, the saleslady mistakes Breezy for his daughter. 'All we add up to is a dirty joke', says Frank, when he decides their relationship is over. Breezy has prepared dinner, but Frank's itching for a fight, telling her to stop calling him 'Frankie': 'It makes me feel like one of those unwashed idiots you hang around with'. 'Why are you throwing us away?' she cries, but he can't cope with what other people think of them. As Breezy leaves, she says that Love-A-Lot will have to stay, she can't afford to feed him, but 'Don't teach him to roll over and play dead'.

    The strength of Frank and Breezy's growing love and Frank's process of defrosting provide Eastwood with some effective scenes. 'I have no secrets from the sun', sings Shelby Flint during the titles, 'and I'll have none from you', which delineates Breezy's straightforward honesty and sincerity. 'Would you mind very much if I love you?' she asks, 'I just would like to be able to say the words once in a while'. 'Don't you ever want to be loved back?' he asks her; 'I thought I was', she hopes. As their relationship develops, Frank finds himself drawn into a full-scale love affair, with social taboos ignored. 'Well Edith Alice', he smiles, 'for a man who likes his privacy and a girl without means of transport, we're sure seeing a lot of each other'. Frank realises that he's been reawakened. Now he has 'a genuine interest in someone other than myself'. There are sappy moments too, as to be expected from a film with a dog called Sir Love-A-Lot, but on the whole, *Breezy* is a mature piece of work by a rapidly developing filmmaker. *Village Voice* deemed it 'Eastwood's most accomplished directorial job so far ... a love story in which almost everything works', while the *New York Post* said that 'Eastwood continues to rise as a director ... [he] hits the bull's-eye with a sentimental April-November romance that could have been awful, but isn't'.

Breezy was released with little fanfare in November 1973 in the US, three months after *High Plains Drifter* and the month before *Magnum Force*. In an effort to entice filmgoers, some posters featured a photograph of Eastwood in the corner of the poster – proclaiming 'Directed by Clint Eastwood'. In the US, it was rated 'R', which was one of the film's problems. Lenz's topless scenes were mostly tastefully filmed in shadow but still garnered an 'R' rating, which meant no admittance to unaccompanied teenagers under the age of 17. Eastwood was angry about the rating and also about Universal's mishandling of the film, which vanished without a trace. *Breezy*, rated 'AA', was released briefly in the UK by CIC in November 1973. It has since been screened on BBC TV in the UK (buried as part of Eastwood film seasons) and is a forgotten film. Perhaps its availability now on DVD will ensure the film is appreciated for its fine performances and Heims' story: it's an interesting companion piece to *Play Misty for Me* and a definite seventies curio.

The Bridges of Madison County (1995)

Eastwood's first love story since *Breezy*, 22 years earlier, *The Bridges of Madison County* is the only time the actor has played a straightforward romantic lead. Robert James Waller's highly praised book had been a bestseller on its publication in 1992. The story was ideal Hollywood material, narrating a chance, four-day romance between *National Geographic* photographer Robert Kincaid and Iowa housewife Francesca Johnson. Eight of Kincaid's photographs illustrate Waller's story. When the book was first published in the UK in 1992 by Sinclair-Stevenson Ltd, it was titled *Love in Black and White*.

Following Francesca Johnson's death, her son Michael (Victor Slezak) and daughter Carolyn (Annie Corley) meet Lawyer Peterson at their mother's house near Winterset, Madison County, Iowa. Francesca is to be buried in the same Prairie Hill plot as her deceased husband Richard, but it transpires she has stipulated in her will that she wants her ashes scattered off nearby Roseman Bridge. Her family questions this odd request and begins to sort through her personal effects: letters, photographs and treasured mementos, including a journal *Four Days*. It soon becomes obvious that in 1965 Francesca had a brief affair and experienced a lost love which has lasted a lifetime.

On Monday 16 August 1965, photographer Robert Kincaid (Eastwood) arrives at an Iowa farmhouse, asking directions to Roseman Bridge. There he meets Francesca (Meryl Streep), the unhappy, bored Italian wife of farmer Richard Johnson (Jim Haynie). Her husband and two teenage kids, Michael and Carolyn, are away for four days at the state fair. Francesca takes Kincaid to Roseman Bridge – he is on a *National Geographic* assignment to photograph the historical covered wooden bridges of Madison County. They enjoy each others' company and she invites him to her farm for dinner. He has visited so many interesting places, including Bari, her birthplace in Italy, and she finds his free spirit refreshing and charming. Over the four days, they grow to love one another, finding a rare bond, but too quickly, it is time for him to leave. He'll still be in town for a couple of days, but her family returns from the fair and Francesca returns to her humdrum life. She agonises over whether to leave with Kincaid, but even seeing him one last time in the pouring rain in the streets of Winterset doesn't convince her and he drives out of her life forever. Finally her family realises why she wishes to be scattered from Roseman Bridge; 'I gave my life to my family', Francesca wrote, 'I wish to give Robert what is left of me'.

Eastwood recognised in the character of Kincaid a kindred free spirit and is convincing in a difficult role. In Waller's book, Kincaid is described as having long silver hair and wearing a silver bracelet, khaki or denims and boots: a modern cowboy. Although no mention or reference is made to cowboys in the film, Eastwood's screen iconography naturally conjures such associations. Interestingly, when Kincaid talks to Francesca about his work, he refers to it as 'making pictures', blurring the character with Eastwood the filmmaker. This symbiosis between character and actor probably helped his performance, especially when he tells Francesca that 'I'm no artist', but 'making pictures' is his 'obsession'. Kincaid may be 'no artist' but he's certainly a poet. He's of Irish decent and reads Yeats, as Frankie would in *Million Dollar Baby*.

Eastwood liked the story, and a script by Richard LaGravenese transformed the highly effective weepy from page to screen. Steven Spielberg was originally going to direct, but Eastwood was in place as 'hyphenate' director-star before shooting began. Several actresses were mooted for Francesca, including Anjelica Huston and Lena Olin, but Eastwood cast Meryl Streep, probably the most lauded actress of her generation. She'd been Oscar-nominated nine times, winning for *Kramer vs. Kramer* in 1979 and *Sophie's Choice* in 1982. She is also adept at speaking in accents and adopts a convincing English-Italian accent in *Bridges*. Eastwood and Streep rehearsed little before the shoot, Eastwood's idea being that they would grow to know each other as actors, as their characters would in the film.

The story is really a two-header and the supporting cast, though vital to the narrative, is peripheral. Jim Haynie is suitably distant as Francesca's hardworking farmer husband. When Kincaid and Francesca enjoy an evening in a roadhouse, the band

3.6 'Making Pictures': Robert Kincaid snaps Francesca Johnson at Roseman Bridge; Clint Eastwood and Meryl Street on location in Iowa in *The Bridges of Madison County* (1995). Author's collection.

onstage playing the sassy 'Jammin' with J.R.' is the James Rivers Band, with Eastwood's son Kyle clearly visible on double bass. Annie Corley as Carolyn and Victor Slezak as Michael do what they can with their supporting roles as Francesca's grown-up children, initially shocked to discover their mother's infidelity but later moved by her account of it. They also provide the story with its final image, as they scatter Francesca's ashes from Roseman Bridge, her remains drifting like smoke in the wind.

The book's moving coda, which doesn't feature in the film, describes the author interviewing John 'Nighthawk' Cummings, a tenor sax player. Kincaid took some promotional pictures of Cummings and later attended the jazzman's gigs, always asking for 'Autumn Leaves'. Kincaid recounted details of his 1965 love affair to Cummings; the latter was so moved he composed the tune 'Francesca' in her honour and Kincaid gave him a photo of Roseman Bridge as a thank you.

With a $22 million budget, *The Bridges of Madison County* was filmed from September to October 1994, the autumnal months passing convincingly for a scorching Iowa August. Jack N. Green's cinematography is exemplary – the hazy sunshine, green fields filled with chirruping crickets and dusty roads depicting a perfect, endless summer of childhood remembered. Authentic Madison County locations were used. The town scenes were shot in Winterset and Adell, while the actual Holliwell and Roseman covered bridges appear. These distinctive wooden bridges had boxed sections covering the central portion of the structure. The story was shot chronologically, with a refurbished Iowa farmhouse used as the rural Johnson residence. Filming progressed well and Eastwood was proud of his work on *Bridges*, citing his favourite directors in interviews: 'I tried to be more in the Ford and Hawks tradition, allowing things to happen onscreen'.

The Bridges of Madison County is a romantic drama in the tradition of the screen's great love stories. It is Eastwood's most European movie, its slow pace, simplicity and visual beauty reminiscent of pastoral French and Italian cinema. Some critics have complained of the film's 129-minute length, but Eastwood spends time developing his characters, through nuance and gesture: this is particularly true of Streep, often an actress seen to be 'acting', who effortlessly transforms from lonely frumpiness to elegance. Eastwood is less expressive, but this is still a great Eastwood performance. His naturalistic acting, no doubt enhanced by their lack of rehearsal, makes his stoicism even more effective than usual: the difference between performance and 'living the character' has never been more obvious than here, as they share memories and cigarettes in Francesca's kitchen. Francesca's voiceover aptly says at one point: 'I was acting like another woman and yet I was more myself than ever before'. In one scene, Francesca wanders idly across Holliwell Bridge, while Kincaid sets up his camera. When she reaches the other side, he has crept around the bridge and surprises her, taking her photograph. She laughs girlishly, as Kincaid captures on film the 'real' Francesca, the Francesca even she has forgotten.

The bridges of Madison County are used in the film as a symbolic link between two places, or rather two hearts. In Eastwood's action films, the bridges would have been blown up. Here they unite two people, but significantly, though they build bridges between their lives during their four-day liaison, by the end of the film, with Kincaid's departure, they end up on opposite banks of the river – separated forever by a gulf neither can span.

As Francesca says of love after Kincaid's departure, 'Its mystery is pure and absolute'. Kincaid is a globetrotting loner, living his own life, a drifting existence with a rucksack that takes him all over the world. Francesca grew up in Bari and Naples, married her husband Richard (a GI posted there during the war) and returned to his native Iowa, but, 'It's not what I dreamed of as a girl'. On his deathbed, Francesca's husband acknowledges that she had her own dreams: 'I'm sorry I couldn't give them to you – I love you so very much'. But in her own way, for those four brief days with Kincaid, Francesca has realised her dreams. The film is at its most effective in their carefree moments of new love: a picnic beside a river, the scenes of Kincaid photographing the covered bridges at evening light and their days spent driving dusty roads through beautiful Iowa countryside: 'We let the day take us where it wanted', remembers Francesca. For their first dinner together at her house, they are both dressed in their everyday clothes. For a later meal, Kincaid dons a clean shirt, while Francesca has bought herself a new dress from Des Moines. She appears, looking radiant, and Kincaid is enraptured. This perfect moment, as they stare at one another, is inopportunely interrupted by the ringing telephone. She answers it: it's her friend Madge, a reminder of the real world encroaching on their dream world. Later they slow dance around the kitchen to Johnny Hartman's smoochy 'I See Your Face before Me'. But this idyll can't last, as these precious moments fall through their fingers like sand.

It is during their agonising farewell at the farm that Eastwood appears to cry on screen, though he turns his head away from the camera to shield his tears, as he had at his wife's graveside in *The Outlaw Josey Wales*. When Kincaid drives away from the farm, she can't leave, even though he has told her, 'This kind of certainty comes but once in a lifetime'. Days later in Winterset, in the pouring rain, Francesca and her husband are in town shopping. Through the teeming downpour, she sees Kincaid, standing drenched and distraught, his tears this time indiscernible from the rain. They stare at one another, a silent, ghastly farewell, before he pulls off in his pickup. Francesca's husband returns and they drive off, pulling up behind Kincaid's vehicle at a stop light. Francesca deliberates, as she sees Kincaid take her silver icon (inscribed 'Francesca') from the glove compartment and hang it from the rear view mirror. The traffic lights change to green, but Kincaid doesn't drive off. Francesca's hand grips the door handle. Is he waiting for her to come to him? Then his pickup's indicator light begins to flash – he's waiting to turn left and finally, finally, he pulls off. We all make our choices and we have to live with them, but seldom has cinema made the choice so difficult.

The Bridges of Madison County was released in the US in June 1995, with a trailer featuring an eloquent voiceover by Streep, accompanied by 'For All We Know'. Roger Ebert in the *Chicago Sun-Times* called the film 'deeply moving', noting that Eastwood and Streep 'have made [the book] into a wonderful movie love story'. The *New York Times* said their love affair was 'as powerful as anything the movies have given us'. The general consensus was that this was highly effective, emotional entertainment. It was rated 'PG-13' in the US, '12' in the UK. The film's burnished poster had no tagline, just the names of the two stars. Its artwork depicted Francesca resting her head on Kincaid's shoulder, with the Roseman Bridge as a backdrop – a faded photograph of a never-forgotten summer, its simple, pastoral beauty an ideal evocation of the film's tone. Eastwood co-composed 'Doe Eyes' – also billed as 'Love Theme from *The Bridges of Madison County*' – with Lennie Niehaus; it appears to emotive effect during Francesca and Kincaid's parting in the rain and over the end titles. A fragmented, delicate piano motif, lushly orchestrated by Niehaus, 'Doe Eyes' was inspired by a new love in Eastwood's life, newscaster Dina Ruiz, whom he later married. *Bridges*' soundtrack also featured songs by Dinah Washington ('Blue Gardenia', 'I'll Close My Eyes') and Johnny Hartman ('It Was Almost Like a Song', 'Easy Living'). These lyrics reinforce the film's emotive power – 'I close my eyes and there you are'; 'For all we know we may never meet again'. Its CD release proved popular; so much so that it spawned a spin-off CD, *Remembering Madison County* (1995).

The Bridges of Madison County was a massive hit with the public, Streep's presence and the book's popularity ensuring a different audience for this Eastwood film and it remains among his most popular. It took over $70 million in the US. Eastwood the director has often surprised critics with his choice of subject matter and he's always willing to try something new, taking new directions, like Kincaid. *The Bridges of Madison County* contains one of Eastwood's most memorable performances and remains one of his finest films – like artful Kincaid's talent, when on form his skill at 'making pictures' is unsurpassed.

PART FOUR
THE COMEDIES

The cover of the January 1978 issue of *Time* magazine featured Clint Eastwood and Burt Reynolds, under the caption 'Hollywood Honchos'. The popularity of Reynolds' *Smokey and the Bandit* the previous year, second only to *Star Wars* in grosses, pushed Reynolds to number one at the box office and made 'good old boy' country and western movies both viable and popular. Often dismissed by critics, too sophisticated to bother with such hick flicks, the film and its sequels were lapped up by folk to whom smart aleck Reynolds was a comedy idol. These car chase films include hits such as Reynolds' all-star *The Cannonball Run* (1981), *The Great Smokey Roadblock* (1976) starring Henry Fonda, and Sam Peckinpah's *Convoy* (1978), which rode on the CB (Citizens' Band) radio craze. This style also transferred to TV, with jokey series including *The Dukes of Hazzard* and *The Fall Guy*. The latter featured Lee Majors as stuntman-cum-trouble-shooter Colt Seavers and the name-checking country and western title song (sung by Majors) that included the lyric, 'I've gotten burned over Cheryl Tiegs, blown up for Raquel Welch. I might jump an open drawbridge or Tarzan from a vine, 'cos I'm the unknown stuntman that makes Eastwood look so fine'. In the hip comedy *The Blues Brothers* (1980), the brothers' rhythm and blues band plays at a redneck bar. 'What kind of music do you usually have here?' the band asks gingerly. 'Oh, we got both kinds – country and western'. So they entertain the baying crowd from behind a protective chicken wire fence with a rousing rendition of the theme from *Rawhide*.

Every Which Way But Loose (1978)

After two hyper-violent action movies, *The Enforcer* (1976) and *The Gauntlet* (1977), Eastwood's *Every Which Way But Loose* would cannily tap into Reynolds' market. Eastwood was approached by Jeremy Joe Kronsberg with a script written with Reynolds in mind, called 'The Coming of Philo Beddoe', about a bare-knuckle boxer and his orang-utan companion Clyde (in the original script, a gorilla). Kronsberg had loosely based the title character on a real fighter. Clint and producer Fritz Manes were interested in the project as a change of pace for the action star.

In *Every Which Way But Loose*, Eastwood starred as Philo – a San Fernando Valley trucker who spends his spare time fighting bare-knuckle bouts for cash. His buddy, mechanic Orville (Geoffrey Lewis) acts as his manager, while orang-utan Clyde (won by Philo in a fight) tags along for the ride. In the Palomino bar, Philo falls for pretty country singer Lynn Halsey-Taylor (Sondra Locke), but after she borrows some cash from him, she skips town with her lover, Schyler. Philo sets off in pursuit, with Orville, Clyde, and Orville's pick-up Echo. After an interstate trek, which takes in Albuquerque, Santa Fe and Georgetown, they arrive in Halsey-Taylor's hometown of Denver. In a bout with local bare-knuckle legend Tank Murdock (Walter Barnes), Philo finally learns some smarts and takes a fall: he doesn't want to topple Murdock and become top dog. Spurned by Lynn, Philo drives back to California. The plot, such as it is, is loose and episodic. Critics joked that James Fargo directed 'every which way but well'. Sidetrack subplot running gags saw Philo pursued by two vengeful LAPD cops, Putnam and Herb (whom Philo humiliates in a bar), and the Pacoima chapter of the Hells Angels, the 'Black Widows'. Further complications arise from Orville's mother 'Ma' (Ruth Gordon) attempting to pass her driving test.

Eastwood, now 48 years old, played brawler Philo, even though he was 29 years old in Kronsberg's script. Blonde Sondra Locke played Lynn, in the original screenplay a brunette. Geoffrey Lewis, fast becoming a Malpaso regular, was goofy sidekick Orville. Kooky Beverly D'Angelo was perfectly cast as Echo (that's 'Echo'), who hitches up with Orville en route to Denver. James McEachin and Gregory Walcott were the idiot LAPD cops, while Ruth Gordon, the testy mother from such comedies as *Where's Poppa?* (1970) and *Harold and Maude* (1971), was perfect as foul-mouthed Ma Boggs, wondering whether she should wear her dark wig or her glasses for her driving test, and then failing for being too old and short-sighted.

For the role of Clyde, Eastwood cast a fresh-faced newcomer, 11-year-old, 165-pound orang-utan Manis, from 'Bobby Beronsini's Performing Orangutan Show', from the MGM Grand in Las Vegas. If there was ever a case of Eastwood being upstaged by a co-star, *Every Which Way* is it. Much of Manis' performance onscreen

4.1 'Beers to You': Barroom buddies Clyde and Philo enjoy a cool brew; Manis and Clint Eastwood in the hit comedy *Every Which Way But Loose* (1978). Author's collection.

was 'controlled' by his trainers off-screen; in some sequences, you can see Clyde's eyes looking for his cue before reacting. As his trainers put it, 'You may say he is a natural method actor'. To critics who despised Eastwood and the film, Clyde made great copy. *Newsweek* jibed, 'The only decent part is played by an orang-utan. One can forgive [his] participation – he couldn't read the script – but what is Eastwood's excuse?' The two co-stars got on well together. As Eastwood noted during the making of the film, Manis was on his best behaviour when he saw 'I was the one signing the cheques'.

Inept biker gang The Black Widows are a superb comic creation: a disaster waiting to happen. Without them, the film would have struggled for laughs. The Black Widders were the cream of Eastwood's Malpaso regulars, decked out in denim, swastikas and army surplus. Roy Jenson and Dan Vadis had both played menacing bikers in *The Gauntlet*, harassing Sondra Locke in a railway truck. Here they played eye-patched, bowler-hatted Woody and headband-wearing Cochise-alike Frank. Bill McKinney looked ridiculous as Dallas, two Viking-style longhorns protruding from his WWII German helmet, while William O'Connell's Elmo boasted the most unconvincing comb-over in celluloid history. Best of all was their pot-bellied leader, played by John Quade. Previously cast as the Comanchero leader in *The Outlaw Josey Wales*, Quade here plays dim-witted Cholla, a travesty in white flying scarf, peaked cap and jackboots. The Widders are middle-aged men, a travelling mid-life crisis, perpetually on the receiving end of ridicule. Ma routs them with a pump-action shotgun from the comfort of her porch and when they hassle some truckers at a truck stop, the diners send them packing – bruised. Chasing Philo's pickup, they find themselves driving through a car wash on their bikes. Their smooth sax break signature tune on the soundtrack, later becoming a fifties-style 'Sha-la-la-sha-la' do-wop, only adds to the fun. When they confront Philo in Georgetown down an alleyway, the face-off is a spaghetti western parody, complete with *The Good, the Bad and the Ugly* theme on the soundtrack.

Budgeted at $5 million, *Every Which Way* was shot on location, en route east from Los Angeles to Denver, the setting for Philo's gonzo odyssey, via Albuquerque, Santa Fe, Taos and Georgetown. Philo is a straightforward character, with straightforward motives. A truck driver for the 'Familian Pipe and Supply Company', he loves fighting, beer, his Chevy Apache pickup and his ape. In his universe, a can of Olympia, a bottle of Bud or Coors or a six-pack solves everything. Philo is also a practical joker, best exemplified when he plants a set of false teeth in a USC student's chowder in the Palomino; she's writing a paper on the 'country and western mentality'. When she leaves screaming, having scooped the teeth up with her spoon, Philo hands them back to Orville smiling, 'This wild clam got out of control'. Philo's love affair with Lynn, though the motivation for the cross-country trek, is the weakest of the Eastwood-Locke collaborations, through a lack of chemistry between the stars and a poor script. Critics have noted that this film actually tells us more about their off-screen relationship, especially the presence of Lynn's lover 'Schyler', perhaps a stand-in for Locke's husband Gordon Anderson. But it's not worth overanalysing Philo and Lynn's liaison; in *Every Which Way* relationships are like the characters: simple.

Eastwood was coached by Al Silvani, a boxing consultant who had worked on *Rocky* (1976). He also played Tank Murdock's manager in *Every Which Way*. The fight scenes are strictly comic strip. There are several barroom scrapes, resembling western saloon punch-ups, accompanied by country and western numbers on the soundtrack, one of the 'good old boy' subgenre's signatures. Bare-chested or in a T-shirt for his bouts, Philo takes on Church, a bruiser at a cement factory, Kincaid at a Santa Fe meatpacking plant festooned with cattle carcasses, and Tank Murdock at the Denver Brick and Pipe Company. Tank is less than a legend – 'a real porker', as Orville puts it. Philo throws this fight, an un-Eastwood-like outcome, but one intended to subvert his heroic screen persona. As *Positif* noted in June 1979, 'Philo prefers the carefree security of anonymity to a fragile and ever-threatened glory'. And I just thought he wanted to spend more time with Clyde.

Although Kronsberg's script included a series of self-penned songs which acted as links throughout the story, Eastwood decided to provide his own soundtrack, thereby owning a percentage of the original songs. He contacted Snuff Garrett, a country and western record producer, who created a soundtrack using country artists and a host of new songs. Garrett was billed as 'Music Supervisor' and co-wrote some of the songs, while Steve Dorff, who also co-wrote some of the songs, was 'Musical Director'. Garrett went on to work on *Smokey and the Bandit II*, and the two 'Cannonball Run' films. The song 'Every Which Way But Loose', sung by Eddie Rabbitt, was released as a single in November 1978 (eventually reaching number one in the country music charts in February 1979), followed by 'I'll Wake You Up When I Get Home' by Charlie Rich. Rich performed his song at the Denver 'Zanza Bar' in the movie. Locke got up on stage at the Palomino and played 'I Seek the Night' and later duetted with Phil Everly on 'Don't Say You Don't Love Me No More'. Other tunes included Mel Tillis's 'Coca Cola Cowboy' and 'Send Me Down to Tucson' (Tillis also appears in the film), a jokey burst of Rich's 'Behind Closed Doors' (as Clyde pays a visit to a female orang-utan in Albuquerque Zoo), 'Ain't Love Good Tonight', 'Red Eye Special', 'Honky Tonk Fever', 'I Can't Say No to a Truck Drivin' Man' and Cliff Crofford's appropriately titled 'Monkey See, Monkey Do'.

Trailers for *Every Which Way* featured a couple discussing the latest Eastwood release: 'What'd'ya think of Clint Eastwood confiding his deepest, darkest secrets to an orang-utan?' asks the husband. 'Now you're really kidding me', laughs his wife. 'It's no joke – it's Eastwood like you've never seen him before. Every which way you look there's action, adventure and fun'. Almost every which one of Eastwood's associates thought it would make peanuts, with some at Warners thinking the film unreleasable, but Eastwood was confident. When it was exhibited in the US in December 1978, business went through the roof. It was rated 'PG' and opened the doors of Eastwood's films to a younger audience, as long as they were accompanied by an adult. In the UK, it was deemed 'AA' for its profanity, though the bad language was much stronger in the novelisation, written by Kronsberg and published by Star Books as a tie-in in 1980. In the US, it took almost $52 million, eventually rising to over $85 million: double any previous Eastwood movie. *Ladies' Home Journal* liked Ruth Gordon and the ape but saw 'an unstructured shambles', *Newsweek* called it 'a Clint Eastwood comedy that could not possibly have been created by human hands…(a) plotless junkheap' and Rex Reed's appraisal of this 'anthropomorphic romance between Big Clint and an orang-utan' pitied audiences: 'Anyone who sees it has suffered enough brain damage already'.

This type of hick-and-miss comedy isn't to everyone's taste: some absolutely love its broad, lewd, crude style, while others emerge visibly harrowed. It is perhaps the film closest to Eastwood's own sense of humour and although he's good as Philo, the film really belongs to Clyde – he's the film's gimmick and, with the Black Widows, provides most of the laughs. The audience of the time agreed with Stuart Byron of *The Village Voice*: 'This is a redneck comedy with no stops pulled. If I could persuade my friends to see it, they'd probably detest it. I loved it'. It was Warner Bros' third biggest all-time success, behind *The Exorcist* and *Superman: The Movie*, at a fraction of their costs. By 1979, Eastwood was the only star to have appeared in the box office top ten for the entire decade. Inflation adjusted, it is still Eastwood's most profitable film.

Bronco Billy (1980)

Having reteamed with director Don Siegel for the bleak prison drama *Escape from Alcatraz* (1979), Eastwood returned to *Every Which Way* territory with his next film, *Bronco Billy*. William 'Bronco Billy' McCoy (Eastwood) runs a low-rent, struggling wild-west show, touring the American Midwest. He employs a gallery of losers, many of whom he met in Fulsom Prison while serving a seven-year sentence for attempting to murder his adulterous wife. His motley crew comprises ringmaster 'Doc' Lynch (Scatman Crothers), one-armed wrangler 'Two-gun Lefty' LeBow (Bill McKinney), rope-trick artist Lasso Leonard James (Sam Bottoms), and Indian rattlesnake charmer Chief Big Eagle (Dan Vadis) and his wife, Lorraine Running Water (Sierra Pecheur). On their travels they harbour Antoinette Lily (Sondra Locke), a New York heiress, who is on her honeymoon in Idaho. Just prior to her thirtieth birthday, she has entered into a marriage of convenience with John Arlington (Geoffrey Lewis), so that she won't jeopardise her inheritance. But Arlington leaves her high and dry, and she hitches a ride with Billy's touring show, initially only to the next town, working as his assistant in a trick shooting and knife throwing act. But through newspapers she learns that she has been reported murdered, all part of a ruse by her stepmother and her attorney to get their hands on her money. The wild-west show is in a constant battle for money. Even so, they give free shows at orphanages and other state institutions, including the Mineral Wells Sanatorium for the mentally ill. When the big top burns down during a performance, the show looks sunk, but the inmates of Mineral Wells repay Billy's generosity over the years and sew together hundreds of American flags to make a new tent. During the course of the story, spoilt little rich girl Antoinette falls for homespun Billy, until by the end she decides to stay with the troupe, now riding high as their latest engagement is a roaring success.

Bronco Billy develops themes explored in *The Outlaw Josey Wales*, and *Billy*'s cast reinforces this. Billy, like Josey, has attracted an extended family of society's outcasts. Several of *Josey*'s actors are recast, including Sondra Locke, Sam Bottoms and Bill McKinney. Eastwood's regular comedy sidekick Geoffrey Lewis appears as disingenuous newlywed Arlington and William Prince played the crooked attorney. Walter Barnes (as Sheriff Dix), Dan Vadis (as Big Eagle, who keeps getting bitten during his rattlesnake dance), Woodrow Parfrey (as Mineral Wells' helpful Doctor Canterbury) and Douglas McGrath (investigator Lieutenant Wiecker) – all marked Malpaso reappearances for the actors. Bill McKinney compared the reliable Malpaso stable to John Ford's famous 'Stock Company' of supporting players, who were recalled for Eastwood's projects time and again. *Bronco Billy* boasted a cameo appearance by slow-talking Hank Worden, an actual member of Ford's 'Stock Company'. His most famous role was as 'Old Mose' Harper in Ford's iconic *The Searchers* (1956); here he plays a Shady Acres gas station mechanic, though he had also appeared briefly in *Every Which Way* as a trailer park manager.

Eastwood was sent the script by its authors Dennis E. Hackin and Neal Dobrofsky. Eastwood liked it and Locke, no doubt recognising a great role for herself as Antoinette Lily, liked it even more and pressed for it to be made. As part of the deal, Hackin and Dobrofsky produced the film for their own company, Second Street Films. Filming took place in Idaho, around Boise, Garden City and Nampa (with fairground scenes at the Meridian County Fair) and Ontario, Oregon. The stepmother-attorney subplot was filmed separately in New York. For the wild-west show performances, Alan Cartwright as Billy staged the trick riding scenes, acrobatically putting steed Buster through his paces. Rodeo roping champion J.W. Stoker doubled for Bottoms as Lasso Leonard for the trick roping act, while the film unit's outside catering was provided by the appropriately named 'High Noon Mobile Caterers'. Budgeted at $5 million and scheduled for eight to ten weeks, *Bronco Billy* cost only a little over $4 million, over a six-week shoot. This is perhaps its problem. The finished film feels rushed, as though more care could have been taken with the narrative. There's a great story in there somewhere and the novelisation tie-in reads much better than the film it publicises.

The eponymous title character bears the same name as Bronco (sometimes spelt Broncho) Billy Anderson, the first great cowboy screen star of the silent era, and Eastwood includes references to his own film mythology and western career. Eastwood sent up his cold gunfighter persona and *Variety* commented on Eastwood's 'comical slow burns', his eye twitching uncontrollably when he's riled. It's as if 'The Man with No Name' has been possessed by the spirit of Gene Autry. Billy talks in cowboy clichés, sings along to the radio and lives by his own high standards, like Autry's 'Cowboy Code'. He drives a bright red Oldsmobile convertible, with Colt pistol door handles and a set of steer's longhorns on the radiator. Billy is supposed to be a dead-eye shot but puts his first assistant in hospital when he grazes her with a throwing knife during 'Bronco Billy's Wheel of Fortune Death-Defying Shootout'. 'I'm the head ramrod', says Billy to his crew, recalling *Rawhide*. When Billy first meets Antoinette Lily, he can't help himself: 'You sure are pretty', he quotes from

Eastwood's own early *The First Travelling Saleslady*. But here the object of his affections scoffs sarcastically, 'Bronco, what an amusing name'. The hip New Yorkers find the country characters quaint, with Arlington calling the wild-west show 'wonderfully corny'. To Antoinette, Billy is, 'nothing but an illiterate cowboy' and 'a phoney ... from New Jersey'. Arriving at Mineral Wells, Billy tells Antoinette: 'It's a home for the criminally insane'; 'They should love your act', she snipes.

But to the children in the film, Bronco Billy is a hero. Billy takes time to talk to his 'little pards', the children who still hero worship him, in a world that doesn't believe in cowboys any more. He jokingly confronts a bunch of kids hanging around his Olds: 'Stick 'em up, or I'll plug ya!' The camera gives us a kid's-eye-view of heroic Billy, silhouetted against the sun. 'Ain't nobody faster than Bronco Billy', he assures them, twirling his pistols. He tells them they shouldn't be playing hooky from school, but they inform him it's Saturday. 'Yea, well I been riding late last night ... man's brain gets kind of fuzzy when he's been on the range'. In a clever piece of publicity, he gives the kids one free ticket each and tells them to bring their folks. At St Patrick's Orphanage, Billy tells the children tall stories of his exploits, of how he disarmed One-eyed Charley, reasoning, 'You should never kill a man unless it's absolutely necessary', which is hilarious given Eastwood's screen track record. The two 'little pards' Eastwood is talking to in this scene are his own children: Alison rides on Billy's horse; then at the picnic table she sits beside her father, while her brother Kyle sits opposite them.

As the film strives for Capraesque comedy-drama, it fails on both counts. Only two scenes realise the material's potential, and both are at the expense of Eastwood's screen persona. In the first, skint Billy pops into town to cash a three-dollar cheque at the Farmers and Merchants State Bank. As Billy deliberates ('I'd like it in two singles and four quarters ... no, make that two quarters and five dimes'), two armed felons try to rob the bank. A young boy is pushed to the ground, smashing his piggy bank. Billy can't stand by and watch such behaviour and, quick-drawing his pistol, disarms both men. 'Wow!' mouths the little boy. This scene plays like a parody of Eastwood's *Dirty Harry* exploits. When the press arrives to interview the hero, Billy uses his interview spot exposure on the news as an advert for the evening's wild-west show performance. Later, with the big top burned down and hard times coming, Billy decides to rob a train. The 'gang' forms up at a level crossing: Billy on Buster, the rest in Billy's Oldsmobile, wearing outlaw neckerchief masks and armed with shotguns, and bows and arrows. Antoinette pleads with Billy: 'You're living in a dream world. There are no more cowboys and Indians – that's in the past'. Billy tells her he was raised in a one-room tenement in New Jersey. He was a shoe salesman until he was 31. As a boy he never saw a cowboy, let alone the wide-open spaces of the west, except at the pictures: 'Deep down in my heart, I always wanted to be a cowboy. You only live once, you gotta give it your best shot'. But when the modern Union Pacific streamer appears, it zooms straight past the gang, who give chase, firing. 'Cowboys and Indians', says a kid, marvelling through the window. 'Of course, dear', answers his half-dozing mother.

The punch line of *Bronco Billy* is spoken by Lorraine Running Water, as she explains to Antoinette the appeal of being in the wild-west show: 'You can be anything you want … all you have to do is go out and become it'. When Antoinette realises Billy's for real, love blooms between these two mismatched characters, the cynic and the dreamer. 'Don't you find anything about your life bizarre?' Antoinette asks Billy. Won over, she becomes his cowgirl. 'Oh my God', she quickly realises, 'I'm even beginning to talk like you'. In the denouement, finally the show is a success, playing to a full house. Billy makes the audience believers and, for a moment, he makes us believers too.

Following previews anticipating its June 1980 release, many critics loved the film, with The *New York Post*, *New York Daily News* and *Variety* (which called it 'genuinely funny') printing positive reviews. *Village Voice* decided, 'It's time to take [Eastwood] seriously, not only as a popular phenomenon, but as one of the most honest and influential movie personalities of our time'. The *New York Times* thought Eastwood's performance as Billy was his 'warmest and most memorable' character. *Newsweek* was more realistic, 'The mock sentimentality is only a cover for the movie's genuine sentimentality about becoming the person you want to be'. It was rated 'PG' in the US, 'A' (later 'PG') in the UK. Star published a paperback tie-in, with country and western-style key art of Eastwood (dressed like Roy Rogers) leaping his horse through a poster advertising 'Clint Eastwood – Bronco Billy'. 'Saints and sinners, losers and winners, they're all in Bronco Billy's Wild West Show!' ran the blurb. Posters featuring this artwork were later replaced with a portrait of Eastwood in a denim shirt, not even wearing a cowboy hat, with the line 'His latest. His fastest. His funniest!' and several positive press quotes, including the *New York Times*'s 'The best and funniest Clint Eastwood movie'.

The trailer, presenting non-stop comedy, wasn't representative of the film and word travelled fast among filmgoers. *Bronco Billy* grossed $15 million in the US, eventually rising to $25 million, which isn't bad for a film costing $4 million, but Eastwood saw it as a financial disappointment. Cowboy Billy was an anachronism in the modern world; unfortunately so was the film. In an interview for the French TV show *Etoiles et Toiles* in December 1982, Eastwood said, 'It was an old-fashioned theme, probably too old fashioned since the film didn't do as well as we hoped. But if, as a film director, I ever wanted to say something, you'll find it in *Bronco Billy*'. It remains one of the star's favourite films.

Following *Every Which Way*'s lead, *Bronco Billy* included a country and western soundtrack, again supervised by Snuff Garrett and music director Stephen Dorff. Singer Merle Haggard (backed by 'The Strangers') appeared on stage in the Ranch Club in the film playing a slowy, 'Misery and Gin', which went to number two in the Country Music Charts. Even better, Haggard's duet with Eastwood on 'Barroom Buddies' (which Billy sings along to on the radio) went to number one. On the back of this success, Eastwood formed his own record label, Viva Records, in partnership with Garrett. Other songs included 'Bayou Lullaby' sung by Penny De Haven, plus two schmaltzy ballads from Ronnie Milsap: 'Cowboys and Clowns' and the triumphant end titles' 'Bronco Billy'. The former, as candyfloss as they come, states that people love 'Cowboys and Clowns' without asking why: 'You're everybody's hero for a while'. 'Bronco Billy' is even more sentimental:

> So dream on Bronco Billy, it's one Hell of a life you chose.
> Keep those spurs a-jingling, 'cos every cowboy knows.
> When you saddle your last pony, he'll be calling by and by.
> And you'll ride that final roundup for the Big Boss in the sky.

Any Which Way You Can (1980)

Eastwood's next film, *Any Which Way You Can*, his third comedy in two years, again relied heavily on barroom buddy-style country and western tracks as its backdrop. It kicks off with 'Beers to You', Eastwood's lilting country duet with Ray Charles: 'Beers to you, old amigo! For all the good times and here's to all the women that we've been through'. Yes folks, it's monkey business as usual for Philo and Clyde.

With *Every Which Way*'s huge success, Kronsberg was contracted to concoct another story but didn't reprise any of the supporting characters, except Clyde. Sanford Sherman instead wrote a direct sequel to the first movie, reprising all the major characters, with a small screen title acknowledging they were 'based on characters created by Jeremy Joe Kronsberg'. Kronsberg had also written another orang-utan movie called *Going Ape!* which he eventually directed in 1981, featuring Jessica Walter. It was seen by Eastwood as direct competition to his orang-utan franchise, and Eastwood and Kronsberg settled the matter out of court.

In *Any Which Way You Can*, Philo, still managed by 24-hour mechanic Orville and accompanied everywhere by Clyde, pummels his latest bare-knuckle opponent and decides to retire because he's becoming desensitised to the violence. But he's approached by New York hood and gambler James Beekman (Harry Guardino) to fight Jack Wilson (William Smith) in a 'Fight of the Century' in Jackson Hole, Wyoming, for a $25,000 purse – win or lose. Philo agrees but is then convinced by Orville, Ma and Lynn (who is back on the scene, now in love with Philo) to renege on the deal. The mob kidnaps Lynn, forcing Philo and crew to travel to Jackson. With punters crowding into Jackson from all over the country, Philo manages to free Lynn, with unexpected help from Wilson. The fight's officially off, but the two brawlers decide to see who will win for their own honour in a long drawn-out bout through the streets of Jackson. 'It's the most knuckle-bustin', gut wrenchin', brain-scramblin', butt-bruisin', lip-splittin' brawl of all time!' as the film's trailer put it. It ends with Philo, his arm broken, defeating Wilson, before heading home with Clyde and Lynn.

Any Which Way wisely recast most of the main actors: Sondra Locke, Ruth Gordon and Geoffrey Lewis returned as Lynn, Ma and Orville. Locke, still Eastwood's off-screen lover, again gets to sing a couple of numbers in the Palomino, including the tactless 'One Too Many Women in Your Life': 'The one you say you love and the one

4.2 'It'll Knock You Out': *Every Which Way But Loose*'s sequel *Any Which Way You Can* (1980) reprised the Philo and Clyde partnership to great success; US one-sheet poster, courtesy Ian Caunce Collection.

you call your wife'. As crotchety Ma, Gordon delivered lines like nobody else could, berating biscuit-thieving Clyde with 'Come back with my Oreos, you hairy ass!' The key Black Widows – John Quade, William O'Connell, Bill McKinney, Dan Vadis and Roy Jenson – all reappeared. Eastwood associates Harry Guardino (*Dirty Harry*, *The Enforcer*) and Michael Cavanaugh (*The Enforcer*, *The Gauntlet*) played the New York mobsters who want a piece of the bare-knuckle action. Singers Glen Campbell and Fats Domino both appeared, performing songs in bars: the Lion Dollar Cowboy Bar and the Palomino, respectively.

Filming took place in the summer of 1980 at Bakersfield in California (the motel and zoo scenes) and at the picturesque town of Jackson Hole in Wyoming, including the elk antler archway in the town square and the Ramada Snow King Inn (where Beekman and the mob check in). With Jackson Hole as the setting for the final bout, what better a name for Philo's opponent than Jack Wilson, also the name of Jack Palance's gunslinger in *Shane*, lensed in the vicinity of Jackson Hole in 1951. Stone-faced tough-guy William Smith, cast as Wilson, shares a little of Palance's viperous menace. His prolonged slugfest with Philo, the most drawn-out punch-up of Eastwood's career, features two signatures that reappear throughout his starring roles: a close-up punch aimed straight into the camera lens (which appears in many of his films, including *A Fistful of Dollars*, *Play Misty for Me* and *The Gauntlet*) and the half-turn feint, as though to turn away from his opponent, before swivelling and releasing an unexpected punch, first seen at the start of his pool room fight in *Coogan's Bluff*.

This time out, Clyde is the star of the show, his contribution much more prominent than his set dressing in *Every Which Way*. This is mostly at the expense of Orville, with Lewis barely featuring here. Manis didn't reprise his role, with an anonymous, younger, livelier-looking ape, 'supplied by Gentle Jungle Inc.' and trained by Boone Narr, cast instead. Clyde wears a wristwatch throughout and like all great actors he steals scenes by hardly doing anything at all. It must be soul-destroying for the supporting players – after all those years at acting school and finally making it onscreen, to know everyone in the audience is looking at the ape. Clyde likes his beer (swigging bottles and cans in bars), enjoys deploying obscene hand gestures, dismantling cars and has a tendency, when left unaccompanied, to defecate in police cars. Clyde again woos a lady orang-utan, with their motel 'love scene' courtship intercut with Philo and Lynn's monkeying around in the next room. In addition to these running gags, Clyde has his own solo showcase, accompanied by Cliff Crofford's 'Orangutan Hall of Fame', swinging on a tyre, rocking in a hammock, playing basketball and other such goofiness. Eastwood, still in denims, T-shirt and cowboy hat, is the ideal underplayed foil to his hairy partner, never surprised by his companion's behaviour. In a bar, a cigar-smoking tough tries to pick a fight with Clyde, who bends a metal handrail, steals the tough's cigar and plants a slurped kiss on his lips, while in another scene, Clyde is sneaked into a motel in drag, disguised as 'Aunt Hortence'. The film's tone is summed up by two fuddy-duddy tourists: while tootling along the highway, the wife complains that Californian folks are 'a little peculiar', as they pass Philo, Orville and Clyde, standing in a row on the verge, urinating.

Any Which Way is an improvement on its sluggish predecessor. It boasts better direction (by Eastwood's stunt co-ordinator Buddy Van Horn) and a coherent story with superior gags. In acknowledgement of their contribution to the first film's success, the Black Widows feature prominently. Still on Philo's trail following their humiliation, the Widows, now bearded, vow to nail Philo. While chasing Philo's General Motors pickup, the bikers drive under a road-resurfacing truck. Now coated in rapidly solidifying tar, the gang members freeze like statues, as they try to confront Philo, and collapse in a blackened heap. When the tar is removed, they lose all their body hair and have to draw on eyebrows and moustaches and adopt a variety of outlandish, brightly coloured wigs. For example, Roy Jenson sports then-fashionable Bo Derek *10*-style beaded braids. A traffic cop who pulls them for speeding can't stop laughing and doesn't have the heart to book them, noting, 'You are a walking violation of the laws of nature'. In the film's best gag, the bikers form up at a stop light beside Philo and Clyde's pickup. 'Right turn Clyde', quips Philo, a signal for Clyde to throw a right turn hand signal out of the passenger window, a swinging hook which clouts Cholla and sends him sprawling, his fall toppling the rest of the Widows, domino fashion.

Trailers promised 'faster, funnier and feistier than ever!' continuing: 'They're coming from every which way they can, any which way they can, cos they're onto a sure thing – Clint 'n' Clyde are Back!' It was rated 'PG' in the US for its Christmas 1980 release and was dismissed by critics, unconverted by the first film's success. In the UK it was 'AA', since re-rated '15'. It ran into problems with a scene depicting the mobsters watching a fight between a mongoose and a rattlesnake, which has since been abridged; TV prints have also toned down the language. In the US, the film took $40 million on its initial release, which has since risen to a lifetime gross of over $70 million. The 'Beers to You' Charles-Eastwood duet was a minor hit, while Glen Campbell's 'Any Which Way You Can' reached number 10 on the country music chart. Other songs featured on the soundtrack, again supervised by Garrett and directed by Dorff, included 'Whiskey Heaven' (sung by Fats Domino), Jim Stafford's 'Cow Patti', 'You're the Reason God Made Oklahoma', 'Any Way You Want Me', the instrumental 'Cotton-Eyed Clint' (played by the Texas Opera Company) and John Durrill's memorable play-out, 'The Good Guys and the Bad Guys'.

As the country and western explosion continued, further films capitalised on the 'Clyde' movies' success. In *The Cannonball Run* (1981), Peter Fonda led a biker gang in a massed fistfight against the Cannonball racers, including Dean Martin, Sammy Davis Jnr, Jackie Chan and Roger Moore. By the time of *Cannonball Run II* (1984 – also scripted by Stanford Sherman), with Shirley MacLaine disguised as a nun (though not called Sister Sara) and Mel Tillis's stretch limo driven by 'Bobby Beronsini's Orang-utan' (as he's billed in the credits) dressed as a chauffeur, it was Reynolds who was aping Eastwood's success.

Pink Cadillac (1989)

Pink Cadillac was a last attempt by Eastwood at a knockabout comedy. Closer in rowdy tone to the 'Clyde' movies than *Bronco Billy*, the film is a strange choice – a not-very-funny comedy with little to recommend it – given that Eastwood had just revisited his 'Dirty Harry' persona with the successful *The Dead Pool* and gained critical acclaim with jazz biopic *Bird*. In *Pink Cadillac*, Eastwood starred as Tommy Nowack, a modern-day bounty hunter who works for 'Buddy's Bail Bonds' in Sacramento. He is a 'track-'em-and-snatch-'em' skip tracer, apprehending criminals who've been granted bail but skipped town. He is assigned to track down Lou Ann McGuinn (Bernadette Peters), who has just taken the rap for her husband Roy's counterfeiting scheme and is out on bail. In revenge, she steals his car – a prized vintage pink Cadillac – and goes on the run to her sister's in Reno, only to discover that the car contains the counterfeit cash. Roy's gang – ex-cons who are now members of the Birthright Militia, a racist organisation which has a redoubt in the sierras – gives chase. Nowack captures Lou Ann in Reno, as she is about to gamble the fake money hoping to win some real cash. But the militia kidnaps her baby, and Tommy and Lou Ann must confront the extremists in their woodland hideaway, escaping with the baby and driving off in the pink Cadillac to a life together in their new capacity as 'Nowack & McGuinn Skip-tracing Bureau'.

Written by John Escrow and directed by Wayne 'Buddy' Van Horn, *Pink Cadillac* has its moments, but they are sprinkled thinly. For openers, Eastwood is too old for Nowack. Given to donning various disguises to apprehend his quarries, Nowack is introduced in the film as 'Crazy Carl Cummings', a fast-talking radio DJ who telephones bail-jumper Randy Bates (Gary Klar) and convinces him he has won a competition to spend a VIP evening with Dolly Parton. Nowack also impersonates a rodeo clown at the 'Frontier Days Rodeo' (to apprehend a bucking bull rider), a moustachioed high roller in a gold lamé jacket (named 'Darryl Hasselbach, casino vice president') and a baccy-chewing racist redneck, 'Will Van Slyke', eager to join the Birthright Militia. These characterisations allow Eastwood to deploy a variety of silly accents and costumes.

Pink Cadillac was shot in late 1988 on location in California and Nevada, including the gambling mecca of Reno, Nevada; the credits thank the 'Eldorado Hotel & Casino' and 'John Ascuaga's Nugget Hotel/Casino'. With Eastwood no longer casting Sondra Locke, his female lead was Bernadette Peters, who had been hilarious opposite Steve Martin in *The Jerk* (1979). Peters' bubbly persona and excellent timing with one-liners worked well opposite Eastwood's underplaying, resembling an odd-couple comedy version of *The Gauntlet*. Nowack tells Lou Ann his 'firm policy on gun control' – 'If there's a gun around, I wanna be the person controlling it'. Outside a casino, a drunken vagrant flashes Lou Ann. 'Waddaya think?' asks the drunk hopefully; 'Looks like a penis', quips Lou Ann, 'Only smaller'. Even so, *Variety* noted that Peters and Eastwood 'developed little visible rapport and zero sexual chemistry'. Hidden among the cast was Frances Fisher, as Lou Ann's sister Dina. Fisher and Eastwood began an off-screen relationship during this film, in the wake of his separation from Locke in late 1988.

James Cromwell (later of *Space Cowboys*) had a supporting role as a motel check-in clerk; Mara Corday (from *Tarantula*) was a dice game croupier; wild-eyed Jimmie F. Skaggs (a drug dealer from *Lethal Weapon*) played militiaman Billy Dunston, while the rest of the militiamen were an unmemorable, rent-a-mob bunch. Eastwood comedy regulars Geoffrey Lewis and Bill McKinney both appear in *Pink Cadillac*, in an attempt to recapture the fun of the 'Clyde' films. Lewis played Ricky Z, a zonked-out hippy forger who runs 'Nirvana Publications', providing false identities to fugitives, while McKinney did his trademark simpleton as a bartender in Colterville. Jim Carrey can fleetingly be seen on stage impersonating Elvis in Reno; 'Post Nuclear Elvis Lounge Act Conceived and Performed by James Carrey', states the end credits. Canadian rock star Bryan Adams also has a cameo, playing a gas station attendant cleaning a car windscreen as Nowack pulls onto the forecourt – Nowack asks him if he's seen a blonde in a pink Cadillac. 'Only in my dreams' answers Adams.

Clearly intended as comic relief in the manner of the Black Widows biker gang, the Birthright Militia is the film's biggest enemy, in more ways than one. Their racist attitudes and survivalist mentality strike a dissonant note. In camouflage gear, they are 'speed freaks with automatic weapons' who plan to use the counterfeit money to stockpile arms. The finale, a familiar Eastwood shootout with car and truck crashes, explosions and hails of machine-gun fire, at least woke audiences up for the fade-out.

Pink Cadillac was unpopular with almost every reviewer who was forced to sit through it and managed only $12 million in the US in May 1989, when it was released opposite *Indiana Jones and the Last Crusade*. Though deemed a failure, this was still six times what *White Hunter Black Heart* took the following year. Richard Freedman of *Newhouse News Services* wrote of its 'general torpid pace; it's almost total lack of any cinematic energy ... a 122-minute dozer'. Fuensanta Plaza in her book *Clint Eastwood/ Malpaso* deemed it 'possibly the most underrated of Malpaso films', while *Variety* reported: 'May be the weakest Eastwood release ever'. *Pink Cadillac*'s trailer aimed low and still missed. It was rated 'PG-13' in the US but wasn't released to UK cinemas, instead suffering the ignominy of 'straight-to-video'. It was rated '12' by the BBFC in November 1989 and then re-rated '15' (for one unnecessary utterance of 'fuck' by militiaman Waycross) for a belated video release by Warner Bros in 1991. Warner Bros at least cashed in on the soundtrack. Again assembled by Steve Dorff, the songs this time were rather more 'Country Rock', the presence of Dolly Parton ('Two Doors Down') and Hank Williams ('There's a Tear in My Beer') notwithstanding. Celine Dion sang Bryan Adams's 'Drive All Night', while rockers Southern Pacific played the film out rousingly with 'Any Way the Wind Blows'.

All of Eastwood's films, even his most violent, contain moments of humour, and it is perhaps on these that Eastwood's comedic skills should be judged. He's fine playing comedy in the 'Clyde' films, where his tough guy persona is depicted just about intact, though when Eastwood 'plays funny' he's often forced. His understated double-takes and one-liners in *For a Few Dollars More*, *The Good, the Bad and the Ugly*, *Kelly's Heroes*, *High Plains Drifter* or even the ultra violent 'Dirty Harry' films provoke more genuine laughs than his comedy roles. Eastwood once said in an interview with Iain Johnstone, 'If [the audience is] not laughing, it's not a comedy', which explains why misfire *City Heat* is discussed in 'The Cops' chapter.

PART FIVE
THE DRAMAS

Throughout his career, Clint Eastwood has made several adult-themed films, whose plots conclude in tragedy – a risky game to play when unhappy endings often spell box office disaster. The stories are sometimes biographical, featuring characters and plots which share themes and dreams, usually a quest to achieve a seemingly unattainable goal against all odds. These quests take the form of a cross-country odyssey to become a star in *Honkytonk Man* (1982), an African elephant hunt in *White Hunter Black Heart* (1990), a lunar mission in *Space Cowboys* (2000), and a boxing world title bid in *Million Dollar Baby* (2004). Six of the seven films discussed in this chapter, including *Bird* (1988), *Midnight in the Garden of Good and Evil* (1997) and *Mystic River* (2003), close with the death of one of the main protagonists. All seven are directed by Eastwood and he appears in four of them. With these films Eastwood has proved not only that his directorial talent for hard-hitting drama can be much more powerful when dealing with subjects outside his action movie cannon, but also that they could be just as lucrative and far more critically revered.

Honkytonk Man (1982)

The American tragedy *Honkytonk Man* was Clint Eastwood's first hint at the path his later career – directorial and acting – would take. Made immediately after the special effects extravaganza *Firefox* (1982), it was a Depression Era story of a drifting Honkytonk player, Red Stovall (Eastwood). It was based on the 1980 novel of the same name by Clancy Carlile, who also adapted the screenplay. Red, whose life is one of smoky barrooms, bootleg whisky, flop houses and late hours, has tuberculosis and suffers coughing fits, which are beginning to destroy his career and his voice. Having received an invitation to audition for a guest spot at the Grand Ole Opry in Nashville, the promised land for country singers, he arrives at his sister Emmy's ranch in Oklahoma in his flashy burgundy Lincoln Continental. Work has dried up for Emmy's family, dust storms ravage their scant crops, and they plan to relocate to California. In bad shape, drunkard Red convinces Emmy to allow her youngest son, Whit (Eastwood's real-life son Kyle), to be his driver on the trip to Tennessee. Grandpa Wagoneer (John McIntire), a native of Tennessee, tags along too, to return to his birthplace. The trio ride the dusty roads through Oklahoma to Arkansas, surviving on their wits, stealing chickens, avoiding the police, racking up traffic violations (Whit doesn't have a licence, the car has no ownership registration) and picking up an unwelcome passenger, Marlene (Alexa Kenin), a 16-year-old girl who also dreams of singing at the Opry. When their car breaks down in Noxpater, Arkansas, Grandpa completes the last leg of his journey by bus, while Red drunkenly sleeps with Marlene, before skipping town. Whit finds Red in Nashville and they attend the audition, which Red fails when a coughing fit curtails his performance. But a representative from Burnside Records offers him a recording deal: $20 a tune and a $100 advance, but no royalties. If one of his songs becomes a hit, success is assured. Red agrees and cuts several songs, including his theme 'Honkytonk Man', a tune which he had written with lyrical help from Whit on the road. But the recording sessions take their toll and having finished the last track, Red isn't fit to carry on. Marlene has caught up with them and in Red's apartment a doctor pronounces that he hasn't got long to go. Soon afterwards, Red dies and is buried in Nashville cemetery. As Whit and Marlene walk away, they pass a car. On the radio, an announcer introduces Red Stovall singing 'Honkytonk Man', which is about to become a hit.

A Warner Bros-Malpaso production, *Honkytonk Man* was shot on location in five weeks for $3 million. The crew lensed action in Carson City and Dayton, Nevada, in Sacramento and Bird's Landing, California, and in Nashville. Red was a character of unusual depth for Eastwood. When he talks about the one true love of his life, Mary Simms, who was married to someone else, it's with sad regret: 'She was a fine, decent, faithful woman – at least until I met her'. Her husband threatened to break Red's fingers, so he could never play the guitar again, and it's to her Red cries out on his deathbed. *Honkytonk Man*'s cast is one of its strengths. The family of sharecroppers, decked out in Dust Bowl dungarees, are living Walker-Evans portraits. Verna Bloom played Red's ruddy-faced sister Emmy; Matt Clark played her husband Virgil. John McIntire, an actor who has close associations with classic westerns and the TV series *Wagon Train*, played Grandpa, Mr Wagoneer, a role originally offered to James Stewart. In *Honkytonk Man*, strong links with the past enhance the drama, as three generations of the same family are presented on screen.

Linda Hopkins made a memorable cameo as jazz singer Flossie King, in the black Top Hat Club, a gin joint which looks like rushes for *Bird*. Eastwood can be seen in her backing band, at the piano, joining in the boogie-woogie. Newcomer Alexa Kenin was enthusiastic as Marlene, who dreams of being a star, 'Marlene Moonbeam', a dream she'll never fulfil. At the close of the film, it's implied that she's carrying Red's baby. Real country singers, including Marty Robbins (who died shortly before the film's release), Ray Price and Porter Wagoner (as fellow Grand Ole Opry hopeful Dusty), also sang in the movie. For the role of Whit (nicknamed 'Hoss' by Red), Eastwood looked no further than his own backyard. He cast Kyle, his own son, in a plum role. Kyle had appeared briefly in *Breezy*, *The Outlaw Josey Wales* and *Bronco Billy*, while a piece of graffiti reading 'KYLE' can be seen on the wall of an underground station in *Dirty Harry*. He was coached by Sondra Locke and his performance was very good – father and son worked well together, their natural chemistry one of the best aspects of the film. As Kyle noted after filming: 'I enjoyed stealing the chickens and I really liked driving the car'. Deciding not to follow his father into acting, Kyle is now an accomplished jazz bass player, who has released the albums *From Here to There* (1998), *Paris Blue* (2004) and *Now* (2006).

Honkytonk Man is filled with country music and Eastwood sings several numbers. As the tall Oklahoman honkytonk man, in his Stetson, suit, bootlace tie and cowboy boots, Eastwood looks like a guitar-picking Walt Coogan but is obviously based on such balladeers as Hank Williams. 'If Clint were a failure', said co-star Verna Bloom, 'He'd be Red'. Eastwood's voice here is his familiar whispered vocal (rather than the richer baritone of his earlier album *Cowboy Favourites*), more appropriate for the cigarette-smoking, TB-ridden crooner, especially on his last ever performance in the recording studio, the sentimental 'Honkytonk Man', a song 'about lost love, in waltz time', as Red describes it:

So I lost my woman and you lost your man
And who knows who's right or who's wrong.
But I've got my guitar and I've got a plan.
Throw your arms around this honkytonk man.

Carlile had written several songs for the book, which Eastwood didn't use. Instead Eastwood enlisted Snuff Garrett and Steven Dorff to write new music, which was released to tie-in with the film, via a soundtrack LP and four singles.

Honkytonk Man is a mixture of knockabout adventure – a life on the road and on the run – and nostalgic tragedy. Early scenes depict Red and Whit's escapades, particularly their brushes with the law, the pair zooming along in their maroon Lincoln Continental (in Carlile's book, a black Packard) and Red bathing in a water trough and then being chased by an irate bull. Permanently sozzled on bootleg liquor ('real panther piss'), Eastwood subtly underplays some of the best comedy scenes of his career. But critics were unconvinced: 'Eastwood never overdoes his acting – maybe he can't', noted the *New York Post*, 'always playing it very close to the vest'. In one scene he is caught chicken rustling and thrown into jail in Tallaboosa. Outside a local picture house, Whit sees a poster advertising the appropriately titled Buck Jones western *When a Man Sees Red* (1934); the poster depicts a jailbreak, with riders dislodging the jail bars with ropes attached to their horses. Inspired, Whit pulls out the jailhouse's bars with the Lincoln. For Eastwood's turn as the bad-living drifter, one of his most famous props is back – Eastwood smokes cigarettes throughout, one of the rare times the health-conscious actor lit up on screen since *High Plains Drifter* (1973).

Honkytonk Man shares the homespun, small-town country atmosphere of *Bronco Billy*, but the realism of the Depression Era setting and the tragic last half-hour mark the film out as a more mature work. The production design is convincing, with authentic sets and costumes by Edward Carfagno. Bruce Surtees' acrid, handsome photography chokes the screen with Ozark authenticity. The mid-thirties deprivation is one familiar to Eastwood's own family. In a notable scene Grandpa gives his grandson Whit his recollections of the Cherokee Strip Land Rush in September 1893. The wistful link between the past and the present has never been stronger in Eastwood's oeuvre than it is here.

The enticing prospect of action man Eastwood as a tubercular country and western singer proved less than contagious at the box office and the film took a disappointing $4.5 million. Hardcore Eastwood fans did show up and then wished they hadn't. The sepia adwork featured portraits of the Eastwoods and the tagline: 'The boy is on his way to becoming a man. The man is on his way to becoming a legend'. It was rated 'PG' in the US, '15' in the UK, on its release in Christmas 1982. The *New York Daily News* thought Red was 'an appealingly good natured but rather dull character'. *Variety* called the film 'a meandering and downbeat tale where [Eastwood] seldom gets to exhibit much of the bravura his fans will long for'. *Motion Picture Product Digest* saw 'a folksy, boring movie that will really test the loyalty of Eastwood's fans'. Iain Johnstone, in *The Man With No Name*, christens it 'Bronchial Billy'. 'Clint looks the classic country and western singer', praised *Newsday*, 'but the scenario's ultimate ambition is kitschy bathos, to make you weep into your popcorn', comparing the finale to Garbo's death scene in *Camille*.

At the other extreme, Norman Mailer called it 'the finest movie made about the country plains life since *The Last Picture Show* ... one of the saddest movies I've seen in a long time, yet, on reflection, terrific'. The *New York Post* was similarly positive: 'The pace is slow, very country, but it rises to touching moments ... not all perfect by any means, but ultimately a story of occasional awkward truths'. In the UK, *The Guardian* dubbed it 'a classic American tragedy'. In France, the film has a reputation as an heir to John Ford's *The Grapes of Wrath* (1940), which must please Eastwood, as Ford's film is one of his personal favourites. François Guérif in *Clint Eastwood: From Rawhide to Pale Rider* (1986) wrote: 'Despite one or two slow passages, *Honkytonk Man* is, to this day, Eastwood's most accomplished film'. Richard Schickel, later Eastwood's official biographer, also praised the film in the 20 December 1982 issue of *Time*, 'Eastwood has fashioned a marvellously unfashionable movie, as quietly insinuating as one of Red's honkytonk melodies ... As both actor and director Eastwood has never been more laconic ... it is persistence rather than big talent or bold stroke heroism that *Honkytonk Man* wants to celebrate'.

But *Honkytonk Man* isn't Eastwood's *Grapes of Wrath*. It's a moving story, constricted by its own star's screen image and audience preconceptions of it, in the same way that *Hang 'Em High* isn't his *The Ox-Bow Incident*, or *High Plains Drifter* his *Hell's Hinges*, but 'Clint Eastwood Movie' variations on these stories. Eastwood strove to make good films for a general audience, films which appealed to the nostalgia in everyone, tugged heartstrings and spoke across generations. Unfortunately with Eastwood still widely regarded at the box office as an action man, his audiences weren't ready just yet for this radical transformation.

Bird (1988)

Following a return to his most famous action man, Dirty Harry Callahan, in *The Dead Pool* (1988), a sure-fire box office hit, Eastwood's lifelong love of jazz reached fruition in *Bird*, his screen biography of alto sax legend Charlie 'Yardbird' Parker (known as 'Bird'). To those who weren't aware of Eastwood's penchant for jazz, *Bird* was an unusual choice. Eastwood had actually seen Parker perform in 1946 on the West Coast in the 'Jazz at the Philharmonic' gig at the Shrine Auditorium in Oakland

and was smitten. By this point in his career, Parker had been a heroin addict for nine years and 1947 saw him take six months off in an effort to kick the habit. Eastwood, an accomplished musician and composer himself, can be seen playing the piano in many of his films: the first time this happens is in *Thunderbolt and Lightfoot* (1974), but he also tinkles the ivories in *Honkytonk Man*, *City Heat* and *In the Line of Fire*, among others. In *Escape from Alcatraz* he plays the accordion and the actor is sometimes photographed at the piano during interviews.

Beginning with Parker's suicide attempt by ingesting iodine in September 1954, *Bird* recounted the life of the altoist through flashbacks, detailing the artist's career highs and lows. Parker (played by Forest Whitaker) rose to prominence in the forties popularising be-bop style jazz with trumpeter Dizzy Gillespie (Samuel E. Wright): if Parker's late-night hedonistic lifestyle (he was an alcoholic junkie) represented the artist at his most self-destructive, then Gillespie was his antithesis, but their collaborations have remained legendary. Parker became so revered that there was even a club in New York called 'Birdland' in his honour. The most important theme in *Bird* is Parker's relationship with young dancer Chan Richardson (Diane Venora), later his wife, with whom he had two children, Pree and Baird (three-year-old Pree died of pneumonia in 1954). Through patches of attempted sobriety, when Parker kicked heroin but drank to compensate, his lifestyle brought soaring Bird crashing to earth. With rock 'n' roll on the rise in the mid-fifties, Parker found his style of jazz out of fashion. On 12 March 1955, he died of a heart attack at the home of Baroness Pannonica de Koenigswarter, known as 'Baroness Nica'. A medical examiner at the scene estimated Parker was 65 years old – Parker was 34.

Bird was written by Joel Oliansky, based on *Life in E-flat*, the memoirs of Chan Richardson. When Warner Bros acquired the script, Eastwood was immediately interested in directing a biography of one of his heroes. *Bird*, then titled 'Yardbird Suite' after a Parker composition, was originally conceived in 1982 as a vehicle for Richard Prior. Later singer Prince was linked to the project, but Forest Whitaker was eventually cast as Parker. Texan-born stage actor Whitaker was perfect as Parker, with his convincingly mimed sax work adding to the authenticity of the film. Whitaker's younger brother Damon played Parker for the flashbacks to Bird's youth in Kansas. Samuel E. Wright played Dizzy Gillespie, while Parker collaborator Red Rodney was portrayed by Michael Zelniker. Despite some awful hairstyles, Diane Venora gave a moving performance as Chan, while Anna Levine (later Anna Thomson) appeared as Parker's one-time lover Audrey.

With a $9 million budget, Eastwood filmed *Bird* over nine weeks, from late 1987 to early 1988, on location in California, in the Sacramento Valley, Los Angeles and Pasadena, with New York's legendary West 52nd Street shot on the standing back-lot street at Warner's Burbank Studios. The street was dressed to resemble the New York of the forties, with neon club signs advertising 'Club Carousel', '18 Club', '3 Deuces' and 'Onyx'. The exterior of Parker's honorary 'Birdland' venue, opened in 1949 at 1678 Broadway, was also lensed there. In reality, Parker was eventually banned from the venue for firing the entire orchestra during his stint as 'Parker with

5.1 Jazz Man: Clint Eastwood directs Forest Whitaker as altoist Charlie Parker, the 'Yardbird', in jazz biopic *Bird* (1988), Eastwood's best film of the eighties. Image courtesy Kevin Wilkinson Collection.

Strings'. Reflecting a shift in public taste as times changed, *Bird*'s 'New York' set was redressed for the fifties scenes: the area now seedier, with sleazy strip clubs replacing the jumping jazz joints.

Throughout the thirties and forties, jazz was developing from the black New Orleans style, to the white 'Dixie Jazz' and swing. Parker and bespectacled trumpeter Gillespie were progenitors of the cult of 'be-bop' on 52nd Street in the early forties, though strangely the film makes no mention of another key Parker collaborator, Miles Davis. If more traditional jazz improvised on the tune, be-bop improvised on the chords. Parker was a dynamic saxophonist and playing the frenetic speed-rush of be-bop established him as one of the finest, most popular sax players of all time. The inflections and variant tones he produced from his instrument are almost vocal in their variety and effect. A listen to Parker's 1946 classic 'Yardbird Suit', with Miles Davis accompanying him on trumpet, confirms his genius: the fluid, seemingly effortless runs and his gift for improvisation. Parker's sense of humour, which doesn't transmit to the film, can be seen in the titles he gave to compositions. His punchy 'Relaxing in Camarillo' from February 1947 with Howard McGee on trumpet was recorded shortly after his release from the State Mental Institution at Camarillo.

Charles Christopher Parker Jnr was born in Kansas City, 29 August 1920. He learned to play the baritone horn at school, then in 1933 he switched to a $45 alto sax his mother Addie bought him from a pawn shop. She worked nights as a cleaner and teenage Parker hung out at the local jazz clubs. He started to play on the Kansas City scene, but a pivotal moment in the young man's life occurred in 1936 when he was laughed off stage for his inept performance while playing with Count Basie's band. During Parker's solo, Jo Jones, the drummer, dropped a cymbal to the ground, the smash halting the band in their tracks. Eastwood uses this moment, known as 'gonging out', in *Bird* and makes the imagery of the flying cymbal a recurrent symbol of this key turning point in Parker's life. In Eastwood's version, the band's sax soloist for this humiliating Reno jam session is Buster Franklin, who asks young Charlie where he's from. 'Just around', is Parker's shy reply. Franklin shows up eight years later on 52nd Street to hear that Gillespie has a new star playing with him: Charlie Parker. Franklin laughs that the last time he saw Parker, 'He couldn't play "Come to Jesus" in whole notes'. Entering the club, Franklin discovers Parker and Gillespie tearing the place apart with their performance. Having witnessed the reborn, transformed 'Charlie from Just Around', Franklin walks home with his saxophone under his arm and then despondently throws his instrument off a bridge into the river.

Bird tells Parker's story via a complicated series of flashbacks and flash-forwards through his life – sometimes the only clue to the shift in eras is Chan Richardson's hairstyle. An authentic jazz milieu is carefully created by Eastwood and his production designer, Edward Carfagno: the neon-lit streets of New York, parties with guests 'cooling out' on reefers, imagery of drifting smoke, blinding spotlights, silhouettes and shades – the cool nocturnal world of hep cats, dolls and frenetic, late-night drug-fuelled performances, half-remembered and woken by weary, bleary dawns. The film's tone is often bleak, as befits the story of a depressive whose search for a fix destroyed his marriage, career and life. Parker had a history of nervous breakdowns and attempted suicide following the death of his daughter. He was busted for possession and temporarily lost his Cabaret Card work permit and was unreliable, uncontrollable and eventually unemployable. By the time of his death, Parker was suffering from perforated ulcers, liver and heart disease, and internal bleeding, after a lifetime of hooch, smack and carousing – a late-night life lived at the wrong end of the day.

There are also moments of tenderness in his wasted story and even humour. One of the most successful passages in the film is when Parker's group is joined by white trumpeter Red Rodney, who secures them society gigs, including a riotous Jewish wedding. Parker embarks on a tour of the Deep South, with his quintet: Rodney, Gillespie, and rhythm section Billy Prince and John Wilson. Rodney is the only member of the otherwise all-black band able to enter 'White Only' shops to buy supplies. Posters advertise 'The King of Bebop Charles "Yardbird" Parker featuring Albino Red – Blues Singer Extraordinaire'. At gigs, performing for black audiences, they pass Rodney off as an albino as he sings his featured number 'Albino Red Blues', actually performed by the real Red Rodney on the soundtrack.

Bird's great strength is its soundtrack, with many Parker originals deployed. The film ends with the legend: 'This picture is dedicated to musicians everywhere'. Leonard 'Lennie' Niehaus, Eastwood's music collaborator from *Tightrope* (1984) onwards, was an alto saxophonist and arranger who had played with Stan Kenton's band. He moved into film and TV scoring in the sixties, working as an arranger for Jerry Fielding. Niehaus's sax style was influenced by Bud Shank, Art Pepper and Parker. Niehaus was an excellent choice as music supervisor for *Bird*; he was also able to teach Whitaker authentic fingering techniques on the sax. While researching, Eastwood met Chan Richardson, who gave him a selection of her husband's old reel-to-reel recordings, some of which were used in the film. On some of the recordings, sax player Charles McPherson filled in overdubs as Parker. The film features Parker numbers 'This Time the Dream's on Me', 'Moose the Mooche' (named after Parker's heroin contact, Emry Byrd), 'Loverman', 'Ram', 'Parker's Mood' (with strings), 'Now's the Time', 'Cool Blues', 'Ko Ko', and the classic 'Ornithology'. The 'Reno Jam Session' track was performed by personnel including Niehaus, James Rivers and Red Rodney. Having abandoned jazz for the latest fad, reinvented sax player Buster Franklin rocks the Paramount Theatre with 'Buster's Last Stand' – 4/4 time, three chord pap. Rock 'n' roll, 'the music of today', may induce stage-invading hysteria, but it's a poor substitute for Parker's bop genius.

Released in October 1988, *Bird* won awards but little box office favour. Posters used a tagline quote that was used at the beginning of the film: 'There are no second acts in American lives – F. Scott Fitzgerald'. Some thought Jack Green's cinematography too dark and smoky: the *Los Angeles Times* noted, 'relentlessly underlit', while Pauline Kael in the *New Yorker* thought that Eastwood mustn't have 'paid his Con Edison bill'. In competition at Cannes in April 1988, Whitaker won Best Actor. In the US, Eastwood won a Golden Globe for his direction, Diane Venora won the New York Critics Award for Best Supporting Actress and Les Fresholtz, Dick Alexander, Vern Poore and Willie D. Burton won Oscars for their work on the film's sound. The *Washington Post* saw 'talents that were never even hinted at in [Eastwood's] earlier pictures'. *Variety* thought Eastwood was charting 'bold new territory for himself... and has pulled it off in impressive fashion', further mentioning that it 'will surprise those stragglers who believe Eastwood's talents lie strictly in mayhem and monkeys'.

Bird took only $11 million in the US, a $2 million profit, though with Bertrand Tavernier's *Round Midnight* (1986), it remains one of the best movies about jazz. *Straight No Chaser* (1989), an Eastwood-produced documentary on jazz pianist Thelonius Monk directed by Charlotte Zwerin, was exhibited in *Bird*'s wake. Eastwood had released a Kansas City jazz documentary, *The Last of the Blue Devils*, in France in 1988 and is among the most high-profile supporters of the form. In 1998, he produced *Monterey Jazz Festival: 40 Legendary Years*. In 2003, Eastwood directed 'Piano Blues', an episode of *The Blues* TV series, and on 17 October 1996 was honoured at Carnegie Hall with a concert – *Eastwood After Hours*.

Eastwood has noted in interviews that the only two original American art forms are westerns and jazz. His love of jazz has permeated his career, a seam of gold which can be traced from that first time he saw Parker in his youth, and he has made crucial contributions to keep both American forms alive. *Bird* was a daring project for

Eastwood and one of his best-directed films, with a strong sense of history, creativity and narrative aided by some good performances and great music. It is also his best film of the eighties and a treat for jazz buffs: it's one of those films where audiences wait until the final credits have unfurled, as fans wait to read the roll call of Parker compositions.

White Hunter Black Heart (1990)

Eastwood followed his endeavours on *Bird* with a return to formulaic knockabout comedy, the woeful *Pink Cadillac* (1989), but surprised everyone with his next project as director-star. In *White Hunter Black Heart*, Eastwood impersonated another famous actor-director, John Huston, although in the film he is called 'John Wilson'. *The Treasure of the Sierra Madre* (1948), Huston's Mexican gold hunt drama, is one of Eastwood's favourite films. *White Hunter* depicts the events of Huston's pre-production visit to Africa prior to shooting *The African Queen* in 1950, as recounted in the 1953 bestseller *White Hunter Black Heart* by Huston's uncredited screenwriter on the film, Peter Viertel. Huston decided to make the film so he could fulfil one of his hunting ambitions: to shoot a bull elephant, a 'Big Tusker'. All names have been changed in the book, but the main players are easily identifiable. Viertel for example is called Pete Verrill in the film.

In England, Wilson and his scriptwriter Verrill (played by Jeff Fahey) work on the latest draft of 'The African Trader', detailing a dangerous river journey by steamboat during the First World War. Their producer (Paul Landers, played by George Dzundza) and the backers at Sunrise Films are worried about filming on location in Africa using expensive colour stock and would rather send the second unit there and film it in the UK on a placid river. Wilson will have none of it and once the film is cast, he sets off with Verrill to the Congo – ostensibly to scout locations, but really to bag a tusker. The film's unit manager Ralph Lockhart (Alun Armstrong) is also there, as a spy to report back to Landers in London. Staying at the Lake Victoria Hotel, Wilson and Verrill labour over the script's ending, while locations are scouted by other crew members. Wilson and Verrill fly to Lake Albert, so they can check on the jet black Ruiki River locations to be used in the film. They stay at a hunting camp run by Zibelinsky (Alex Norton), who organises a safari for them to hunt big game. On his recce, Wilson recruits local tribal guide Kivu (Boy Mathias Chuma) as his elephant tracker. Eventually the film's cast and crew land at Entebbe airport in British Uganda and arrive to begin the film, now shifted by Wilson to Kivu's village. Fortuitous prolonged rain further delays filming, enabling Wilson to continue his quest. As the rains clear and the crew prepares the first shot, Wilson receives a message that there is a tusker nearby. Verrill, Wilson, hunter Kemp Ogilvy and Kivu set off and find the bull elephant protecting a herd including cows and young. Ogilvy warns of the danger, but Wilson ignores him and confronts the tusker. Wilson can't shoot and when the animal charges, Kivu tries to save Wilson's life but is gored to death on the bull's tusks. Wilson and the party return to Kivu's village, where the cast and crew are waiting to commence. The villagers spread the bad news of Kivu's death via drums; Ogilvy notes that such messages always start with the same words: 'White hunter, black heart'. Wilson sits down in his director's chair, the crew is ready for scene one, take one. There's a long pause, then Wilson finally announces, 'Action'.

There were several differences between Viertel's book and the screenplay, which had further revisions by James Bridges and Burt Kennedy. In the book, Wilson did indeed shoot his 'Big Tusker'; Eastwood altered the ending, retaining the death of Kivu, but ensuring that Wilson didn't commit such a crime against nature. This doesn't make Wilson any more sympathetic (he's known as 'The Monster'), but it does make the film's ending more powerful. The last shot, with Wilson saying, 'Action', then the fade to black, was Kennedy's idea.

Made immediately after Eastwood's lengthy separation case with Sondra Locke, settled out of court, *White Hunter* was filmed on location over two months in the summer of 1989. The far-flung African locations were essential to the story, with Zimbabwe standing in for the Belgian Congo and Uganda. Some location footage was lensed around Lake Karibu. The crew then travelled to the UK, to Pinewood Studios, with Edgerton Gardens, Wilson's grand estate residence, being shot at West Wycombe House, West Wycombe Park, a National Trust property previously used by Don Siegel for *Rough Cut* (1980).

Huston's *The African Queen*, based on a novel by C.S. Forester, starred Humphrey Bogart and Katherine Hepburn as Charlie Allnut and Rose Sayer, mismatched travelling companions escaping from the Germans aboard Allnut's steamer. The actual making of *Queen* was hideous, with floods, ants, malaria, humidity and dysentery. In *White Hunter*, Marisa Berenson gave an excellent performance as Katherine Hepburn, or rather 'Kay Gibson'. Richard Vanstone was 'Phil Duncan', cynic Bogart, while Jamie Koss was 'Mrs Duncan', otherwise known as Lauren Bacall. Paul Landers, the film's producer (played by George Dzundza), was really producer Sam Spiegel and cinematographer Basil Fields (played by Richard Warwick) was Jack Cardiff. The actual producers of *African Queen* were Horizon Pictures; in *White Hunter* they're Sunrise Films. Jeff Fahey was excellent as Pete Verrill, the romantic optimist, agog at the wonders of Africa and aghast at Wilson's contempt for its natural riches.

In this British colonial setting, African actor Boy Mathias Chuma was cast as guide Kivu and was doubled in the stunt scenes by David Mabukane. Eastwood was stunt doubled by his regular collaborator George Orrison; Eastwood's riding double was Bill Weston in the opening estate scene, where Wilson gallops through the countryside dressed in a red hunting jacket, a sequence that recalls *The List of Adrian Messenger* (1963), Huston's Irish-set murder mystery. *White Hunter* deployed several faces familiar to British audiences, among them Timothy Spall as 'Hod' Hodkins Wilson's daredevil safari pilot and Clive Mantle as the racist general manager of the Lake Victoria Hotel.

White Hunter Black Heart looks at how the white's black hearts destroyed Africa, as interlopers and exploiters. In the UK, prior to setting off for Africa, Wilson and

5.2 Out in Africa, director-star Clint Eastwood plays 'John Wilson', a thinly disguised John Huston, who is loaded for elephant in *White Hunter Black Heart* (1990). Image courtesy Kevin Wilkinson Collection.

his crew dine in a fancy restaurant. After the meal, they enjoy the African-themed cabaret: a blonde damsel in distress attempts to escape the clutches of a wild gorilla (or rather a man in a gorilla suit), while a bongo player dressed as a native warrior thumps on the jungle drums. 'Doesn't that make you long for the dark continent?' Wilson asks his date. Out in Africa, this clichéd depiction of the country is seen to be untrue: the sheer majesty of the place is overwhelming, but the white interlopers treat the Africans like dirt. The ugly side of Africa – the colonialism, the racism and the white's hunting – is contrasted with the natural beauty of the country. The film's photography by Jack N. Green was outstanding, his cinematography capturing the golden glow of sunrise over lakeside savannah and bush, stretching to the horizon. There is much second-unit wildlife footage, of antelope, lions, buffalo herds and bird life, and for Wilson's plane trips there was splendid aerial photography of the wilderness scrubland spread below. Lennie Niehaus's percussive score is driven by traditional African instruments (flutes, drums, Congolese marimba); the percussionists are Emil Richards and Efrain Toro, with flute work by Bill Perkins. Eastwood ends the film with burnished sundown panoramas. As the sun sets, even someone as monstrous as Wilson has no impact on the landscape.

Wilson is a flamboyant, arrogant character – a rip-roaring, hard-drinking, cigar-smoking, womanising braggart – and the role required a most un-Eastwood-like performance from the star. Katherine Hepburn thought Huston's macho 'big game hunter' act was a sham. A maverick survivor who at the beginning of this film is massively in debt, Wilson is depicted as a crazy egocentric who sees film directors as 'lousy little gods'. The new film will save his neck he hopes (*The African Queen* eventually did), but the carefree gambler in Wilson is always willing to risk everything for the thrill. Eastwood studied footage of Huston, who had died in 1987. Huston had appeared in many films as an actor, most notably as land grabber Noah Cross in *Chinatown* (1974), but these were performances, not Huston. Eastwood does a passable impersonation of the director and towards the film's conclusion – as the dramatic hunt unfolds and the shock of seeing the normally reticent actor gesticulate and showboat has worn off – the fact that Eastwood is 'playing' Huston is forgotten.

Wilson is in Africa for one thing: to shoot animals first, the film later. From licensed hunter Dickie Marlowe, Wilson learns that there are two sure-fire ways to kill an elephant: either aim for the heart, or plant a bullet six inches down from between the elephant's eyes. Wilson acknowledges, 'It's a sin to kill an elephant', but it's a sin you can go out and buy a license to commit. Verrill despises Wilson's wanton attitude to one of God's creatures. On the big hunt, Wilson's mania results in him taking risks, even when advised by Ogilvy not to. The tusker is something he must confront, as though the animal represents something within his own psyche, the beast inside, which drives him on. Many potential victims have found themselves staring down the barrel of Eastwood's gun, but the scene when the mighty bull approaches, to go nose-to-nose with Wilson, is among the most tension-filled of Eastwood's career. Following the death of Kivu, Wilson is visibly choked, almost moved to tears, as the villagers' drums – not part of a cabaret act – spread the bad news. Earlier Verrill and Wilson have argued over their script's downbeat ending. As Wilson looks at the weeping villagers, he reflects, 'You were right Pete, the ending is all wrong'.

White Hunter Black Heart was released in the US in September 1990 to good reviews and terrible business. The poster for the film, advertised as 'An Adventure in Obsession', featured the rugged Eastwood physiognomy smoking a cigar, in a vain effort to make John Wilson look as much like 'The Man with No Name' as possible. *Variety* recorded that 'as a director [Eastwood] ... is more than just a fine craftsman, and his willingness to tackle difficult subjects is commendable'. Eastwood's regular detractors were nevertheless impressed. 'Brilliant, witty and exciting', thought Rex Reed in *Coming Attractions*, 'Big Clint gives the finest performance of his career ... one of the best films of 1990'. Janet Maslin in the *New York Times* deemed it 'a gutsy fascinating departure'. Michael Wilmington in the *Los Angeles Times* gave the film the most perceptive, enduring review, however: 'It's a fine film in many ways – even if Huston's persona becomes Eastwood's own big tusker: the prey he can't quite shoot. He doesn't bring back the Big One, but he doesn't return empty-handed; intellectually and morally, there's plenty of game for the pot'. But the film was a severe disappointment at the box office for Warner Bros and its lifetime gross is just over $2 million – it cost $24 million.

Midnight in the Garden of Good and Evil (1997)

On something of a literary roll, following *The Bridges of Madison County* (1995) and *Absolute Power* (1996), Eastwood's next project was yet another adaptation of a best-seller, though this time only as director. Based on a factual murder case, *Midnight in the Garden of Good and Evil* by John Berendt was published to great success in the US by Random House in 1994. The screenplay was fashioned by John Lee Hancock, who had written *A Perfect World* (1993) for Eastwood, and the film is similarly meandering.

John Kelso (John Cusack), a New York journalist writing for *Town and Country*, arrives in Savannah, Georgia, in America's 'Deep South'. He's there to cover a society Christmas party being thrown by gay, nouveau riche antiques dealer Jim Williams (Kevin Spacey) at his home, Mercer House. After the party, on the night of 19 December 1981, Williams shoots dead Billy Hanson (Jude Law), a hustler who is Williams' lover. Kelso decides to forget about his *Town and Country* piece and to write a book on Williams and the case. Williams, pleading self-defence, has since been charged with Murder One and is remanded in custody until his trial. Through Kelso's association with various marginal Savannians, including Lady Chablis (a vaudeville entertainer and ex-housemate of Hanson's), Minerva, a practising voodoo priestess, and Mandy, a florist neighbour of Williams', he discovers proof that Williams fired in self-defence. But Williams secretly confides in Kelso that Hanson had the safety catch on and in the precious few seconds, Williams shot Hanson dead, engineering the scene to look like self-defence. Williams is acquitted but dies shortly thereafter of a heart attack that may have been caused by Minerva as revenge for his deceit. Kelso meanwhile settles down in Savannah to pen a best-selling book.

John Cusack was cast as 'John Kelso', actually pseudonymous author Berendt. The same year Cusack narrated an excellent documentary, *Eastwood on Eastwood* (TNT Productions, 1997), based on Richard Schickel's book *Clint Eastwood: A Biography*. The documentary was written, produced and directed by Schickel and featured much behind-the-scenes footage of the making of *Midnight in the Garden of Good and Evil*. The always-excellent Kevin Spacey had been Oscar-nominated for *The Usual Suspects* (1995) and had just made *L.A. Confidential* (1997), where he starred as Jack Vincennes, showbiz cop. Behind a becoming moustache, he essays the best southern accent of the non-Savannah leads. Eastwood's own daughter Alison played Mandy Nichols, Kelso's superfluous love interest. Paul Hipp was good as louche gadabout Joe Odom, another swanky Savannah party-thrower, given to spouting lines such as 'Where's my libation?' and 'My ice cubes are getting a little bit dry'. British actor Jude Law was hustler Billy Hanson, 'A good time, but a good time not yet had by all'. Eastwood stalwart Geoffrey Lewis appeared as Luther Driggers, a local eccentric.

Two key subplots feature two of the film's best performances. In the first, Chablis Deveau helps Kelso when she agrees to testify about Billy's drug use and temper. Chablis, a real character from the book, plays herself in the film. When Kelso asks her why she's listed in the phone book as 'F. Deveau', she answers the 'F' is for Frank. 'The Lady Chablis' is actually a famous Savannah drag act and emcee. She is undoubtedly one of the highlights of the film and illuminates the screen with her purring, over-the-top, sequinned performance. She provokes shocked expressions when she sashays into a posh Alpha Phi Beta ball and later memorably opens her testimony in the witness stand with the confession, 'I have a man's tool box'.

For the other subplot, Williams decides not to take any chances with his trial and enlists the help of Minerva, a voodoo priestess (played by Irma P. Hall), as part of his 'defence team'. Williams and Kelso meet her in the graveyard (which she refers to as the 'garden') at the grave of her recently deceased husband, Dr. Louis Buzzard. She tells them about 'Dead Time', the 30 minutes either side of midnight: the half-hour before is for doing good, the half-hour after for evil, hence the film's title. Minerva is present at the trial and the juju works in acquitting Williams, but for his sins it seems Billy will take revenge from beyond the grave. You can outwit the living, but you can't outrun the dead.

The film was shot on location in Savannah, Georgia, in the spring of 1997. The scene where Mandy sings 'Come Rain or Come Shine' was filmed in Churchill's, an authentic English pub, with a sign over the door featuring Winston. In *Eastwood on Eastwood*, the director can be seen joking around on set and showing Paul Hipp how to crack a whip, with a shout of 'Rawhide!' The bestseller's cover had featured a photograph of the distinctive sculpture 'Bird Girl', by Sylvia Shaw Judson, which also appears in the film in the Bonaventure Cemetery scenes. The sculpture depicts a girl in a long dress, her head quizzically tilted sideways, holding two plates in her outstretched hands, like a bizarre, bird-feeding crucifixion, or the scales of justice. Savannah is a beautiful city and the sumptuous architecture is the film's main asset. The central Forsyth Park, with its trees and tiered fountain, features extensively in the film. As Kelso notes, 'This place is fantastic. It's like *Gone with the Wind* on mescaline'. Everyone is 'heavily armed and drunk' – just the kind of combustible atmosphere for a good story.

The story may be good, but its telling is convoluted. An indication of the film's missed opportunities is its lame symbolism. Williams shows Kelso a painting from his collection: Stubbs' 'Newmarket Heath with the Rubbing-down House', painted near Newmarket racecourse. Kelso recognises it as an 'over paint'. There is another picture hidden underneath, but Williams asserts, 'I rather enjoy not knowing'. This metaphor for Williams' sexuality – his 'outing' in court is one of the key scenes in the film – is without resonance amid the saggy melodrama and hokey voodoo.

Considering the vivid setting and characters, Lennie Niehaus's score is among his most colourless, but the soundtrack is redeemed by a selection of great Johnny Mercer songs; lyricist Mercer was born in Savannah in 1909. The film is bookended by a soaring rendition of Mercer and Hoagy Carmichael's 'Skylark', performed by k.d. lang. Other Mercer classics deployed were 'Fools Rush In (Where Angels Fear to Tread)', 'Autumn Leaves', 'Tangerine', 'In the Cool Cool of the Evening', 'This Time the Dream's on Me', 'Laura', 'Jeepers Creepers' and the lush 'Days of Wine and Roses', co-written with Henry Mancini. In fact, the soundtrack 'Music from and Inspired By' the film, released on Warners, is worth buying for its classic collection of Mercer tunes and unusual cameos: Spacey sings 'That Old Black Magic', while Eastwood himself gives a snappy rendition of Mercer's 'Ac-Cent-Tchu-Ate the Positive'.

Midnight in the Garden of Good and Evil was released by Warner Bros during Christmas 1997. Posters featured the 'Bird Girl', while the trailer warned: 'Here in the heart of Dixie, southern hospitality never dies – but people do'. The film took only $25 million: $5 million less than it cost. Many reviews were positive, making it difficult to understand the film's failure – perhaps Minerva jinxed it. Todd McCarthy in *Variety* summed up the results very well: '*Midnight in the Garden of Good and Evil* is an outstanding lean film trapped in a fat film's body … the picture's aimless, sprawling structure and exceedingly leisurely pace finally come to weigh too heavily upon its virtues'. The book's massive success and its associated expectations may have worked against the film here. Put simply, the film, like its title, is just too long. It may be *Midnight in the Garden of Good and Evil*, but where's the Bad and the Ugly when you need them?

Space Cowboys (2000)

Since *The Bridges of Madison County* in 1995, Eastwood's directorial career has relied almost totally on literary adaptations, with varying degrees of success. *Space Cowboys* is one of the few Eastwood projects based on an original screenplay (by Ken Kaufman and Howard Klausner) and is an anomaly in Eastwood's canon, combining human drama, heroics and a sense of nostalgia with special effects and, for the only time in his career, science fiction and space travel.

In 1958, four-man US Airforce Team Daedalus, who test supersonic X-2 jets, is ready to fly into space but have the chance snatched away from them when chimpanzee Mary-Ann is chosen by Major Bob Gerson (James Cromwell) as the first American into orbit. Over 40 years later, the National Aeronautics and Space Administration (NASA) has a problem. Ikon, a huge Soviet communications satellite, has suffered a total system failure – it is dropping out of space and will crash to earth in approximately 30 to 40 days. The Russians want to save it, but its guidance system and technology are long out of date. Only someone like Frank Corvin (Eastwood) of Team Daedalus would be able to reactivate the satellite, realigning its 'geosync orbit'. Corvin agrees only if his long-retired comrades from the 1958 project can come too. Major Gerson, now at NASA, reluctantly agrees to this blackmail and Project Daedalus is resurrected. Corvin contacts navigator 'Tank' Sullivan, now a Baptist preacher (James Garner), structural engineer and designer Jerry O'Neill (Donald Sutherland), now designing fairground roller coasters, and ace pilot William 'The Hawk' Hawkins (Tommy Lee Jones), who spends his time taking kids for loop-the-loop thrills in his biplane. Corvin and Hawkins blame each other for blowing their chances in 1958 but agree to work together to finally get into space. On the NASA training program, the quartet struggles to meet the physical requirements but eventually pass. During training it's discovered that Hawkins has inoperable pancreatic cancer, but the others refuse to go without him. Embarking on their mission in the space shuttle, with Ethan Glance and Roger Hines, two younger astronauts on board as back up, they reach Ikon and discover they've been duped. The communications satellite is actually a nuclear launch platform, housing a missile silo armed with six warheads. The missiles are targeted at strategic installations in the US, in large metropolitan areas, and Glance and Gerson are in league with the Russians to reactivate the station. But following a collision with the satellite which damages the shuttle, Project Daedalus seizes the day: in a selfless act, Hawkins pilots the satellite into deep space, and destruction, while Corvin brings the shuttle, battered and low on fuel, safely back to earth.

Another director-star vehicle for Eastwood, *Space Cowboys* enabled him to work with Tommy Lee Jones, James Garner (reunited from their 1959 *Maverick* episode 'Duel at Sundown') and Donald Sutherland (from *Kelly's Heroes*). Barbara Babcock played Corvin's wife, Barbara, William Devane (ex of *Knots Landing*) gives a punchy performance as gum-chewing NASA flight director Gene Davis, while the always-excellent James Cromwell is suitably menacing as Corvin's adversary who is revealed to be an enemy of the state. Marcia Gay Harden is well cast as Sara Holland, NASA's mission director, who falls in love with charming-but-rough Hawkins. One of the film's major assets is the warmth of Team Daedalus's scenes together, especially in Eastwood's reunion with Garner. Each of the team members has his quirks, with Corvin, for instance, known by reputation for not being a 'team player'. But whoever cast Sutherland as Jerry O'Neill, the 'babe magnet' every woman swoons over, should be fired into space.

Made after edgy thriller *True Crime* (1999), *Space Cowboys* was budgeted at $65 million and shot over three months, beginning in July 1999. This included footage lensed in Johnson Space Centre in Houston, Texas, for the training scenes, and at the Kennedy Space Centre at Cape Canaveral, Florida, for actual footage of the space shuttle's lift-off. The crew enjoyed the co-operation of NASA, though the space shuttle and Ikon interior, the flight simulator and the mission control were built at Warners Bros. The impressive special visual effects and animation were staged by George Lucas Film's Industrial Light and Magic and replicas of the space shuttle were provided by Wonder Works. One of the film's most impressive moments occurs when Ikon collides with the shuttle. Involved in the effects process, which was often slow and tedious, Eastwood also contributed an acoustic guitar lament, 'Espacio' (performed by Mitch Holder), to the soundtrack, which also featured the punchy 'Space Cowboys (Yippie-Ti-Yay)' by boy band *NSYNC.

Throughout *Space Cowboys,* there is a sense of the old folks showing the youngsters how it's done. In the 1958 scenes, Team Daedalus are ousted by a chimpanzee, and later Eastwood complains that NASA had 'replaced my ass with a monkey' – not the first time he's been upstaged by a primate. Under computer guidance in the space shuttle flight simulator, Hawkins crashes it into a wood; when allowed to operate it manually, the same way he'd pilot a plane, he executes a perfect landing. The old ways are the best. As one of Eastwood's familiar ruminations on ageing, *Space Cowboys* has its moments, mostly at the stars' expense. Corvin asks bespectacled O'Neill if he really needs to wear his glasses: 'Why no, just to read, go to movies, drive, walk ... you know'. The only reason Corvin is in demand is that he's 'proficient in obsolete technology'; a Russian general liasing with NASA notes that the last time Team Daedalus was together, 'people were driving cars with fins on them'. Prior to being thumped in a barroom brawl, Eastwood's character notes these days 'I've got Medicare – go ahead'. *USA Today* calls Team Daedalus 'the Ripe Stuff' and the team appears on *Tonight with Jay Leno*. Their host learns that the Daedalus crew all have military backgrounds – 'North or south? Which side were you on?' deadpans Leno.

In terms of Eastwood's career, two of the most striking aspects of the film are how well he's aged and how much special effects have improved in the 18 years since *Firefox*. The scenes in outer space have a grounding in reality, despite the film's fanciful conclusion. In Greek mythology, Daedalus was the designer of the Labyrinth, imprisoned on Crete with his son Icarus, who constructed feathered wings affixed with wax to effect their escape, but Icarus flew too near the sun. Eastwood saw his team not as literal 'cowboys', but as 'pioneers in space'. The mission scenes are magnificently staged, with Corvin finally achieving his dream of seeing Earth from afar, his home planet reflected in his helmet visor as he gazes in awe, drifting through the star field. Especially eerie is the moment when they find Ikon, the huge, ghostly sleeping satellite, which when reactivated slowly begins to rotate and majestically spins back to life, rather like reawakened Team Daedalus themselves.

'Space Will Never Be the Same', ran the poster tagline. Critics deemed the movie just okay, but audiences who avoided the darker *True Crime* and *Absolute Power* flocked to enjoy *Space Cowboys*, proving the four stars' continued pulling power. It took more than these two previous films combined, raking in $90 million in the US, following its release in August 2000. Despite being too long, *Space Cowboys* remains quite a charming, moving story, in an old-fashioned Hollywood way. It's unfortunate that it ends with one of the most inappropriate and tactless deployments of a popular standard in the history of cinema. Back on earth, Corvin and his wife Barbara wonder if Hawkins made it to the moon. The camera pans heavenwards, eventually craning along the Moon's grey, dusty surface, through various spaceship debris, before settling on a shot of Hawkins's space-suited corpse, accompanied on the soundtrack by Frank Sinatra's 'Fly Me to the Moon'.

Mystic River (2003)

With this film, Eastwood is back on terra firma and back to literature as a source. He had first read Dennis Lehane's *Mystic River* as a synopsis in a newspaper during the making of *Blood Work* (2002). Eastwood liked the treatment, which matched his penchant for sinister modern moral fables. Brian Helgeland, who was then adapting Michael Connelly's novel *Blood Work* for Eastwood, was commissioned to turn *Mystic* into a screenplay. Helgeland is actually from Boston, the setting for Lehane's tale of guilt, misunderstanding, betrayal and lost youth.

In 1975, as three boys play on the streets of their Boston neighbourhood, one of them is abducted by two men posing as cops. The boy, Dave Boyle, is imprisoned in a shed and abused by the men for four days, after which he escapes, but the experience shatters his life; 25 years later, the three childhood friends still live and work around the same neighbourhood. Dave (Tim Robbins) has married Celeste (Marcia Gay Harden) and has a son Michael; Sean Devine (Kevin Bacon) is an officer on Boston's homicide squad and has split from his wife, while Jimmy Markum (Sean Penn) is a shopkeeper and small-time hoodlum, now apparently on the straight-and-narrow and is married to Annabeth (Laura Linney). When Jimmy's 19-year-old daughter Katie (Emmy Rossum) is found in Pen Park, beaten and shot dead on her way home from McGill's Bar after a Saturday night out with friends, a murder hunt engulfs the community. There are two prime suspects: her boyfriend Brendan Harris (Thomas Guiry), with whom she had planned to elope to Las Vegas, and Dave Boyle. On the night of the murder, Dave came home covered in blood, his stomach slashed, telling Celeste that he had confronted a mugger and he may have killed him. Sean is the investigating officer on Katie's murder, with his partner Sergeant Whitey Powers (Laurence Fishburne). Jimmy dispatches the three Savage brothers to find the killer before the police do, to exact revenge, giving the police a deadline. The police discover that the murder weapon is a .38 Smith & Wesson, which was used in 1984 in a robbery of Looney Liquors. It transpires that the chief suspect, never convicted, was Ray Harris (Brendan's father), who has also been involved in crime enterprises with Jimmy. When no newspapers report the discovery of the mugger's body, Celeste implicates her husband in Katie's murder. Jimmy and the aptly named Savages take Dave to a bar near Boston harbour; there Jimmy forces drunk Dave to confess to the crime and kills him, dumping his body in the Mystic River. The next morning Jimmy is visited by Sean, informing him they have solved the case. Brendan's mute brother 'Silent Ray Harris' and his friend John O'Shea stole the pistol and shot Katie, to stop Brendan from leaving for Vegas – they were supposed to scare her, but the prank went disastrously wrong. Now an innocent man is dead and the Mystic River has swallowed another victim.

Mystic River was filmed in Boston, Massachusetts, on a $30 million budget. The Boston Harbour and its girder bridge feature prominently, with location filming taking place on the city streets. Eastwood often ranges his camera across the cityscape, with helicopter shots seeking out an abandoned car at a murder scene or sweeping across the waters of the bay. Tom Stern's Panavision cinematography is a notable improvement on Jack Green's work, with darkness and shadow deployed more poetically than at any point in Eastwood's films since *Unforgiven*.

Eastwood noted that he acquired his first choice actors for all the main roles, including the pivotal trio of leads. Eastwood cast Sean Penn as Jimmy Markum. Formerly best known as a movie brat and bad boy with a fiery temper, and for his action-packed marriage to Madonna, whirlwind Penn had quietened somewhat by 2003. He had also started directing in 1991 with *The Indian Runner* and had proved to be a talented actor when able to harness his energies onscreen. On meeting his director, Penn said of Eastwood, 'He's the least disappointing American icon' he had ever met. Penn had previously played opposite Al Pacino in *Carlito's Way* (1993) and Penn infuses vengeful Jimmy with a little of Pacino's bile; his extraordinary performance here is a revelation. Tim Robbins, cast as Dave Boyle, had appeared to critical and commercial success in *Bull Durham* (1988), *The Player* (1992), *Bob Roberts* (1992) and *The Shawshank Redemption* (1994). Robbins had directed Penn to a Best Actor nomination in *Dead Man Walking* (1995), with Robbins nominated for Best Director. Kevin Bacon, playing Sean Devine, became a star via such films as *Footloose* (1984), *Flatliners* (1990), *JFK* (1991) and *Apollo 13* (1995). Laurence Fishburne was well cast as Sean's partner Powers, who is convinced that Sean's closeness to the case is clouding his judgement. To Powers, Dave is definitely the culprit; 'Why's your wife acting like she's afraid of you?' asks the bullying cop of Dave. In this 'real world', bullish Powers' methods, which resemble Harry Callahan's, are unsettlingly callous. Laura Linney, as Jimmy's cold wife, Annabeth, and Marcia Gay Harden, as Dave's paranoid, untrusting wife Celeste, had both worked for Eastwood before (on *Absolute Power* and *Space Cowboys* respectively), while Eli Wallach, from *The Good, the Bad and the Ugly*, gave an unbilled cameo as genial Mr Looney, the loony proprietor of 'Looney Liquor'.

The murder at the centre of the film reunites the three friends, located at the points of a triangular police investigation as the cop, the victim and the accused. Although Dave and Jimmy haven't managed more than a 'hello' on the street for many years, they are still invisibly bound by what happened to Dave. In the immediate aftermath of Katie's death, Jimmy seems to find comfort in chatting to Dave on his porch, but this changes when Dave is implicated. Later, Jimmy says to Sean that the last time they saw Dave was 25 years ago, looking back at them terrified from the rear window of his abductors' car. 'Dave', the boy they once knew, no longer exists.

As the police investigation proceeds, they try to establish motive. Sceptical Powers impounds Dave's car, the boot of which is splattered with blood, but the police can't tie Dave to Katie's murder. As in *Blood Work*, a mysterious 911 telephone call proves to be the vital clue. The emergency call from the scene of the crime, which sounds like two teenage boys, says that they have found a bloodstained car, but somehow they know the victim is female (referring to 'her'), even though the body was found in a nearby park. How would they know the victim's gender? Sean realises the connection to Brendan's teenage friends. On the morning following Dave's death, when Sean visits Jimmy with the news that the case is closed, the cop says they have discovered a body in the woods behind McGill's Bar, that of a convicted paedophile. On his way home from the bar, Dave had seen the man engaged in a sexual act with a boy in his car and intervened, in his rage killing the man: 'He was a wolf... a vampire'. Dave had hidden the body in his car, which is why no reports of a body being discovered appeared in the local papers. The shocking ending, with the death of an innocent man, echoes that of Eastwood favourite *The Ox-Bow Incident* (1943).

It is the Mystic River which holds the secret to the mystery. Brendan plans to run away with Katie; his mother snaps that he was going to disappear, just like his father did. Esther thinks Ray is still alive somewhere – he 'sends' her $500 a month, but it is revealed that Jimmy killed him years ago (Ray ratted on Jimmy to avoid a jail term) and dumped him in the Mystic. It is Jimmy who sends the money to Ray's wife to continue the subterfuge. 'You gonna send Celeste Boyle 500 a month too?' asks Sean flatly following Dave's 'disappearance'.

As director-only, Eastwood seems able to invest his films with a depth sometimes absent from those he has acted in. *Mystic River* is the closest Eastwood has come to making a 'Godfather' movie and the powerful ties between the three main protagonists, from youth to adulthood, recall his mentor Leone's haunting *Once Upon a Time in America* (1984), another film with dark secrets. Author Dennis Lehane called *Mystic River* a 'street opera' and Penn's dominating performance, introverted and self-persecutory, bursting into elemental rage, certainly enforces this. The powerful score, composed by Eastwood, with Lennie Niehaus conducting the Boston Symphony Orchestra and the Tanglewood Festival Chorus, gives the tragedy added dimension. Jimmy is initially destroyed by Katie's death, but he comes back stronger and meaner. Cop Sean knows in his gut that Dave isn't the killer; Jimmy's instincts are more feral and his retribution swift and irreversible. Eastwood intercuts the murder scene with Jimmy and his family attending his daughter Nadine's first communion, an image of death, religion and violence intertwined, further recalling the 'Godfather' films.

The chilling opening scenes cast a discomforting shadow across the entire film. Three young boys play hockey in the street, until they lose their ball down the sewer drain. They find a recent repair to the sidewalk and begin vandalising it, writing their names in the patch of wet concrete. Jimmy and Sean write theirs, but Dave is interrupted by two men in a car who appear to be police officers. They tell Dave to get in the vehicle with them, to be taken home to his mother for a scolding. Dave's name, incomplete, like his youth, lies cemented forever on the sidewalk, a stark reminder of this fateful, life-changing moment. Celeste, Dave's disbelieving wife who doesn't understand his trauma, is unnerved by his odd behaviour and thinks the 'mugger' is a figment of Dave's overactive imagination. It is her gossiping and her weak faith and understanding which result in his murder. Dave's story about the mugger masks his real motive for killing the paedophile: his own loss of innocence. Throughout his life, Dave is always running from these predatory 'wolves' and 'vampires', but he never escapes them. Days later, at the neighbourhood street parade, Sean mimes firing a bullet at Jimmy, who, like a kid, mimes an explosive impact. In this make-believe world, Jimmy gets away with murder. As Sean notes, 'Sometimes I think all three of us got in that car and all of this is just a dream'. They are still 11-year-old boys locked in a cellar: 'Imagining what our lives would have been, had we escaped'.

Released in the US and UK in October 2003, the film was critically praised and a great success. The trailer solemnly observed: 'There are places that make us who we are, moments that give us hope, feelings that make us question our beliefs, fears that trigger our darkest emotions'. The poster featured the tagline; 'We bury our sins, we wash them clean': Jimmy's remark to Dave prior to the latter's death on the banks of the Mystic. 'Remarkable, Powerful', wrote the *Los Angeles Times*, 'a masterpiece' thought *Newsday*, 'a fine American Hollywood beauty', echoed *Entertainment Weekly* and 'a masterfully crafted tale' enthused *The Dallas Morning News*. *The Sun* called the film 'a haunting masterpiece and probably [Eastwood's] best film to date'. It took $90 million in the US. With several nominations at the Academy Awards, for Best Direction, Best Picture, Best Supporting Actress (Marcia Gay Harden) and Best Screenplay, the film deservedly took two top awards: Robbins was named Best Supporting Actor and Penn took Best Actor. Robbins' pained portrayal truthfully depicts one of the most moving, troubled protagonists of modern drama through nuance and depth, while Penn's incredible performance rises in intensity, until the moment his daughter is avenged, and then subsides. He roars like a tidal wave, crashing over the film, before ebbing, calm, like the lapping waters of the Mystic River.

Million Dollar Baby (2004)

On the coat-tails of *Mystic River*, Eastwood's next film was equally hard-hitting. *Million Dollar Baby*, written by Paul Haggis, was based on *Rope Burns: Stories from the Corner* by boxing writer F.X. Toole, published in 2000, which included 'The Monkey Look', 'Fightin in Philly', 'Frozen Water' and 'Million Dollar Baby'. The rights were bought by Albert S. Ruddy, the producer behind the 'Godfather' movies. Ruddy had also produced *Matilda* (1978), a children's film about a six-foot tall boxing kangaroo, with Elliott Gould as a promoter and Gary Morgan in the kangaroo suit. Ruddy drafted in Haggis to incorporate Toole's stories into a screenplay. Haggis wanted to direct as well, but when Warner Bros became involved, Eastwood took the reins. The emotional result was both life-affirming and nihilistic.

A 31-year-old hopeful, Maggie Fitzgerald (Hilary Swank), shows up at The Hit Pit, a rundown Los Angeles boxing gym run by trainer Frankie Dunn (Eastwood), and pleads with him to coach her as a fighter. Frankie says, 'I don't train girls' and is occupied with his prize-fighter, Big Willie Jones (Mike Colter). But when overly cautious Frankie loses Big Willie to a rival manager with the promise of a shot at the title, Frankie takes Maggie on. She is an apt pupil, and with help from Frankie's old pal, ex-boxer Eddie Scrap-Iron Dupris (Morgan Freeman), she is soon knocking down opponents with ease, gaining a following and a reputation. Frankie christens her 'Mo Cuishle' and her fans take up the Gaelic cry whenever she fights. Moving up a weight, Maggie is equally successful and soon she has a shot at the WBA Welterweight title in Las Vegas for a million dollar prize against Billie 'The Blue Bear' Osterman (Lucia Rijker), a fighter renowned for fighting dirty. During the bout, Billie punches Maggie after the bell. Maggie falls awkwardly, cracking her head on her corner stool. The fight and her career are over. Maggie lies in hospital, paralysed from the neck down and can't breathe properly, relying completely on a respirator attached to her throat. She is categorised 'C1 and C2 Complete': her spinal cord is irreparably broken and it is two months before she is even moved back to Los Angeles to a rehab centre. Frankie blames himself for her condition and visits her every day, often spending hours reading Gaelic poetry to her. Trapped, unable to move in bed, she develops skin ulcers, which become infected. Her family visits her once, vultures scratching for a share of her fortune. Soon afterwards, Maggie loses her left leg to infection. Unable to cope, Maggie asks Frankie to put her out of her misery, but Frankie can't bring himself to kill the girl whom he has grown to love like a daughter. After Maggie attempts suicide by biting her tongue, Frankie wrestles with his conscience and decides to grant her her wish. When he unplugs her air supply and injects her with adrenaline, he kisses her and tells her 'Mo Cuishle' means 'My darling, my blood', as she slips into unconsciousness, a tear rolling down her cheek.

With a $30 million budget, filming took place on location in LA (often in authentic boxing venues and gyms) and at Warner Bros Studios over 38 days during June and July 2004. Eastwood played Frankie, another ideal role for the aged actor. Once one of boxing's great 'cut men' and trainers in the sixties, he is now a man of doubts and moral flaws with a troubled family background, who recognises his need for forgiveness and redemption in the eyes of God. Eastwood was obviously taking the project seriously with the heavyweight casting of Morgan Freeman. As always Freeman is excellent, here as 'Scrap-Iron' Dupris, another boxer who could have been a contender but unfortunately lost an eye in a fight. Scrap wasn't present in Toole's 'Million Dollar Baby' story and was introduced by Haggis from another chapter. Canadian Jay Baruchel was stringy, inexperienced Texan boxer Danger Barch, or, to give him his full name, 'Dangerous Dillard Fightin' Flippo Bam-bam Barch'. Barch is keen but talentless, even though Scrap-Iron offers nothing but encouragement. Barch is taunted by

5.3 To the Bone: Glacial artwork promoting *Million Dollar Baby* (2004); left to right: Frankie Dunn (Clint Eastwood), Maggie Fitzgerald (Hilary Swank) and 'Scrap Iron' Dupris (Morgan Freeman). Author's collection.

his fellow trainees, especially Shawrelle Berry (Anthony Mackie), who at one point harshly beats Barch, forcing the broken youngster to quit. Eastwood's seven-year-old daughter Morgan Colette, his child with his second wife Dina Ruiz (whom he married on 31 March 1996), also appears in the film. She is the girl playing with her pet dog who smiles and waves at Maggie from a pickup parked on a gas station forecourt.

For the key role of the Million Dollar Baby, Eastwood cast Hilary Swank, who had already won an Oscar as Brandon Teena, or rather Teena Brandon, the man born a woman in *Boy's Don't Cry* (1999). When production company Lakeshore sent her the *Million Dollar Baby* script, 'Hilary flipped when she read it', said producer Ruddy. As Maggie Fitzgerald, a waitress from the Ozark town of Theodosia, with boundless self-belief and a great right hook, Swank is perfectly cast. Eastwood has acted opposite some great actresses, especially Jessica Walter in *Play Misty for Me* and Meryl Streep in *The Bridges of Madison County*, but Swank's heartbreaking performance is the best in Eastwood's oeuvre. Swank's weight trainer was Grant Roberts. Billie 'The Blue Bear', her formidable, terrifying opponent, was played by real-life boxing and kick-boxing champion, Netherlands-born Lucia Rijker, who also acted as boxing technical advisor and trained Swank for the fight scenes.

As in *Unforgiven*, Eastwood depicts women on the fringes of society: women's boxing is still not well thought of in mainstream society. The story uses boxing as a metaphor for life's lost opportunities and failures. Maggie arrives in LA from the 'scratch-ass Ozark town of Theodosia, set in the cedars and oak trees somewhere between nowhere and goodbye', where 'she grew up knowing one thing: she was trash'. 'She'd come 1,800 miles but Theodosia was still just over the hill', notes Scrap. 'My daddy's dead,' Maggie tells Frankie, 'and my momma weighs 312 pounds'; her brother's in prison and her sister still collects welfare for her long-dead baby. For Maggie, boxing is 'the only thing I ever felt good doing'. 'To make a fighter', says Scrap, 'you gotta strip them down to the bare wood'. Watching her gruelling training sessions, he observes that 'she might just be a natural', so Frankie agrees.

Though visually dark throughout, thanks to Tom Stern's shadowy, almost monochrome, Panavision cinematography and Joel Cox's editing, the film initially appears to be *Rocky*-style rags-to-riches, air-punching, life-affirming fluff, with underdog Swank as a 'Rockette' from the bad side of the tracks. As it turned out, fluff it isn't. Following the training scenes, which hardly resemble their montage, power ballad equivalents in other boxing movies, Maggie's early fights are exuberant, with her leaping around like a kid in celebration. 'It didn't take Maggie long to hit her stride', notes Scrap, as she glides from one flattened opponent to the next. She becomes so proficient that Frankie has to pay managers sweeteners to ensure her a supply of opponents.

Soon the sport's dark side emerges, in the form of Billy 'The Blue Bear', a former prostitute from East Berlin who fights dirty. Their bout, for the million dollar WBA Welterweight world championship is a step too far. *Million Dollar Baby* is Eastwood's most moving film. From the film's 88th minute, when Billie's punch connects with Maggie and sends her sprawling, the tone changes in an instant: the boxing crowd's dumbfounded silence was echoed by cinema audiences. Thereafter, with Maggie's horrific deterioration, there's a gnawing hole in the pit of your stomach, a feeling of nausea and a wave of emotion, which makes the film very difficult to watch.

The story is narrated by Freeman, as reflective, wise old boxer Scrap. There is a poetic bleakness to the narration's plain speaking and cold imagery, delivered by Freeman in his trademark rich tone, at once reassuring and chilling. 'If there's magic in boxing', he intones, 'It's the magic of fighting battles beyond endurance – beyond cracked ribs, ruptured kidneys and detached retinas. It's the magic of risking everything for a dream that nobody sees but you'. Freeman's spellbinding voice had been used to narrate films before, most famously *The Shawshank Redemption* (1994), for which he was Oscar-nominated. Scrap's narration was present in Haggis's script and adds weight to the final emotive punch: the revelation that the narration's recounted story is a letter to Frankie's absent daughter, Katie, telling her what kind of man

5.4 Clint Eastwood behind the camera on *Million Dollar Baby* (2004), which won him his second Best Director Oscar. Image courtesy Kevin Wilkinson Collection.

her father was. Frankie sends her letters, but they are always returned unopened and he has attended mass regularly for 23 years; whatever he has done, his lifelong regrets, he feels within himself that he is unforgiven. Of Irish heritage (like author Toole), Frankie reads poetry by W.B. Yeats and christens Maggie 'Mo Cuishle', which becomes her fans' battle cry while she enters the ring decked out in an emerald green robe. 'Seems there are Irish people everywhere', says Scrap, 'Or people who wanna be'. Maggie becomes Frankie's replacement for his own daughter, making the filial killing merciful and sympathetic. 'I got nobody but you, Frankie', Maggie once tells her surrogate father figure; 'But you've got me', he assures.

Maggie is also trying to prove something to her worthless family. Maggie buys her ungrateful mother a house, who then worries about her benefit being stopped. When the Fitzgeralds hear about her injury, they come to visit, stopping off at Universal Studios first. They arrive with a lawyer, for Maggie to sign her assets over to her mother, but she refuses. 'So anytime I feel like it', Maggie curses, 'I can sell that house from under your fat, lazy, hillbilly asses'. To them she'll always be 'Mary M', the waitress with no future.

'Some wounds are too deep or too close to the bone', says Scrap in his narration, speaking both of Frankie's estrangement from his daughter and Maggie's injury, 'and no matter how hard you work at it, you just can't stop the bleeding'. Maggie's mercy killing is mirrored in a moment from her childhood, when her father had to put down the family's crippled pet dog. 'Don't let me lie here 'til I can't hear those people chanting no more', Maggie pleads. *Million Dollar Baby* becomes more resonant on repeated viewings, even knowing the outcome. In the oblique conclusion following Maggie's death, Scrap recalls that he never saw Frankie again. The final image shows a blurred image of Frankie sitting at the counter of Ira's Roadside Diner, the same diner where he and Maggie had eaten lemon pie. She used to go there with her father and Frankie says that he has some savings and wonders if it's for sale. Whether he bought it or not, it is where Frankie will remain emotionally forever, 'Somewhere between nowhere and goodbye'.

Million Dollar Baby was released by Warner Bros, in only eight theatres, in December 2004. Bleak posters featured Eastwood, Freeman and Swank, her distinctive plaited braid, angular beauty and icy, marble shoulders catching the cold light. The trailer gave little indication of what audiences could expect. Edited, as per the boxing genre, with a pumping soundtrack, only Freeman's narration hinted at the story's dark heart. Audiences hoping for frivolous, odd couple fare detailing old hand Eastwood teaching 'girlie' Swank were shocked by the powerful ending, as devastating a half-hour as has ever been put on film. Fearing spoilers, reviews hardly mentioned these latter stages. *Variety* praised Eastwood, 'Staying at the top of his game when most of his contemporaries have long since hung up their gloves, [he] delivers another knockout punch'. In the US, Christian groups attacked the film for its assisted suicide. As Eastwood recalled, 'People who hadn't even seen the movie were saying that it's pro-euthanasia, but it wasn't'. It became a hundred-million-dollar baby in the US alone, making it Eastwood's fourth most successful film of all time, as either actor or director, after *Gran Torino*, *In the Line of Fire* and *Unforgiven*. In the UK also, it did well, taking £5 million. The *Mail on Sunday* called it 'a masterpiece', while the *Independent on Sunday* raved, 'A film that takes your breath away'. Reviewers and audiences totally agreed on an Eastwood film for the first time since *Unforgiven*. The BBFC deemed it '12A' at the cinema and '12' on DVD. The blisteringly honest film may not be exceptionally strong stuff in terms of visual violence, but emotionally it is the cinematic equivalent of a death in the family.

At the 2005 Oscars, *Million Dollar Baby* took on all comers and won. Nominated for Editing (Cox), Adapted Screenplay (Haggis) and Lead Actor (Eastwood), Swank collected Best Actress and Freeman won Best Supporting Actor. Even more impressive, Eastwood again won Best Director and the movie, Best Motion Picture. It was a deserved honour for a film streets ahead of its competitors. It also did well at the Golden Globes, garnering Best Actress (Swank) and Best Director, while failing in its nominations for Supporting Actor (Freeman), Motion Picture Drama and for Eastwood's delicate, moving score, with its twinkling descending piano motif. The score, incorporating Bruce Forman's guitar work, was orchestrated and conducted by Lennie Niehaus. Eastwood composed 'Blue Morgan' for the film, while his son Kyle co-wrote 'Boxing Baby' and 'Blue Diner' (both with Michael Stevens) and 'Solferino' (with Stevens and David Potaux-Razel).

Toole's source novel *Rope Burns* was republished following the film's success as *Million Dollar Baby: Stories from the Corner*. Toole had actually been a trainer and a 'cut man', who had spent 40 years attempting to get his stories published. He was almost 70 when *Rope Burns* was issued and he died in 2002. Haggis won a Best Picture Oscar of his own for *Crash* (2005), which he also directed, and continues to be highly successful working on the re-branded Bonds *Casino Royale* (2006) and *Quantum of Solace* (2008). *Million Dollar Baby* also proved that Eastwood the actor still wasn't out for the count. But as Scrap-Iron notes of his own career, it's just a case of knowing when to quit – 'Everybody's got a particular number of fights in them'.

PART SIX
THE THRILLERS

In addition to his many urban cop action movies, Clint Eastwood has made several thrillers which are more difficult to categorise. These films often featured Eastwood attempting to solve a mystery or as a protagonist engulfed in an exhilarating race against the clock. They cast Eastwood in such uncharacteristic roles as a hit man (*The Eiger Sanction*), a resourceful prisoner (*Escape from Alcatraz*), a master art thief (*Absolute Power*), a journalist (*True Crime*), an FBI profiler (*Blood Work*) and an on-the-lamb bank robber (*Thunderbolt and Lightfoot*). Interestingly, like his westerns, they often place him outside the law, but Eastwood is always the heroic 'good guy' – whether he's playing the outlaw Josey Wales, a bank robber or an art thief.

Thunderbolt and Lightfoot (1974)

During the preparations for *Magnum Force* in 1973, Eastwood received a script from Michael Cimino called *Thunderbolt and Lightfoot*. Eastwood liked its idiosyncrasy and asked Cimino to help out with rewrites on *Magnum Force*, when writer John Milius left to direct *Dillinger* (1973). With *Magnum Force* completed, Cimino stipulated that he also wanted to direct his script, even though he had made only documentaries and commercials. Eastwood agreed and so one of his most underrated films was born, a comedy thriller with more thrills than comedy, and more tragedy than either.

Ex-bank robber John Doherty (Eastwood) is hiding out, posing as a country reverend, until Dunlop, one of his old comrades, tracks him down. By chance, Lightfoot (Jeff Bridges), a young drifter, saves Doherty's life, killing Dunlop. The two form a friendship as they travel aimlessly through Idaho and Montana. Lightfoot discovers that Doherty is the famous criminal 'The Thunderbolt', who robbed the bank vault at the Montana Armory with the help of electronics expert Dunlop, safecracker Red Leary (George Kennedy), driver Eddie Goody (Geoffrey Lewis), planner Billy Lamb and a 20mm cannon with armoured-piercing shells. They succeeded and Lamb and Doherty hid the $500,000 haul behind the blackboard in the one-room schoolhouse Lamb attended as a child. But the gang fell out, Lamb died and Leary told Dunlop and Goody that Thunderbolt had double-crossed them, so Doherty went into hiding as the 'preacher'. Thunderbolt and Lightfoot return to the schoolhouse in Warsaw, Montana, to discover that the old one has been demolished and a new one built in its place. Leary and Goody show up and they decide to join forces and take the Montana Armory again: maybe exactly the same plan can work twice. Lightfoot, in drag, distracts the warning alarm operator, while Leary and Thunderbolt raid the Armory, again blasting the vault with a cannon. With Goody as their getaway driver, the heist works, but the police give chase. Goody is shot dead, Leary takes the loot and is killed, but not before administering a severe beating to Lightfoot. In an epic twist, as Thunderbolt and Lightfoot wander through the countryside after the robbery, they find the Warsaw school, moved intact to a new location. Inside they find the cash, but Lightfoot is obviously badly injured. Earlier he'd told Thunderbolt that it has always been his dream to walk into a showroom and buy a brand new white Cadillac convertible. He achieves his dream, but as Thunderbolt drives them away 'to see what's over the next mountain', Lightfoot dies in the passenger seat of his injuries and Thunderbolt snaps his celebratory cigar: their partnership is over.

Thunderbolt and Lightfoot was filmed with a $4 million budget, from July to September 1973, in the rolling countryside of Montana around Great Falls, Ulm, Hobson, Fort Benton, Choteau and August. This majestic backdrop of valleys, cornfields, rivers, lakes, girder bridges and the Rockies, photographed by Frank Stanley (from *Magnum Force* and *Breezy*), makes this Eastwood's most scenic film of the seventies. The story's structure and banter resemble *Butch Cassidy and the Sundance Kid* (1969), with its similarly tragic turn, and the exploits of *Bonnie and Clyde* (1967). The scenes with Lightfoot in drag, wearing a blond wig, make this even more apparent.

Cimino had written the role of laconic 'Thunderbolt' with Eastwood in mind, but his light-footed foil would have to carry the film: a teaming of effervescence and cool. The flashy, garrulous, hopelessly optimistic Lightfoot was played by 24-year-old, LA-born Jeff Bridges, the son of Lloyd Bridges (from *High Noon* and the 'Airplane'

6.1 Crazy Preacher: John 'The Thunderbolt' Doherty travels incognito in an unlikely disguise; Clint Eastwood smiles in *Thunderbolt and Lightfoot* (1974). Image courtesy Kevin Wilkinson Collection.

films). Bridges was carving a career for himself as a promising star, having received a Best Supporting Actor Oscar nomination for his role as Duane Jackson in *The Last Picture Show* (1971).

It is with *Thunderbolt* that the Malpaso stock company of actors began to evolve – actors whom Eastwood liked working with would be rehired on future projects, including Bill McKinney and Geoffrey Lewis. McKinney, who had appeared as the rapacious hillbilly mountain man in *Deliverance* (1972) and as an assassin in *The Parallax View* (1974), was cast as a crazy bumpkin driver who picks up hitchhikers Thunderbolt and Lightfoot – he has a racoon in a cage on his front seat, the car's exhaust piped into the car and a boot full of white rabbits. He suddenly pulls over and starts shooting the rabbits with a pump action shotgun, in one of the bizarre vignettes that pepper the film. Geoffrey Lewis had appeared in *The Culpepper Cattle Company, Bad Company* (both 1972, the latter opposite Bridges) and *High Plains Drifter*. *Thunderbolt* was the first film where he was cast as a bumbling comedy sidekick. George Kennedy played Leary, a sadist. He is the character who most undercuts the film's humour with his pugnacious greed and crabby, sweaty demeanour. Kennedy went on to appear in *The Eiger Sanction*, but he never made it as a full-fledged member of the Malpaso company. Gregory Walcott appeared as duped used car salesman, Pete and Lightfoot's one-night-stand, Melody, was played by Catherine Bach, five years prior to becoming pin-up girl Daisy Duke in *The Dukes of Hazzard* (1979–85).

Thunderbolt and Lightfoot is the most nostalgic of Eastwood's early films and is filled with references to America, American history and the American dream. When Thunderbolt and Lightfoot stumble upon the Warsaw schoolhouse, preserved as a national treasure, Thunderbolt marvels, 'History, dammit'. 'Do you think...?' wonders Lightfoot of the hidden cash. 'I don't know', answers Thunderbolt, 'But it do present mind-boggling possibilities'. The ferry launch they hitch a ride on from Hell's Canyon on the Snake River is called *Idaho Dream* and both Thunderbolt and Lightfoot dream big – the sky's the limit in Montana's 'Big Sky Country'. The film also details the rural battle against the undertow of modernisation. The dreamers' landscape is partly small-town America, partly idyllic breathtaking countryside, with long, dusty roads tapering to tomorrow's horizon. As the white Cadillac drives off at 'The End', the melancholy title song 'Where Do I Go from Here?', written and performed by Cat Stevens sound-alike Paul Williams, sums up the characters' aimless existence and shattered dreams:

> *If I knew the way, I'd go back home*
> *But the countryside has changed so much I'd surely end up lost*
> *Half-remembered names and faces, so fond in the past*
> *On the other side of bridges that were burned once they were crossed*

This America of pickup trucks and guitar-pickin' country music, populated by folksy, whimsical characters, would soon become even more important to Eastwood.

Thunderbolt bears the hallmarks of road movies such as *Vanishing Point* and *Two-Lane Blacktop* (both 1971); one critic actually called it 'a right-wing *Easy Rider*', but *Thunderbolt* is lighter and more scatological in tone, at least until its finale. The film even harks back to Depression Era gangster movies and contrasts them with their modern counterparts. Leary, Goody and Dunlop, dressed in black suits, look like Al Capone hitmen, old style gangsters in an old-style Ford. In their brightly patterned shirts, Thunderbolt and Lightfoot, speeding along in a Firebird (which Lightfoot steals by pretending to have a wooden leg), are altogether more hip, though the film never feels like it's set in the seventies – the shirt collars are the only giveaway of that – but rather in a timeless blur somewhere between the two eras. Dunlop blasts away at Thunderbolt with a 9mm Mauser Broomhandle, original vintage 1896, while 'The Thunderbolt' demolishes a safe with armoured-piercing shells from his 20mm cannon.

Thunderbolt is difficult to pigeonhole and is all the better for its anarchic mixture of styles. The central characters are contrasted both with mainstream society and its oddball fringes. The film is peppered with eccentrics: a talkative gas station attendant (played by irascible Dub Taylor) who hates credit cards and is convinced the entire country's financial security is dependant on one little old lady, and McKinney's rabbit-shooter, a crazed Elma Fudd. A humorous passage sees the gang forced to rejoin society, in the short-term, taking regular jobs to bankroll their heist. Thunderbolt works in a welding plant, Lightfoot as a landscape gardener for Pinski Bros, while Goody becomes a Frosty's ice cream man, with Leary reading out his route. But the heroes, like Butch, Sundance, Bonnie and Clyde, are forever outsiders.

There are also several references to Thunderbolt's age and Lightfoot's youth. When Thunderbolt spends the night with Gloria, his much younger date, he tells her he fought in Korea; 'Oh yea, I heard about that war', she answers. 'Thunderbolt and Lightfoot – that sounds like something, doesn't it?' enthuses Lightfoot, but the older man's dynamic duo days are behind him. In a diner, Thunderbolt makes his case with quoted poetry: 'Clock uncoils the working day and wakes up feeling his youth has gone away'. 'You stick with me kid', answers Lightfoot, ignoring Thunderbolt's pessimism, 'You gonna live forever!' Cimino's sharp script is what makes the film so successful. Lightfoot explains to Thunderbolt, still disguised as a reverend, that he mistook him for a cop. 'Do I look like heat?' blurts Thunderbolt; 'You look like one crazy son-of-a-bitch for a preacher!' Thunderbolt asks blond, blue-eyed, light-fingered Lightfoot if he's an Indian; 'No, just American', a typically liberal sentiment – Indians in cinema were no longer 'Injuns', but Native Americans. Early on, when Thunderbolt tries to give Lightfoot a watch, Lightfoot says, 'I want your friendship...we're good together'. 'Kid', replies Thunderbolt resignedly, 'You're 10 years too late'. 'You're as young as you feel', answers Lightfoot.

It was Cimino's plan to get Bridges to make Eastwood laugh, as Cimino said Eastwood didn't smile onscreen. During their dialogues, Eastwood did indeed smile and laugh – and laugh naturally, not his usual forced grimace. Eastwood's easygoing

6.2 'They have exactly seven minutes to get rich quick': US one-sheet Style 'A' poster promoting *Thunderbolt and Lightfoot* (1974), starring Clint Eastwood and Jeff Bridges as the bank robbing title duo. Poster courtesy Ian Caunce Collection.

charm and broad grin, most noticeable in the scene where Lightfoot has some racoon excrement on his hand and threatens to wipe it on Thunderbolt's shirt, make this one of Eastwood's most spontaneous, believable performances. Bridges' acting is equally impressive. His switch from fearless, leather-trousered dude with his whole life ahead of him, to a man suffering horrific creeping paralysis, caused by internal injuries and brain damage, is very moving. Such pessimism would reappear in Eastwood's later directorial work. Youth withers and dies – nobody lives forever.

Thunderbolt and Lightfoot was released via United Artists in the US at the end of May 1974. The film's posters and trailer celebrated Eastwood and the action, at the expense of all else. United Artists seemed determined to cash in on Eastwood's cop movies, which were made at rival Warners. Eastwood disliked UA exploiting this angle and condemned their mishandled promotional campaign when the film took only $21 million in the US – a shock after *Magnum Force*'s $40 million. It was the first time UA had handled an Eastwood film since *Hang 'Em High* and their fumbling proved fatal. Eastwood has never worked for UA since. It was rated 'R' in the US, for violence, nudity and profanity, an 'X' in the UK. Subsequent UK releases on video and DVD are rated '18'. One strong line of dialogue that is missing from all UK TV prints is the moment when Goody and Leary are serving ice cream from their float and a boy keeps asking for a flavour they haven't got. 'Hey kid', snaps Leary, 'Go fuck a duck'.

The film received largely favourable notices, with *Film Weekly* liking Eastwood and Bridges and warning: 'Watch out for new director Cimino'. But Rex Reed in the *New York Daily News* was unconvinced, calling it 'a demented exercise in Hollywood hackery', deploying 'lame gags that would have been rejected by the Three Stooges'. Not an Eastwood fan, Reed didn't just dislike the film, he hated it: 'Cheap pot-boilers like this shouldn't be released. They should be recycled and used to catch droppings on the floors of chicken coops'. Bridges was nominated for the Best Supporting Actor Oscar again, this time losing out to Robert De Niro as Vito Corleone in *The Godfather Part II* (1974). Rex Reed had noted that Cimino was a director 'about whom you're unlikely to hear more'. Cimino went on to win the Best Director Oscar for the Best Film Oscar-winner *The Deer Hunter* (1978), before destroying his career, and several others, with *Heaven's Gate* (1980), when the budget rocketed horrifically from $7.5 million to $44 million. United Artists lost out again: hit film *The Deer Hunter* had been made for Universal, while UA were unlucky enough to finance *Heaven's Gate*, which almost bankrupted them.

The Eiger Sanction (1975)

Eastwood immediately followed *Thunderbolt and Lightfoot* with *The Eiger Sanction*, based on a 1972 best-seller by Trevanian. Eastwood directed and also starred – somewhat implausibly – as Dr Jonathan Hemlock, a Californian lecturer in the History of Art, who is a retired killer formerly employed by the clandestine government assassination bureau, C2. When their agent 'Wormwood' has his throat slit in Zurich and the microfilm detailing a new formula for germ warfare is stolen, C2 contacts Hemlock for one last job to 'sanction' his two killers. An avid art collector, Hemlock visits his old boss, Mr Dragon (Thayer David), who convinces him to undertake one sanction in Zurich, for $20,000 and an IRS certificate validating his large illegal collection of paintings. Hemlock sanctions the first murderer, Garcia Kruger. When Hemlock finds out that 'Wormwood' was the codename for his old comrade Henri Bach, Hemlock agrees to carry out the second killing for $100,000. C2 doesn't actually know the killer's identity, but they do know he will be part of an international team embarking on a 'Goodwill Climb' of the notoriously difficult North Face of the Eiger. Hemlock's only clue is that the target walks with a limp. Hemlock used to be a mountaineer and trains at the climbing camp of his friend Ben Bowman (George Kennedy). The expedition team are Hemlock, German Karl Freytag, Austrian Anderl Meyer and Frenchman Jean-Pierre Montaigne, with Bowman as their ground man. During the ascent, Montaigne is badly injured, then the weather turns worse, with a freeze. With the party stranded in snow, Montaigne dies, while the survivors attempt the descent. Bowman leads the rescue mission, but both Meyer and Freytag are killed in accidents, and Hemlock is left dangling. At this vital moment, when he must trust Bowman with his life, Hemlock notices that Bowman walks with a limp. Hemlock trusts Bowman and is rescued, he then lets his old friend live, as it was knifeman Kruger who actually killed Bach. Bach was sacrificed by C2 because the microfilm was a fake, but in order for the 'other side' to be convinced it was authentic we had to trawl through this pantomime for the past two hours.

In the 1971 *Photoplay Film Annual*, Steve McQueen mentions that his next project is *Man on a Nylon String*, 'a mystery adventure story about mountaineers who attempt to conquer Switzerland's giant Eiger', but the project never materialised. *The Eiger Sanction* unfortunately did. Owing plenty to James Bond films, to Euro-thriller sagas depicting ruthless hit men working in international locales, and Cold War espionage of *The Ipcress File* variety, it seems like three separate films glued together, or as if Alain Delon's hitman *Le Samouraï* had decided to take a holiday and tackle Mont Blanc. *Sanction* begins in familiar Euro-thriller territory, with the death of Wormwood in chilly Zurich. This first section has bespectacled Hemlock enticed out of retirement by his old employers, with a fee that will enable him to buy 'Woman Digging in an Orchard', an 1882 painting by Camille Pissarro. C2 is an odd bunch, almost parodic. Its boss is Dragon, a portly, reptilian, pink-eyed albino with a whispering, raspy voice. Ultra-sensitive to light, cold and germs, he hides in his headquarters, bathed in red-light Bond villain décor. His secretary Miss Cerberus is named after the three-headed Hellhound of mythology, which the dead encounter once across the River Styx. Thuggish C2 operative Pope, a degenerate in smudge sunglasses, is played by Eastwood regular Gregory Walcott, who in the Swiss scenes dons a horrible chequered jacket that makes him look like a Battenburg cake.

Hemlock's home scenes were filmed in Carmel, while the training section was shot on location in Zion National Park, Utah, and in Monument Valley. For one impressive scene, Hemlock and Bowman scale the Totem Pole in the valley (an icon familiar from many John Ford westerns) and enjoy a beer in triumph atop the sandstone spire. The Eiger expedition scenes were shot in Switzerland, including the city of Zurich and the River Limmat. All the Eiger footage was filmed on the actual mountain in the Swiss Alps. The Eiger is situated in the Bernese Oberland above Bern and is 13,025 feet (3,970 metres) high. The route took the team up the 'Northwall', the infamous North Face of the Eiger. The crew arrived in Grindelwald and the chalet-style, balconied Hotel Bellevue des Alpes was used as the climbers' base in the film. The hotel, in Kleine Scheidegg, near Wengen, had a railway station as part of the mountain rail link. Helicopters ferried the actors and a specialist international climbing team to the mountain. Norman Dyhrenfurth was the leader of the expedition, with Mike Hoover as climbing advisor. The mountain sequences were photographed by Hoover, John Cleare, Jeff Schoolfield, Peter Pilafian and Pete White. The sheer rock faces, often wreathed in billowing clouds or sheathed in ice and snow, look extraordinarily dangerous, with the climbers perched high above the green valley. The climbers employed crampons (boot spikes), ice axes, carabiners (metal looped rings) and a network of ropes to negotiate the precipitous ascent. A team of climbers from the Dougal Haston International School of Mountaineering, including Haston himself, worked on the film. The others were David Knowles, Ben Clark, Martin Boysen, Guy Neithardt and Charles Scott (27-year-old Knowles was accidentally killed during the shoot by a falling rock).

Thanks to the underwritten script, seductive C2 agent Jemima Brown (blaxploitation actress Vonetta McGee) is little more than a cardboard Mata Hari. Hemlock's personal trainer is Native American beauty George, Bowman's busty daughter (Brenda Venus), with long dark hair and cut-off denim shorts. All the other female roles in *Sanction* are sexy stereotypes of the worst kind – from the blonde art student who tries to bed Hemlock to 'maintain a B average', to the scantily clad beauties hovering around the swimming pool at Bowman's training camp. The fact that Susan Morgan, playing a brief role wearing a brief pink bikini, is billed simply as 'Buns' gives a fair indication of the film's attitude to its female characters. *Sanction* is guilty at various points of sexism, racism and homophobia. When he tries to catch George on one of their jogging excursions, Hemlock mumbles comments about wishing Custer had won and 'Screw Marlon Brando', a reference to Brando's championing of Native American issues at the 1973 Oscars. Hemlock's insulting language, to Jemima, George, even albino Dragon, strikes a sour note. For its proliferation such racism and sexism, satirised so well in the *Dirty Harry* movies, loses all irony here.

At the training camp, we are sidetracked by a subplot, involving Miles Mellough, who fought in Indochina with Bach and Hemlock. Mellough knows who killed Bach and offers to exchange the information for his life. As played by all-round-entertainer Jack Cassidy (father of singer David) in an embroidered safari suit, Errol Flynn moustache and russet complexion, Mellough is the kind of seventies camp stereotype that

6.3 'His lifeline held by the assassin he hunted': US one-sheet poster advertising Clint Eastwood's cliffhanging thriller *The Eiger Sanction* (1975). Poster courtesy Ian Caunce Collection.

looked ridiculous then, but even more so now. He even has a hunky henchman called Dewayne and a pet terrier called Faggot. When Hemlock shoots Dewayne dead in the middle of the desert, Mellough wails, 'Jonathan, you are an animal!' Mellough is abandoned in parched Monument Valley without water, while Faggot hops aboard Hemlock's jeep. Bowman later reports that the police found Mellough's corpse, 'Dead as Kelsey's Nuts'.

Hemlock has failed to climb the Eiger twice before (and fails once again here), while he doesn't carry out his sanction either, ending the film on a strangely dissatisfying note. Trevanian, who followed *The Eiger Sanction* with *The Loo Sanction* (1973), worked on an early draft of the film adaptation as 'Rod Whitaker' (his real name is Rodney William Whitaker), along with Warren B. Murphy and Hal Dresner. Eastwood's decision to make *The Eiger Sanction* may be baffling now, but cunning marketing ensured its success. Posters exclaimed in Bondian fashion, 'Eastwood is the man … Eiger is the location … and the sanction – is a license to kill!' In the US, the film was released in May 1975 rated 'R'; the UK release, through CIC, was rated 'AA' after being cut from 125 to 119 minutes. The *Monthly Film Bulletin* noted, 'All the villains have been constructed from pre-fabricated Bond models … Eastwood the director asks of Eastwood the actor only the faint curling of the lip as every female character topples before him'. *Variety* praised the suspenseful Swiss and

Monument Valley climbs, *Film Weekly* deemed it 'a good film to sleep to', while the *Wall Street Journal* noticed distastefully that the villains were 'homosexuals and physically disabled men'. It still took over $14 million in the US – at least someone made a killing.

Escape from Alcatraz (1979)

Wedged between *Every Which Way But Loose* (1978) and *Bronco Billy* (1980), during Eastwood's whimsical 'light comedy period', his next thriller incarcerated him in the most escape-proof detention centre in the US. The star had found himself locked up onscreen before, in *The Good, the Bad and the Ugly*, *Hang 'Em High* and *Joe Kidd*. But in his thriller *Escape from Alcatraz*, directed by Don Siegel, his captors are determined he'll remain behind bars.

Alcatraz was Eastwood and Siegel's fifth, and last, collaboration. Siegel had made the prison classic *Riot in Cell Block 11* (1954). Eastwood plays inmate Frank Lee Morris, a detainee at Atlanta State Prison, who on 18 January 1960 is transferred to the island prison of Alcatraz, built on a rock in San Francisco Bay. Although the Warden (Patrick McGoohan) vows that his prison is escape-proof, Morris, plus the Anglin brothers, Clarence and John (Jack Thibeau and Fred Ward), plot their escape. They improvise tools and dig by night, tunnelling through the concrete walls, which are moisture-damaged by the sea air around the rusty latticed ventilation grilles. With cardboard dummies left in their beds, the trio escapes into the vent ducts, climbs onto the roof, and then doggy-paddles across the bay on a homemade raft, wearing makeshift lifejackets. The next day, on nearby Angel Island, a pouch containing photographs and a notebook belonging to Clarence is found, and the Warden discovers a chrysanthemum, a genus not native to the island, but grown on Alcatraz by green-fingered prisoners.

Though this story sounds pure Hollywood fiction, it is, in fact, based on a true story. On 11 June 1962, Frank Morris and the Anglin brothers did tunnel out of the concrete maximum-security prison with modified spoons, construct papier-mache dummies of themselves and float to freedom on a raft made of raincoats. They were never seen again and no bodies were ever found, leading to speculation that they had succeeded, making them the only inmates ever to do so. Of the 39 who attempted to escape, 26 were recaptured, seven were shot dead and three drowned.

Alcatraz Prison, now a popular tourist attraction, was named by Spanish explorers, who saw an island covered in pelicans: 'Isla de los Alcatraces'. In 1848, it was bought by the US government and it remained army property until 1934, when it became a maximum-security prison, known as 'The Rock' or 'America's Devil's Island'. Its brightly lit central corridor, illuminated 24 hours a day, was named 'Broadway' by inmates. On foggy nights, prisoners were driven mad by blasting foghorns, the 'Alcatraz Symphony'. Insanity was a merciful release for some, while other tried suicide, charging their cell bars or concrete walls headfirst like bulls, or slashing their wrists, tendons or throat with razorblades or the tiny blade from a pencil sharpener. Closed as a prison in 1963, Alcatraz was used memorably in Lee Marvin's crime thriller *Point Blank* (1967) and Eastwood had filmed the climax of *The Enforcer* there.

Written by Richard Tuggle, the film was an adaptation of *Escape from Alcatraz: A Farewell to the Rock* (1963), a book by J. Campbell Bruce. Siegel had read Campbell's book in 1966 and had even prepared a treatment of it called 'The Rock', but when he read Tuggle's version he paid $100,000 of his own money to secure the rights. It became a Malpaso-Siegel Production for Paramount, budgeted at $8 million. Even with the Siegel-Eastwood team, the film was still a gamble. Its static setting meant that the actors, particularly Eastwood, would have to carry the film. Shooting began in October 1978 and worked around the tours of sightseers who flocked to the island, with much of the shoot done at night in freezing, damp conditions; Eastwood equated it with 'working in a meat locker'. Paramount spent $500,000 renovating the prison, which had fallen into disrepair, while some cell interiors were filmed at Paramount Studios on sets.

Alcatraz is populated with a roster of 'Big House' archetypes. The Anglin brothers were typical jailhouse rocks, ready for a breakout. Charley Butts (played by Larry Hankin) decides to join the escape attempt when he learns that his mother is terminally ill but loses his nerve on the fatal night. When his wife comes to visit, they have to communicate by telephone, separated by glass, their hands reaching for one another either side of the pane. Paul Benjamin played black librarian English, given back-to-back 99-year sentences for killing two white knife-wielding Alabama rednecks. Bruce M. Fischer played Wolf, the psychosexual thug who wants Morris as his 'punk'. Frank Ronzio was scrounger Litmus, who feeds spaghetti to his pet mouse and dies of a heart attack when provoked by the Warden; the mouse fares better and travels in Morris's pocket during the escape attempt. Most affecting is elderly Chester 'Doc' Dalton (Roberts Blossom), an artist who lives for his painting. When the Warden sees a portrait of himself, he hates Doc's representation of him and takes away Doc's privileges: 'Painting's all I have', pleads Doc, before he chops off the fingers of his own right hand with a hatchet, ensuring he'll never paint again. The Alcatraz Warden, an authoritarian, inflexible sadist, was played by Patrick McGoohan, who once upon a time had been incarcerated himself, as Number Six in TV's *The Prisoner* (1967–68).

The power play between Morris and the Warden provides the film with its best dialogue, with McGoohan on excellent, callous form. 'If you disobey the rules of society', he tells Morris, 'they send you to prison. If you disobey the rules of prison, they send you to us...Alcatraz is not like any other prison in the United States'. Morris steals a nail clipper from the Warden's office, which later becomes his tool for chipping at the concrete vent surround. 'Alcatraz was built to keep all the rotten eggs in one basket', the Warden continues, 'I was especially chosen to make sure the stink from the basket does not escape...No one has ever escaped from Alcatraz and no one ever will'.

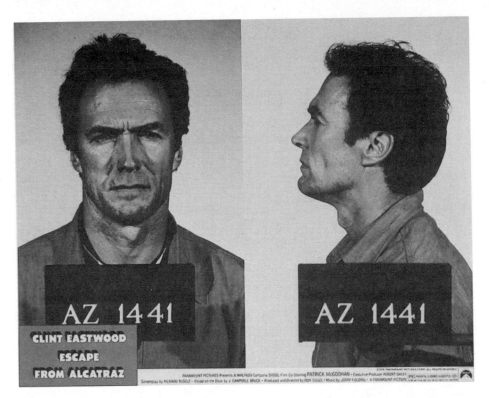

AZ 1441

AZ 1441

CLINT EASTWOOD
ESCAPE
FROM ALCATRAZ

6.4 'All The Bad Eggs': A mugshot of Frank Lee Morris, otherwise known as AZ 1441, in this US lobby card promoting *Escape from Alcatraz* (1979). Courtesy Ian Caunce Collection.

Escape from Alcatraz is Eastwood's fourth San Francisco-set movie of the seventies, following the dark *cinema vérité* of *Dirty Harry*, the sun-drenched *Magnum Force* and *The Enforcer*, and returning to darkness (and Siegel) for *Alcatraz*. It is Eastwood's most static, claustrophobic film, almost documentary-like in its realistic depiction of the prison's living conditions and the prisoners' escape. By night, the compound is strafed with searchlights, from watchtowers and a lighthouse, in contrast to its foreboding majesty when photographed bathed in beautiful Bay dawns. The regulated, compartmented hours and days are unflinchingly depicted; the film takes place over an 18-month period, though the sense of passing time is completely lost on the audience. This edgy, disorientating atmosphere is enhanced by Jerry Fielding's dissonant score. The robotic guards (or 'bulls') guide the robotic inmates through soulless chores – a life governed by headcounts, frisks and clanging, electronically operated gates and doors. As the Warden notes, 'We don't make good citizens, but we make good prisoners'.

But Morris, prisoner number AZ 1441 with a 'Superior I.Q.', is different and won't be broken by the Warden's regime. Initially a 'Fresh Fish' (new arrival), he soon settles into prison life, working in the library and as a carpenter, and trying to avoid trouble. The inmates' meticulous escape preparations are engrossing, as are the ingenious ways in which they collate and create their 'tools', often under the guards' noses. An electric drill is assembled using a drill bit, an extension cable and the motor from an electric desktop fan. Human hair is collected from the barber's by Clarence to provide convincing eyebrows and hairstyles for their papier-mache 'heads'. John Anglin steals raincoats from the clothing shop by wearing them. Morris makes himself a primitive scalpel-like chipping utensil by welding a spoon handle to a piece of the Warden's stolen nail clippers, using a dime as flux and a bundle of sulphur matches as his oxyacetylene torch.

Much has been written by critics concerning the film's 'unsatisfying' coda. Siegel's original ending closed with the guards' discovery of the dummy in Morris's bed, leaving the escape attempt's success hanging in the air. Eastwood disliked this and improved the ending, by inserting a brief scene of the Warden searching Angel Island and discovering a chrysanthemum on the rocks. The Warden is thus defeated and informed by his aide that he has been summoned to catch the next plane to Washington to face his superiors: the rotten egg stench has apparently escaped after all. The night fog was light, the tides mild. It is left up to the audience as to the prisoners' success.

Posters depicted Eastwood's face framed through a fractured slab of Alcatraz concrete, his sweating face granite and resolute as he chips his way to freedom. Quoting the Warden, the tagline ran: 'No one has ever escaped from Alcatraz... and no one

6.5 'The Rock': The bleak Maximum Security prison known as America's Devil's Island on Alcatraz in San Francisco Bay was used as the setting for *Escape from Alcatraz* (1979) and the climax of *The Enforcer* (1976); it is still a popular tourist attraction. Photograph courtesy Sonya-Jayne Stewart.

ever will'. It was rated 'PG' in the US, '15' in the UK and opened to the best reviews of Eastwood's career so far. Vincent Canby in the *New York Times* decreed, 'This is a first-rate movie. Terrifically acted', though he asked of Eastwood, 'Is it acting? I don't know, but he's a towering figure in [the film's] landscape'. *Time* urged audiences to 'rediscover the simple, classic pleasures of moviegoing ... *Alcatraz*'s cool, cinematic grace meshes ideally with the strengths of its star'. *Newsweek* called it 'splendid', *New York Daily News* deemed it 'neat and suspenseful', *New Republic* saw 'crystalline cinema', while Rex Reed thought it was 'thoughtful, sobering, gratifying ... [which] bobs pretty close to the top of its genre'. *Alcatraz* was also successful at the box office. It was the 15th most successful film of the year, taking over $20 million in the US when released in June 1979, though with its steely blue photography (by Bruce Surtees) and characters dressed in greatcoats and woolly hats, it's a very 'cold' summer movie. It remains one of the star's best performances and the only time Eastwood has played a named historical figure.

Absolute Power (1996)

Like the acclaimed *The Bridges of Madison County* which preceded it, *Absolute Power* was a literary adaptation. Based on the 1995 bestseller by David Baldacci, the screenplay, originally titled 'Executive Power', was written by Oscar-winner William Goldman, honoured for his scripts for two Robert Redford movies, *Butch Cassidy and the Sundance Kid* (1969) and *All the President's Men* (1976), the latter a dramatisation of the Watergate investigation which brought down President Nixon.

In *Absolute Power*, Eastwood plays master thief Luther Whitney, a Korean War veteran who hasn't been arrested in 30 years and who everyone presumes has retired. But Whitney is far from inactive and breaks into the country residence of rich industrialist and kingmaker Walter Sullivan. Hiding behind a two-way mirror looking out onto Sullivan's bedroom, Whitney sees Sullivan's wife, Christy (Melora Hardin) and Allen Richmond (Gene Hackman), the president of the United States. Their passionate encounter turns increasingly violent and when Richmond slaps Christy, she fights back. Richmond tries to strangle her, but she grabs a letter-opener and stabs him in the shoulder. She is about to kill him when two Secret Service agents, Bill Burton (Scott Glenn) and Tim Collin (Dennis Haysbert), burst in and shoot her dead. A quick cleanup operation engineered by White House Chief-of-Staff Gloria Russell (Judy Davis) ensures that it looks as though Christy encountered a burglar. Whitney manages to escape and takes the bloodstained letter-opener with him, incriminatingly covered in Christy's and the president's fingerprints. The Secret Service set about tracking him down as the chief 'suspect'. Walter Sullivan (E.G. Marshall) returns from his holiday in Barbados; it appears that he is an old friend of Richmond's, effectively buying him the presidency. Disgusted with Richmond's hypocrisy during a TV broadcast, Whitney resolves to expose the president as the liar he is. Sullivan hires McCarty, a professional assassin, to kill Christy's murderer, for a $1 million bounty and '$2 million a bullet', while the Secret Service keeps tabs on the police investigation, led by homicide detective Seth Frank (Ed Harris). Frank encourages Whitney's estranged daughter Kate (Laura Linney) to contact her father. In a rendezvous at Café Alonzo, both the Secret Service and Sullivan's sniper attempt to kill Whitney, but he eludes them. The Secret Service tries to kill Kate, shunting her car off a cliff, though she too survives. Posing as Sullivan's chauffeur, Whitney drives him to the White House and en route explains who is really responsible for Christy's slaying. Sullivan takes the letter-opener and confronts Richmond in his office, while Frank arrests Chief-of-Staff Russell. Soon afterwards, reports begin to surface of breaking news at the White House. Sullivan informs the press that the president has taken his own life, by stabbing himself with a letter-opener.

Filmed from June to July 1996, *Absolute Power*'s location scenes were lensed in Baltimore, Maryland, and in Washington DC. The exterior of the White House can be glimpsed, as can the Watergate Hotel, a reference to Nixon's downfall. The scene where Whitney sketches an El Greco was the Corcoran Gallery of Art and Detective Frank interviews Luther in the gallery's café. Frank knows that Whitney is one of only a few men capable of pulling such a complicated burglary. His interview with Whitney, when the old man claims to be inactive and have a pacemaker, is well acted by smiling, affable Eastwood and delving Ed Harris. The meeting between Kate and Whitney is engineered at the outdoor Café Alonzo, while following her 'car accident' she is rushed to Lafayette Medical Centre. The setting for the murder, the opulent county mansion of Walter Sullivan, with its crenellations and stone mullions, was the Maryvale School for Girls in Brooklandville.

Absolute Power provides interesting contrasts with *In the Line of Fire*, offering several reversals of the earlier story's ingredients. Here the shadowy Secret Service is the villain and the president isn't worth protecting. Eastwood was reunited with Gene Hackman from *Unforgiven* as the president, though, apart from the murder (where a two-way mirror separates them), they share no scenes. As in Petersen's film, a master of disguise eludes government agents. Whitney is ready to flee the country, with a selection of passports and personas, but when Richmond attempts to clear his own conscience by exploiting Sullivan on TV, shedding a crocodile tear, Whitney hisses at the screen, 'You heartless whore. I'm not about to run from you'. Whitney engineers the president's disgrace, by feeding unnerving clues to the president's immediate staff: Russell and her two agents, Burton and Collin.

Whitney's exposure of the president is excellently handled but lacks urgency and doesn't match *In the Line of Fire* for thrills. *Absolute Power* has an unremarkable piano and strings score by Lennie Niehaus but does boast two more Eastwood compositions, the 'Power Waltz' and 'Kate's Theme'. The lack of momentum is especially noticeable in the Café Alonso scene; this set-up, with two snipers, assassin McCarty (in an upper-story window) and Secret Service man Collin (hidden in a Maintenance van), should be a Kennedy-inspired highlight, but the slack pacing and unintentional humour spoil the scene. Supposedly trying to look inconspicuous, Whitney appears on a bright sunny day dressed in trench coat, hat and shades, like Inspector Clouseau. In a crucial change from Baldacci's book, Whitney survives to exact revenge on the president – the assassins at Café Alonzo are better shots in the book. Sullivan also fares better in the film, surviving to kill the president, and several characters are missing from the film, including attorney Jack Graham. Kate's love story subplot with Graham is shifted to become a relationship with Detective Frank.

The key difference between *Absolute Power* and *In the Line of Fire* is the lack of love interest for Eastwood. Here his screen relationship is between father and daughter. The family scenes between Whitney and Kate are most effective; these were expanded by Goldman from initial drafts of the screenplay and Laura Linney makes the most of the role's poignancy. Whitney was never there for her and since the death of his wife a year ago, she hasn't seen him. Now a successful attorney, Kate thinks he has missed out on all her successes. But when she and Detective Frank search Whitney's house, they discover dozens of family photographs, including many of her: at her graduation, at work after she won her first case, at all the key moments in her life, when she thought he wasn't there. This strong family thread is continued by the casting of two of Eastwood's daughters in bit parts. Alison plays the art student who admires Whitney's sketches in the Corcoran, and Kimber Eastwood, from his relationship with Roxanne Tunis, appeared as a White House tour guide who shows around a party which includes a heavily disguised, bearded Whitney.

A subplot dealing with Secret Service agent Bill Burton is particularly well handled – Burton keeps track of the investigation and Scott Glenn's performance is one of the film's standouts. In the climax, Burton is found slumped over his desk, dead from a self-inflicted bullet wound, and the evidence against Richmond, Russell and the Secret Service carefully documented on cassettes.

Absolute Power was released in the US on Valentine's Day 1997 to generally favourable reviews. Stanley Kaufman in *The New Republic* wrote: 'Eastwood understands, as a director, what his star's face is worth – a testament of life lived, of victories missed and defeats redeemed, of a worn but persistent beauty', while the *Los Angeles Times* referenced Whitney's love of fine art and called Eastwood 'the last Old Master in Hollywood, just as reliable in his sphere (at least when he's not co-starring with orang-utans) as Rembrandt and Rubens were in theirs'. It took $50 million in the US. In the UK, it was released in May; 'This classy thriller grips from first to last', wrote the *Daily Star*. Posters blended a portrait of the star, a detail of the presidential seal and Christy's slain corpse with the predictable tagline, quoting Lord Acton: 'Absolute Power…Corrupts Absolutely'.

True Crime (1999)

Following Eastwood's stint behind the camera in *Midnight in the Garden of Good and Evil*, *True Crime* featured another of his mature acting roles, which further developed the 'reformed alcoholic' character the actor was fond of revisiting, from *The Gauntlet* through to *Unforgiven*. An adaptation of Andrew Klavan's 1995 novel of the same name, the film had a screenplay written by Larry Gross, Paul Brickman and Stephen Schiff, contrasting stories of two very different men and their families.

Frank Louis Beechum (Isaiah Washington) is on death row in the California State Prison at San Quentin. Six years ago mechanic Beechum was found guilty of murder in the first degree. On 4 July, he shot 20-year-old Amy Wilson, who was working behind the till of Pocum's Grocery and Liquor store in Richmond – she owed him $96 for work done on her car. Amy was expecting and both she and her baby died as a result of a gunshot to the chest. There were two witnesses: Nancy Larson, who saw Beechum escaping through the car park, and accountant Dale Porterhouse, who entered the store and saw Beechum standing over Amy's body brandishing a pistol. Michelle Ziegler (Mary McCormack), a reporter on the *Oakland Tribune*, is scheduled to interview Beechum on his final day and then watch his execution by lethal injection at one minute past midnight, but she is killed in a car crash the night before at notorious 'Dead Man's Curve'. Her colleague at the *Tribune*, veteran journalist Steve 'Ev' Everett (Eastwood), is assigned the job, to produce a human-interest article on Beechum's last hours. As he researches his subject, Everett begins to suspect that Michelle was onto something: it appears there was a third witness who was never investigated. As the hours tick by, Beechum is prepared for his death and bids his wife and daughter goodbye, while Everett frantically tries to piece together the fragments. With the lethal dose seeping into Beechum's veins, Everett finds the key to the mystery and saves the innocent man's life.

True Crime is a simple story, well told, with an especially strong cast. Isaiah Washington, who received glowing notices from critics, gave a moving portrayal of Beechum, the car mechanic who simply went to Pocum's to pick up some 'A-1 Steak Sauce'. In Klavan's book, Beechum (spelt 'Beachum') is white and the setting is Missouri, with Michelle writing her article for the *St Louis News*. Washington's scenes with his wife Bonnie (played by Lisa Gay Hamilton) and little daughter Gail (Penny Bae Bridges) convincingly enact the most awful moment in a condemned man's life, when the time comes to say goodbye to his loved ones. Beechum is a 'born again' – as cynical Everett observes, most prisoners on death row are – and is calm and contemplative of his fate. Washington's noble performance convincingly depicts extreme moments of emotional release, as when he realises that his daughter is being torn from him for the last time – her 'Goodbye daddy' visibly shakes him up. At one point little Gail asks why she can't come to see Daddy tomorrow, but for Beechum tomorrow is a long way away.

The rest of the cast enhance the powerful drama. Bernard Hill, Yosser Hughes in UK TV's *Boys from the Black Stuff* (1982), was cast as Warden Plunkitt. Mike McKean, guitarist David St Hubbins in *This is Spinal Tap*, appeared as San Quentin's Reverend Shillerman and comedian and actor Denis Leary was cast as Bob Findley, Everett's boss at the *Tribune*. Their antagonism is further enhanced by the fact that Everett is sleeping with Findley's wife. Findley has always hated Everett, but the affair has provided him with an 'ethical mandate to annihilate' Everett. Apart from Washington, the casting highlight is James Woods, one of the most respected actors of his generation, who plays the snapping, motor-mouth *Tribune* editor-in-chief Alan Mann, a fast-talking newspaperman in extremis: Jimmy Cagney on speed. 'Stop fucking Bob's wife', he deadpans to Everett at one point, 'He doesn't like it'. 'What'd he do?' asks bemused Everett, 'Put it in the company newspaper?' Sparks fly in the Eastwood–Woods scenes, as Mann warns Everett what he thinks of reporters with hunches: 'Cos honest to God, I don't know whose ass you're trying to save here – Beechum's or your own – but if your nose for a story has gone my friend, you are gone too'.

Some critics have noted that 69-year-old Eastwood is a little mature for Everett (aged 35 in the novel), but this doesn't detract from his driven performance. Everett is a philanderer and a recovering alcoholic (now 'sober as an ex-drunk') who is 'chasing salvation' via a big story. During his drinking period, he made a fool of himself on the Mike Vargas rape case, where he campaigned for the man's innocence. When threatened with a DNA test, Vargas confessed. But when on-form, Everett has also brought down the mayor of New York on corruption charges. His reputation and nose for a story are second to none.

Unfortunately, when his 'nose is working' all else in his life suffers, including his family. Caught up in his investigation, he forgets that he is due to take his daughter Kate (played by Eastwood's own daughter Francesca Fisher-Eastwood) to the zoo. When he takes her there in a rush, he plonks her on a trolley and whizzes her around, playing 'Speed Zoo', until on a bend the trolley topples over and Kate sprawls across the gravel. Everett returns Kate to Barbara, his wife (Diane Venora), with plasters on her grazed face. Francesca's mother, Frances Fisher, also appears in the film, as a red-head DA who delights in putting paid to Everett's theories, telling him that Beechum took a lie-detector test and 'flunked it, big time'. The actor-director's second wife, Dina Eastwood (nee Ruiz), also crops up as Wilma Francis, a reporter interviewing protesters outside San Quentin.

While *True Crime* doesn't take place in 'reel time', the cross-cutting and the appearance of several clock faces – as the hands swing inexorably towards 12.01 – recall suspenseful *High Noon*. *True Crime* creates a believable milieu through its use of location filming at San Quentin and in Oakland – the actual *Tribune* exterior, the Alameda County Courthouse and the Oakland Zoo all appear. The bar seen in the film, The Washoe House, is also a real place.

Michele tells Everett that she suspects something 'stinks' about the case and *True Crime* incorporates biographical flashbacks to Beechum's early life and re-enactments of the robbery and murder. Everett realises that shrewish accountant Dale Porterhouse couldn't have seen whether Beechum was holding a pistol in his hand, because of a stand displaying Granny Goose potato chips. He also finds that Michelle has unearthed another witness at the scene, a young black man named Warren Russell, who claimed that he just went into the store to buy a soda. In her interview notes, Michelle has scrawled 'something fishy here' and when Everett tracks down Russell's grandmother Angela (Hattie Winston), she is wearing murder victim Amy's heart-shaped necklace.

When Everett visits San Quentin to interview Beechum, a guard warns him that condemned prisoners have a tendency to lie to reporters: 'Well everyone lies pal', answers Everett, 'I'm just here to write it down'. He asks Beechum, point-blank: 'Did you kill that woman or what?'; 'What?' blurts Beechum, both questioning and answering the audacious query. Everett's crusade for the truth is highlighted in the finale. Everett has been told by the warden, 'There's no such thing as Santa Claus'. Months later, now jobless and without a wife, Everett encounters a vagrant collecting for charity dressed as Santa Claus, while out Christmas shopping. Santa moans that he has to work alone – he has no wife, no elves: 'You wanna be Santa Claus these days, baby', he tells Everett, 'You're on your own'. 'You're right there, pal', Everett agrees, 'Santa Claus rides alone'.

Eastwood said of *True Crime*, 'It's not the kind of movie they're doing today ... it's hampered by having a story. But I think there's somebody out there who appreciates that, so I'll keep on trying'. *True Crime* also benefits from a familiar-yet-suspenseful jazz-inflected score from Lennie Niehaus. The end titles are accompanied by 'Why Should I Care', written by Eastwood, Carole Bayer Sager and Linda Thomson and sung by Diana Krall, which was released as a tie-in. Klavan's novel was also republished with a new cover. *True Crime* was rated 'R' in the US and '15' in the UK, for its frequent but justified profanity. Despite its association with a best seller, it failed to be as profitable as Eastwood's other literary adaptations. It was his least successful film of the period when it was released in the US in March 1999, taking over $16.5 million.

Blood Work (2002)

Following *Space Cowboys*, Eastwood was back in thriller mode for *Blood Work*, yet another bestseller adaptation. This one was written by Michael Connelly (a former police reporter for the *Los Angeles Times*) and was published in 1998. Eastwood purchased the book rights after he had met Connelly and even suggested some changes, which were then incorporated into the story; Eastwood is thanked in Connelly's acknowledgements. Brian Helgeland, who had turned James Ellroy's lengthy *L.A. Confidential* into a script so impressively, worked on the screenplay. This was a cat-and-mouse cop thriller with a twist – the only arrests in the movie are cardiac.

Blood Work cast Eastwood as an idiosyncratic investigator, Terrell 'Terry' McCaleb. He is an ageing FBI profiler working with the LAPD investigating the 'Code Killer', a serial slayer who holds a particular grudge against McCaleb. At the murder scenes of his fifth and sixth victims, there are bloody messages: 'McCaleb Catch Me 903 472 568'. No one can crack the code, but when McCaleb gives chase to a suspect who is wearing bloodstained Converse sneakers, he collapses, suffering a serious heart attack. Two years later, McCaleb, now retired and recovering from a recent heart transplant, is living on his boat *The Following Sea* in Los Angeles harbour. He is approached by Graciella Rivers (Wanda De Jesus), who is searching for the murderer of her sister, Gloria Torres. McCaleb now has Gloria's heart – his blood type is a rare AB with CMV negative. Gloria was shot dead by a killer in a ski mask, during the hold-up of Kang's Valley Market, a discount convenience store. After she was shot, a Good Samaritan passer-by tried to save her and called 911, but she died in hospital. With help from Graciella, Buddy Noone (Jeff Daniels), McCaleb's neighbour in the marina, and Jaye Winston (Tina Lifford), a detective and old friend in the County Sheriff's office, McCaleb begins to investigate the robbery, examining CCTV footage. He discovers that the same killer struck at an ATM machine outside the Soledad Canyon Bank, Canoga Park, two weeks before, but due to a mix-up with the address, the ambulance was too late and the victim, James Cordell, was pronounced dead at the scene. McCaleb realises that the culprit is the Code Killer and both murders were engineered to provide McCaleb with a new heart, ensuring their battle of wits continues – both Cordell and Gloria matched McCaleb's blood group. The 'Good Samaritan' in the CCTV is actually the killer and the call he made to the hospital for an ambulance was made seconds before the murder, to ensure it arrived in time. Gloria's little son Raymond (Mason Lucero), now in Graciella's care, works out that the cryptic code includes all the digits (903 472 568) but there is 'no one'. When the Code Killings resume, McCaleb finds that the culprit is none other than his marina neighbour, Buddy No/one. Buddy kidnaps Graciella and Raymond, hiding them on a partially submerged wreck in the harbour, but McCaleb manages to free them and kills Noone, who drowns pleading, 'I saved you'.

Eastwood's adaptation differs significantly from Connelly's novel, considerably simplifying the plot. In the book, there is a third killing, which preceded the ATM slaying – Donald Kenyon, a fraudster under house arrest, was killed when the murderer used the wrong type of bullet, killing him instantly before his organs could be harvested. The killer in the film's CCTV footage mouths, 'Happy Valentine's Day', in the book, 'Don't forget the cannoli' (a reference to *The Godfather*). In the book, McCaleb's marina neighbour, Buddy Lockridge, chauffeurs McCaleb and nicknames him 'Terror' McCaleb but is not the culprit. That killer is James Noone, the witness present at the cash point murder, who is eventually given away by a distinctive scar on his hand and when he fakes a trance under hypnosis during a police interview. For much of the book, McCaleb is the number one suspect, implicated by the real killer, Noone – a pseudonym for 32-year-old Daniel Crimmins ('an LAPD academy washout'), who studied computer security, enabling him to hack the BOPRA computer blood database. The Code Killer's story is secondary for most of the book and the final showdown between McCaleb and Crimmins takes place on a Mexican beach at Playa Grande. Graciella and Raymond are held hostage in the septic tank of a half-constructed house nearby. When Crimmins' dead body is found, the police deem it suicide.

Jeff Daniels, an actor well known by cinema audiences for shocks and comedy, via *Arachnophobia* (1990) and *Dumb and Dumber* (1994), was well cast as hazy, harmonica-playing Buddy Noone. At first a boating beer bum, living a perpetual Sunday afternoon, then a bumbling sidekick in McCaleb's investigations, he convincingly transforms into a goading psychopath who would make Scorpio and Booth proud. Anjelica Huston played McCaleb's cardiologist, Doctor Bonnie Fox, who is aghast that he is involved in an energetic case when he should be recuperating. Wanda De Jesus was cast after Eastwood saw her in *Almost a Woman* (2001), a PBS TV production. Her affecting, understated performance is *Blood Work*'s best. Paul Rodriguez and Dylan Walsh played LAPD detectives: fiery Mexican Arrango and his largely silent Anglo partner, Waller (called Walter in the novel). Eastwood's wife Dina played a reporter at the Code Killer's latest crime scene, asking McCaleb, 'Did you think this was over?' Tina Lifford played Detective Winston, providing a partner for McCaleb when the film begins to resemble a 'Dirty Harry' movie.

Blood Work was filmed in the spring of 2002 on location at Long Beach and in Los Angeles, California, on a $50 million budget in 38 days. The scenes of McCaleb's moorings in the Cabrillo Marina were Los Angeles harbour and San Pedro. Cinematographer Tom Stern was in top form in his first film as director of photography at Malpaso in place of Jack N. Green. The plotting, which takes McCaleb location-hopping, owes something to previous Eastwood cat-and-mouse pursuits: *Dirty Harry*, *Tightrope* and *In the Line of Fire*. As Graciella notes, 'You have Gloria's heart, she'll guide you'. If only Eastwood had been working with such fine source material in the late-seventies and eighties, what different propositions *The Enforcer*, *Sudden Impact* and others would have been.

The idea that a criminal would commit murder to extract his victim's organs – to resurrect his sworn enemy and to then go on killing – is among the most macabre plots touted in the name of entertainment. *Blood Work* also includes elements of serial killer movies, with the Code Killer collecting trophy souvenirs from his victims. If it does have a failing, it is slightly too long, even at only 106 minutes. *Blood Work* begins along familiar lines, with helicopter shots of a neon-lit city. Even Lennie Niehaus's lounge piano and trumpet bossa nova can't dispel the ghost of Harry Callahan. The opening action, with McCaleb surveying a bloody crime scene and then his pursuit of the Code Killer down dark alleys, is equally reminiscent of Harry's many chases through the streets of San Francisco. The book's plot begins much more leisurely, with Graciella (or 'Graciela', as spelt in the novel) tracking down McCaleb to the Cabrillo Marina. But almost immediately the audiences' expectations are shattered, as Eastwood's cop hero clutches his chest while attempting to scale a wire fence and suffers a massive coronary.

At this late stage in his career, Eastwood was addressing his own mortality, via his now destructible screen heroes. Eastwood had 'died' twice on screen, in *The Beguiled* and *Honkytonk Man*, but this film and *Million Dollar Baby* would take a hard look at mortality and feature extensive scenes set in hospitals, not a usual Eastwood locale. With the gift of life restored by a mysterious but well-timed donor, McCaleb is reawakened. This resurrection is a theme prevalent in Eastwood's oeuvre: in his early action movies, Eastwood's heroes often suffer a heavy beating or torture, almost to the point of death, and their recovery to defeat the villains is a symbolic 'rebirth'. In the ghostly *High Plains Drifter* and *Pale Rider*, this resurrection is even more explicit. The horrible scar down the middle of McCaleb's torso is a constant reminder of the fine line he treads, and McCaleb is forever popping pills and being berated by Dr Fox for his exertions – only 60 days post-transplant, he could suffer from 'infection or rejection'. It is usually Eastwood's screen companions who die: Lightfoot in *Thunderbolt and Lightfoot*, Jaime in *The Outlaw Josey Wales*, Frank DiGeorgio in *The Enforcer*, or Ned Logan in *Unforgiven*. Suspensefully, in *Blood Work*, we wonder if McCaleb's ticker is up to the challenge.

Interviewed in the documentary *Making Blood Work*, Wanda De Jesus noted, 'It's a story how loss redefines a person'. Graciella's relationship with McCaleb is one of the most moving, but also one of the strangest, of Eastwood's career. As he lies in a hospital bed for a check-up, he tells her, 'I lost a little something, but knowing you ... I feel a little bit of it coming back'. The film's dark romance has Graciella falling for McCaleb, who now has her sister's heart. Through him, she feels closer to her deceased sibling and through her love, he realises how fortunate he is to be alive. But Noone offers an even more ghoulish scenario. 'Every breath you take belongs to me ... every beat of that stolen heart is the echo of my voice in your head, every day, always'.

Eastwood was 72 when he filmed *Blood Work*, though he still handled himself ably in the action spots, including the shootout aboard the foggy, half-sunken trawler. In another scene, McCaleb takes out a pump-action shotgun and ventilates the stalking Code Killer's speeding car, a wild-west shootout disrupting the peace of sunny San Fernando Valley. When McCaleb realises that Gloria's killer has access to the blood donor database, his rant ('If you can't protect the integrity of the system, then there is no system') has a familiar ring. When the Code Killer announces his return, predictably with a corpse, Arrango looks at the message – 'McCaleb Happy Valentine's Day' written in blood – and laughs bitterly: 'Some people get flowers, some people get chocolates. You get a dead guy'. 'Now I'm back', realises McCaleb, 'And so is he'. As he kills Noone, McCaleb utters, 'Ten ring', a reference to the highest score in an FBI marksmanship contest, which involved shooting a circle of bullet holes around the target's heart.

Blood Work arrived in US cinemas in August 2002, rated 'R'; it was a '15' in the UK. Connelly's book was reissued as a tie-in, with a new Eastwood portrait cover. 'He's a Heartbeat Away from Catching the Killer', ran the poster tagline. The trailer featured a rippling blood pool effect and the voiceover: 'On the trail of a killer, his career changed in a heartbeat. Until somebody else's death saved him. The only link to the killer beats within him'. There are allusions in the trailer to *In the Line of Fire*, with a face-to-face conversation between McCaleb and Noone (with Noone comparing them to 'Cain and Abel, Kennedy and Oswald'), re-edited to resemble a threatening telephone call. Like *Midnight in the Garden of Good and Evil*, best-selling book sales didn't translate into box office mega hit, and *Blood Work* took just over $26 million in the US, a substantial loss.

Eastwood's thrillers have been a mixed bag, providing him with one of his finest acting performances (as Frank Morris), some of his most formulaic work as actor and director (*Absolute Power, True Crime* and *Blood Work*), one of his very worst films (*The Eiger Sanction*) and one of his greatest, the magnificent *Thunderbolt and Lightfoot*, a film that jumps out from Eastwood's oeuvre as a quirky cult classic.

PART SEVEN
THE WAR MOVIES

'I'm against war – period', Clint Eastwood is on record as saying, 'When I was in the army I was against the Korean War, and after that – although I wasn't a protester – I was against Vietnam'. In the years before he became an actor, Eastwood was drafted into the US army, arriving at Fort Ord on the Monterey Peninsula in the autumn of 1951. But even though the Korean War, in which the US military was involved via the UN, lasted until July 1953, Eastwood never saw active service – like John Wayne, another heroic American actor who appeared in a raft of war movies. Wayne's Second World War combat movies, including *The Fighting Seebees* (1944), *Back to Bataan* (1945) and *Sands of Iwo Jima* (1949), were jingoistic anti-Axis propaganda, with Big John's patriotic Americanism writ large. Just as Eastwood's cowboy heroes were markedly different from Wayne's, so too were his war heroes.

Where Eagles Dare (1968)

During the sixties, the Second World War was used as the setting for several popular action movies featuring do-or-die missions. The heroes were always 'daring', the odds invariably 'massive'. MGM wanted to capitalise on the success of such films as *The Dirty Dozen* (1967). Alistair MacLean had recently written a story entitled *Adler Schloss* ('Eagle Castle'), detailing a fictitious raid on a German mountaintop stronghold in the Austrian Alps. Retitling the story *Where Eagles Dare*, MGM decided to make it into a film, directed by Brian G. Hutton.

For this British production, Eastwood – fresh from his success in the 'Dollars' films, *Hang 'Em High* and *Coogan's Bluff* – was cast almost as a US guest star, in the role of Lieutenant Morris Schaffer. He is part of a special mission mounted by British Intelligence (MI6) to spring US General Carnaby from imprisonment in a Nazi Secret Service fortress at Schloß Adler, 'The Castle of the Eagles'. Carnaby is one of the planners of the invasion of Europe that would become the D-Day landings. Led by Major John Smith (Richard Burton), the squad includes Schaffer, five British soldiers – Christiansen, Berkeley, Thomas, Harrod and MacPhearson – and female agent Mary Ellison (Mary Ure) visiting her 'cousin' Heidi (Ingrid Pitt), another agent, who works in a local bar. They parachute into the locality disguised as German Alpenkorps, but Harrod is killed upon landing, and MacPhearson is mysteriously murdered shortly afterwards in the village of Werfen. Realising that Christiansen, Berkeley and Thomas are traitors, Smith and Schaffer rig various booby traps in preparation for their escape and then infiltrate the fortress, which can be reached only by cable car. They free Carnaby (who is actually an actor named Cartwright Jones impersonating the general) and make good their escape, firstly by cable car and then by bus, in a five-mile dash to the Oberhausen military airfield, where they rendezvous with their rescue plane.

Principal photography began in Austria on 2 January 1968 and was completed at MGM's Borehamwood studios in Hertfordshire the following May, though second unit work dragged on until July. Eastwood was paid $800,000, for only his sixth star-ring role. The 'Schloß Adler' was an actual 11th Century castle: the Burg Hohenwerfen, perched like an eagle's nest above the village of Werfen in the snowy Salzach Valley. When the commandos first spot the inaccessible castle through the pines, Schaffer observes, 'Somebody's got to be crazy'.

In 1968, the angular, gothic schloß, with its fortified turrets and crenellations, was a police training school and had been used in the past as an escape-proof prison.

7.1 Easy Rider: Lieutenant Morris Schaeffer attempts a great escape in *Where Eagles Dare* (1968); Clint Eastwood, on location in the Austrian village of Lofer, is filmed in close-up by a cameraman positioned in the sidecar. Image courtesy Kevin Wilkinson Collection.

All interiors were constructed back at Borehamwood. Some of the cable car scenes were lensed in picturesque Ebensee, Austria; the exterior of 'Zum Wilden Hirsch' ('The Wild Stag'), the tavern where Heidi works, was in Lofer; and the Oberhausen Airfield was filmed at Aigen Im Ennstal. There have been few war movies as handsomely photographed; the film is memorable for the white letterbox of Arthur Ibbetson's Panavision snowscape nocturnes. As the action unfolds, with explosions and hardware tearing through the fairytale locations, *Eagles* resembles an apocalyptic war movie unfolding on a Christmas card.

As Schaffer, Eastwood is even less talkative than in his 'Dollars' films. In *Where Eagles Dare: On Location* Eastwood noted, 'It's certainly unusual wearing war uniforms as opposed to ponchos', while Burton discussed their variant acting styles: '[Eastwood is] tall and slow and drawly, sort of a la Gary Cooper, and he's as good as Gary Cooper, perhaps even better – and I'm short and thick and fast-talking'. Burton liked Eastwood's 'dynamic lethargy'. In MacLean's original draft, there were references to Schaffer being a cowboy from Montana, which were excised from the script; Burton noted that Eastwood could reduce four lines to four words.

Eastwood's role in the film was twofold: to ensure an American audience for a film with an almost exclusively British cast and to kill Germans by the dozen in the spectacular action sequences. Eastwood kills more people here than he did in the entire 'Dollars' trilogy; his killings include the assassination of the Schloß Adler's senior staff, one of whom is a woman (he shoots her in the back). In Eastwood's most memorable scenes, he takes on the innumerable, well-equipped German garrison in a castle corridor, armed with a Schmeisser machine-gun. He even has time to pick up activated grenades and throw them back, and at one point he blasts away with a Schmeisser in each hand – as Eastwood himself observed, 'If you thought that I shot a lot of people with a six-shooter, you should see how we can do with a machine gun'.

The film develops its own kind of rolling, destructive momentum, as the raiders effect their mind-boggling escape amid the exploding castle. There are motor bike chases, fistfights while dangling from cable cars, tonnes of explosives, falling telegraph poles, blasted vehicles and dynamited bridges. The film opens with the Junkers transport plane soaring out of the Alps, en route to dropping the paratroopers into Werfen, and ends with the same plane whisking them back to England. These scenes, and much of the action, are accompanied by Ron Goodwin's enduring score, the opening ascending chords and machine-gun percussion growing in menace like a gathering storm.

Released in the UK rated 'A' after cuts, in December 1968, *Eagles* came out in the US the following March, rated 'M' (later 'PG'). Posters publicised, 'Alistair MacLean's epic adventure story of a wartime mission that cannot succeed – but dare not fail'. US posters featured the heroes in disguise and the tagline: 'They look like Nazis but... the Major is British... the Lieutenant is American... The beautiful Frauleins are Allied Agents!' The *Monthly Film Bulletin* loved the film's 'cunningly devious script... with a sublime contempt for logic', *Variety* thought it was the best war movie since *The Great Escape* and Rex Reed concurred, calling it 'genuinely entertaining, chockful of equal doses of suspense, action and well-timed anxiety'. Hutton said that he intended the film to be a spoof of action movies, but few recognised it as such. It is the perfect fantasy war film, an extravagant, *Boy's Own*-style adventure. *Eagles* soared to the top of the charts and was MGM's top earner of 1969, taking $21 million worldwide and was Eastwood's biggest success so far. His first non-X certificate film, it guaranteed his style exposure to a younger audience.

Kelly's Heroes (1970)

From *Where Eagles Dare* to 'Where Opportunists Dare' for Eastwood's next Second World War offering, an unconventional 'special mission' movie that could have been equally great but somehow lost its way. Made immediately after he finished work on *Two Mules for Sister Sara*, *Kelly's Heroes* was again directed by Brian Hutton, with a rather different tone to the patriotic, selfless heroics of *Eagles*.

Following their landing on Omaha Beach, Big Joe's squad of GIs has been slogging through France towards Berlin. The unit is on the brink of taking the town of Nancy but is being withdrawn from the frontline by their superior Captain Maitland, so that reserve troops in clean uniforms can take the glory. Kelly (Eastwood), one of Joe's squad, captures German colonel Dunkhepf, who is carrying a gold bar in his attaché case. Under interrogation, Dunkhepf reveals that the bar is part of Operation Tannenbaum ('Fir Tree'), a $16 million bullion shipment currently sitting in a bank guarded by three Tiger tanks in Clermont, 30 miles behind German lines. With three days to kill, Kelly hits upon 'the perfect crime'. Sergeant Big Joe (Telly Savalas) and his 12 men are recruited, plus black market hustler Crapgame (Don Rickles) and three freelance Sherman tanks commanded by the aptly named Oddball (Donald Sutherland) – all for 'a piece of the action'. They breeze through war-torn France, breaking through enemy lines and heading for Clermont; their enthusiasm is misconstrued by General Colt (Carroll O'Connor) as bravery and he mobilises his forces to capitalise on their success. Eventually the treasure hunters arrive in Clermont and strike a deal with the German Tiger tank commander to share the gold: as Crapgame notes, 'Business is business, right?' Having cleaned out the bank, Kelly's heroes split, just as General Colt's column arrives, to be greeted by the flag-waving populace as liberators.

Written by Troy Kennedy Martin as 'The Warriors', and for part of its production known as 'Kelly's Warriors', *Kelly's Heroes* was another, multi-million dollar MGM enterprise – this time a US-Yugoslavian co-production, shot for $4 million on location in Yugoslavia over five months in 1969. The crew was based at the Petrovaradin Fortress in Novi Sad (now in Serbia) and in Umag, a port on the Adriatic.

Nine starring roles into his screen career and Eastwood must have begun to wonder if he was ever going to escape 'The Man with No Name' label: Eastwood may be dressed as a GI, but Kelly's greedy motivation is almost identical. At the end of *Kelly's Heroes*, Hutton even stages a homage to Leone: during the stand-off in Clermont, having knocked out two Tigers but lost their last Sherman, Kelly, Big Joe and Oddball

7.2 'We Could Be Heroes': Kelly leads his mercenary troops on a treasure hunt through France in *Kelly's Heroes* (1970); Clint Eastwood on location in Yugoslavia. Image courtesy Kevin Wilkinson Collection.

decide to try to reason with the Tiger commander. As they stride down the town's main street to parlay, they could be walking into San Miguel, while on the soundtrack Lalo Schifrin provides harmonicas, drums, electric guitars, trumpets and wailing voices, pastiche Morricone, in case audiences didn't spot the reference.

Eastwood thought that the disparate elements in the film, the drama and the comedy, the satire and the parody, didn't gel, and nor did the different actors: 'Our styles were inconsistent. People off on different trips – no cohesion'. For many,

Sutherland's hippy Oddball is the best aspect of the film. He may be 25 years out, historically, but he and his crew definitely liven the film up. Dressed in a leather flying helmet and jacket, rose-tinted goggles and sporting a shaggy dog beard and 'stache, Sutherland seems to have beamed down from another planet, recreating his Hawkeye Pierce from the hugely successful *M*A*S*H*. He's backed by an equally odd crew, including fez-wearing Turk and flaky, pessimistic Moriarty, given to lounging around listening to Arabic music – a doped-out hippy commune running at half-speed. Berating his crew for clouding his day with 'negative waves' ('Have a little faith, baby'), Oddball would rather be spending the war catching rays, eating cheese, drinking wine: 'But for $1.6 million we could be heroes for three days'. Memorably, Oddball's Shermans emerge from a railway tunnel and attack a Nazi marshalling yard, while Hank Williams Junior's 'All for the Love of Sunshine' and 'I've Been Working on the Railroad' blast from the tanks' speakers. *Kelly's Heroes* title song, the ironic 'Burning Bridges' (performed by The Mike Curb Congregation, who sound like The Mamas and the Papas) is in a similarly playful vein. This poppy sixties sing-along has the funkiest drumbeat ever deployed in a war movie. Eastwood himself also recorded a cover of the song, with 'When I Loved Her' on the B-side.

Kelly's Heroes opened almost simultaneously with Eastwood's own *Two Mules for Sister Sara* (for rivals Universal) in June 1970 but still took $5.2 million in the US, rated 'GP'. Judith Crist wrote that Eastwood as Kelly 'manages not to change expressions once', while *Variety* saw a 'very commercial WWII comedy drama'. The *Los Angeles Times* reviewer deemed it 'the noisiest picture I have ever sat through' and *Argosy* loved it, raving, '*Kelly's Heroes* abounds with brilliance! It's a superbly acted, exquisitely photographed, howling spoof of wartime heroics'. *Films and Filming* dubbed it 'The Sons of Patton's Dirty Dozen Go Where Eagles Dare'. Posters proclaimed, 'Clint Eastwood is the leader of *Kelly's Heroes* – They set out to rob a bank... and damn near won a war instead!'

Firefox (1982)

Following his massive success with *Any Which Way You Can* (1980), the second of his comedies with Clyde the Orang-utan, Eastwood decided to embark on his costliest Malpaso film to date – a war movie set in a very different type of conflict, the Cold War, where Eastwood's solitary persona fitted well into a story of spies and clandestine espionage. Based on a best-selling 1977 book by Welsh schoolteacher-turned-novelist Craig Thomas, *Firefox* saw its loner hero embark on a daring mission behind the Iron Curtain.

British Intelligence, the SIS, discovers that the Russians have developed and built a supersonic jet fighter, the MIG-31, codenamed by NATO 'Firefox'. The project is based in a complex at Bilyarsk, to the west of Moscow. The Firefox is so advanced it can outrun any NATO plane (reaching speeds of Mach 6), is invisible to radar and has a thought-controlled weapons system. SIS boss Kenneth Aubrey (Freddie Jones) plans to steal it and employs US Vietnam-vet Mitchell Gant (Eastwood), who has a Russian

7.3 *ABC Film Review* (price: 5 pence) celebrates the UK release of *Kelly's Heroes*, *Paint Your Wagon* and *The Beguiled* in November 1971 with cover star Clint Eastwood. This issue also offers lucky readers the chance to win the title 'Miss Cinema 1972', a Holiday in Tunisia (courtesy of Clarksons Holidays) and a Ford Capri 1600 GTXLR worth £1200. Author's collection.

mother, is fluent in the language and is the same build as the Russian test-pilot Yuri Voskov. Gant's mission is made near impossible by his recurring bouts of Delayed Stress Syndrome: an ace pilot in the 'Aggressor' squadron in Vietnam, he was shot down, leading to his imprisonment in a bamboo cage by the Vietcong. As a result of this, he is reduced to a quaking jelly in times of crisis. Gant arrives in Moscow, under the guise of heroin peddler Leon Sprague. Soon afterwards, Gant meets his Russian contact, Pavel Upenskoy (Warren Clarke), who murders the real Sprague at a rendezvous at the Krasnokholmskiy Bridge and dumps him in the Moscow River. The KGB, state secret police led by Colonel Kontarsky (Kenneth Colley), is soon on their trail. Upenskoy and Gant (now posing as 'Boris Glanzunov') make contact with the dissident Jewish scientists forced to work in the Bilyarsk compound: Doctors Semelovsky (Ronald Lacey) and Baranovich (Nigel Hawthorne). As the appointed hour for a highly publicised test flight approaches, to be witnessed by the country's first secretary, Gant infiltrates the hangar. While his comrades cause a diversion, he steals the MIG. All seems to be going as planned, as Gant jets across the Urals, into the Gulf of Kara, and heads for the Arctic Circle to refuel from 'Mother One', a US nuclear submarine, evading missile sites, the Wolfpack border squadrons and the missile cruiser Riga. But a second MIG prototype has evaded sabotage and sets off in pursuit, with ace Russian pilot Voskov at the controls. Gant overcomes his nerves ('Let's see what this baby can do') and defeats Voskov in an aerial duel to the death.

Craig Thomas's book was a good read – fast moving, straightforward, but tightly crafted, with a fine Cold War atmosphere. Intertitles split the raid into chapters, including 'The Murder', 'The Journey', 'The Rip-Off', culminating with 'The Duel'. Warners bought the rights to the story in 1979, to be produced in tandem with Malpaso with Eastwood directing, though the screen adaptation is rather less riveting.

With a budget of $18 million, Eastwood shot much of the 'Moscow' action in Vienna, Austria, including Sprague's riverside murder. The Vienna subway was redressed as Moscow's Metro. Other location shooting was done in Montana, California, London and Thule Air Base in Greenland. Eastwood employed John Dykstra to create the special effects of the Firefox in action; Dykstra had worked with George Lucas on Star Wars.

Eastwood's performance is very out-of-character. As 'Sprague', he wears glasses and a moustache – bad news for an Eastwood hero, as neither suits him. Eastwood tries to articulate Cold War issues in his own simple movie terms. Gant asks the dissidents: 'What is it with you Jews – don't you ever get tired of fighting City Hall?' There is none of Eastwood's usual cool asides and macho action. For release, the film's trailer cunningly featured a specially filmed 'buddy' scene that wouldn't have been out of place in Any Which Way You Can. Gant, in blue T-shirt and with a bottle of beer in his hand, tells his off-screen companions: 'There's not a one of you who think I have a chance in the world of pulling this off, is there?' This moment bodes well but doesn't appear anywhere in the finished film. On its release in June 1982, Firefox took almost $47 million, while critics were apathetic. Posters ran with the

7.4 'His Job…Steal It!': French poster advertising *Firefox* (1982), with Clint Eastwood as ace pilot Mitchell Gant. Author's collection.

tagline: 'The most devastating Soviet killing machine ever built...his job...steal it!' Thomas's book was reissued, with an Eastwood tie-in cover, billed as a 'supersonic thriller'. Thomas also wrote a sequel, *Firefox Down*, published in 1983, dedicated: 'For Clint Eastwood, Pilot of the Firefox'. Unlike the film itself, the trailer is fast-paced, action-packed entertainment. Trimmed DVD and video prints of the film now run 119 minutes (it originally ran 137); TV prints prune the film's violence, shortening the massacre of the dissidents as Gant steals the Firefox. When *Firefox* was released, a Grandstand *Firefox F-7* handheld computer game was issued as a tie-in. Watch the trailer, read the book, play the game – just avoid the film, it's another *Eiger Sanction*. Less a 'Firefox', it's more of a damp squib, or at best a smouldering turkey.

Heartbreak Ridge (1986)

'What warriors do when they haven't got a war has always interested me', Eastwood said of his next war effort. Having won the Second World War and turned the tide of the Cold War, Eastwood looked to another, more contemporary, conflict. Following his return west with *Pale Rider* (1985) and side-stepping the political morass that was the Vietnam War (he had turned down the role of Captain Willard in *Apocalypse Now* [1979]), Eastwood chose to make *Heartbreak Ridge*, actually named after a battle in the Korean War, but largely focussing on the 1983 invasion of Grenada by the US military.

Heartbreak Ridge begins on the weekend of 20–21 July 1983. Gunnery Sergeant Tom 'Gunny' Highway (Eastwood), a hard-drinking ex-marine, is currently stuck working in the 1st Air Delivery supply depot, though he's a veteran of Korea, Dominica and three tours of 'Nam. At his request and with retirement looming, he's transferred to the 2nd Reconnaissance ('Recon') Battalion, in the 2nd Marine Division. He immediately clashes with his superior, battalion commander Major Powers (Everett McGill), and is assigned to whip a useless, undisciplined Recon platoon into shape: 'I'll make life-takers and heartbreakers of them, sir', he promises. Meanwhile, Highway becomes reacquainted with his ex-wife Aggie (Marsha Mason) and tries to woo her back from bar owner Roy Jennings (Bo Svenson), who has asked her to marry him. In predictable fashion, the platoon, initially unresponsive to Highway, eventually welds into a compact fighting unit, which is just as well as in October they are dispatched to Grenada, a Caribbean island that has suffered a coup d'état. Their mission: to rescue a party of American students held hostage in St George's, the island's capital, at the University's School of Medicine. The operation is a success, leading to commendations all round. On their arrival back in the US, Highway is reunited with Aggie, who isn't going to marry Jennings after all.

Heartbreak Ridge is about as formulaic as can be, mixing the 'mission' aspect of Eastwood's previous war excursions with a training programme reminiscent of a hundred other combat films. It was based on an original script by Vietnam veteran James Carabatsos, which was then purchased by Warners in 1984. Dennis Hackin and Joseph Stinson worked on it uncredited, until Eastwood was finally satisfied with the screenplay. He began filming, as director-star, in the summer of 1986 with a $15 million budget. It was originally set in the US army regulars, who decided that Highway's ways were outmoded in their modern era, which is partly the point of the film. The army refused to co-operate, so the script was altered to make Highway a marine. The marines were perfectly happy to offer technical support and hardware for the film. Their re-enactment of the invasion of Grenada (involving an aircraft carrier, amphibious landing craft and helicopters) was an actual marine exercise, with real marines as extras. The training camp was Camp Pendleton Marine Corps Base, California, while Vieques Island, Puerto Rico subbed as Grenada for the amphibious invasion and a private school at Solano Beach stood in for St George's University. Lieutenant Colonel Fred Peck acted as military advisor and liased with Eastwood and producer Fritz Manes, an ex-marine himself. But when the Department of Defence saw the finished film, with its strong profanity, it balked, withdrawing its whole-hearted endorsement. Apparently the language was too much even for the marines.

As 'Gunny' Highway, Eastwood is at his toughest and his voice at its most gravelly, while his scarred forehead and neck and his snarling grimace make him resemble a *GI Joe* cartoon – the ultimate battle-scarred jarhead 'vet'. His antagonism at Camp Pendleton with Major Powers ('a walking clusterfuck') provides some humour. Highway boasts, 'I eat concertina wire and piss napalm, and I can put a round through a flea's ass at 200 metres', while Major Powers observes that Highway should be kept in a locked case, reading 'Break Glass Only in the Event of War'. But the ongoing inter-platoon enmity has all the depth of college football rivalry and as Highway gains his men's respect, the boot camp training scenes drag – cue footage of marines jogging, marching, abseiling, shooting, crawling under barbed wire and jumping out of Chinook helicopters. Lennie Niehaus's rumbling score provides exactly the backing you'd expect for such antics. In contrast to all the tough-talking, there are strong homoerotic undertones in the film's imagery, as the muscled, sweaty, bare-chested marines jog in tight shorts, or wrestle in a waterhole. Pendleton isn't the only camp element in the film. *Heartbreak Ridge* is Eastwood's *Green Berets* (1969), John Wayne's Vietnam War folly – a misguided but well-meaning military movie casting its star as a war hero.

The addition of the topical Grenada invasion references were Eastwood's idea. The US did indeed invade the tiny Caribbean island of Grenada (occupied by 1,500 local troops and 700 Cubans) with 7000 men plus armour and air support, which was the military equivalent of driving a Sherman tank at an anthill. On 25 October 1983, six days after a coup on the island, the US launched 'Operation Urgent Fury', their first major action since Vietnam, to free American students held hostage.

The most interesting aspect of *Heartbreak Ridge*, and of Eastwood's performance, is his relationship with his estranged wife Aggie (Marsha Mason), a name which bears a resemblance to Eastwood's own ex-wife's name, Maggie. Aggie hates Highway for never being around, for volunteering to take every mission on offer and for being so out-of-touch when dealing with human emotions. Highway tries to become more considerate, mouthing relationship theories he's read about in *Femme*, *Bazaar* and *Woman*, but she second-guesses his 'changed tactics'.

Highway's Recon platoon consists of the usual disparate movie mix of socially inept troublemakers, including Herculean muscleman 'Swede' Johanson, cocky, shades-wearing Italian-American Fragatti and motormouth rapper and self-proclaimed 'Duke of Cool' Stitch Jones, played by Mario Van Peebles. Peebles gets to deliver lines such as 'Word, am I fresh!' and perform rock 'n' roll numbers in the Palace Bar. Wearing a bandanna and wielding a leopardskin guitar, he sings a self-penned number entitled 'I Love You, But I Ain't Stupid'. Van Peebles had just starred as a rapping ex-con in *Rappin'* (1985). The light, bantering tone of *Heartbreak Ridge* unfortunately carries over into the combat scenes, where there should be little room for levity when dealing with such recent operations. The Recon platoons' taking of a bridge objective with a commandeered bulldozer is strictly *A-Team* and when they are trapped in a house by armoured militia, they call in an airstrike by phoning up their base in North Carolina, reversing the charges.

Heartbreak Ridge invaded US cinemas in May 1986, to surprisingly good reviews and encouraging box office. *USA Today* even went so far as to note, 'Eastwood's best performance since *Dirty Harry* – tough, funny, credible, even tender'. Eastwood also co-wrote 'How Much Can I Care' with Sammy Cahn, sung by Jill Hollier. The film was rated '15' in the UK, 'R' in the US, and was backed by a tie-in paperback, adapted by Joseph Stinson from Carabatsos's screenplay. 'Some men are born to win', ran the blurb, 'Some men are born to lose. Highway was born to fight'. *Heartbreak Ridge* eventually took $42 million in the US, more than *City Heat* and *Pale Rider*, no doubt due in part to the handy publicity surrounding its vulgarity.

Flags of Our Fathers (2006)/ Letters from Iwo Jima (2006)

Eastwood's most recent war films again deal with the US marines, though he portrays them in a markedly different light to that of *Heartbreak Ridge*. With the resounding Oscar success of *Million Dollar Baby* (2004) proving that Eastwood had risen to the peak of his profession as director, he embarked on an ambitious project: to tell the story of the Battle of Iwo Jima in the Second World War through two parallel films. *Flags of Our Fathers* told the story of America's amphibious assault and its aftermath, and *Letters from Iwo Jima* was the same engagement told from the perspective of the embattled Japanese defenders.

The American attack on Iwo Jima island was part of a final push through the Pacific Islands. Gaining such footholds would enable the US to capture enemy air-fields, essential for their assault on Japan itself. The volcanic island, five-and-a-half miles long and two-and-a-half miles wide, was dominated at the southern tip by Mount Suribachi. On 19 February 1945, the US 5th Amphibious Corps landed on the beach at the southern sector of the island and by 23 February, the marines had captured Suribachi. Men of the 2nd Battalion, 28th Regiment of the 5th Marine Division raised the US flag, 'Old Glory', atop the mountain and the moment was captured by war photographer Joe Rosenthal. This photograph, of six men struggling to erect the flagpole, became one of the most iconic images of the Second World War.

Eastwood looked to two primary sources to tell each side of the story. *Flags of Our Fathers*, written by James Bradley and Ron Powers, was published in 2000, based on interviews with US participants in the battle. Bradley was the son of John 'Doc' Bradley, one of the men in Rosenthal's famous photograph. This account was turned into a screenplay by Paul Haggis and William Broyles Jnr. *Letters from Iwo Jima* was based on *Picture Letters from Commander in Chief* by Tadamichi Kuribayashi, edited Tsuyuko Yoshida and published by Shogakukan-Bunko; Kuribayashi was the general in command of Japanese forces. A story based on this account with the working title 'Red Sun, Black Sand' was written by Iris Yamashita and Haggis, with a screenplay in Japanese by Yamashita.

In *Flags of Our Fathers* James Bradley interviews his father's comrades-in-arms about their celebrity status following the Battle of Iwo Jima. John 'Doc' Bradley (Ryan Phillippe) was a navy medic involved in the amphibious landings. He became famous, together with five marines, for raising the US flag in Rosenthal's photograph. Only Bradley and two others, Rene Gagnon (Jesse Bradford) and Ira Hayes (Adam Beach), survive the battle and are shipped back to the US to be fêted as heroes. Their fame is also exploited by Bud Gerber (John Slattery), who recruits them for a publicity tour advertising War Bonds, a fundraising ploy. Gagnon is fame-hungry, Bradley thinks the tour will help their comrades still fighting the war, but Hayes, a Native American, is particularly troubled by the farce, especially when it becomes clear that Gagnon has misidentified one of the other three soldiers in the photograph. Even worse, Rosenthal's photograph isn't of the actual triumphant flag-raising. US Secretary Forrestal wanted to have the victory flag as a souvenir, but the marines' commander decided to switch flags, to ensure his regiment retained the banner. A second party of marines, including Bradley, Hayes and Gagnon, plus Sergeant Mike Strank, Harlon Block and Franklin Sousley, is despatched to swap the flags and it is the erection of this second 'fake' flag which becomes the iconic image. Years later, wracked by guilt, Hayes died an alcoholic, Bradley never talked about the events on Iwo Jima and Gagnon soon found himself 'yesterday's hero', ending up working as a janitor.

In *Letters from Iwo Jima*, the arrival on the island of new Imperial commander General Kuribayashi (Ken Watanabe, from *The Last Samurai* [2003]) causes friction among the officers, especially when he drastically changes their stratagem, fortifying Mount Suribachi and digging a tunnel network. Kuribayashi realises that Iwo Jima must stand alone: there will be no reinforcements. Young Saigo (Kazunari Ninomiya) is one of the Japanese soldiers on Iwo Jima. He sees his friends die of dysentery due to the infected water and becomes disillusioned with fighting for his homeland. Under siege and living a hellish existence in dimly lit caves, the Japanese defenders are reduced to moles. Mount Suribachi is lost and Saigo's squad is ordered to commit suicide rather than fall into enemy hands. Saigo doesn't and manages to scramble across

7.5 The commander directs his troops: Clint Eastwood on manoeuvres during the filming of *Flags of Our Fathers* (2006). Image courtesy Kevin Wilkinson Collection.

the island to Kuribayashi's HQ, witnessing many horrors en route. But the situation is hopeless. Surrounded by the marines, Kuribayashi instructs Saigo to burn all documentation in the HQ, and the general leads one final attack, which fails. But Saigo buries many of the records instead, including letters from Kuribayashi to his wife back in Japan. Rather than fall into enemy hands, mortally wounded Kuribayashi shoots himself and Saigo conceals the body, before being captured by marines. Years later archaeologists excavating the island discover the never-delivered letters from Iwo Jima, revealing the true story of the battle for the island.

Ryan Phillippe, cast as young Bradley on Iwo Jima, had appeared in Paul Haggis' Oscar-winning *Crash* (2005), as well as in teen fodder such as *I Know What You Did Last Summer* (1997) and *Cruel Intentions* (1999). Jesse Bradford, as preening Gagnon, had popped up in *Bring it On* (2000) and *Swimfan* (2002). Adam Beach, a Sioux from Canada, was cast as Hayes and gave the film's best performance. Barry Pepper, cast as platoon sergeant Strank, had appeared in *The Three Burials of Melquiades Estrada* (2005). Jaime Bell, from *Billy Elliot* (2000), played 'Iggy' Ignatowski, one of Strank's men. Lundsford, one of the marines on board the transporter, looks like a young Clint Eastwood – uncannily so, in fact. It's no surprise to discover that he is played by 20-year-old actor Scott Reeves, Eastwood's son from his longstanding relationship with Jacelyn Reeves.

The films were shot back-to-back in 2006 for approximately $70 million, under the same production aegis (Warner Bros, Amblin Entertainment, Malpaso, DreamWorks) by essentially the same personnel: director Eastwood, cinematographer Tom Stern, editor Joel Cox, production designer Henry Bumstead and costume designer Deborah Hopper. The actual island of Iwo Jima is a protected site, essentially a mass war grave, and little location footage was shot there. *Flags of Our Fathers* was filmed on location in the US (Illinois, Los Angeles, Chicago and Texas), on Iwo Jima and partly in Iceland. The black Icelandic sand was a good match for Iwo Jima's ashen-hued beaches. The credits also thank *SS Lane Victory* (used as a cargo troop ship), *Leatherneck Magazine* (the official publication of the Marine Corps) and Marine Corps Base Camp Pendleton (which had appeared in *Heartbreak Ridge*). *Letters from Iwo Jima* was mostly filmed in California, with some brief shots actually on Iwo Jima. The production design is of the highest standard, with the re-enactment of the island assault a highlight of both films.

Flags and *Letters* are the most epic productions of Eastwood's career. Much of the colossal battle footage was created using special effects, enabling Eastwood to create an authentic depiction of the engagement at a fraction of the cost of an actual recreation. Battle and invasion fleet footage from the first film reappears in the second – now filmed and presented from the Japanese point of view, and this dual view of the battle is the project's most interesting achievement. Both films must be watched in order, *Flags* first, as having seen the assault from the marines' point of view, the Japanese defence gains emotionality.

Flags of Our Fathers takes place within three time frames: the present day (for James Bradley's interviews), the battle for the island, and the fundraising publicity tour and its aftermath. Eastwood is primarily concerned with how the 'Heroes of Iwo Jima' were used to political ends back in the US, and how it affected the heroes' lives. On the War Bond tour, filling stadiums and attending honorary receptions, they are accompanied by Bud Gerber, an unscrupulous charlatan, to whom the 'heroes' are simply an opportunity to gull the nation for every bond it's worth, prying open public wallets. Gerber cares little that the wrong names have been assigned to the dead flag heroes, telling the trio: 'I don't give a shit. You're in the picture, you raised the flag. That's the story we're selling boys'. Native American Hayes never really recovered from his stint as a 'national hero' and died a broken, disillusioned man, but not before he had hitchhiked 1,300 miles from Arizona to Texas to inform Harlon Block's father that it is his son in the picture, as Block's parents had always suspected.

Letters from Iwo Jima was filmed entirely in Japanese, with Japanese actors in all the principal roles, and for Eastwood was something of a circuitous return to his cinematic roots. He had long been a fan of the work of Japanese film director Akira Kurosawa. Eastwood's breakthrough role had been in *A Fistful of Dollars*, a remake of Kurosawa's *Yojimbo*, which Eastwood still rates among his favourite films. Now here he was, making a film in Japanese, which included several stylistic nods to the master. There is even a reference to Kurosawa's signature 'screen wipe' transitional effect, whereby the current shot is 'wiped' by a vertical line passing across the frame, introducing another scene. In *Letters* the 'wipe' is the frame of Kuribayashi's map board. The humble Japanese conscripts echo characters in Kurosawa's cinema, in particular the two peasant 'everymen' in *The Hidden Fortress* (1958); the 'Hidden Fortress' in Eastwood's film is Mount Suribachi. Saigo and Shimizu are too young to die: 'You haven't lived enough', says Saigo, 'to know what you are sacrificing'.

The link between officers and men in *Letters* is their correspondence with their loved ones back in Japan – many of their letters were never posted, due to the strict army censor. As he digs trenches on the beach, Saigo wonders, 'Am I digging my own grave?' As with several Eastwood-directed films, characters from the present are enveloped by past events. The final image is of the letters being emptied from a bag, silent voices fluttering to the ground.

A major plus for both films is their scores. *Flags* was composed by Eastwood himself and is probably his best: it draws on Niehaus's lushly orchestrated approach but adds another dimension, with resonant strings and echoing flutes evoking menace and terror in the Iwo Jima scenes, and recalling Ennio Morricone's pan-pipes score for the Vietnam-set *Casualties of War* (1989). *Flags*' score was orchestrated and conducted by Niehaus, with 'special arrangements' by Eastwood's son Kyle and Michael Stevens. The film also deploys period songs, including 'I'll Walk Alone' by Dinah Shore. Interestingly, *Flags* begins with Eastwood himself softly singing the lyrics, a cappella, which recalls the similarly eerie opening of *The Beguiled*. Almost inaudibly, Eastwood whispers:

> *I'll walk alone, because to tell you the truth I am lonely,*
> *I don't mind being lonely when my heart tells me you are lonely too.*
> *They'll ask me why and I'll say that I'd rather, there are dreams I must gather.*

Letters score is equally atmospheric, this time composed by Kyle Eastwood and Michael Stevens (orchestrated and conducted by Niehaus). This simple arching theme, played on piano and trumpet, is particularly powerful. Elsewhere, dissonant strings, piano chords and a twanging cimbalom create an unnatural atmosphere – as in the scene when the Japanese soldiers commit suicide with grenades. It's a very unusual score, which in its understated, threatening way, adds much to the film.

Flags, the more accessible film of the two for general audiences, was released first in October 2006. The film's poster – depicting the flag-raising, which still resonates today, evoking events from Vietnam to 9/11 – was accompanied by the tagline: 'A single shot can end the war'. Perhaps memories of the cinematic disaster that was *Pearl Harbor* (2001) discouraged audiences, because despite good reviews *Flags* took only $33 million in the US. *Rolling Stone* was typical, calling it 'a film of awesome power and blistering provocation'. A film subtitled in Japanese stood even less chance of becoming a hit, though *Letters* received better notices. *Time* called it 'another masterpiece from Clint Eastwood'. *Rolling Stone* concurred: 'The result is unique and unforgettable'. Philip French in *The Observer* called the films 'masterpieces of humanist cinema... a magnificent diptych'. The *New York Times* named *Letters* as the best American movie of the year, adding, 'Eastwood just gets better and better'. Eastwood was nominated for a Best Director Golden Globe and the film won a Globe for Best Foreign Language Picture. At the 2007 Oscars, *Flags* was nominated for Best Sound and Best Director. Eastwood was nominated again for *Letters*, which was also shortlisted for Best Picture and Best Screenplay. The only Academy Award given to *Letters* was to Alan Robert Murray and Bub Asman for their work on the film's sound design, particularly effective in the whizzing, bullet-peppered action scenes. *Letters* took only $13 million on its US release in December 2006 but was successful worldwide (especially in Japan) and is now available, with *Flags*, on DVD. While promoting his own WWII movie *Miracle at St Anna* (2008) detailing a black unit fighting in Italy, director Spike Lee complained publicly that Eastwood hadn't included any black marines in *Flags*: 'That was his version', Lee said, 'The negro version did not exist'. Eastwood responded that there were black soldiers on Iwo Jima as part of a munitions company, but they weren't involved in the flag raising and as such had no place in his film – he couldn't rewrite history.

Flags is a good film, with the 'flags of our fathers' being the sometimes unseen legacy our fathers leave behind. But *Letters* is far superior to its companion piece, perhaps because it concentrates more on the actual battle, rather than its aftermath, or perhaps because the characters are more sympathetic, but mainly because it is the better written and acted of the two. *Letters* is one of the great antiwar movies. It's also one of the best films Eastwood has directed and is fully deserving of the term 'masterpiece'.

EPILOGUE

Eastwood's current critical acclaim seems a long way from the Clyde the Orang-utan films and 'Beers to You', and even the media's initial negative response to 'The Man with No Name' and Dirty Harry. In fact, Eastwood's directorial legacy has now equalled, if not surpassed, his film stardom. It is a unique achievement: of all the great film stars or great directors, masters of a single discipline, only the legacies of Charlie Chaplin and Buster Keaton approach Eastwood's accomplishments of critical and commercial success. And at the time of writing, prolific Eastwood shows no signs of slowing down.

In 2008, Eastwood directed *Changeling*, an atmospheric Los Angeles-set period piece. Angelina Jolie starred as single mother Christine Collins, whose nine-year-old son Walter (Gattlin Griffth) is kidnapped on March 10, 1928. Five months later, the police succeed in locating Walter but on his return Christine knows intuitively that he's not the same boy: 'That's not my son', she insists when presented with a Walter impostor (Devon Conti). It is revealed that the new 'Walter' is three inches shorter than her son and has been circumcised, but Christine is convinced by Captain J.J. Jones (Jeffrey Donovan) to take the foundling home. Despite much evidence and the testimony of many who knew Walter, the police refuse to admit the switch and Christine is taken to the psychiatric wing of LA hospital, for shock treatment for her delusional behaviour – they try to make her admit that it is she who is wrong, that she is running away from her responsibilities as a mother. Meanwhile a separate investigation in Wineville County into the abduction and murder of children unearths evidence that one of the victims may have been Walter. With this news, Christine is released and the web of corruption and duplicity in the LAPD leads to the courts.

Changeling is a familiarly bleak tale from Eastwood, produced by Imagine Entertainment, Relativity Media and Malpaso, for Universal Pictures. J. Michael Straczynski's script was based on a true case, the 'Wineville Chicken Murders', which he researched from archival records. The $55 million film was shot between October and November 2007, on location in Los Angeles, and in Pasadena (Daniel Webster Elementary School), Lancaster, Long Beach and San Dimas, California. The railway station where Christine is reunited with 'Walter' was Santa Fe Railroad Depot in San Bernardino. Studio shots were filmed at Universal, with Eastwood back at the studio where years ago he began his career as a contract player. Photographed by cinematographer Tom Stern in Panavision, *Changeling* convinces in its authentic period setting and is a more successful drama than the similarly noir-ish *The Black Dahlia* and *Hollywoodland* (both 2006). Eastwood also composed the moving jazz-inflected score (disparagingly described by one critic as 'washes of mournful gloop'), in his trademark understated style, with long, low strings backing piano motifs. *Changeling*'s milieu recalls dark noirs such as the corruption-ridden *L.A. Confidential*, and the child abduction dredges the troubling depths of *Mystic River*. 'I'm always particularly appalled by crimes against children', said Eastwood, 'And that had something to do with me wanting to make this film'. Like *Flags of Our Fathers*, *Changeling* also deals with the misrepresentation of facts to the media – like the flag-raising heroes of Iwo Jima, the 'Walter' paraded before the press isn't who he seems.

Changeling reunited Eastwood with John Malkovich (from *In the Line of Fire*) as Reverend Gustav Briegleb, who drums up support for Christine and condemns the LAPD for incompetence and hidden dishonesty. Jolie, a Best Supporting Actress Oscar winner for *Girl, Interrupted* (1999), was cast in the lead, though Hilary Swank and Reese Witherspoon had both sought to play Christine, a woman convinced her son is still out there somewhere, alive. Jolie is particularly convincing in a scene when the 'changeling', settled into his new home, says, 'Goodnight mommy', and she screams at him to stop calling her that, she's not his mother. Michael Kelly appeared as Detective Lester Ybarra, an honest cop on the Wineville case. Colm Feore was LAPD chief James E. Davis and Jeffrey Donovan scored as despicable Captain Jones, who tries to convince Christine of the deception – 'Why should we be looking for somebody we've already found?' – and convinces Christine to take 'Walter' home on a 'trial basis'. Jason Butler Harner was particularly effective as Gordon Northcott, the perpetrator of the Wineville murders. Eastwood's 11-year-old daughter, Morgan, who was glimpsed in *Million Dollar Baby*, can be seen briefly riding a tricycle.

Like some of Eastwood's other directorial efforts, *Changeling* is slightly overlong at 141 minutes – it starts well but gets bogged down navigating the endless investigation and subsequent trial of the disturbing Wineville murders, an interesting subject worthy of a film of its own. *Changeling* premiered in May 2008 at the Cannes Film Festival as *L'Échange* ('The Exchange'). It was released in the US in October 2008 rated 'R', with the tagline 'To Find Her Son, She Did What No One Else Dared', to largely positive reviews and widespread commercial success. The *Hollywood Reporter* announced in November that Jolie was the highest paid female star in Hollywood and her popularity and regular appearances in the media no doubt helped the film's profile. She was nominated for a 'Best Actress' Oscar and the film also garnered nominations for cinematography and art direction. It was released in the UK at the end of November, again to positive reviews, though some had problems with the film's length. Most agreed, however, that Jolie's tearful, impassioned performance made the film a superior melodrama and that Eastwood's artistry had again brought an atypical, undiscovered story to life. *Changeling* wasn't aimed at a popcorn audience, who can just about follow a piece of string, and Eastwood liked the story's complexity, noting that it was 'made for people who want to think along with you'.

In July 2008, Eastwood began shooting *Gran Torino* which was rumoured to be a sixth Dirty Harry movie, though this has proved unfounded: 'There are certain age limits on police officers', noted Eastwood, 'They'd have retired me out at 65'. He again worked as actor-director, playing the role of recently widowed Walt Kowalski, a Korean War veteran and owner of the title vehicle, a 1972 vintage Ford Gran Torino. Walt is now retired from his civilian job on the production line at a Ford plant, while his son now sells Japanese cars. The story follows Walt's developing relationship with his Hmong neighbours, including young Thao (Bee Vang), who tries to steal Walt's car as his initiation into a violent Hmong street gang led by Thao's cousin Spider (Doua Moua). As Walt gets to know the Hmong families, especially Thao's sister Sue (Ahney Her), he realises that he has more in common with them than with his own greedy, covetous family: Walt's two sons are trying to convince him to move into a retirement home, while his granddaughter Ashley (Dreama Walker) has her eye on the shiny Gran Torino. Racist Walt, his worldview coloured by his traumatic war experiences, learns to be more tolerant of his neighbours and teaches Thao good values, even getting him a job on a construction site run by his Irish friend Tim Kennedy (William Hill). A heavy smoker, Walt begins coughing up blood and discovers that he's terminally ill. The friction between Walt, Thao and the gangs escalates, eventually climaxing in a drive-by attack on Thao's house in which he's wounded, and the gang members abduct and savagely rape Sue. Walt and Thao swear revenge, but Walt locks Thao in his basement before facing the gangsters alone.

Gran Torino is based on a story by Nick Schenk and David Johannson, with the screenplay written by Schenk. It was filmed on location in Michigan for $35 million, using many Asian actors in the cast – Vang and Her are excellent as brother and sister, and Choua Kue played Youa, Thao's love interest, whom Walt calls 'Yum-Yum'. Walt allows Thao to borrow his Gran Torino to take Youa on a date. Walt mispronounces Thao 'Toad' and enjoys mock-racist banter with his 'Italian prick' barber Martin (John Carroll Lynch); later his own surname is mispronounced by a health clinic's Muslim receptionist. Father Janovich (Christopher Carley), the persistent padre determined to save Walt's soul, has promised Dorothy, Walt's wife, that he would comfort her husband after her death. Eastwood's son Scott Reeves has a small role as Sue's cowardly 'white trash' boyfriend Trey. Regular Eastwood collaborator Tom Stern provided the cinematography and Lennie Niehaus orchestrated the music, which was composed by Kyle Eastwood and Michael Stevens. *Gran Torino* references several films by Eastwood and others: for example, the opening funeral sequence echoes the beginning of *Unforgiven*; his helping Thao find a job has echoes of Frank helping Maggie in *Million Dollar Baby* and Harry Callahan drove a Ford Torino sedan in *The Enforcer*. Walt smokes cigarettes throughout the film, like many of Eastwood's screen heroes, and there's even a disclaimer about the prominent 'depiction of tobacco products' during the end titles. Walt's spitting habit recalls Josey Wales's, the warring gangs from *A Fistful of Dollars* have resonance in the warring street gangs and a photograph of Walt on active duty in Korea is a still from *Kelly's Heroes*. Eastwood's 'Korean War Vet growl' is back from *Heartbreak Ridge* (as Walt's gravely delivery) and his home, an 'outpost' in a largely Hmong neighbourhood with the US flag flying on the porch, resembles resolute *Fort Apache*.

The ending is a replay of the climax of Don Siegel's western *The Shootist* (1976), which saw John Wayne's aged, cancer-stricken gunfighting legend J.B. Books go out in style, by putting his house in order and then setting up a confrontation with his adversaries. Eastwood had died on screen twice before – in the box office flops *The Beguiled* and *Honkytonk Man* – but this is the first time he has done so in a shootout.

Having been told by Father Janovich to 'go in peace', Walt arrives at Spider's house and challenges the gang. He refers to the hoods as 'miniature cowboys' and mimes shooting them with his finger. With a cigarette in his mouth, he notes, 'I've got a light', and reaches inside his jacket. The gang riddles him with a spluttering flurry of automatic fire and Walt falls dead, his arms outstretched, as though crucified. It is revealed later that he wasn't armed but was reaching for his Zippo, decorated with his Korean War unit's emblem, the 1st Cavalry. There are witnesses to the crime and the perpetrators will go to jail, granting Sue and Thao peace. Walt has already gifted Thao his Korean War medal; at the reading of Walt's will, it is revealed that he has left his house to the church and his Gran Torino to Thao. The film's final shot has Thao, Walt's beloved dog Daisy by his side, driving the car along a sunny waterfront, as Eastwood himself sings the first verse of 'Gran Torino', the moving end title song. Co-composed by Eastwood, Jaime Cullum, Kyle Eastwood and Michael Stevens, the remainder of the vocal is performed by Cullum: 'Engines hum and bitter dreams grow. Heart locked in a Gran Torino, beats a lonely rhythm all night long'. Eastwood the filmmaker does 'visceral' effortlessly, creating powerful cinema, and audience emotions run high in *Gran Torino* long before the martyred finale. As Walt says of his ancient, reliable freezer, they don't make 'em like this any more. When *Gran Torino* was released in the US in January 2009 it earned Eastwood his biggest ever opening weekend, taking $29 million and surpassing *Space Cowboys*' $18 million in 2000. It has since gone on to become Eastwood's most successful film of all time, crashing through the $100 million mark.

Another recent Eastwood project sees the director reunited with Morgan Freeman, cast as Nelson Mandela for *The Human Factor* – the actor has a singularly appropriate name for portraying the most famous 'Free Man' on earth. The film details Mandela's campaign to host the 1995 Rugby World Cup in South Africa during his first term as president. Its source is John Carlin's book *Play the Enemy – Nelson Mandela and the Game that Made a Nation*, published in August 2008. Yet again Eastwood wasn't afraid of tackling important, difficult subjects – his films of the 21st Century have addressed euthanasia, abuse, organ harvesting and child kidnapping.

In addition to critical acclaim, Eastwood has reaped considerable financial rewards as both director and star. His 11 biggest blockbusters at the box office as an actor are *Gran Torino, In the Line of Fire, Unforgiven, Million Dollar Baby* (all of which have broken the $100 million mark in the US), *Space Cowboys, Every Which Way But Loose, The Bridges of Madison County, Any Which Way You Can, Sudden Impact, Absolute Power* and *Tightrope*. His six most financially successful films as director are *Gran Torino, Unforgiven, Million Dollar Baby, Space Cowboys, Mystic River* and *The Bridges of Madison County*. Having watched Eastwood's entire filmography during the research for this book, my selection for his '10 best' movies as an actor would be *The Beguiled, The Good, the Bad and the Ugly, Dirty Harry, Unforgiven, Play Misty for Me, Thunderbolt and Lightfoot, The Outlaw Josey Wales, The Bridges of Madison County, For a Few Dollars More* and *Million Dollar Baby*, all of which have been acknowledged as classics. Of his films as director, I would

8.1 The Beguiler: Clint Eastwood (in costume as Corporal John McBurney) behind the camera on Don Siegel's *The Beguiled* (1971), prior to starting work on his directorial debut, *Play Misty for Me* (1971). Author's collection.

suggest *Mystic River, The Bridges of Madison County, Bird, Unforgiven, The Outlaw Josey Wales, Play Misty for Me, Million Dollar Baby, Letters from Iwo Jima* and *Gran Torino* as career highlights representative of his talent.

Eastwood's personal favourites are more offbeat – he often cites *Bronco Billy, The Outlaw Josey Wales* and *Bird* as his favourite films. These are probably closer to Eastwood's heart, more representative of his psyche, than some of his more perennially popular films – the 'Dollars' films or the 'Dirty Harrys'. The 'American Dream', a tale of the settling of the west, is refracted through Eastwood's vengeful gunslinger in *The Outlaw Josey Wales*. Homespun sentimentality and a small-town success story is the crux of *Bronco Billy* and an American Tragedy with no second act is the driving force behind *Bird*. All three depict America, and Eastwood is an unequivocally American filmmaker. His films have entertained, impressed and moved audiences for over 40 years and as he approaches 80, older and wiser, but still full of energy, the master craftsman remains convinced that the heart is still worth aiming for.

EASTWOOD FILMOGRAPHY

This is a complete filmography of all Clint Eastwood's feature-length releases, as either director or star. Before achieving stardom Eastwood appeared in *Revenge of the Creature* (1955, dir: Jack Arnold), *Francis in the Navy* (1955, dir: Arthur Lubin), *Lady Godiva* (1955, dir: Arthur Lubin), *Tarantula* (1955, dir: Jack Arnold), *Never Say Goodbye* (1956, dir: Jerry Hopper), *Away all Boats* (1956, dir: Joseph Pevney), *Star in the Dust* (1956, dir: Charles Haas), *The First Travelling Saleslady* (1956, dir: Arthur Lubin), *Escapade in Japan* (1957, dir: Arthur Lubin), *Lafayette Escadrille* (1958, dir: William Wellman) and *Ambush at Cimarron Pass* (1958, dir: Jodie Copeland).

A Fistful of Dollars (1964)
Director: Sergio Leone
Jolly Film/Ocean Film/Constantin Film (Italian/Spanish/West German)
97 Minutes
Clint Eastwood, (Joe the Stranger), Marianne Koch (Marisol), Gian Maria Volonte (Ramon Rojo), Wolfgang Lukschy (Sheriff John Baxter), Sieghardt Rupp (Esteban Rojo), Josef Egger (Piripero, undertaker), Antonio Prieto (Don Miguel Rojo), Margherita Lozano (Consuela Baxter), Jose Calvo (Silvanito, cantina owner), Daniel Martin (Julio), Fredy Arco (Jesus), Bruno Carotenuto (Antonio Baxter), Benito Stefanelli (Rubio, Ramon's lieutenant), Mario Brega (Chico), Jose Riesgo (Mexican Captain), Luis Barboo, Antonio Molino Rojo and Lorenzo Robledo (Baxter gunmen who spook mule), Jose Halufi and Nazzareno Natale (Rojo gunmen unloading corpses at Rio Bravo), Fernando Sanchez Polack (Rojo gunman crushed by wine cask), Jose Canalejas, Aldo Sambrell and Umberto Spadaro (Rojo gunmen), Bill Thompkins and Joe Kamel (Baxter gunmen guarding Marisol at hostage exchange), Julio Perez Taberno and Antonio Pico (Baxter gunmen) with Manuel Peña, Jose Orjas, Juan Cortes and Antonio Moreno

For a Few Dollars More (1965)
Director: Sergio Leone
PEA/Arturo Gonzales/Constantin (Italian/Spanish/West German)
126 minutes
Clint Eastwood (Manco), Lee Van Cleef (Colonel Douglas Mortimer), Gian Maria Volonte (El Indio), Mara Krup (Mary, hotelier), Josef Egger (Prophet in El Paso), Rosemary Dexter (Colonel's sister), Jose Marco Davo (Red 'Baby' Cavanagh), Antonio Ruiz (Fernando, Mexican boy), Lorenzo Robledo (Tomaso), Diana Faenza (Tomaso's wife), Francesca Leone (Tomaso's son), Roberto Camardiel (Tucumcari ticket seller), Riccardo Palacios (Tucumcari bartender), Sergio Mendizabal (Tucumcari banker), Guillermo Mendez (Sheriff of White Rocks), Kurt Zipps (Mary's husband), Jesus Guzman (Carpetbagger on train), Tomas Blanco (Shorty, Santa Cruz telegrapher), Karl Hirenbach (Mortimer's sister's lover), Jose Terron (Guy Callaway), Diana Rabito (Callaway's girl), Carlo Simi (El Paso bank manager), Dante Maggio (Indio's cellmate), Enrique Navarro (Sheriff of Tucumcari), Giovanni Tarallo (Bank vault guard), Mario Meniconi (Train conductor), Roman Ariznavaretta (Morton, in White Rocks), Furio Meniconi (Prison governor), Indio's gang: Mario Brega (Niño), Werner Abrolat (Slim), Klaus Kinski (The Wild One), Luigi Pistilli (Groggy), Benito Stefanelli (Huey), Aldo Sambrell (Cuchillo), Frank Braña (Blacky), Antonio Molino Rojo (Frisco), Jose Canalejas (Chico), Nazzareno Natale (Paco), Panos Papadopoulos (Sancho Perez), Massimo Carocci (Mexican bandit in poncho) with Eduardo Garcia, Rafael Lopez Somoza, Jose Felix Montoya, Aldo Ricci, Enrique Santiago and Luis Rodriguez

The Good, the Bad and the Ugly (1966)
Director: Sergio Leone
PEA/United Artists (Italian/US)
169 minutes

Clint Eastwood (Blondy), Lee Van Cleef (Angel Eyes, alias 'Sergeant Allen Crane'), Eli Wallach (Tuco Pacifico Juan Maria Ramirez, alias 'Bill Carson'), Aldo Giuffre (Captain Clinton, at bridge), Luigi Pistilli (Padre Pablo Ramirez), Rada Rassimov (Maria, prostitute), Antonio Casas (Stevens, farmer), Livio Lorenzon (Baker), Antonio Casale (Corporal Jackson, alias 'Bill Carson'), Angelo Novi (Young monk at San Antonio), Antonio Molino Rojo (Captain Harper, at prison camp), Mario Brega (Corporal Wallace), Al Mulock (Elam, bounty hunter), Frank Braña and Saturnino Cerra (Bounty hunters in ghost town), John Bartho (Marshal of Mesilla), Franco Doria (Marshal's deputy), Jesus Guzman (Hotel owner in Santa Fe), Chelo Alonso (Stevens' wife), Antonio Ruiz (Stevens' son operating waterwheel), Enzo Petito (Milton, gunsmith), Jose Terron (Thomas 'Shorty' Larson), Victor Israel (Confederate Sergeant at fort), Silvana Bacci (Mexican prostitute in Socorro), Mimmo Maggio, Claudio Scarchilli and Aysanoa Runachagua (Tuco's hired guns), Roman Ariznavaretta (Blond bounty hunter), Nazzareno Natale (Mexican bounty hunter), Riccardo Palacios (Socorro bartender), Sergio Mendizabal (Socorro dignitary), Lorenzo Robledo (Clem), Romano Puppo (Slim), Benito Stefanelli, Luigi Ciavarro and Aldo Sambrell (Angel Eyes' gang)

The Witches (1967 – episode: *An Evening like the Others*)
Director: Vittorio De Sica
Dino De Laurentiis Cinematografica/Les Artistes Associes (Italian/French)
19 minutes (of 119 minute film)

Silvana Mangano (Giovanna), Clint Eastwood (Charlie), Armando Bottin (Nembo Kid), Pietro Torrisi (Batman), Gianni Gori (Diabolik), Paolo Gozlino (Mandrake the magician), Angelo Santi (Flash Gordon), Franco Moruzzi (Sadik), with Valentino Macchi, Corinne Fontaine

Hang 'Em High (1968)
Director: Ted Post
United Artists/Malpaso/Leonard Freeman Productions (US)
110 minutes

Clint Eastwood (Deputy Marshal Jedediah Cooper), Inger Stevens (Rachel Warren), Ed Begley (Captain Wilson), Pat Hingle (Judge Adam Fenton), Arlene Gononka (Jennifer), James MacArthur (Preacher at Fort Grant), Ruth White (Madam Peaches Sophie), Ben Johnson (Sheriff Dave Bliss), Bruce Dern (Miller, rustler), Richard Gates (Ben, rustler), Bruce Scott (Billy Joe, rustler), Dennis Hopper (The Prophet), Alan Hale Jnr (Matt Stone, Red Creek blacksmith), Bob Steele (Jenkins), L.Q. Jones (Em Loomis), Joseph Sirola (Reno), Russell Thorson (Mr Maddow), Ned Romero (Charlie Blackfoot), Jonathan Lippe (Tommy), Charles McGraw (Ray Calhoun, Sheriff of Red Creek), Jack Ging (Marshal Hays), James Westerfield (Prisoner chewing tobacco), Michael O'Sullivan (Francis Elroy Duffy), Bert Freed (Schmidt, executioner), Herbert Ellis (Swede), Joel Fluellen (William, Tumbleweed wagon driver), Robert B. Williams (Elwood, undertaker), Hal England (Son of rancher murdered by Miller), Richard Angarola (Mexican posse member), John Wesley and Roy Glenn (Prison guards at Fort Grant), Mark Lenard (Prosecution attorney), Tod Andrews (Defence attorney), Bill Zuckert (Sheriff guarding Swede), Roxanne Tunis (Prostitute at hanging) with Richard Guizon, Paul Sorenson, Larry J. Blake, Ted Thorpe, Robert Jones, Barry Cahill, Dennis Dengate, Tony Di Milo

Coogan's Bluff (1968)
Director: Donald Siegel
Universal/Malpaso (US)
91 minutes

Clint Eastwood (Deputy Sheriff Walt Coogan), Lee J. Cobb (Lieutenant McElroy), Susan Clark (Julie Roth), Tisha Sterling (Linny Raven), Don Stroud (James Ringerman), Betty

Field (Ellen Ringerman), Tom Tully (Sheriff McCrea), Melodie Johnson (Millie), James Edwards (Sergeant Wallace, cop disguised as tramp), Rudy Diaz (Running Bear), David F. Doyle (Pushie), Louis Zorich (Cab driver), Marjorie Bennett (Mrs Fowler), Seymore Cassel (Joe), Joe Coe (Golden Hotel bellboy), Albert Popwell (Wonderful Digby), Skip Battyn (Omega), Albert Henderson (Desk sergeant), James McCallion (Golden Hotel clerk), Syl Lamont (Apartment manager), Jess Osuna and Doug Reid (Bellevue Hospital guards), Antonia Rey (Mrs Amador), Marya Henriques (Abseiling stripper), James Dukas (Bellevue doctor), Scott Hale (Dr. Scott), Meg Myles (Big Red), James Gavin (Ferguson), Conrad Bain (Madison Avenue man), Jerry Summers (Good Eyes), Eve Brent (Hooker in Golden Hotel)

Where Eagles Dare (1968)
Director: Brian G. Hutton
Metro-Goldwyn-Mayer/Winkast Productions (GB)
149 minutes
Richard Burton (Major John Smith, alias 'Major Johann Schmidt'), Clint Eastwood (Lieutenant Morris Schaffer, OSS agent), Mary Ure (Mary Ellison, alias 'Maria Schenk'), Patrick Wymark (Colonel Wyatt Turner), Michael Hordern (Admiral Rolland, MI6), Donald Houston (Captain James Christiansen), Peter Barkworth (Edward Berkeley), William Squire (Captain Philip Thomas), Robert Beatty (Corporal Cartwright Jones, alias 'General George Carnaby'), Brook Williams (Sergeant Harrod), Neil McCarthy (Sergeant Jock MacPhearson), Vincent Ball (Wing Commander Cecil Carpenter), Anton Diffring (Colonel Paul Kramer), Ferdy Mayne (Reichsmarschall Julius Rosemeyer), Derren Nesbitt (Major Von Happen, Gestapo), Victor Beaumont (Colonel Weissner, SS Field Security officer), Ingrid Pitt (Heidi), John Heller (German Major at table in tavern), Guy Deghy (Major General Wilner, Kesselring's Chief of Intelligence), Olga Lowe (Lieutenant Anne-Marie Kernitser, Kramer's secretary), Ivor Dean (German officer) Richard Beale (Telephone orderly), Lyn Kennington (German woman), Nigel Lambert (Young German soldier), Michael Rooney (Radio operator), Ernst Walder (Airport control officer)

Paint Your Wagon (1969)
Director: Joshua Logan
Paramount Pictures/Alan Jay Lerner Productions (US)
148 minutes
Lee Marvin (Ben Rumson), Clint Eastwood (Sylvester Newel, called 'Pardner'), Jean Seberg (Elizabeth Woodling), Harve Presnell (Rotten Luck Willie), Ray Walston (Mad Jack Duncan), Tom Ligon (Horton Fenty), Alan Dexter (Parson), William O'Connell (Horace Tabor), Ben Baker (Haywood Holbrook), Alan Baxter (Mr Fenty), Paula Trueman (Mrs Fenty), Robert Easton (Ezra Atwell), Geoffrey Norman (Foster), H.B. ['Hard Boiled'] Haggerty (Steve Bull, the blacksmith), Terry Jenkins (Joe Mooney, Irish prospector), Karl Bruck (Gus Schermerhorn, barman), John Mitchum (Jacob Woodling), Sue Casey (Sarah Woodling), Eddie Little Sky (Indian in bar), Harvey Parry (Higgins), H.W. Gim (Wong, Willie's sidekick), Roy Jenson (Hennessey), Pat Hawley (Clendennon), William Mims (Frock-coated man), The Nitty Gritty Dirt Band (No Name City band)

Two Mules for Sister Sara (1970)
Director: Don Siegel
Universal/Malpaso/Sanen (US/Mexico)
109 minutes
Shirley MacLaine (Sarita, alias 'Sister Sara'), Clint Eastwood (Hogan, alias 'Tex Hamilton'), Manolo Fabregas (Colonel Beltran, Juarista leader), Alberto Morin (General LeClaire, Chihuahua commander), Armando Silvestre, John Kelly and Enrique Lucero (Bandits who attack Sara), David Estuardo (Juan, cantina barman), Ada Carrasco and Pancho Cordova (Juan's parents), Jose Chavez (Horatio, the candle maker) with Jose Angel Espinosa, Rosa Furman, Pedro Galvan, Margarito Luna, Xavier Marc, Javier Masse, Aurura Munoz, Hortensia Santovena and Jose Torvay

Kelly's Heroes (1970)
Director: Brian G. Hutton
Metro-Goldwyn-Mayer, The Warriors Company, Avala Films (US/Yugoslavia)
138 minutes

Clint Eastwood (Kelly), Telly Savalas (Big Joe), Don Rickles (Crapgame), Donald Sutherland (Oddball), Carroll O'Connor (General Colt), Gavin MacLeod (Moriarty, Oddball's crewman), Gene Collins (Babra), Perry Lopez (Petchuko), Dick Balduzzi (Fisher), Harry Dean Stanton (Willard), Hal Buckley (Captain Maitland), Stuart Margolin (Little Joe), Jeff Morris (Cowboy), Fred Pearlman (Mitchell), Tom Troupe (Job), Richard Davalos (Gatowsky), Len Lesser (Sergeant Bellamy, Bridging Engineers), George Savalas (Sergeant Mulligan, artillery), Michael Clark (Grace), George Fargo (Penn), Dee Pollock (Jonesy), Shephard Sanders (Turk, Oddball's crewman), Frank J. Garlotta, Sandy Kevin, Phil Adams (Sherman tank commanders), Read Morgan (ADC driver), David Hurst (Colonel Dankhopf), Robert McNamara (Roach), John Heller (German lieutenant at minefield ambush), James McHale (Clermont hotel guest), Ross Elliott (Booker, General Colt's communications officer), Tom Signorelli (Bonsor, General Colt's aide), Karl Otto Alberty (German tank commander in Clermont), Hugo de Vernier (Mayor of Clermont), Donald Waugh (Corporal Roamer, Engineers), Vincent Maracecchi (Old man in Clermont), Harry Goines (Supply sergeant), David Gross (German captain)

The Beguiled (1971)
Director: Don Siegel
Universal/Malpaso (US)
105 minutes

Clint Eastwood (Corporal John McBurney), Geraldine Page (Martha Farnsworth, Seminary Headmistress), Elizabeth Hartman (Edwina Dabney), Jo Ann Harris (Carol), Darleen Carr (Doris), Mae Mercer (Hallie), Pamela Ferdin (Amelia, called 'Amy'), Melody Thomas (Abigail), Peggy Drier (Lizzie), Pattye Mattick (Janie), Charlie Briggs (First Confederate Captain leading patrol), Charles Martin (Second Confederate Captain at seminary), George Dunn (Sam Jefferson, Confederate patrol member), Matt Clark (Scoggins, Confederate soldier), Patrick Culliton and Wayne Van Horn (Soldiers)

Play Misty for Me (1971)
Director: Clint Eastwood
Universal/Malpaso (US)
102 minutes

Clint Eastwood (Dave Garver), Jessica Walter (Evelyn Draper), Donna Mills (Tobie Williams), John Larch (Sergeant Paul McCallum), Jack Ging (Dr Frank Dewan), Irene Hervey (Madge Brenner, Malpaso TV Productions executive), James McEachin (Al Monte, DJ), Clarice Taylor (Birdie, Dave's housekeeper), Donald Siegel (Johnny Murphy, Sardine Factory bartender), Duke Everts (Jay Jay, Tobie's boss), George Fargo and Paul E. Lippman (Men outside Sardine Factory), Mervin W. Frates (Locksmith in Carmel), Tim Frawley (Deputy Sheriff), Otis Kadani (Policeman at Dave's), Brit Lind (Angelica, Tobie's first roommate), Jack Kosslyn (Yellow Cab driver), Ginna Patterson (Madalyn, Tobie's second roommate), Malcolm Moran (Dave's neighbour in window), The Johnny Otis Show (themselves), The Cannonball Adderley Quintet (themselves)

Dirty Harry (1971)
Director: Don Siegel
Warner Bros/Malpaso (US)
98 minutes

Clint Eastwood (Inspector Harry Francis Callahan), Harry Guardino (Lieutenant Alfred J. 'Al' Bressler), Reni Santoni (Inspector Charles 'Chico' Gonzales), Andy Robinson ('Scorpio'), John Vernon (Mayor of San Francisco), John Larch (San Francisco Chief of Police), John

Mitchum (Inspector Frank DiGeorgio), Mae Mercer (Mrs Russell, victim's mother), Lyn Edgington (Norma Gonzales), Ruth Kobart (Marcella Platt, bus driver), Woodrow Parfrey (Mr Jaffe, 'Burger Den' proprietor), Josef Sommer (District Attorney William T. Rothko), William Paterson (Judge Bannerman of the Appellate Court), James Nolan (Liquor store proprietor), Maurice S. Argent (Sid Kleinman, radio expert), Jo de Winter (Miss Willis, Rothko's secretary), Craig G. Kelly (Sgt Jim Reineke, Russell murder scene), Charles Washburn (Steve, police doctor), Diana Davidson (Sandra Benson, rooftop swimmer), Lois Foraker (Hot Mary), Marc Hertsens (Park Emergency doctor), Debralee Scott (Ann Mary Deacon), Stephen Zacks (Boy fishing in reservoir), Albert Popwell (First bank robber), Ernest Robinson (Getaway driver), Diane Darnell (Mayor's secretary), Bill Couch (Suicidal jumper), Charles Murphy (Old man in payphone), Max Gail, John Garber and Christopher Pray (Muggers in Fort Mason tunnel) with Pamela Tanimura, Richard Samuelson, Sean Maley, Derek Jue, Jack Hanson, Diane and Denise Dyer (Children on hijacked school bus)

Joe Kidd (1972)
Director: John Sturges
Universal/Malpaso (US)
87 Minutes

Clint Eastwood (Joe Kidd), Robert Duvall (Frank Harlan), John Saxon (Luis Chama), Stella Garcia (Helen Sanchez), Don Stroud (Lamarr Sims), James Wainwright (Olin Mingo), Paul Koslo (Roy Gannon), Gregory Walcott (Bob Mitchell, Sheriff of Sinola), Dick Van Patten (Grand Hotel manager), Lynne Marta (Elma, Harlan's companion), John Carter (Sinola County Judge), Pepe Hern (Arroyo Blanco padre), Joaquin Martinez (Manolo, Chama's lieutenant), Ron Soble (Ramon), Pepe Callahan (Naco), Clint Ritchie (Deputy Sheriff Calvin), Gil Barreto (Emilio, Kidd's foreman), Maria Val (Emilio's wife), Ed Deemer (Harry, Railroad Saloon bartender), Chuck Hayward (LJ), Michael R. Horst (Sinola Deputy)

High Plains Drifter (1973)
Director: Clint Eastwood
Universal/Malpaso (US)
101 minutes

Clint Eastwood (The Stranger), Verna Bloom (Sarah Belding), Marianna Hill (Callie Travers), Mitchell Ryan (Dave Drake), Jack Ging (Morgan Allen), Stefan Gierasch (Mayor Jason Hobart, general storekeeper), Ted Hartley (Lewis Belding, hotelier), Billy Curtis (Mordecai), Geoffrey Lewis (Stacey Bridges), Anthony James (Cole Carlin), Dan Vadis (Dan Carlin), Ron Soble (Ike Sharp, first hired gun), Scott Walker (Billy Borders, second hired gun), Russ McCubbin (Fred Morris, third hired gun), Walter Barnes (Sam Shaw, Sheriff of Lago), Paul Brinegar (Lutie Taylor, barman), Richard Bull (Asa Goodwin, undertaker), Robert Donner (Lago Preacher), John Hillerman (Bootmaker), William O'Connell (Barber), John Quade (Jake Ross, haulier), Wayne 'Buddy' Van Horn (Marshal Jim Duncan), Reid Cruickshanks (Gunsmith), Jack Kosslyn (Saddle maker), Jane Aull (Townswoman), James Gosa (Tommy Morris), Belle Mitchell (Mrs Lake), John Mitchum (Territorial Prison warden), Carl C. Pitti (Teamster), Chuck Waters (Stableman)

Breezy (1973)
Director: Clint Eastwood
Universal/Malpaso (US)
106 minutes

William Holden (Frank Harmon), Kay Lenz (Edith Alice Breezerman, called 'Breezy'), Roger C. Carmel (Bob Henderson), Marj Dusay (Betty Tobin), Joan Hotchkis (Paula Harmon), Jamie Smith Jackson (Marcy, Breezy's friend), Norman Bartold (Man in car who picks up Breezy), Lynn Borden (Frank's overnight date), Shelley Morrison (Nancy Henderson), Dennis Olivieri (Bruno, Breezy's lover), Eugene Peterson (Charlie Eisen, lawyer), Lew Brown (Police officer who arrests Breezy), Richard Bull (Doctor), Johnny Collins III (Norman), Don Diamond

(Maitre D'), Scott Holden (Veterinarian), Sandy Kenyon (Real Estate agent), Jack Kosslyn (Passing driver as Frank tends dog), Mary Munday (Restaurant waitress), Frances Stevenson (Boutique saleswoman), Buck Young (Paula's date), Priscilla Morrill (Boutique customer), Kyle Eastwood (Boutique customer's son), Clint Eastwood (Man leaning on harbour railing), Earle (Sir Love-A-Lot)

Magnum Force (1973)
Director: Ted Post
Warner Bros/Malpaso (US)
122 minutes

Clint Eastwood (Inspector Harry Francis Callahan), Hal Holbrook (Lieutenant Neil Briggs), Mitchell Ryan (Officer Charlie McCoy), David Soul (Officer John Davis), Tim Matheson (Officer Phil Sweet), Kip Niven (Officer Red Astrachan), Robert Urich (Officer Mike Grimes), Fenton Perry (Inspector Early Smith), Maurice Argent (Nat Weinstein, Ricca's defence attorney), Margaret Avery (Prostitute killed in taxi), Richard Devon (Carmine 'Bubby' Ricca), Tony Giorgio (Frank Palancio), Jack Kosslyn (Walter Smathers, ballistics expert), Bob March (Estabrook), Bob McClurg (Cab driver), John Mitchum (Inspector Frank DiGeorgio), Russ Moro (James Cantina, aka 'Gino', Ricca's driver), Clifford A. Pellow (Lou Guzman), Albert Popwell (J.J. Wilson, pimp), Christine White (Carol McCoy), Adele Yoshioka (Sunny), Will Hutchins (Cop at store hold-up armed with shotgun)

Thunderbolt and Lightfoot (1974)
Director: Michael Cimino
United Artists/Malpaso (US)
110 minutes

Clint Eastwood (John 'The Thunderbolt' Doherty), Jeff Bridges (Lightfoot), George Kennedy (Red Leary), Geoffrey Lewis (Eddie Goody), Gary Busey (Curly, worker in garden), Roy Jenson (Dunlop, assassin at church), Bill McKinney (Crazy driver), Gregory Walcott (Pete, used car salesman), Catherine Bach (Melody), June Fairchild (Gloria), Dub Taylor (Gas station attendant), Jack Dodson (Montana Armory manager), Vic Tayback (Mario Pinski, contractor), Luanna Roberts (Housewife posing naked in window), Gene Elman and Lila Teigh (Tourists in church), Burton Gilliam (Welder), Claudia Lenear (Secretary at welding plant), Erica Hagen (Waitress taking orders), Stuart Nisbet (Arnold, driver at gas station), Virginia Baker (Arnold's wife), Alvin Childress (Janitor at department store), Irene K. Cooper (Cashier in bank), Cliff Emmich (Fat man in telegraph office), Ted Foulkes (Little boy ordering ice cream), Karen Lamm (Girl on motorcycle), Leslie Oliver and Mark Montgomery (Teenagers), Tito Vandis (Counterman)

The Eiger Sanction (1975)
Director: Clint Eastwood
Universal/Malpaso (US)
124 minutes

Clint Eastwood (Dr. Jonathan Hemlock), George Kennedy (Ben Bowman), Vonetta McGee (Jemima Brown, C2 agent), Jack Cassidy (Miles Mellough), Heidi Brühl (Anna Montaigne), Thayer David (Dragon, Head of C2), Reiner Schoene (Karl Freytag, German climber), Michael Grimm (Anderl Meyer, Austrian climber), Jean-Pierre Bernard (Jean-Paul Montaigne, French climber), Brenda Venus (George Bowman, Ben's daughter), Gregory Walcott (Pope, C2 agent), Candice Rialson (Art student with crush on Hemlock), Elaine Shore (Miss Cerberus, C2 secretary), Dan Howard (Dewayne, Mellough's bodyguard), Jack Kosslyn (Reporter), Walter Kraus (Garcia Kruger, assassin), Frank Redmond (Henri Bach, alias 'Wormwood'), Siegfried Wallach (Hotel Bellevue Des Alpes manager), Susan Morgan (Buns), Jack Frey (Airport cab driver)

The Outlaw Josey Wales (1976)
Director: Clint Eastwood
Warner Bros/Malpaso (US)
130 minutes

Clint Eastwood (Josey Wales), Chief Dan George (Lone Watie), Sondra Locke (Laura Lee Turner), Paula Trueman (Grandma Sarah Turner), Geraldine Keams (Little Moonlight), John Vernon (Fletcher), Bill McKinney (Captain 'Redlegs' Terrill),Sam Bottoms (Jamie), Woodrow Parfrey (Major Best, carpetbagger on ferry), Will Sampson (Ten Bears, Comanche war chief), John Quade (Comanchero leader), John Russell (William 'Bloody Bill' Anderson), Joyce James (Rose), Sheb Wooley (Travis Cobb), William O'Connell (Sim Carstairs, ferryman), Royal Dano (Ten Spot), John Mitchum (Al, first trapper), Bruce M. Fischer (Yoke, second trapper), John Davis Chandler (Blond bounty hunter),Tim Roy Lowe (Second bounty hunter),Charles Tyner (Zukie Limmer, trading post owner), Matt Clark (Kelly),Cissy Wellman (Josey's wife), Kyle Eastwood (Little Josey), Clay Tanner (First Texas Ranger), Bob Hoy (Second Texas Ranger), Erik Holland (Union army sergeant reading Union Pledge), Madeline T. Holmes (Grannie Hawkins, at ferry), Faye Hamblin (Grandpa Turner), Buck Kartalian (Shopkeeper in Towash), John Verros (Chato, farm hand), Frank Schofield (Senator Jim Lane), Len Lesser (Abe, first hunter), Doug McGrath ('Lige, second hunter), Danny Green (Lemuel, Carstairs' ferryman)

The Enforcer (1976)
Director: James Fargo
Warner Bros/Malpaso (US)
93 minutes

Clint Eastwood (Inspector Harry Francis Callahan), Tyne Daly (Inspector Kate Moore), Harry Guardino (Lieutenant Alfred J. 'Al' Bressler), Bradford Dillman (Captain Bradford McKay), John Mitchum (Inspector Frank DiGeorgio), DeVeren Bookwalter (Bobby Maxwell), John Crawford (Mayor of San Francisco), Samantha Doane (Wanda), Robert Hoy (Buchinski, massage parlour owner), Jocelyn Jones (Miki Waleska), M.G. Kelly (Father John), Nick Pellegrino (Martin), Albert Popwell (Big Ed Mustapha, leader of UHURU), Rudy Ramos (Mendez), Bill Ackridge and Bill Jelliffe (Andy and Johnny, Western Gas & Electric Co. employees), Joe Bellan (Freddie the Fainter), Tim O'Neill (Police sergeant at liquor hold-up), Jan Stratton (Mrs Grey, interview panel), Will MacMillan (Lieutenant Charles Dobbs, interview panel), Jerry Walter (Inspector Mike Kraus, interview panel), Steve Eoff (Bustanoby, interview candidate), Tim Burrus (Henry Lee Caldwell, gang member), Michael Cavanaugh (Lalo, gang member), Dick Durock (Karl, gang member), Ronald Manning (Tex, gang member), Adele Proon (Irene DiGeorgio), Glenn Leigh Marshall (army sergeant demonstrating LAWS), Robert Behling (Autopsy surgeon), Terry McGovern (Disk Jockey), Stan Richie (Third Street swing bridge operator), John Roselius (Jimmy, mayor's assistant), Brian Fong (Scoutmaster with kids on tour), Art Rimdzius (Porn film director), Chuck Hicks (Huey, Massage parlour bouncer), Ann Macy (Madam of Tiffany's massage and sauna), Gloria Prince (Massage girl), Kenneth Boyd (Abdul, UHURU member), Bernard Glin (Koblo, UHURU member), Fritz Manes (First detective)

The Gauntlet (1977)
Director: Clint Eastwood
Warner Bros/Malpaso (US)
105 minutes

Clint Eastwood (Detective Ben Shockley), Sondra Locke (Augustina 'Gus' Mally), Pat Hingle (Meynard 'Josie' Josephson), William Prince (Commissioner E.A. Blakelock), Bill McKinney (Deke, Las Vegas Constable 315), Michael Cavanaugh (Assistant D.A. John Feyderspiel), Carole Cook (Vegas waitress), Mara Corday (Clark County Jail matron), Douglas McGrath (Vegas bookie), Jeff Morris (Desk Sergeant Grady, Clark County Jail),

Samantha Doane, Roy Jenson, Dan Vadis ('Noblemen' bikers), Carver Barnes (Southwest Trail Lines bus driver), Robert Barrett (Vegas Paramedic), Roger Lowe (Paramedic driver), Teddy Bear (Lieutenant), Mildred J. Brion (Old lady on bus), Ron Chapman (Veteran cop), Don Circle (Southwest Trail Lines bus clerk), James W. Gavin and Tom Friedkin (Helicopter pilots), Darwin Lamb (Police captain), Fritz Manes (Helicopter sniper), John Quiroga (Vegas cab driver), Joe Rainer (Rookie cop), Art Rimdzius (Phoenix judge), Al Silvani (Police sergeant)

Every Which Way But Loose (1978)
Director: James Fargo
Warner Bros/Malpaso (US)
110 minutes

Clint Eastwood (Philo Beddoe), Manis (Clyde), Sondra Locke (Lynn Halsey-Taylor), Geoffrey Lewis (Orville Boggs), Ruth Gordon (Ma Boggs), Beverly D'Angelo (Echo), Walter Barnes (Tank Murdock), George Chandler (Clerk at Dept. of Motor Vehicles), John Quade (Cholla, leader of the Black Widows), Gregory Walcott (Officer Putnam), James McEachin (Officer Herb), Hank Worden (Trailer court manager), Jerry Brutsche (Road sweeper driver), Janet Louise Coleman (Carol, student at Palomino), Al Stellone (Big Al, in Carter's Place), Sam Gilman (Big Al's friend), Chuck Hicks (Trucker), Timothy P. Irvin (MC at Zanza Bar), George Wilbur (Church, first opponent), Michael Mann (Church's manager), William J. Quinn (Kincaid, second opponent), Cary Michael Cheifer (Kincaid's manager), Tim Irwin (Bandleader), Billy Jackson (Bettor), Joyce Jameson (Sybil, owner of Sybil's Café), Richard Jameson (Harlan Toothaker), Jackson D. Kane (Man who Lynn picks up at bowling alley), Jeremy Kronsberg (Bruno), Fritz Manes (Bartender at Zanza Bar), Lloyd Nelson (Bartender), George Orrison (Spectator at fight), Thelma Pelish (Lady customer at Echo's roadside grocers), Tom Runyon (Bartender at Palomino), Bruce Scott (Schyler, Lynn's lover), Al Silvani (Tank Murdock's manager), Hartley Silver (Bartender), Jan Statton (Waitress), Mike Wagner (Lester, trucker), Guy Way (Bartender), Mel Tillis (Himself), Charlie Rich (Himself), Phil Everly (Himself, duetting with Lynn), The Black Widows: Roy Jenson (Woody), William O'Connell (Elmo), Bill McKinney (Dallas), Dan Vadis (Frank), Gary Davis, Scott Dockstader, Orwin Harvey, Gene LeBell, Chuck Waters and Jerry Wills (Biker gang members)

Escape from Alcatraz (1979)
Director: Don Siegel
Paramount Pictures/Malpaso-Siegel (US)
107 minutes

Clint Eastwood (Frank Lee Morris), Patrick McGoohan (Warden of Alcatraz), Roberts Blossom (Chester 'Doc' Dalton), Jack Thibeau (Clarence Anglin), Fred Ward (John Anglin), Paul Benjamin (English, the librarian), Larry Hankin (Charley Butts), Bruce M. Fischer (Wolf), Frank Ronzio (Litmus), Fred Struthman (Johnson), David Cryer (Wagner), Madison Arnold (Zimmerman, guard), Blair Burrows (Fight guard), Bob Balhatchet (Medical technical assistant), Matthew J. Locricchio and Stephen Bradley (Exam guards), Don Michaelian (Beck), Ray K. Goman (Cellblock captain), Jason Ronard (Bobs), Ed Vasgersian (Cranston), Ron Vernan (Stone), Regie Baff (Lucy Butts, Charley's wife), Hank Brandt (Associate warden), Candice Bowen (English's daughter), Joseph Miksak (Police Sergeant), Garry Goodrow (Weston), Ross Reynolds (Helicopter pilot), Al Dunlap (Visitors' guard), Dennis Berkfeldt, Jim Haynie, Tony Dario, Fritz Manes, Dana Derfus, Don Cummins, Gordon Handforth, John Scanlon, Don Watters, Dan Leegant, Joseph Knowland, James Collier, R.J. Ganzert, Robert Hirschfeld, Lloyd Nelson, George Orrison, Gry F. Warren, Joe Whipp, Terry Wills, John Garabedian (Prison guards), Dale Alvarez, Sheldon Feldner, Danny Glover, Carl Lumbly, Patrick Valentino, Gilbert Thomas Jnr, Eugene W. Jackson (Prisoners)

Bronco Billy (1980)
Director: Clint Eastwood
Warner Bros/Second Street Films (US)
108 minutes

Clint Eastwood (William 'Bronco Billy' McCoy), Sondra Locke (Antoinette Lily), Geoffrey Lewis (John Arlington), Scatman Crothers ('Doc' Lynch, ringmaster), Bill McKinney ('Two-gun Lefty' LeBow), Sam Bottoms (Lasso Leonard James, trick rope artist), Dan Vadis (Chief Big Eagle), Sierra Pecheur (Lorraine Running Water), Walter Barnes (Sheriff Dix), Woodrow Parfrey (Dr. Canterbury), Beverlee McKinsey (Irene Biddle Lily), Douglas McGrath (Lieutenant Wiecker), Hank Worden (Shady Acres gas station mechanic), William Prince (Edgar Lipton, attorney), Pam Abbas (Mother Superior Gabrielle), Edye Byrde (Eloise Ebby, Irene's maid), Douglas Copsey and Roger Dale Simmons (Reporters at bank robbery), John Wesley Elliott Jnr (Mineral Wells Sanatorium attendant), Chuck Hicks and Bobby Hoy (Oaktree Jones and Donald, cowboys who attack Antoinette), Jefferson Jewell (Boy at bank robbery), Dawnee Lee (Bank teller), Don Mummert (Antoinette's Chauffeur), Lloyd Nelson (Chuck, Sanatorium policeman), George Orrison (Cowboy in bar), Michael Reinbold (King Tucker, fairground owner), Tessa Richarde (Miss Mitzi Fritts, Billy's first assistant), Tanya Russell (Doris Duke, Billy's second assistant), Valerie Shanks (Sister Maria), Sharon Sherlock (Muriel Moody, license clerk), James Simmerhan (I.V. Collarton, bank manager), Jenny Sternling (Reporter at Mineral Wells), Chuck Waters and Jerry Wills (Bank robbers), Kyle and Alison Eastwood (Orphans at St Patrick's Orphanage), Merle Haggard (Himself)

Any Which Way You Can (1980)
Director: Wayne 'Buddy' Van Horn
Warner Bros/Malpaso (US)
110 mins

Clint Eastwood (Philo Beddoe), Sondra Locke (Lynn Halsey-Taylor), Geoffrey Lewis (Orville Boggs), Ruth Gordon (Ma Boggs), William Smith (Jack Wilson), Harry Guardino (James Beekman), Michael Cavanaugh (Patrick Scarfe), Barry Corbin (Fat Zack, Texan punter), Al Ruscio (Tony Paoli Snr, aka 'Big Tony'), Camila Ashlend (Hattie), Michael Brockman (Moustachioed officer), Julie Brown (Candy), Glen Campbell (Himself), Dick Christie (Jackson officer), Rebecca Clemons (Buxom Bess), Reid Cruickshanks (Bald-headed trucker), Michael Currie (Wyoming officer), Gary Lee Davies (Husky officer), James Gammon (Bartender in Palomino), Dick Durock (Joe Casey, Philo's first opponent), Michael Fairman (CHP Captain), Weston Gavin (Beekman's butler), Lance Gordon (Biceps, tough in bar), Lynn Hallowell (Honey Bun), Peter Hobbs (Motel clerk), Dan Barrows (Baggage man), Art La Fleur (Second baggage man), Ken Lerner (Tony Paoli Jnr), John McKinney (Officer), Robin Menken (Tall woman), George Murdock (Sergeant Cooley), Jack Murdock (Little Melvin, Fat Zack's friend), Sunshine Parker (Motel clerk who flashes Clyde), Ann Nelson (Harriet), Kent Parkins (Trucker), Anne Ramsey and Logan Ramsey (Loretta and Luther Quince, tourists), Michael Reinbold (Officer with glasses), Tessa Richarde (Sweet Sue), Jeremy Smith (Intern), Bill Sorrells (Bakersfield officer), Jim Stafford (Long John), Michael Talbot (Officer Morgan), Mark Taylor (Desk clerk), Jack Thibeau (Head muscle), Charles Walker (Officer), Fats Domino (Himself), John Quade (Cholla, leader of the Black Widows), The Black Widows: Roy Jenson (Moody), William O'Connell (Elmo), Bill McKinney (Dallas), Dan Vadis (Frank), Jerry Brutsche, Orwin Harvey, Larry Holt, John Nowak, Walt Robles, Mike Tillman (Biker gang members)

Firefox (1982)
Director: Clint Eastwood
Warner Bros/Malpaso (US)
119 minutes

Clint Eastwood (Major Mitchell Gant), Freddie Jones (Kenneth Aubrey), David Huffman (Captain Buckholz), Warren Clarke (Pavel Upenskoy), Ronald Lacey (Dr. Semelovsky),

Kenneth Colley (Colonel Kontarsky), Klaus Lowitsch (General Vladimirov), Nigel Hawthorne (Dr. Pyotr Baranovich), Stephan Schnabel (First Secretary), Thomas Hill (General Brown), Clive Merrison (Major Lanyev), Kai Wulff (Lt. Col. Yuri Voskov), Dimitra Arliss (Natalia), Austin Willis (Walters), Michael Currie (Captain Seerbacker), James Staley (Lt. Commander Fleischer), Ward Costello (General Rogers), Alan Tilvern (Air Marshall Kutuzov), Oliver Coitton (Dmitri Priabin), Bernard Behrens (William Saltonstall), Hugh Fraser (Police Captain Tortyev), John Grillo (Customs Officer), Richard Derr (Admiral Curtin), Barrie Houghton (Boris Glazunov), Curt Lowens (Dr Schuller), Alfredo Michelson (KGB Interrogator), George Orrison (Leon Sprague),Olivier Pierre (Borkh), George Pravda (General Borov), Woody Eney (Major Dietz), Grisha Plotkin (GRU officer), Alex Rodine (Captain of the Riga), Lance Rosen (Agent), Eugene Scherer (Russian Captain), Warwick Sims (Shelley), Mike Spero (Russian Guard), Malcolm Storry, Eugene Lipinski, David Gant, Bernard Erhard, Lev Mailer (KGB agents), Wolf Kahler (KGB Chairman Andropov), John Yates (Admiral Pearson), Fritz Manes (Captain)

Honkytonk Man (1982)
Director: Clint Eastwood
Warner Bros/Malpaso (US)
1118 minutes

Clint Eastwood (Red Stovall), Kyle Eastwood (Whit, known as 'Hoss'), John McIntire (Grandpa Wagoneer), Alexa Kenin (Marlene Mooney), Verna Bloom (Emmy), Matt Clark (Virgil), Barry Corbin (Derwood Arnspringer), Jerry Hardin (Snuffy), Tim Thomerson (Highway patrolman), Macon McCalman (Doctor Hines), Joe Regalbuto (Henry Axle, Burnside Records), Gary Grubbs (Jim Bob, police officer), Rebecca Clemons (Belle), John Gimble (Bob Wills), Linda Hopkins (Flossie King, singer), Bette Ford (Lulu, owner of 'Pair a Dice Café'), Jim Boelsen (Junior), Tracey Walter (Pooch), Susan Peretz (Miss Maud), John Russell (Jack Wade), Charles Cyphers (Stubbs), Marty Robbins (Smoky, singer), Ray Price (Bob Wills, singer), Shelly West and David Frizzell (Opry singing duo), Porter Wagoner (Dusty), Bob Ferrera (Howarth), Tracy Shults (Margery), R.J. Ganzert (Rancher), Hugh Warden (Grocer), Kelsie Blades (Veteran), Jim Ahart (Waiter), Steve Autry (Mechanic repairing car), Peter Griggs (Mr Vogel), Frank Reinhard (Standin), Julie Hoopman (Whore), Rozelle Gayle (Top Hat Club manager), Robert V. Barron (Undertaker), DeForest Covan (Gravedigger), Lloyd Nelson (Radio announcer), George Orrison and Glen Wright (Escaped jailbirds), Roy Jenson (Dub), Sherry Allurd (Dub's wife), Gordon Terry, Tommy Alsup and Merle Travis (Texas Playboys instrumentalists), Robert D. Carver (First bus driver), Thomas Powels (Second bus driver).

Sudden Impact (1983)
Director: Clint Eastwood
Warner Bros/Malpaso (US)
113 minutes

Clint Eastwood (Inspector Harry Francis Callahan), Sondra Locke (Jennifer Spencer), Pat Hingle (Chief Lester Jannings, San Paulo Police), Bradford Dillman (Captain Briggs), Paul Drake (Mick), Audrie J. Neenan (Ray Parkins), Jack Thibeau (Kruger), Wendell Wellman (Tyrone, storekeeper), Matthew Child (Alby), Michael Maurer (George Wilburn), Michael Currie (Lieutenant Donnelly), Albert Popwell (Horace King, SFPD), Mark Keyloun (Officer Bennett, San Paulo Police), Kevyn Major Howard (Hawkins), Bette Ford (Leah, gallery curator), Nancy Parsons (Mrs Kruger), Mara Corday (Loretta, coffee shop waitress), Russ McCubbin and Robert Sutton (Eddie and Carl, the Stagnaro brothers), Nancy Fish (San Paulo historical society woman), Barmen Argenziano (D'Ambrosia, prosecutor), Lisa Britt (Elizabeth 'Beth' Spencer), Bill Reddick (Police Commissioner), Lois De Banzie (Judge M. Lungstrom), Michael Johnson and Nick Dimitri (Mob assassins), Pat DuVal (Bailiff), Christian Phillips and Steven Kravitz (Hawkin's crony), Joe Bellan (Burly detective), Dennis Royston, Melvin Thomson, Jophery Brown and Bill Upton (Young Chicano guys in street), Lloyd Nelson (San Paulo desk sergeant), Christopher Pray (Detective Jacobs), James McEachin (Detective

Barnes), Maria Lynch (Hostess at hotel), Ken Lee (Loomis), Morgan Upton (San Paulo bartender), John X. Heart (Uniform policeman), David Gonzales, Albert Martinez, David Rivers and Robert Rivers (Gang robbing coffee shop), Harry Demopoulos M.D. (Dr Barton), Lisa London (Las Vegas hooker), Tom Spratley (Senior man), Eileen Wiggins (Hysterical woman), John Nowak (Bank robber in San Paulo), Michael V. Gazzo (Threlkis, crime lord who suffers heart attack)

Tightrope (1984)
Director: Richard Tuggle
Warner Bros/Malpaso (US)
110 minutes
Clint Eastwood (Detective Wes Block), Genevieve Bujold (Beryl Thibodeaux), Dan Hedaya (Detective Joe Molinari), Alison Eastwood (Amanda Block), Jennifer Beck (Penny Block), Marco St John (Leander Rolfe), Rebecca Perle (Becky Jacklin, fifth victim), Regina Richardson (Sarita, prostitute), Randi Brooks (Jamie Corey, third victim, murdered in Jacuzzi), Jamie Rose (Melanie Silber, second victim), Margaret Howell (Judy Harper, fourth victim), Rebecca Clemons (Prostitute with whip), Janet MacLachlan (Dr Yarlofsky, psychologist), Graham Paul (Luther), Bill Holliday (Police Chief), John Wilmot (Forensic surgeon), Margie O'Dair (Mrs Ruth Holstein, babysitter), Joy N. Houck Jnr (Massage parlour owner), Stuart Baker-Bergen (Blond surfer), Donald Barber (Shorty, Gello wrestling referee), Robert Harvey (Lonesome Alice), Ron Gural (Investigator), Layton Martens (Sergeant Surtees), Richard Charles Boyle (Dr Fitzpatrick), Becki Davis (Nurse), Jonathan Sachar (Male prostitute), Valerie Thibodeaux (Black prostitute), Lionel Ferbos (Plainclothes Gus), Eliott Keener (Sandoval), Cary Wilmot Alden (Secretary), Dave Valdes (Manes), Fritz Manes (Valdes), James Borders (Carfagno), Jonathan Shaw (Quono), Don Lutenbcher (Dixie Brewery President), George Wood (Sales rep), Kimberly Georgoulis (Sam, a prostitute), Glenda Byars (Lucy Davis), John Schluter Jnr (Piazza cop), Nick Krieger (Rannigan), Lloyd Nelson ((Patrolman Restic, guarding Beryl's house), David Dahlgren (Patrolman Julio), Rod Masterson (Patrolman Gallo), Glenn Wright (Patrolman Redfish), Angela Hill (Reporter), Ted Saari (TV News technician)

City Heat (1984)
Director: Richard Benjamin
Malpaso/Deliverance/Warner Bros (US)
97 minutes
Clint Eastwood (Lieutenant Joe Speer), Burt Reynolds (Michael Twitchell 'Mike' Murphy), Jane Alexander (Addy), Madeline Kahn (Caroline Howley), Rip Torn (Primo Pitt), Irene Cara (Ginny Lee), Richard Roundtree (Dehl Swift), Tony Lo Bianco (Leon Coll), William Anderson (Lonnie Ash), Nicholas Worth (Troy Roker), Robert Cavi (Nino, Pitt hood), Jude Farese (Dub Slack, Pitt hood), John Hancock (Fat Freddy, club owner), Gerald S. O'Loughlin (Louie, diner owner), Bruce M. Fischer and Art LaFleur (Repo men), Jack Nance (Aram Strossell, bookkeeper), Dallas Cole (Redhead Sherry), Lou Fillipo (Boxing referee), Preston Sparks (Keith Stoddard Esq. party guest), Michael Maurer (Vint Diestock, Pitt hood), Ernie Sabella (Ballistics expert), Christopher Michael Moore (Cop outside Roxy), Harry Caesar (Boxing club locker attendant), Charles parks (Dr. Breslin), Hamilton Camp (Garage attendant), Tab Thacker (Tuck, bouncer), Arthur Malet (Doc Loomis), Carey Loftin (Roxy driver), Jim Lewis (Roxy Patron), Jack Tibeau, Gene LeBell, Nick Dimitri, George Fisher, Bob Herron, Bill Hart (Garage hoods), Fred Lerner (Lefty, Pitt roof sniper), George Orrison (Pitt Doorman), Beau Starr (Pitt lookout), Anthony Charnota, Walter Robles, Richard Foronjy (Bordello poker players), Joan Shawlee (Peggy Barker, madame), Darwyn Swalve (Bordello bouncer), Wiley Harker and Bob Maxwell ('Mr Smiths'), Tom Spratley (Chauffeur), Bob Terhune (Hood playing billiards), Holgie Forrester (Marie 'Little Red Riding Hood'), Harry Demopoulos M.D. (Roman orgy patron), Edwin Prevost (Butler), Alfie Wise (Short guy), Hank Calia (Shorter friend), Alex Plasschaert (Shortest friend), Daphne Eckler (Agnes), Lonna Montrose (Didi)

Pale Rider (1985)
Director: Clint Eastwood
Warner Bros/Malpaso (US)
111 minutes

Clint Eastwood (The Preacher), Michael Moriarty (Hull Barret), Carrie Snodgress (Sarah Wheeler), Christopher Penn (Josh LaHood), Sydney Penny (Megan Wheeler, Sarah's daughter), John Russell (Marshal Stockburn), Richard Dysart (Coy K. LaHood), Richard Kiel (Club), Doug McGrath (Spider Conway), Charles Hallahan (McGill), Marvin J. McIntyre (Jagou), Fran Ryan (Ma Blankenship), Richard Hamilton (Jed Blankenship, storekeeper), Graham Paul (Ev Gossage, prospector), Chuck LaFont (Eddie Conway), Jerry Weissman (Teddy Conway), Allen Keller (Tyson), Tom Oglesby (Elam), Herman Poppe (Ulrik Lindquist, Swedish prospector), Kathleen Wygle (Bess Gossage), Terrence Evans (Jake Henderson), Jim Hitson (Biggs), Loren Adkins (Bossy), Tom Friedkin (Miner Tom), S.A. Griffin (Deputy Folke), Jack Radosta (Deputy Grissom), Robert Winley (Deputy Kobold), Billy Drago (Deputy Mather), Jeffrey Josephson (Deputy Sledge), John Dennis Johnson (Deputy Tucker), Clay Lilley, Gene Hartline, R.L. Tolbert, Mike Adams, Cliff Happy, Ross Loney, Larry Randles,Gerry Gatlin and Mike McGaughy (LaHood horsemen), Lloyd Nelson (Bank teller), Jay K. Fishburn (Telegrapher), George Orrison (Stationmaster Whitey), Milton Murrill (Station porter), Mike Munsey (Dentist-cum-barber), Keith Dillin (Blacksmith), Fritz Manes and Glenn Wright (Stage riders), Wayne Van Horn (Stage driver)

Heartbreak Ridge (1986)
Director: Clint Eastwood
Warner Bros/Malpaso/Jay Weston Productions (US)
125 minutes

Clint Eastwood (Gunnery Sergeant Thomas 'Gunny' Highway), Marsha Mason (Aggie), Everett McGill (Major Malcolm A. Powers), Moses Gunn (Staff Sergeant Webster, 1st Platoon, Marine Corps), Eileen Heckart (Little Mary Jackson, 'Globe and Anchor' bar), Bo Svenson (Roy Jennings, owner of Palace Inn), Boyd Gaines (Lieutenant M.R. Ring, Recon platoon leader), Mario Van Peebles (Corporal 'Stitch' Jones), Arlen Dean Snyder (Sergeant Major Choozoo), Vincent Irizarry (Lance Corporal Fragatti), Ramon Franco (Aponte), Tom Villard (Profile), Mike Gomez (Quinones), Rodney Hill (Collins), Peter Koch ('Swede' Johanson), Richard Venture (Marine Colonel Meyers), Peter Jason (Major Devin), J.C. Quinn (Quartermaster sergeant), Begona Plaza (Mrs Aponte), John Eames (Judge Zane), Tom Sharp and John Gallagher (Palace Inn emcees), John Hostetter (Officer Reese), Holly Shelton-Foy (Sarita Dwayne, singer in Palace Inn), Nicholas Worth (Jil Binger), Timothy Fall (Kid in jail), Jon Pennell (Jail Crier), Trish Garland (Female marine officer), Dutch Mann and Darwyn Swalve (Tough guys in Palace Inn), Christopher Lee Michael and Alex M. Bello (Marines), Steve Halsey and John Sasse (Bus drivers), Rebecca Perle (University student in shower), Annie O'Donnell (Telephone exchange operator), Elizabeth Riscio (Waitress), Lloyd Nelson (Deputy), Sergeant Major John H. Brewer (Sergeant Major in court), Michael Maurer (Bouncer in bar), Tom Ellison (Marine Corporal)

The Dead Pool (1988)
Director: Wayne 'Buddy' Van Horn
Universal/Malpaso (US)
88 minutes

Clint Eastwood (Inspector Harry Francis Callahan), Patricia Clarkson (Samantha Walker, reporter), Liam Neeson (Peter Swan), Evan C. Kim (Inspector Al Quan), David Hunt (Harlan Rook, alias 'Ed Butler'), Michael Currie (Captain Donnelly), Michael Goodwin (Lieutenant Ackerman), Darwin Gillett (Patrick Snow), Anthony Charnota (Lou Janero), Christopher P. Beale (D.A. Thomas McSherry), John Allen Vick (Lieutenant Ruskowski), Jeff Richmond, Patrick Van Horn and Sigrid Wurschmidt (Freeway reporters), James Carrey (Johnny Squares), Deborah A. Bryan (Girl playing Regan in *Exorcist* rock video), Nicholas Love (Jeff Howser, special effects supervisor), Maureen McVerry (Vicky Owens, secretary), John X. Heart (Bob, cameraman), Victoria Bastel (Suzanne Dayton, Johnny's girlfriend), Kathleen Turco-Lyon and Michael Faqir (Police officers at Trailer murder scene), Ronnie Claire Edwards (Molly Fisher), Mallace Choy (Chinese store manager), Melodie Soe (Chinese restaurant waitress), Kristopher Logan and Scott Vance (Gunmen who hold up restaurant), Glenn T. Wright (Detective Hindmark), Stu Klinster (Minister), Karen Kahn (TV associate producer), Shawn Elliott (Chester Docksteder), Ren Reynolds (Perry), Ed Hodson (Paramedic attending elevator shooting), Edward Hocking (Warden Hocking, San Quentin), Diego Chairs (Butcher Hicks, prisoner), Patrick Valentino (Pirate captain on tug boat), Cal vin Jones and Melissa Martin (Pirate tug reporters), Phil Dacey (Detective Dacey), Louis Giambalvo (Gus Wheeler, pyromaniac), Peter Anthony Jacobs (Sergeant Holloway), Bill Wattenburg (Nolan Kennard, victim blown up in car), Hugh McCann and Suzanne Sterling (Man and woman on talk show), Lloyd Nelson (Sergeant Waldman), Taylor Gilbert and Charles Martinet (Police station reporters), George Orrison and Marc Alaimo (Bodyguards on dock), Justin Whalin (Jason), Kris LeFan (Carl), Katie Bruce (Girl on sidewalk during car chase), Harry Demopoulos M.D. (Doctor in Quan's room), John Frederick Jones (Dr. Friedman, psychologist), Martin Ganapoler (Reporter at pier), James W. Gavin and Craig Hosking (Helicopter pilot), Guns n' Roses (Mourners at Johnny Squares' funeral).

Bird (1988)
Director: Clint Eastwood
Warner Bros/Malpaso (US)
154 minutes
Forest Whitaker (Charlie 'Yardbird' Parker), Diane Venora (Chan Parker, nee Richardson), Michael Zelniker (Red Rodney), Samuel E. Wright (Dizzy Gillespie), Keith David (Buster Franklin), Michael McGuire (Brewster), James Handy (Esteves, police officer), Damon Whitaker (Young Charlie Parker), Morgan Nagler (Kim), Arlen Dean Snyder (Dr Heath at Belleview), Sam Robards (Moscowitz), Penelope Windust (Bellevue nurse), Glenn T. Wright (Alcoholic patient), George Orrison (Patient playing Checkers), Bill Cobbs (Dr Caulfield, at morgue), Hamilton Camp (Mayor of 52nd Street), Chris Bosley (First 52nd Street doorman), George T. Bruce (Second 52nd Street doorman), Joey Green (Gene), John Witherspoon (Sid), Tony Todd (Frog), Jo de Winter (Mildred Berg), Richard Zavaglia (Ralph the Narc), Anna Levine (Audrey, Parker's lover), Al Pugliese (Three Deuces owner), Hubert Kelly (John Wilson, Parker band member), Billy Mitchell (Billy Prince, Parker band member), Karl Vincent (Stratton), Lou Cutell (Bride's father), Roger Etienne (Parisian MC), Jason Bernard (Benny Tate), Gretchen Oehler (Southern nurse), Richard McKenzie (Southern doctor), Tony Cox (Pee Wee Marquette), Diane Salinger (Baroness Nica, aka Baronness Pannonica de Koenigswarter), Johnny Adams (Birdland bartender), Natalia Silverwood (Red's girlfriend), Duane Matthews (Engineer), Slim Jim Phantom (Grainger), Matthew Faison (Judge), Peter Crook (Parker's lawyer), Alec Paul Rubinstein (Recording producer), Patricia Herd (Nun), Steve Zettler (Oasis Club owner), Ann Weldon (Violet Welles, singer), Chaley Lang (MC at the Paramount), Tim Russ (Harris), Richard Jeni (Chummy Morello), Don Starr (Doctor at Baroness Nica's), Richard Mawe (Medical examiner at Baroness Nica's)

Pink Cadillac (1989)
Director: Wayne 'Buddy' Van Horn
Warner Bros/Malpaso (US)
116 minutes
Clint Eastwood (Tommy Nowack), Bernadette Peters (Lou Ann McGuinn), Timothy Carhart (Roy McGuinn), Michael Des Barres (Alex, Birthright Militia leader), John Dennis Johnston (Waycross, militiaman), Jimmie F. Skaggs (Billy Dunston, militiaman), Bill Moseley (Darrell, militiaman), Michael Champion (Ken Lee), Michael Hickey (Mr Barton), Geoffrey Lewis (Ricky Z, forger), Bill McKinney (Colterville bartender), Gary Klar (Randy Bates, first bail jumper), Gary Leffew (John Capshaw, second bail jumper),

Julie Hoopman (Waitress), Paul Benjamin (Judge at Lou Ann's trial), Cliff Bemis (Jeff, Lou Ann's brother-in-law), Frances Fisher (Dinah, Lou Ann's sister), Mara Corday (Craps croupier in Reno), Bob Feist (Frontier Days Rodeo announcer), Wayne Storm (Jack Bass), Richie Allen (Drunken flasher), Roy Conrad (Barker outside Reno casino), James Cromwell (Motel desk clerk), Tiffany Gail Robinson and Angela Louise Robinson (Lou Ann's baby), Travis Swords (Capshaw's lawyer), Randy Kirby (District Attorney), Linda Hoy (Lou Ann's attorney), Bryan Adams (Gas station attendant), Sue Ann Gilfillan (Clothes shop sales-lady), John Fleck (Lounge lizard), Bill Wattenburg (Pit Boss), Jim Carrey (Casino comedian), Eric G. Westby (Room service waiter), Robert Harvey (Skip tracer in diner), Gerry Bamman (Buddy, Tommy's boss)

White Hunter, Black Heart (1990)
Director: Clint Eastwood
Warner Bros/Rastar/Malpaso (US)
108 minutes

Clint Eastwood (John Wilson), Jeff Fahey (Pete Verrill), Charlotte Cornwell (Miss Wilding, Wilson's secretary), Norman Lumsden (George, butler), George Dzundza (Paul Landers), Edward Tudor Pole (Reissar), Roddy Maude-Roxby (Thompson), Richard Warwick (Basil Fields), John Rapley (Gun salesman), Catherine Neilson (Irene Saunders), Marisa Berenson (Kay Gibson), Richard Vanstone (Phil Duncan), Jamie Koss (Mrs Duncan), Anne Dunkley (Scarf girl in cabaret act), David Danns (Bongo man in cabaret act), Myles Freeman (Ape man in cabaret act), Geoffrey Huchings (Squadron Leader Alec Laing), Christopher Fairbank (Tom Harrison), Alun Armstrong (Ralph Lockhart, unit manager), Clive Mantle (Harry Longthorn, Lake Victoria Hotel General Manager), Mel Martin (Margaret MacGregor), Martin Jacobs (Dickie Marlowe, hunter), Norman Malunga (Desk clerk), Timothy Spall ('Hod' Hodkins), Alex Norton (Zibelinsky, boss of hunting camp), Eleanor David (Dorshka Zibelinsky), Boy Mathias Chuma (Kivu, guide), Andrew Whalley (Photographer), Conrad Asquith (Kemp Ogilvy, hunter)

The Rookie (1990)
Director: Clint Eastwood
Warner Bros/Malpaso/Kazanjian-Siebert (US)
116 minutes

Clint Eastwood (Nick Pulovski), Charlie Sheen (David Ackerman), Raul Julia (Strom), Sonia Braga (Liesl), Tom Skerritt (Eugene Ackerman), Lara Flynn Boyle (Sara), Pepe Serna (Lt. Ray Garcia), Marco Rodriguez (Loco Martinez), Pete Randall (Cruz, Strom henchman), Donna Mitchell (Laura Ackerman), Xander Berkeley (Blackwell), Tony Plana (Morales, Strom henchman), David Sherrill (Max, garage worker), Hal Williams (Powell), Pat DuVal, Mara Corday, Jerry Schumacher (Interrogators), Matt McKenzie (Wang), Joel Polis (Lance), Rodger LaRue (Maître D'), Robert Dubac (Waiter), Lloyd nelson (Freeway motorist), Anthony Charnota (Romano), Jordan Lund (Bartender), Paul Ben-Victor (Little Felix, police informant), Jeanne Mori (Connie Ling, TV reporter), Anthony Alexander (Alphonse, casino owner), Paul Butler (Captain Hargate), Seth Allen (David as a child), Coleby Lombardo (Joey, David's brother), Roberta Vasquez (Heather Torres), Joe Farago (Anchorman), Robert Harvey (Whalen), Nick Ballo (Vito), Jay Boryea (Sal), Marylou Kenworthy (Ackerman's receptionist), George Orrison (Detective Orrison), James W. Gavin (Aerial co-ordinator/pilot), Thomas Friedkin and Craig Hosking (Pilots)

Unforgiven (1992)
Director: Clint Eastwood
Warner Bros/Malpaso (US)
130 minutes

Clint Eastwood (William Munny, alias 'William Hendershot'), Gene Hackman (Sheriff William 'Little Bill' Daggett), Morgan Freeman (Ned Logan), Richard Harris (English

Bob), Jaimz Woolvett (The Schofield Kid), Saul Rubinek (W.W. Beauchamp), Frances Fisher (Strawberry Alice), Anna Thomson (Delilah Fitzgerald), Tara Dawn Frederick (Little Sue), Beverley Elliott (Silky), Liisa Repo-Martell (Faith), Josie Smith (Crow Creek Kate), Anthony James (Skinny Dubois), Rob Campbell (Davey Bunting), David Mucci (Quick Mike), Shane Meier and Aline Levasseur (Will and Penny Munny), Cherrilene Cardinal (Sally Two Trees, Ned's wife), Ron White (Deputy Clyde Ledbetter), Jeremy Ratchford (Deputy Andy Russell), John Pyper-Ferguson (Deputy Charley Hecker), Jefferson Mappin (Deputy Fatty Rossiter), Walter Marsh (I.B. Bell, barber), Mina E. Mina (Muddy Chandler, coach driver), Henry Kope (German Joe Schultz, storekeeper), Robert Koons (Crocker), Garner Butler (Eggs Anderson), Larry Reese (Tom Luckinbill), Lochlyn Munro (Texas Slim), Blair Haynes (Paddy McGee), Sam Karas (Thirsty Thurston), Frank C. Turner (Fuzzy), Ben Cardinal (Johnny Foley), Philip Haynes (Lippy MacGregor), Michael Charrois (Wiggens), Bill Davidson (Buck Barthol), Larry Joshua (Bucky), George Orrison (The Shadow), Greg Goossen (Fighter), Paul McLean, James Herman and Michael Maurer (Train passengers)

In the Line of Fire (1993)
Director: Wolfgang Petersen
Columbia Pictures/Castle Rock Entertainment (US)
124 minutes

Clint Eastwood (Secret Service Agent Frank Horrigan), John Malkovich (Mitch Leary, alias 'Joseph McCrawley', 'Booth', 'James Carney'), Rene Russo (Agent Lilly Raines), Dylan McDermott (Agent Al D'Andrea), Gary Cole (Agent-in-Charge Bill Watts), Fred Dalton Thomson (Harry Sargent), John Mahoney (Sam Campagna), Gregory Alan-Williams (Agent Matt Wilder), Jim Curley (President of United States, codenamed 'Traveller'), Sally Hughes (First Lady), Clyde Kusatsu (FBI Agent Jack Okura), Steve Hytner (FBI Agent Tony Carducci), Tobin Bell (Marty Mendoza, counterfeiter), Bob Schott and Juan A. Riojas (Jimmy Hendrickson and Raul, Mendoza's henchmen), Elsa Raven (McCrawley's landlady), Arthur Senzy (Paramedic called to Horrigan), Patrika Darbo (Pam Magnus, South West Savings employee), Mary Van Arsdel (Sally, Pam's housemate), Ryan Curtona (LAPD commander), Lawrence Lowe (FBI fingerprint technician), Brian Libby (FBI supervisor), Eric Bruskotter (Young agent), Patrick Caddell (Political speaker), John Heard (Professor Riger, Pasadena College), Alan Toy (Walter Wickland, Leary's friend in Phoenix), Carl Ciarfalio (CIA Agent Collins), Walt MacPhearson and Robert Peters (Hunters killed by Leary), Tyde Keirney (Police Captain Howard), Anthony Peck (FBI Official), Rick Hurst (Bartender), Doris E. McMillon (D.C. News Anchor), Robert Sandoval (Robert Stermer, Bonaventure Hotel bell-boy), Joshua Malina (Agent Chavez), Willia G. Schilling (Sanford Riggs), Michale Kirk (Bates, computer technician), Richard Camphuis (Party fatcat), Marlan Clarke (Marge, bank employee), Robert Alan Beuth (Man at bank), Susan Lee Hoffman (Woman at bank), Donna Hamilton (Reporter at Dulles Airport), Bob Jiminez (Reporter at Bonaventure Hotel), Cylk Cozart (Agent Cozart), Michael Zurich (Agent Zurich), Rich DiDonato and Jeffrey Kurt Miller (Undercover agents at Hotel), Kirk Jordan (Agent)

A Perfect World (1993)
Director: Clint Eastwood
Warner Bros/Malpaso (US)
133 minutes

Kevin Costner (Robert 'Butch' Haynes, alias 'Edgar Poe'), Clint Eastwood (Chief Red Garnett), Laura Dern (Sally Gerber), TJ Lowther (Phillip 'Buzz' Perry), Keith Szarabajka (Terry Pugh), Leo Burmester (Tom Adler), Paul Hewitt (Dick Suttle), Bradley Whitford (Bobby Lee, FBI agent), Ray McKinnon (Bradley, Texas Ranger), Jennifer Griffin (Gladys Perry), Leslie Flowers (Naomi Perry), Belinda Flowers (Ruth Perry), Darryl Cox (Mr Hughes), Jay Whiteaker (Billy Reeves, kid dressed as Superman), Taylor Suzzanna McBride (Tinkerbell), Christopher Reagan Ammons (Dancing Skeleton), Mark Voges (Larry Billings), Vernon Grote (Prison guard), James Jeter (Old neighbour with shotgun), Ed Geldart (Fred Cummings), Bruce

McGill (Paul Sanders), Nik Hagler (General Store manager), Gary Moody (Local sheriff in Ben Hur), George Haynes (Farmer on tractor), Marietta Marich (Farmer's wife), Roder Boyce (Mr Willits, Friendly's Store boss), Lucy Lee Flippin (Lucy, shop employee), Elizabeth Ruscio (Paula, shop employee), David Kroll (Newscaster on TV), Gabriel Folse (Officer Terrence), Gil Glasgow (Officer Pete), Dennis Letts (Governor), John Hussey (Governor's aide), Margaret Bowman (Lady who is 'Trick or Treated'), John M. Jackson (Bob Fielder, picnicker), Connie Cooper (Bob's wife), Cameron Finley (Bob Fielder Jnr), Katy Wottrich (Patsy Fielder), Marco Perella (Roadblock officer), Linda Hart (Eileen, waitress), Brandon Smith (Officer Jones), George Orrison (Officer Orrison), Wayne Dehart (Mack, the farmer), Mary Alice (Lottie, Mack's wife), Kevin Woods (Cleveland, Mack's grandson), Tony Frank (Arch Andrews, farm owner), Woody Watson (Lieutenant Tom Hendricks, FBI), James W. Gavin and Craig Hosking (Police helicopter pilots)

The Bridges of Madison County (1995)
Director: Clint Eastwood
Warner Bros/Amblin Entertainment/Malpaso (US)
129 minutes
Clint Eastwood (Robert L. Kincaid), Meryl Streep (Francesca Johnson), Annie Corley (Carolyn Johnson), Victor Slezak (Michael Johnson), Jim Haynie (Richard Johnson), Sarah Kathryn Schmitt (Young Carolyn), Christopher Kroon (Young Michael), Phyllis Lyons (Betty Johnson), Debra Monk (Madge), Richard Lage (Lawyer Peterson), Michelle Benes (Lucy Redfield, nee Delaney), Alison Wiegert and Brandon Bobst (Children), Pearl Faessler (Wife), R.E. 'Stick' Faessler (Husband), Tania Mishler and Billie McNabb (Waitresses in Winterset café), Art Breese (Cashier in store), Lana Schwab (Saleswoman), Larry Loury (UPS driver), James Rivers, Mark A. Brooks, Peter Cho, Eddie Dejean Snr, Jason C. Brewer and Kyle Eastwood (James Rivers Band), George Orrison, Ken Billeter, Judy Trask, David Trask, Edna Dolson, Dennis McCool, Michael C. Pommier, Jana Corkrean, M. Jane Seymour, Karla Jo Soper (Patrons in Winterset café).

Absolute Power (1997)
Director: Clint Eastwood
Warner Bros/Malpaso/Castle Rock Entertainment (US)
121 minutes
Clint Eastwood (Luther Whitney), Gene Hackman (President Allen Richmond), Ed Harris (Senior Homicide Detective Seth Frank), Laura Linney (Kate Whitney), Scott Glenn (Bill Burton), Dennis Haysbert (Tom Collin), Judy Davis (Gloria Russell), E.G. Marshall (Walter Sullivan), Melora Hardin (Christy Sullivan), Ken Welsh (Sandy Lord, attorney), Penny Johnson (Laura Simon, detective), Richard Jenkins (Michael McCarty, hired assassin), Mark Margolis (Red Brandsford, owner 'Red's Bar'), Elaine Kagan (Valerie, forger), Alison Eastwood (Student in gallery), Yau-Gene Chan (Café Alonzo waiter), George Orrison (Airport bartender), Charles McDaniel (Medical examiner), John Lyle Campbell (Repairman), Kimber Eastwood (White House tour guide), Eric Dahlquist Jnr (Oval Office agent), Jack Stewart Taylor (Watergate Hotel doorman), Joy Ehrlich (Reporter), Robert Harvey (Cop)

Midnight in the Garden of Good and Evil (1997)
Director: Clint Eastwood
Warner Bros/Silver Pictures/Malpaso (US)
149 minutes
Kevin Spacey (Jim Williams), John Cusack (John Kelso), Jack Thompson (Sonny Seiler), Irma P. Hall (Minerva), Jude Law (Billy Carl Hanson), Alison Eastwood (Mandy Nichols), Paul Hipp (Joe Odom), Lady Chablis (Chablis Deveau), Dorothy Loudon (Serena Dawes), Anne Haney (Margaret Williams, Jim's mother), Kim Hunter (Betty Harty), Richard Herd (Henry Skerridge), Geoffrey Lewis (Luther Driggers), Leon Rippy (Detective Frank Boone), Bob Gunton (Finley Largent, prosecuting attorney), Michael O'Hagan (Geza Von Hapsburg,

art dealer), Gary Anthony Williams (Bus driver), Tim Black (Jeff Braswell, official photographer), Muriel Moore (Mrs Loreen Baxter), Sonny Seiler (Judge Samuel White), Terry Rhoads (Assistant D.A.), Victor Brandt (Bailiff), Patricia Herd and Nick Gillie (Jurors), Patrika Darbo (Sara Warren R.N. admitting nurse), J. Patrick McCormack (Doctor), Emma Kelly (Herself, known as the 'Lady of 6,000 Songs'), Tyrone Lee Weaver (Ellis), Gregory Goossen (Prison cell lunatic doing dog impression), Shannon Eubanks (Mrs Hamilton), Virginia Duncan, Rhoda Griffis, Judith Robinson (Married Women's Card Club players), Joann Pflug (Cynthia Vaughn), James Moody (Mr Glover, imaginary dog walker), John Duncan (Gentleman in park), Bess S. Thompson (Pretty girl), Jin Hi Soucy (Williams' receptionist), Michael Rosenbaum (George Tucker, Billy's friend), Dan Biggers (Harry Cramm, guest with .25 calibre Derringer), Georgia Allen (Lucille Wright, party caterer), Collin Wilcox Paxton (Woman party guest), Charles Black (Alpha guest), Aleta Mitchell (Alphabette), Michael Kevin Harry (Phillip), Dorothy Kingery (Jim Williams' sister), Amanda Kingery (Jim Williams' niece, Amanda), Susan Kingery (Jim Williams' niece Susan), Ted Manson (Passer-by), Margaret R. Davis (Ruth), Danny Nelson (Senator), Bree Luck (Woman necking at club), Ann Cusack (Delivery woman), Jerry Spence (Himself, hairdresser).

True Crime (1999)
Director: Clint Eastwood
Warner Bros/Zanuck/Malpaso (US)
122 minutes

Clint Eastwood (Steve 'Ev' Everett), Isaiah Washington (Frank Louis Beechum), Lisa Gay Hamilton (Bonnie Beechum), James Woods (Alan Mann, editor), Denis Leary (Bob Findley), Bernard Hill (Warden Luther Plunkitt), Diane Venora (Barbara Everett), Michael McKean (Reverend Shillerman), Michael Jeter (Dale Porterhouse, CPA), Mary McCormack (Michelle Ziegler, journalist), Hattie Winston (Angela Russel), Penny Bae Bridges (Gail Beechum), Francesca Fisher-Eastwood (Kate), John Finn (Reedy, San Quentin typist), Laila Robins (Patricia Findley), Sydney Poitier (Jane Marsh, journalist), Erik King (Vagrant playing Santa Clause), Graham Beckel (Arnold McCardle), Frances Fisher (D.A. Cecilia Nussbaum), Marissa Ribisi (Amy Wilson, reporter), Christine Ebersole (Bridget Rossiter, editor), Anthony Zerbe (Henry Lowenstein), Nancy Giles (Leesha Mitchell, Beechum's defence lawyer), Tom McGowan (Tom Donaldson, journalist), Lucy Alexis Liu (Toy shop attendant), Dina Eastwood (Wilma Francis, TV reporter), William Windom (Neil), Don West (Dr Roger Waters), Leslie Griffiths and Dennis Richmond (TV anchors), Frank Sommerville (Afternoon news anchor), Dan Green (Field producer), Nicolas Bearde (Reuben Skycock), Frances lee McCain (Mrs Lowenstein), Rev. Cecil Williams (Rev Williams in San Quentin), Casey Lee (Warren Russell), Jack Kehler (Mr Ziegler, Michelle's father), Colman Domingo (Wally Cartwright, lawyer), Linda Hoy (Pocum's Grocery worker), Danny Kovacs (Atkins), Kelvin Han Yee (Zachary Platt), Kathryn Howell (Nurse), George Maguire (Frederick Robertson), Bill Wattenburg (Radio reporter), Cathy Fithian (Nancy Larson, first witness), Roland Abasolo (First night guard), Michael Halton (Execution day guard), Jade Marx-Berti (Bread Company restaurant waitress), Velica Marie Davis (Purse whacker), John B. Scott (Colonel Drummond), Edward Silva (Colonel Hernandez), Jordan Sax (Colonel Badger), Rob Reece (San Quentin executioner), Walter Brown (Beechum family member)

Space Cowboys (2000)
Director: Clint Eastwood
Warner Bros/Village Roadshow Pictures-Clipsal Films/Malpaso/Mad Chance (US)
125 minutes

Clint Eastwood (Colonel Francis D. Corvin), Tommy Lee Jones (William 'The Hawk' Hawkins), Donald Sutherland (Jerry O'Neill), James Garner (Reverend 'Tank' Sullivan), James Cromwell (Major Bob Gerson), Marcia Gay Harden (Sara Holland), William Devane (Eugene Davis), Loren Dean (Ethan Glance), Courtney B. Vance (Roger Hines), Barbara Babcock (Barbara Corvin), Rade Serbedzija (General Vostov),Blair Brown (Dr Anne Caruthers), Jay Leno (Himself), Nils Allen Stewart (Tiny, bar bouncer), Deborah Jolly (Bar waitress), Toby

Stephens (Frank in 1958), Eli Craig (Hawk in 1958), John Mallory Asher (Jerry in 1958), Matt McColm (Tank in 1958), Billie Worley (Bob Gerson in 1958), Chris Wylde (Jason, birthday boy), Anne Stedman (Jason's girlfriend), James McDonald (Capcom), Kate McNeil, Karen Mistal and John K. Linto (Astronauts), Mark Thomason (Mission Control tech), Georgia Emelin (Cherie), Rick Scarry (State Dept. Official), Paul Pender (JBC security guard), Tim Halligan (Qualls), Manning Mpinduzi-Mott and Artur Cybulski (Press reporters), Steve Monroe (Waiter), J.M. Henry (Centrifuge tech), Steven West (Construction tech), Cooper Huckerbee (Trajectory engineer), Hayden Tank (Boy at NASA tour), Jock MacDonald (1958 press reporter), Gerald Emerick (T-38 pilot), Renee Olstead (Little girl), Don Michaelson (NASA doctor), Gordon Owens (Simsupe), Steve Stapenhorst (Vice president), Lauren Cohn (Teacher at NASA tour), Michael Loundon and Jon Hamm (Young pilots), Deborah Hope and Erica Grant (Female engineers), Lamont Lofton (KSC guard), Alexander Kuznetsov (Russian engineer)

Blood Work (2002)
Director: Clint Eastwood
Warner Bros/Malpaso (US)
106 Minutes
Clint Eastwood (Terrell 'Terry' McCaleb), Jeff Daniels (Jasper 'Buddy' Noone), Anjelica Houston (Dr Bonnie Fox, cardiologist), Wanda De Jesus (Graciella Rivers), Tina Lifford (Jaye Winston), Paul Rodriguez (Detective Ronaldo Arrango), Dylan Walsh (Detective John Walker), Mason Lucero (Raymond Torres), Gerry Becker (Mr Toliver), Rick Hoffman (James Lockridge), Alix Koromzay (Mrs Cordell), Igor Jijikine (Michel Bolotov), Dina Eastwood (First reporter at Lockridge murder), Beverly Leech (Second reporter), June Kyoko Lu (Mrs Kang), Chao Li Chi (Mr Kang), Glenn Morshower (Police Captain), Robert Harvey (Graciella's manager in restaurant), Matt Huffman (Young detective), Mark Thomason (James Cordell), Maria Quiban (Gloria Torres), Brent Hinkley (Haley Cab Company driver), Natalia Ongaro (Toliver Industrial Metals receptionist), Amanda Carlin (Office manager), Ted Rooney and P.J. Byrne (Forensic experts at Bolotov murder), Sam Jaeger (Deputy), Derric Nugent (LAPD officer), Craig Hosking and James W. Gavin (Helicopter pilots)

Mystic River (2003)
Director: Clint Eastwood
Warner Bros/Village Roadshow Pictures/NVP Entertainment/Malpaso (US)
132 minutes
Sean Penn (Jimmy Markum), Tim Robbins (Dave Boyle), Kevin Bacon (Sean Devine), Laurence Fishburne (Sergeant Whitey Powers), Marcia Gay Harden (Celeste Boyle, Dave's wife), Laura Linney (Annabeth Markum, Jimmy's wife), Kevin Chapman (Val Savage), Thomas Guiry (Brendan Harris), Emmy Rossum (Katherine 'Katie' Markum), Spencer Treat Clark (Silent Ray Harris), Andrew Mackin (John O'Shea), Adam Nelson (Nick Savage), Robert Wahlberg (Kevin Savage), Jenny O'Hara (Esther Harris, Brendan's mother), John Doman (Driver), Cameron Bowen (Young David Boyle), Jason Kelly (Young Jimmy Markum), Connor Paolo (Young Sean Devine), Bruce Page (Jimmy's father), Miles Herter (Sean's father), Cayden Boyd (Michael Boyle), Toris Davis (Lauren Devine), Jonathan Togo (Pete), Shawn Fitzgibbon (Funeral director), Will Lyman (FBI agent Birden), Celine Du Tertre (Nadine Markum), Ari Graynor and Zabeth Russell (Eve Pigeon and Diane Cestra, Katie's friends), Joe Stapleton (Drew Pigeon), Susan Willis (Mrs Prior, murder witness), Jose Ramon Rosario (Lieutenant Friel), Tom Kemp (CSS Tech), Charles Broderick (Medical examiner), Lonnie Farmer (Lab technician), Celeste Oliva (Trooper Jenny Coughlin), Bates Wilder (Loudmouthed cop), Douglass Bowen Flynn (Cop at barricade), Bill Thorpe (Neighbour at barricade), Matty Blake (Cop in park), Ken Cheeseman (Dave's friend in McGill's Bar), Scott Winters (Detective), Thomas Derrah (Headstone salesman), Jim Smith (Reporter), Patrick Shea (Handcuffed man), Duncan Putney (Solicitor in car), Ed O'Keefe (Communion priest), Dave Zee Garison (1975 police officer), Michael McGovern (1975

reporter), Bill Richards and Michael Paevey (Helicopter pilots), Kevin Conway (Theo), Eli Wallach (Mr Looney, Liquor store owner)

Million Dollar Baby (2004)
Director: Clint Eastwood
Warner Bros/Lakeshore Entertainment/Ruddy Morgan/Malpaso (US)
127 minutes

Clint Eastwood (Frankie Dunn), Hilary Swank (Margaret 'Maggie' Fitzgerald), Morgan Freeman (Eddie 'Scrap-Iron' Dupris), Jay Baruchel ('Danger' Barch), Mike Colter (Big Willie Little Jones), Lucia Rijker (Billy 'The Blue Bear' Osterman), Brian O'Byrne (Father Horvak), Anthony Mackie (Shawrelle Berry), Margo Martindale (Earline Fitzgerald), Riki Lindhome (Mardell Fitzgerald), Michael Peña (Omar), Benito Martinez (Billie's manager), Bruce MacVittie (Mickey Mack), David Powledge (Counterman at Broadway Diner), Joe D'Angerio (Cut man), Marcus Chait (J.D. Fitzgerald), Tom McCleister (Fitzgeralds' Lawyer), Erica Grant (Nurse), Naveen (Pakistani), Morgan Eastwood (Little girl at gas station), Jamison Yang (Paramedic), Dean Familton (First referee), Dr. Louis Moret (Second referee), V.J. Foster (Third referee), John D. Schorle II (Fourth referee), Marty Sammon (Fifth referee), Steven M. Porter (Sixth referee), Ray Corona (Seventh referee), Ming Lo (Rehabilitation doctor), Miguel Perez (Restaurant owner), Jim Cantafio and Ted Grossman (Ringside doctors), Ned Eisenberg (Sally Mendoza), Marco Rodriguez (Second at Las Vegas Arena title fight), Roy Nugent (Fan in Las Vegas), Don Familton (Ring announcer in Las Vegas), Mark Thomason (Radio commentator), Brian T. Finney, Spice Williams-Crosby, Kim Strauss, Rob Maron, Kirsten Berman (Irish fans at fight), Susan Krebs, Sunshine Chantal Parkman and Kim Danenberg (Rehab nurses), Eddie Bates (Rehab resident)

Flags of Our Fathers (2006)
Director: Clint Eastwood
DreamWorks SKG/Warner Bros/Amblin Entertainment/Malpaso (US)
126 minutes

Ryan Phillippe (John 'Doc' Bradley), Jesse Bradford (Rene Gagnon), Adam Beach (Ira Hayes), John Benjamin Hickey (Keyes Beech), John Slattery (Bud Gerber), Barry Pepper (Sergeant Michael 'Mike' Strank), Jaime Bell (Ralph 'Iggy' Ignatowski), Paul Walker (Henry 'Hank' Hansen), Robert Patrick (Colonel Chandler Johnson), Neal MacDonough (Marine Captain Dave Severance), Melanie Lynskey (Pauline Harnois, later Gagnon), Tom McCarthy (James Bradley), Chris Bauer (Commandant Vandegrift), Judith Ivey (Belle Block), Myra Turley (Madeline Evelley), Joseph Cross (Franklin Sousley), Benjamin Walker (Harlon Block), Alessandro Mastrobuono (Lindberg), Scott Reeves (Lundsford), Stark Sands (Walter Gust), George Grizzard (Elderly John Bradley), Harve Presnell (Elderly Dave Severance), George Hearn (Elderly Walter Gust), Len Cariou (Elderly Keyes Beech), Christopher Curry (Ed Block, Harlon's father), Bubba Lewis (Belle's younger son), Beth Grant (Mother Gagnon), Connie Ray (Mrs Sousley), Ann Dowd (Mrs Strank), Mary Beth Peil (Mrs Bradley), David Patrick Kelly (President Trueman), Jon Polito (Borough president), Ned Eisenberg (Joe Rosenthal, war photographer), Gordon Clapp (General 'Howlin' Mad' Smith), Michael Cumpsty (Secretary Forrestal), V.J. Foster (Major on plane), Kirk B.R. Woller (Bill Genaust), Tom Verica (Lieutenant Pennel), Jason Gray-Stanford (Lieutenant Schrier), Matt Huffman (Lieutenant Bell), David Hornsby (Louis Lowery), Brian Kimmet (Sergeant 'Boots' Thomas), David Rasche (Senator), Tom Mason (John Tennack), Patrick Dollaghan (Businessman), James Newman (Local politician), Steven M. Porter (Tourist taking photo of Hayes), Dale Waddington Horowitz (Tourist's wife), Lennie Loftin (Justice of the Peace), David Clennon (White House official), Mark Thomason (Military censor), Oliver Davis (Young James Bradley answering telephone), Sean Moran (Waiter), Lisa Dodson (Iggy's mother), John Nielsen (Senator Boyd), Jon Kellam (Senator Haddigan), Ron Fassler (Senator Robson), Denise Bella Vlasis-Gascon, Jenifer Menedis, Vivian Lesiak, Loie Shettler (Luncheon singers), John Henry Canavan (Jailer), Don Emerson (Navy lieutenant on plane), Jayma Mays (Nurse tending

Bradley in Hawaii), Yukari Black (Voice of 'Tokyo Rose'), John Hoogenakker (Funeral home employee), Barry Sigismondi (Police sergeant), William Charlton (Bartender), Beth Tapper, Shannon Gayle (Women fans in train Bar Car), Jim Cantafio (Mark Colson (LA reporters), Danny McCarthy, Patrick New (Chicago reporters), James Horan (New York reporters), Michael Canavan (Reporter at Hansen's), Erica Grant (Secretary), Silas Weir Mitchell, George Cambio (Lab techs), David S. Brooks (Sergeant 'A' Company), Johann Johannsson (Marine sergeant on beach), Martin Delaney (Marine at cave), Daniel Forcey (Marine on beach), Bjorgvin Franz Gislason (Impaled Marine), Darrin Ingolfsson, Hilmar Gudjonsson (Wounded marines), Jeremy Merrill (Marine in shell hole), Jeremiah Bitsui (Young Indian), John Maloney, Skip Evans, Karl Gulledge (Pilots).

Letters from Iwo Jima (2006)
Director: Clint Eastwood
DreamWorks SKG/Warner Bros/Amblin Entertainment/Malpaso (US)
135 minutes

Ken Watanabe (General Tadamichi Kuribayashi), Kazunari Ninomiya (Saigo, a soldier), Tsuyoshi Ihara (Lieutenant Colonel 'Baron' Nishi), Ryo Kase (Shimizu), Shido Nakamura (Lieutenant Ito), Hiroshi Watanabe (Lieutenant Fujita), Takumi Bando (Captain Tanida), Yuki Matsuzaki (Nozaki, a soldier), Takashi Yamaguchi (Kashiwara, soldier who dies of dysentery), Eijiro Ozaki (Lieutenant Okubo), Nae (Hanako Saigo, wife of Saigo), Nobumasa Sakagami (Admiral Ohsugi), Akiko Shima (Lead woman), Lucas Elliot (Sam, wounded US Marine), Sonny Seiichi Saito (Medic Endo, tending Sam), Steve Santa Sekiyoshi (Kanda), Hiro Abe (Lieutenant Colonel Oiso), Toshioya Agata (Captain Iwasaki), Yoshi Ishii (Private Yamazaki), Yoshi Toda (Colonel Adachi), Ken Kensai (Major General Hayashi), Ikuma Ando (Ozawa), Masashi Nagadoi (Admiral Ichimaru, Ohsugi's replacement), Mark Moses (Bertie, American officer at dinner), Roxanne Hart (Bertie's wife), Yoshio Iizuka (Tired soldier), Mitsu Kurokawa (Suicidal soldier), Takuji Kuramoto (Ono), Koji Wada (Hashimoto), Akia Kaneda, Shoji Hattori, Mitsuyuki Oishi, Mark Tadashi Takahashi (Japanese soldiers), Evan Ellingson (Kid Marine), Kazuyuki Yonezawa (Ito's soldier), Hiroshi Tom Tanaka (Hopeless soldier), Mathew Botuchis (American Marine), Daisuke Nagashima (Prisoner), Yukari Black (Mother), Kirk Enochs (Marine Officer), Ryan Kelly, Michael Lawson, Jonathan Oliver Sessler (US Marines), Taishi Mizuno, Daisuke Tsuji (Cave soldiers), Yoshi Ando, Yukata Takeuchi (Excavators on Iwo Jima), Tsuguo Mizuno (Lead excavator), Mark Ofuji (Kuribayashi's guard), Hallock Beals, Ryan Carnes (Marines in clearing), Jeremy Glazer (Marine lieutenant), Ryoya Katsuyama (Boy), Masashi Odate (Cook), London Kim (Okubo's soldier), Skip Evans, Wanliss E. Armstrong (Pilots)

Changeling (2008)
Director: Clint Eastwood
Universal/Imagine Entertainment/Relativity Media/Malpaso (US)
140 minutes

Angelina Jolie (Christine Collins), Gattlin Griffith (Walter Collins), John Malkovich (Rev. Gustav Briegleb), Michelle Gunn (Sandy), Frank Wood (Ben Harris), Morgan Eastwood (Girl on tricycle), Colm Feore (Chief James E. Davis), Devon Conti (Arthur Hutchins), Jeffrey Donovan (Captain J.J. Jones), Peter Gerety (Dr. Earl W. Tarr), John Harrington Bland (Dr. John Montgomery), Pamela Dunlap (Mrs Fox), Roger Hewlett (Officer Morelli), Michael Kelly (Detective Lester Ybarra), Jason Butler Harner (Gordon Northcott), Eddie Alderson (Sandford Clark), Amy Ryan (Carol Dexter), Denis O'Hare (Dr. Jonathan Steele), Kelly Lynn Warren (Rachel Clark), Colby French (Bob Clark), Geoff Perison (S.S. Hahn), Reed Birney (Mayor Cryer), Peter Breitmayer (Chairman Thorpe), Lily Knight (Leanne Clay), Jeffrey Hutchinson (Mr Clay), Ryan Cutrona (Judge), Mary Stein (Janet Hutchins), Asher Axe (David Clay), Jan Devereaux, Erica Grant, Antonia Bennett and Kerri Randles (Telephone operators)

Gran Torino (2008)

Director: Clint Eastwood

Warner Bros/Village Roadshow Pictures/Double Nickel/Malpaso (US)

116 minutes

Clint Eastwood (Walt Kowalski), Christopher Carley (Father Janovich), Bee Vang (Thao Vang Lor), Ahney Her (Sue Lor), Brian Haley (Mitch Kowalski), Geraldine Hughes (Karen Kowalski), Dreama Walker (Ashley Kowalski), Brian Howe (Steve Kowalski), John Carroll Lynch (Barber Martin), William Hill (Tim Kennedy), Brooke Chia Thao (Vu), Chee Thao (Grandma), Choua Kue (Youa), Scott Reeves (Trey), Xia Soua Chang (Kor Khue), Sonny Vue (Smokie), Doua Moua (Spider), Greg Trzaskoma (Bartender), John Johns (Al), Davis Gloff (Darrell), Tom Mahard (Mel), Cory Hardrict (Duke), Nana Gbewonya (Monk), Arthur Cartwright (Prez), Austin Douglas Smith (Daniel Kowalski), Connor Liam Callaghan (David Kowalski), Michael E Kurowski (Josh Kowalski), Julia Ho (Dr Chang), Maykao K Lytongpao (Gee), Stephen Kue (Officer Chang), Carlos Guadarrama (Head Latino), Andrew Tamez-Hull, Ramon Camacho and Antonio Mireles (Latino gang), Ia Vue Yang and Zoua Kue (Hmong flower women), Elvis Thao, Jerry Lee, Lee Mong Vang (Hmong gang), Tru Hang (Hmong grandfather), Alice Lor (Hmong granddaughter), Tong Pao Kue (Hmong husband), Nelly Yang Sao Yia (Hmong wife), Douacha Ly (Hmong man), Parng D Yarng (Hmong neighbour), Marty Bufalini (Lawyer), My-Ishia Cason-Brown (Muslim receptionist), Clint Ward (Officer), Rochelle Winter (Waitress), Claudia Rodgers (White neighbour), Vincent Bonasso (Tailor)

BIBLIOGRAPHY AND SOURCES

BOOKS, MAGAZINES AND ARTICLES

Allison, Darren, 'Do You Feel Lucky?', *Cinema Retro* (Volume 3: Issue #9, 2007)

Atkinson, John, *The Oscars* (Pocket Essentials, 2001)

Baldacci, David, *Absolute Power* (Warner Books, 1996)

Barry, Lieutenant Colonel Simon, *D-Day to VE Day: The Liberation of Europe* (Castle Books, 1995)

Beacher, M.D., Milton Daniel, *Alcatraz Island: Memoirs of a Rock Doc* (Zymurgy Publishing, 2003)

Berendt, John, *Midnight in the Garden of Good and Evil* (Random House, 1994)

Bergen, Ronald, *The United Artists Story* (Octopus, 1986)

Betts, Tom (ed.) *Westerns All'Italiana!* (Anaheim, CA, 1983–present)

Bierce, Ambrose, *Tales of Soldiers and Civilians and Other Stories* (Penguin, 2000)

Biskind, Peter, *Easy Riders, Raging Bulls: How the Sex-Drugs-And-Rock 'n' Roll Generation Saved Hollywood* (Simon & Schuster, 1998)

———— *Gods and Monsters: Thirty Years of Writing on Film and Culture* (Bloomsbury, 2005)

Blevins, William, *Dictionary of the American West* (Wordsworth, 1995)

Bosworth, Patricia, *Marlon Brando* (Phoenix, 2002)

Botting, Douglas, *Wilderness Europe* (Time-Life, 1976)

Bruckner, Ulrich P., *Für ein paar Leichen mehr* (Schwarzkopf & Schwarzkopf, 2002)

Buscombe, Edward, *Cinema Today* (Phaidon, 2003)

Butler, Michael and Dennis Shryack, *The Gauntlet* (Star, 1977)

Carlson, Michael, *Clint Eastwood* (Pocket Essentials, 2002)

Carr, Ian, Digby Fairweather, Brian Priestly, *Jazz: The Essential Companion* (Grafton Books, 1987)

Chandler, Frank, *A Fistful of Dollars* (Star, 1972)

Cole, Gerald and Peter Williams, *Clint Eastwood* (W.H. Allen, 1983)

Connelly, Michael, *Blood Work* (Orion, 1998)

Connolly, William, *Spaghetti Cinema* (Hollywood, CA, 1984–present)

Cox, Alex and Nick Jones, *Moviedrome – The Guide* (Broadcasting Support Services, 1990)

Cumbow, Robert C., *Once Upon a Time: The Films of Sergio Leone* (Scarecrow, 1987)

De Agostini, *The Clint Eastwood Collection: Volume 1 (Dirty Harry); Volume 2 (Unforgiven); Volume 3 (Magnum Force); Volume 4 (The Outlaw Josey Wales); Volume 5 (Space Cowboys); Volume 6 (Heartbreak Ridge); Volume 7 (Kelly's Heroes); Volume 8 (The Enforcer); Volume 9 (Pale Rider); Volume 10 (The Gauntlet); Volume 11 (Firefox), Volume 12 (Sudden Impact), Volume 13 (Absolute Power), Volume 14 (True Crime), Volume 15 (In the Line of Fire), Volume 16 (The Dead Pool), Volume 17 (The Bridges of Madison County), Volume 18 (Blood Work), Volume 19 (A Perfect World), Volume 20 (Where Eagles Dare), Volume 21 (Tightrope)* (De Agostini, 2004)

De Fornari, Oreste, *Sergio Leone: The Great Italian Dream of Legendary America* (Gremese, 1997)

Douglas, Peter, *Clint Eastwood – Movin' On* (Star, 1975)

Downing, David and Gary Herman, *Clint Eastwood: All-American Anti-hero* (Quick Fox, 1977)

Duncan, Paul (ed.), *Movie Icons: Clint Eastwood* (Taschen, 2006)

Ferguson, Ken (ed.), *Photoplay Film Annual 1971* (Argus, 1971)

Ferguson, Ken and Sylvia Ferguson (eds.), *Western Stars of Television and Film* (Purnell, 1967)

Fox, Brian, *A Dollar to Die For* (Star, 1968)

Fox, Keith and Maitland McDonagh (eds), *The Tenth Virgin Film Guide* (Virgin, 2001)

Franchi, Rudy and Barbara, *Miller's Movie Collectibles* (Octopus 2002)

Frank, Alan, *The Films of Roger Corman 'Shooting My Way out of Trouble'* (Batsford, 1998)

────── *Frank's 500 – The Thriller Film Guide* (Batsford, 1997)

Frayling, Christopher, *Clint Eastwood* (Virgin, 1992)

────── *Sergio Leone – Once Upon a Time in Italy* (Thames and Hudson, 2005)

────── *Sergio Leone – Something to Do with Death* (Faber and Faber, 2000)

French, Philip, *Go Ahead, Make My Day: Philip French Meets Clint Eastwood* (*The Observer*, 25 February 2007)

────── *Westerns: Aspects of a Movie Genre* (Carcanet, 2005).

────── 'The suspense is killing them': Review of *Zodiac* (*The Observer*, 20 May 2007)

Gillette, Paul J., *Play Misty for Me* (Star, 1972)

Giré, Jean- François, *Il Était une Fois… Le Western Européen* (Dreamland, 2002)

Goodenough, Simon, *War Maps: Great Land, Sea and Air Battles of World War II* (Macdonald & Co, 1982)

Graysmith, Robert, *Zodiac* (St Martin's, 1992)

Guérif, François, *Clint Eastwood: From Rawhide to Pale Rider* (Roger Houghton Ltd, 1986)

Guttmacher, Peter, *Legendary Westerns* (Metrobooks, 1995)

Hackin, Dennis E. and Neal Dobrofsky, *Bronco Billy* (Star, 1980)

Hardy, Phil (ed.), *The Aurum Film Encyclopedia – Gangsters* (Aurum, 1998)

────── *The Aurum Encyclopedia – Science Fiction Movies* (Aurum, 1984)

────── *The Aurum Film Encyclopedia – The Western* (Aurum, 1983)

Hart, John Mason, *Revolutionary Mexico* (University of California Press, 1997)

Hartman, Dane, *Dirty Harry No. 1: Duel for Cannons* (New English Library, 1982)

Hirschhorn, Clive, *The Warner Bros. Story* (Octopus, 1983)

Horan, James D. and Paul Sann, *Pictorial History of the Wild West* (Spring, 1954)

Hughes, Howard, *Crime Wave: The Filmgoers' Guide to the Great Crime Movies* (I.B.Tauris, 2006)

────── *Once Upon a Time in the Italian West: The Filmgoers' Guide to Spaghetti Westerns* (I.B.Tauris, 2004)

────── *Stagecoach to Tombstone: The Filmgoers' Guide to the Great Westerns* (I.B.Tauris, 2008)

Hurwood, Bernhardt J., *Burt Reynolds* (Quick Fox, 1979)

Jewell, Richard B. and Vernon Harbin, *The RKO Story* (Octopus, 1982)

Johnstone, Iain, *The Man with No Name* (Plexus, 1981)

Josephy Jr., Alvin M., *The Civil War in the American West* (Random House, 1993)

Kaminsky, Stuart M., *Don Siegel: Director* (Curtis, 1974)

Katz, Ephraim, *The Macmillan International Film Encyclopedia* (HarperCollins, 1998)

Kinnard, Roy, *The Blue and the Gray on the Silver Screen* (Birch Lane, 1996)

Kronsberg, Jeremy Joe, *Every Which Way But Loose* (Star, 1980)

Lackman, Ron, *The Encyclopedia of 20th Century American Television (Post World War II to 2000)*, (Checkmark Books, 2003)

Lloyd, Ann (ed.), *Good Guys and Bad Guys* (Orbis, 1982)

────── *Movies of the Seventies* (Orbis, 1984)

────── *Movies of the Sixties* (Orbis, 1983)

Lloyd, Ann and Graham Fuller, *The Illustrated Who's Who of the Cinema* (Orbis, 1983)

Love, Damien, *Way of the Gun* (Uncut Magazine, Take 53, October 2001)

Luck, Steve (ed.), *Philip's Compact Encyclopedia* (Chancellor, 1999)

MacDonald, John, *Great Battles of the Civil War* (Grange Books, 1995)

MacLean, Alistair, *Where Eagles Dare* (Fontana Books, 1969)

Macnab, Geoffrey, *Key Moments in Cinema* (Hamlyn, 2001)

Madsen, Alex, *John Huston A Biography* (Robson Books Ltd, 1979)

Maltin, Leonard, *2001 Movie and Video Guide* (Dutton/Signet, 2001)

Masheter, Philip, *Broadsword Calling Danny Boy – Where Doubles Dare: The Making of Where Eagles Dare* (Volume Two, Issue Two, 14 March 1995)

McCabe, Bob, *Clint Eastwood 'Quote Unquote'* (Parragon, 1996)

McClure, Arthur F. and Ken D. Jones, *Western Films: Heroes, Heavies and Sagebrush of the 'B' Genre* (Barnes, 1972)

McGilligan, Patrick, *Clint Eastwood – The Life and Legend* (HarperCollins, 1999)

Medved, Harry and Michael, *The Fifty Worst Films of All Time (And how they got that way)* (Angus & Robertson, 1978)

Millard, Joe, *Blood for a Dirty Dollar* (Star, 1974), *A Coffin Full of Dollars* (Star, 1972), *The Devil's Dollar Sign* (Star, 1973), *For a Few Dollars More* (Star, 1968), *The Good, the Bad and the Ugly* (Star, 1968), *The Million-Dollar Bloodhunt* (Star, 1974)

Miller, David (ed.), *The Illustrated Directory of Uniforms, Weapons and Equipment of the Civil War* (Salamander Books, 2001)

Morgan, Wesley, *The Enforcer* (Star, 1978)

Mulherin, Jennifer, *Jazz Greats 11: Charlie Parker* (Marshall Cavendish, 1996)

———— *Jazz Greats 28: Dizzy Gillespie – Early Years* (Marshall Cavendish, 1997)

———— *Jazz Greats 34: Jazz City – Kansas City* (Marshall Cavendish, 1997) Series of magazines, each with a free CD

Müller, Jürgen (ed.), *Best Movies of the 90s* (Taschen, 2005)

———— *Movies of the 60s* (Taschen, 2004)

Naughton, John, *Movies* (Simon & Schuster, 1998)

Newman, Kim, *Wild West Movies: How the West was Found, Won, Lost, Lied About, Filmed and Forgotten* (Bloomsbury, 1990)

Nourmand, Tony and Graham Marsh, (eds) *Film Posters of the 60s: The Essential Movies of the Decade* (Aurum, 1997)

O'Brien, Daniel, *Clint Eastwood – Film-Maker* (Batsford, 1996)

O'Neal, Bill, *The Pimlico Encyclopedia of Western Gunfighters* (Pimlico, 1998)

Parkinson, Michael and Clyde Jeavons, *A Pictorial History of Westerns* (Hamlyn, 1983)

Philbin, Tom, *The Rookie* (Warner Books, 1991)

Richie, Donald, *The Films of Akira Kurosawa* (University of California Press, 1965)

Rock, Phillip, *Dirty Harry* (Star, 1977)

Rosa, Joseph G., *Age of the Gunfighter* (Oklahoma Press, 1995)

Sarf, Wayne Michael, *God Bless You, Buffalo Bill: A Layman's Guide to History and the Western Film* (Cornwall, 1983)

Scheuer, Steven H. (ed.), *Movies on TV* (Bantam Books, 1977)

Schickel, Richard, *Clint Eastwood* (Arrow, 1997)

Shadwick, Keith, *Jazz: Legends in Style* (Eagle Books, 2001)

Shepherd, Donald and Robert Slatzer with Dave Grayson, *Duke: The Life and Times of John Wayne* (Time Warner, 2003)

Siegel, Don, *A Siegel Film* (Foreword by Clint Eastwood) (Faber and Faber, 1993)

Sinyard, Neil, *Clint Eastwood* (Bison, 1995)

Stinson, Joseph C., *Heartbreak Ridge* (Arrow Books, 1986)

Tchernia, Pierre, *80 Grands Succés Du Western* (Casterman, 1989)

Thomas, Craig, *Firefox* (Sphere Books Ltd, 1978)

Thomson, Douglas, *Clint Eastwood: Billion Dollar Man* (John Blake, 2005)

———— *Clint Eastwood: Sexual Cowboy* (Warner Books, 1993)

Valley, Mel, *Magnum Force* (Star, 1978)

Verdone, Luca (ed.): *Per Un Pugno Di Dollari* (Italian Script) (Cappelli, 1979)

Waller, Robert James, *The Bridges of Madison County* (Arrow Books, 1997)

Weldon, Michael J., *The Psychotronic Video Guide* (St Martin's Griffin, 1996)

Whiting, Charles, *'44: In Combat on the Western Front from Normandy to the Ardennes* (Century Publishing, 1984)

Whitman, Mark, *Clint Eastwood* (LSP, 1982)

Whitney, Steven, *Charles Bronson – Superstar* (Dell, 1975)

Wilkinson, Frederick, *Handguns: A Collector's Guide to Pistols and Revolvers from 1850 to the Present* (Apple, 1993)

Williams, Major George F., *The Memorial War Book: As Drawn from Historical Records and Personal Narratives of the Men Who Served in the Great Struggle* (Arno, 1979)

Witcombe, Rick Trader, *Savage Cinema* (Lorrimer, 1975)

Zmijewsky, Boris and Lee Pfeiffer, *The Films of Clint Eastwood* (Citadel, 1993)

FURTHER SOURCES

DOCUMENTARIES

Clint Eastwood – The Man from Malpaso, The Making of Play Misty for Me, Eastwood… A Star, All on Accounta Pullin' a Trigger (*Unforgiven* documentary), *Eastwood & Co: Making Unforgiven* (narrated by Hal Holbrook), *Mystic River: From Page to Screen, The Producer's Round 15* (*Million Dollar Baby* documentary), *Born to Fight* (Boxing training documentary for *Million Dollar Baby*), *James Lipton Takes on Three* (Lipton interviews Eastwood, Freeman and Swank), *Eastwood on Eastwood* (narrated by John Cusack and based on *Clint Eastwood: A Biography* by Richard Schickel), *Arena – Clint Eastwood* (Two-part BBC documentary), *Viva Leone!, The Spaghetti West, The Hero Cop: Yesterday and Today* (The Making of *Magnum Force*)

WEBSITES

The Internet Movie Database (www.imdb.com), the official British Board of Film Classification site (www.bbfc.co.uk), Amazon UK (www.amazon.co.uk) and the Motion Picture Association of America (www.mpaa.org)

INDEX

Film titles in bold type denote a section devoted to the film; page numbers in bold denote an illustration. TV = TV series; doc. = documentary.

10 128
12 Angry Men 18

Absolute Power 147, 151, 153, 165, 178–180, 187, 212, 230
Adams, Bryan 130, 228
Adderley, Julian 'Cannonball' 104, 218
Adios Sabata 22
Adler, Steven 76
African Queen, The 143, 144, 146
Agar, John xix, xx
Age-Scarpelli 12
Agony and the Ecstasy, The 89
Alessandroni, Alessandro 7
Alexander, Dick 142
Alexander, Jane 72, 74, 225
All the President's Men 178
Almeida, Laurindo 40
Almost a Woman 185
Amazing Stories (TV) episode: *Vanessa in the Garden* 66
Ambush at Cimarron Pass xxii–xxiv, **xxiii**, xxv, 215
Anders, Luana xxix
Anderson, Gordon 32, 119
Andrews, Julie 74, 92
Anthony, Tony 7
Any Which Way You Can xvi, 125–128, **126**, 196, 198, 212, 233
Apocalypse Now 200
Apollo 13 153
Arachnophobia 184
Arlen, Harold 74
Armstrong, Alun 143, 228
Arness, James xxi
Arnold, Jack xix–xx, 215
Asman, Bub 207
A-Team, The (TV) 202
Autumn Child (see – *Reflection of Fear*)
Away all Boats xx, 215

Babcock, Barbara 150, 231
Bacall, Lauren 144
Bach, Catherine 96, 167, 220
Bacon, Irving xxii
Bacon, Kevin 152–153, 232
Bad Company 167
Bad Day at Black Rock 25
Baldacci, David 168

Balsam, Martin xxvii
Bandolero! 15
Barnes, Walter 117, 122, 219, 222, 223
Barron, Baynes xxii
Barton, Dee 28, 37, 104, 105
Barton, James 94
Baruchel, Jay 156, 233
Baseheart, Richard xxix
Battyn, Skip 48, 217
Beach, Adam 205, 233
Beatles, The 3
Begley, Ed xxx, 16, 18, 216
Beguiled, The xiii, xvi, xvii, 27, 50, 68, 95–101, **97**, **99**, 106, 185, **197**, 206, 211, 212, **213**, 218
Bell, Jaime 205, 233
Benjamin, Paul 175, 222, 228
Benjamin, Richard 72, 225
Berendt, John 147–148, 237
Bergman, Alan 107
Bergman, Marilyn 107
Beronsini, Bobby 118, 128
Bible, The 89
Bierce, Ambrose 99
Big Country, The 3
Big Silence, The 26, 35
Big Valley, The (TV) xxxi
Billy Elliot 205
Bird xvi, 129, 135, 136, 138–143, **140**, 214, 227
Black Scorpion, The 67
Blazing Saddles 74
Blood Work xvi, 152, 154, 165, 183–187, 232
Bloom, Claire 96
Bloom, Verna 28, 136–137, 219, 224
Blossom, Roberts 175, 222
Blues Brothers, The 117
Blues, The (TV) 142
Bob Roberts 153
Boetticher, Budd 21–22
Bogart, Humphrey 73, 144
Bolognini, Mauro 89
Bonanza (TV) xxxi
Bonnie and Clyde 85, 166, 168
Bookwalter, DeVeren 59, 68, 221
Boone, Richard xxi
Bottoms, Sam 32, 121–122, 221, 223
Boy's Don't Cry 157
Boys from the Black Stuff (TV) 181
Boysen, Martin 172

Bradford, Jesse 203, 205, 233
Bradley, James 203, 205, 233
Bradley, John 'Doc' 203, 205, 233,
Brady, Mathew 98
Brady, Scott xxii–xxiv, **xxiii**
Braga, Sonia 78, 228
Brando, Marlon xiii, 172
Breakfast at Tiffany's 3
Breezy xvi, 53, 57, 105–108, 136, 166, 219
Brega, Mario 12, 215, 216
Brennan, Walter xxvi
Brent, Eve 48, 217
Brickman, Paul 181
Bridges of Madison County, The xiii, xvi,
    108–113, **110**, 147, 149, 157, 178, 212, 214,
    230
Bridges, James 144
Bridges, Jeff 165–166, **169**, 170, 220
Bridges, Lloyd 166
Bridges, Penny Bae 181, 231
Brinegar, Paul xxvi, **xxviii**, xxx, 4, 219
Bring it On 205
Bronco Billy 8, 121–125, 129, 136, 137, 174,
    214, 223
Bronson, Charles xxxi, 3, 8, 16, 61, 69
Broyles Jnr., William 203
Bruce, J. Campbell 175
Buchanan, Edgar xxv
Buckskin 36
Bujold, Genevieve 70, 225
Bull Durham 153
Bullit 51, 52, 76
Bumstead, Henry 28, 39, 205
Burrus, Tim 59, 221
Burton, Richard 191, 193, 217
Burton, Willie D. 142
Butch Cassidy and the Sundance Kid 166,
    178
Butler, Michael 35, 63
Byrd, Emry 142

Caan, James 50
Cagney and Lacey (TV) 59
Cagney, James 45, 72, 73, 182
Cahn, Sammy 202
Calhoun, Rory 3
Calvo, Pepe 5, 215
Camille 138
Campbell, Glen 127–128, 223
Canby, Vincent 49, 178
Cannonball Adderley Quintet, The 104,
    218
Cannonball Run, The 117, 128
Cannonball Run II 120, 128
Cara, Irene 72, 74–75, 225

Carabatsos, James 200, 202
Cardiff, Jack 144
Carfagno, Edward 137, 141
Carley, Christopher 211, 235
Carlile, Clancy 35, 135, 137
Carlin, John 212
Carlito's Way 153
Carmel, Roger C. 106, 219
Carmichael, Hoagy 149
Carrey, Jim 76, 130, 226, 228
Carroll, Leo G. xx
Carter, Forrest 31, 33, 35
Cartwright, Alan 122
Cash, Johnny 84
Casino Royale 161
Cassidy, Jack 172, 202
Casualties of War 83, 206
Cattle Empire xxvi
Cavanaugh, Michael 59, 127, 221, 223
Chan, Jackie 128
Chandler, Jeff xx
Chandler, John Davis 34, 66, 221
Changeling 209–210, 234
Channing, Carol xxi–xxii
Chaplin, Charlie 209
Charles, Ray 125
Charlie Varrick 48
Charlie's Angels (TV) 48
Cheap Detective, The 74
Chernus, Sonia 31
Cheyenne (TV) xxvi, xxxi
Chinatown 146
Chuma, Boy Mathias 143–144, 228
Cimino, Michael 53, 165–166, 168, 170, 220
City Heat 36, 72–75, **73**, 131, 139, 202, 225
Clark, Ben 172
Clark, Matt 32, 136, 218, 221, 224
Clark, Susan 45, 48, 216
Clarke, Warren 198, 223
Clarkson, Patricia 75–76, 226
Cleare, John 172
Clift, Montgomery xxvi
Cobb, Lee J. 45, 48, 216
Coburn, James 3
Code of Silence 69
Colley, Kenneth 198, 224
Colter, Mike 156, 223
Comanche Station 21
Connelly, Michael 152, 183–184, 186
Conti , Devon 209, 234
Convoy 117
Coogan's Bluff xvi, 21, 22, 26, 45–49, **47**,
    63, 83, 89, 101, 127, 191, 216
Cooper, Gary 3, 19, 27, 193
Coote, Robert xxix

Copeland, Jodie xxii–xxiv, 215
Corday, Mara xx, 67, 130, 221, 224, 228
Corley, Annie 108, 110, 230
Corman, Roger 102
Costner, Kevin 84–85, 229
Cox, Joel 42, 158, 205
Crash 161, 205
Creature from the Black Lagoon xix
Crist, Judith 30, 65, 99, 196
Crofford, Cliff 120, 127
Cromwell, James 130, 150, 228, 231
Crothers, Scatman 121, 223
Cruel Intentions 205
Cujo 77
Cullinan, Thomas xvii, 95, **97**
Cullum, Jaime 211
Culpepper Cattle Company, The 167
Curley, Jim 80, 229
Currie, Michael 76, 223–224, 226
Curtis, Billy 27, 219
Cusack, John 147–148, 230

D'Angelo, Beverly 118, 222
Dalton, Abby xxv
Daly, Tyne 58–59, 221
Daniels, Jeff 184, 232
Dano, Royal 32, 221
Das Boot 79
David, Thayer 171, 220
Davidson, Diana 51, 219
Davis Jnr, Sammy 128
Davis, Judy 178, 230
Davis, Miles 140
Day of the Jackal, The 81, 82
De Haven, Penny 124
De Jesus, Wanda 183, 185–186, 232
De Laurentiis, Dino 89, 216
De Niro, Robert 170
De Sica, Vittorio 19, 89, 216
Dead Man Walking 153
Dead Pool, The 75–78, 129, 138, 226
Dean, James xiii, xxvii, 49
Dean, Margia xxii, **xxiii**, xxiv
Death Valley Days (TV) xxv
Death Wish 35, 61, 68
Deer Hunter, The 170
Dehart, Wayne 84, 230
Deliverance 167
Delon, Alain 171
Dern, Bruce 18, 216
Dern, Laura 84–85, 229
Devane, William 150, 231
Deveau, Chablis 147–148, 230
Dexter, Alan 94, 217
Diddley, Bo 184

Dillinger 165
Dillman, Bradford 58–59, 66, 221, 224
Dion, Celine 130
Dirty Dozen, The 191, 196
Dirty Harry xiii, xvi, 25, 32, 45, 49–53, **50,**
    54, 55, 56, 57, 58, 59, 60, 62, 64, 66, 68, 69,
    70, 74, 75, 76, 77, 78, 79, 81, 89, 105, 123,
    127, 131, 136, 172, 176, 185, 202, 209, 212,
    214, 218
Dobrofsky, Neal 122
Domino, Fats 127–128, 223
Donahue, Troy xxvii
Donati, Sergio 8, 12
Donner, Robert xxix, 219
Donovan, Jeffrey 209–210, 234
Dorff, Steve 120, 124, 128, 130, 137
Doyle, David 48, 217
Drake, Paul 66, 68, 224
Dresner, Hal 173
Dufour, Val xxvii
Dukes of Hazzard, The (TV) 117,
    167
Dumb and Dumber 184
Durrill, John 128
Duryea, Dan xxx
Dusay, Marj 106, 219
Duvall, Robert 25–27, 219
Dykstra, John 198
Dysart, Richard 35–36, 226
Dzundza, George 143–144, 228

Earle 106, 220
Eastwood (nee Ruiz), Dina 112, 131–132,
    157, 182, 185,
Eastwood, Alison 70–71, 123, 148, 180, 223,
    225, 230
Eastwood, Clinton Snr xix
Eastwood, Jeanne xix
Eastwood, Kimber 180, 230
Eastwood, Kyle 106, 110, 123, 135–136, 160,
    206, 212, 220, 221, 223, 224, 230
Eastwood, Margaret 'Maggie' (nee
    Johnson) xix, xxiv, 65, 201
Eastwood, Morgan Colette 157, 210, 233,
    234
Eastwood, Ruth xix, 42
Easy Rider 168
Ebert, Roger 112
Edwards, Blake 72
Egger, Josef 5, 215
Eiger Sanction, The 165, 167, 170–174, **173,**
    187, 200, 220
El Condor 28
El Dorado 26
El Gringhero 15

El Maladetto Gringo 15
Ellroy, James 183
Enforcer, The 58–62, **60**, 66, 75, 78, 117, 127, 175, 176, **177**, 185, 186, 211, 221
Enter the Dragon 76
Escapade in Japan xxii, 215
Escape from Alcatraz 8, 32, 121, 139, 165, 174–178, **176**, **177**, 222
Escrow, John 129
Evening Like the Others, An (episode in *The Witches*) 89, 91, 216
Everly, Phil 120, 222
Every Which Way But Loose 64, 117–121, **118**, 122, 124, 125, 126, 127, 128, 174, 212, 222
Exorcist, The 76, 121

Fabregas, Manolo 21, 217
Faddis, Jon 64
Fahey, Jeff 143–144, 228
Fall Guy, The (TV) 117
Fame 74
Feore , Colm 210, 234
Ferdin, Pamela 95–96, 218
Field, Betty 48
Fielding, Jerry 59, 64, 142, 176
Figueroa, Gabriel 22
Fincher, David 52
Fink, Harry Julian 49–50
Fink, Rita 49–50
Firefox 135, 151, 196–200, **199**, 223
First Travelling Saleslady, The xxi–xxii, 123, 215
Fischer, Bruce M. 32, 175, 221, 222, 225
Fishburne, Laurence 152–153, 232
Fisher, Frances 38–39, 130, 182, 228, 229, 231
Fisher-Eastwood, Francesca 182, 231
Fistful of Dollars, A xiv, xvi, xxv, xxix, 3–8, 9, 10, 26, 28, 40, 78, 89, 91, 127, 206, 211, 215
Fitzgerald, F. Scott 142
Flack, Roberta 69, 104–105, 107
Flags of Our Fathers 202–207, **204**, 210, 233
Flatliners 153
Fleming, Eric xxvi, **xxviii**, xxx
Flint, Shelby 107
Flynn, Errol 172
Fonda, Henry 3, 8, 19, 117
Fonda, Peter 128
Footloose 153
For a Few Dollars More xiii, xiv, 3, **4**, 8–10, **11**, 12, 19, 28, 89, **90**, 131, 212, 215
Ford, John 18, 34, 111, 122, 138, 172
Forester, C.S. 144

Forman, Bruce 160
Francis in the Navy xix, 215
Frasier (TV) 81
Frazetta, Frank 65
Freeman, Leonard 16, 216
Freeman, Morgan 38–39, 156–158, **157**, 160, 212, 228, 233
French Connection, The 28
French, Philip 207
Fresholtz, Les 142
Friday the 13th 76
Frontiere, Dominic 19

Gagnon, Rene 203, 205, 233
Garcia, Stella 25, 219
Gardner, Alexander 98
Garner, Erroll 101, 104
Garner, James xxv, xxxi, 150, 231
Garrett, Snuff 120, 124, 128, 137
Gauntlet, The xvi, xx, 46, 62–65, **64**, 66, 67, 78, 117, 119, 127, 129, 180, 221
Gazzo, Michael V. 68, 225
George, Chief Dan 32, 221
Gerstle, Frank xxii, xxiv
Giant Claw, The 67
Gibson, Don 84
Gilkyson, Terry xxi
Gillette, Paul J. 102
Giuffre, Aldo 12, 216
Glenn, Scott 178, 180, 230
Godfather, The 154, 155, 184
Godfather Part II, The 68, 170
Going Ape! 125
Gold Diggers of 1933 72
Gold, Bill 52, 57
Goldberg, Mel 16
Goldman, William 178, 180
Goldsmith, Clio 74
Golonka, Arlene 18
Gone With the Wind 18, 149
Good, the Bad & the Ugly, The xiii, xiv, xvi, 3, 10–16, **13**, 32, 34, 89, 91, 98, 119, 131, 153, 174, 212, 216
Goodwin, Michael 76, 226
Goodwin, Ron 193
Gordon, Rita 94
Gordon, Ruth 118, 120, 125, 222, 223
Gran Torino 160, 210–212, 214, 235
Grapes of Wrath, The 138
Graysmith, Robert 52
Great Escape, The 193
Green Berets 201
Green, Jack N. 39, 84, 110, 142, 146, 153, 185
Griffin, Jennifer 84

Griffith, Gattlin 209, 234
Grimaldi, Alberto 12
Gross, Larry 181
Guardino, Harry 50, 59, 125, 127, 218, 221, 223
Guarino, Ann 104
Guérif, François 138
Guiry, Thomas 152, 232
Gun Law (TV – see *Gunsmoke*)
Gunfight at the O.K. Corral 25
Guns 'n' Roses 76, 149, 227
Gunsmoke (TV) xxvi, xxxi

Hackin, Denis E. 122, 200
Hackman, Gene 38–39, 42, 77, 178–179, 228, 230
Haggard, Merle 124, 223
Haggis, Paul 155–156, 158, 160, 161, 203, 205
Hall, Irma P. 148, 230
Halloween 76
Hamilton, Lisa Gay 181, 231
Hancock, John Lee 84, 147
Hang 'Em High 16–21, **17, 20**, 27, 45, 48, 53, 64, 78, 89, 138, 170, 174, 191, 216
Hankin, Larry 175, 222
Harden, Marcia Gay 150, 152–153, 155, 231, 232
Hardin, Melora 178, 230
Harner, Jason Butler 210, 234
Harold and Maude 118
Harris, Ed 179, 230
Harris, Jo Ann 68, 95–96, **99**, 106, 218
Harris, Richard 38–39, 228
Harrison, Richard 3
Hart, William S. 27–28
Hartman, Dane 62
Hartman, Elizabeth 95–96, 100, 218
Hartman, Johnny 112
Haston, Dougal 172
Have Gun Will Travel (TV) xxxi
Hawks, Howard xxvi, 111
Hawkshaw, Alan 37
Hawthorne, Nigel 198, 224
Haynie, Jim 109, 222, 230
Haysbert, Dennis 178, 230
Hayward, Susan 65
Hearst, Patty 59
Heart is a Lonely Hunter, The 32
Heartbreak Ridge 75, 200–202, 205, 211, 226
Heaven's Gate 170
Hedaya, Dan 70, 225
Heims, Jo 102, 105, 108
Helgeland, Brian 152, 183

Hell Bent for Glory (see *Lafayette Escadrille*)
Hell's Hinges 27, 28, 138
Hemingway, Margaux 68
Hemingway, Mariel 68
Hepburn, Katherine 144, 146
Her, Ahney 211, 235
Hern, Pepe 26, 219
Hickman, Gail Morgan 58
Hidden Fortress, The 206
High Chaparral, The (TV) xxx, xxxi
High Noon xxi, xxvi, 19, 27, 166, 182
High Plains Drifter 27–31, **29**, 35, 37, 39, 41, 53, 56, 96, 105, 106, 108, 131, 137, 138, 167, 186, 219
Highway Patrol (TV) xxv
Hill, Bernard 181, 231
Hill, Marianna 28, 96, 219
Hill, William 211, 235
Hingle, Pat 16, 18, 48, 64, 66, 216, 221, 224
Hipp, Paul 148, 230
Holbrook, Hal 42, 53, 56, 66, 220
Holden, Scott 106, 220
Holden, William 105–107, 219
Holder, Mitch 151
Hollier, Jill 202
Honkytonk Man 35, 66, 135–138, **139**, 185, 211, 224
Hoover, Mike 172
Hopkins, Linda 136, 224
Hopper, Deborah 205
Hopper, Dennis 18, 216
Horse Feathers 72
Hotchkis, Joan 106, 219
Hotel Satan 75, 76
Hour of the Gun 25
How the West Was Won 12
Hudson, Rock xx
Huston, Anjelica 109, 132, 185
Huston, John xvi, 143–147
Hutton, Brian G. 191, 194, 217, 218

I Know What You Did Last Summer 205
I Spit on Your Grave 68
Ibbetson, Arthur 193
In the Line of Fire 79–83, **82**, 84, 85, 139, 160, 179, 180, 185, 186, 210, 212, 229
Indiana Jones and the Last Crusade 130
Ipcress File, The 171
Ireland, John xxvii, xxix
Isaak, Chris 84
It's Alive III 77
Ito, Bernard 52

James Rivers Band, The 110, 230
James, Anthony 27, 39, 219, 229

Jarreau, Al 74
Jenson, Roy 64, 119, 127, 128, 217, 220, 222, 223, 224
Jerk, The 129
JFK 153
Joe Kidd 25–27, 48, 53, 174, 219
Johannson, David 211
Johnny Otis Show, The 104, 218
Johnson, Arch xxix
Johnson, Ben 16, 18, 216
Johnson, Melodie 48, 217
Johnson, Tommy 40
Johnstone, Iain 131, 138
Jolie, Angelina 209–210, 234
Jolly, Pete 75
Jones, Freddie 196, 223
Jones, Jo 141
Jones, L.Q. xxx, 18, 216
Jones, Tommy Lee 150, 231
Julia, Raul 78, 228

Kael, Pauline 38, 53, 57, 59, 77, 142
Kahn, Madeline 72, 74, 225, 227
Kamp, Irene 96
Kaufman, Ken 149
Kaufman, Phil 31–32
Kaufman, Stanley 180
Keams, Geraldine 31–32, 221
Keaton, Buster 209
Kelly, Jack xxv
Kelly, Michael 210, 234
Kelly's Heroes 32, 64, 89, 95, 131, 150, 194–196, **195, 197**, 211, 218
Kenin, Alexa 135–136, 224
Kennedy Martin, Troy 194
Kennedy, Burt 144
Kennedy, George 165, 167, 171, 220
Kenton, Stan 104, 142
Kentucky Fried Movie, The 76
Kibbee, Roland 45
Kiel, Richard 37, 226
Kim, Evan C. 75–76, 226
Kirshner, Irvin 49
Klar, Gary 129, 227
Klausner, Howard 149
Klavan, Andrew 180
Knots Landing (TV) 150
Knowles, David 172
Knox, Mickey 12
Koch, Marianne 5, 215
Koehler, Ted 74
Koslo, Paul 25, 219
Krall, Diana 183
Kramer vs. Kramer 109

Kronsberg, Jeremy Joe 117–118, 120, 125, 222
Krup, Mara **90**, 215
Kue, Choua 211, 235
Kuribayashi, Tadamichi 203–204, 206, 234
Kurosawa, Akira 3–4, 206

L.A. Confidential 148, 183, 209
Lacey, Ronald 198, 223
Ladd, Alan 3, 49
Lady Godiva of Coventry (see *Lady Godiva*)
Lady Godiva xix–xx, 215
Lafayette Escadrille xxii, 215
LaGravenese, Richard 109
Laine, Frankie xxvi
Laird, Jack 45
Lake, Veronica 68
Lang, Jennings 110
lang, k. d. 149
Lang, Mike 75
Larch, John 50, 101, 218
Last of the Blue Devils, The (doc.) 142
Last Picture Show, The 138, 167
Last Samurai, The 203
Laura 105
Law, Jude 147–148, 230
Lawman (TV) xxxi
Lawrence of Arabia 9
Laws, Eloise 74
Lawson, Linda xxv
Leary, Denis 181, 231
Lee, Ruta xxix
Lee, Spike 207
Legrand, Michel 107
Lehane, Dennis 152, 154
Leno, Jay 151, 231
Lenz, Kay 105–108, 219
Leonard, Elmore 26
Leone, Sergio 3–16, 18, 21, 22, 24–25, 27, 30–32, 34, 41, 74, 98, 154, 194, 215, 216
Lerner, Alan Jay 91–92, 217
Lesser, Len 32, 221, 218
Lethal Weapon 78, 130
Lethal Weapon 3 81
Letters from Iwo Jima xvi, 202–207, 214, 234
Lewis, Geoffrey 27, 117–118, 121, 125, 130, 148, 165, 167, 219–220, 222–223, 227, 230
Life and Legend of Wyatt Earp, The (TV) xxvi, xxxi
Lifford, Tina 184–185, 232
Lindfors, Viveca xxix
Linney, Laura 152–153, 179–180, 230, 232
Lipstick 68

List of Adrian Messenger, The 144
Lo Bianco, Tony 72, 74, 225
Locke, Sondra 31, 32, 62–66, **64**, 68, 74, 76, 100, 106, 117–122, 125, 129–130, 136, 144, 221, 222, 223, 224
Loewe, Frederick 91
Logan, Joshua 92, 217
London, Dirk xxii, xxiv
Losey, Joseph 100
Lowther, TJ 84, 229
Lubin, Arthur xix, xxi, xxii, xxv, 215
Lucas, George 151, 198
Lucero, Mason 184, 232
Lynch, John Carroll 211, 235

M*A*S*H 196
Mabukane, David 144
Mack, Tom 95
Mackenna's Gold 16
Mackie, Anthony 157, 223
MacLaine, Shirley xxi, 21–24, **23**, 128, 217
MacLean, Alistair 191, 193
Madigan 48
Magnificent Seven, The 3, 12, 25
Magnifico Straniero, Il 15
Magnum Force xiv, xvi, 42, 46, 53–58, **55**, 59, 66, 77, 96, 108, 165, 166, 170, 176, 220
Maguire, Jeff 79
Mahoney, John 81, 229
Maier, John xxii
Mailer, Norman 138
Major Dundee 21
Maledon, George 18
Malkovich, John 81, 210, 229, 234
Maltz, Albert 21, 24, 96
Mamas and the Papas, The 196
Man Called Horse, A 39
Man from Shiloh, The (TV – see *The Virginian*)
Mancini, Henry 149
Mandela, Nelson 212
Manes, Fritz 36, 63, 70, 117, 201, 221, 222, 224, 225, 226
Mangano, Silvana 89, 216
Manis **118**, 118–119, 127, 222
Mantle, Clive 144, 228
Marshall, E.G. 178, 230
Martin, Dean 128
Martin, Steve 129
Martinez, Joaquin 26, 219
Marvin, Lee 8, 91–94, **93**, 175, 217
Maslin, Janet 147
Mason, Marsha 74, 200, 201, 226
Matheson, Tim 56, 220

Maverick (TV) xxv–xxvi, xxxi, 150
Maverick episode: 'Duel at Sundown' xxv–xxvi
Mayer, Ken xxii
McCarthy, Todd 149
McCormack, Mary 181, 231
McCrea, Joel xxvi
McCubbin, Russ 28, 219, 224
McDermott, Dylan 80–81, 229
McEachin, James 118, 218, 222, 224
McGee, Howard 140
McGee, Vonetta 172, 220
McGill, Everett 200, 226
McGoohan, Patrick 174–175, 222
McGrath, Doug 32, 122, 221, 223, 226
McGraw, Charles 18, 216
McIntire, John 135, 136, 224
McKagan, Duff Rose 76
McKean, Mike 181
McKinney, Bill 31, 64, 119, 121–122, 127, 130, 167, 220, 221, 222, 223, 227
McPherson, Charles 142
McQueen, Steve xxxi, 49, 171
Mercer, Johnny 149
Mercer, Mae 50, 96, 218, 219
Merrick, John xxii
Midnight in the Garden of Good and Evil 135, 147–149, 180, 186, 230
Mifune, Toshiro 5
Mike Curb Congregation, The 196
Milius, John 50, 53, 165
Millard, Joe 15
Miller, Herman 45
Million Dollar Baby xiii, xvi, 109, 135, 155–161, **157**, **159**, 185, 202, 210, 211, 212, 214, 233
Mills, Donna 96, 101, 218
Milsap, Ronnie 124
Mission: Impossible (TV) 51
Mitchum, John 32, 50, 56, 59, 95, 217, 219, 220, 221
Mitchum, Robert 21, 29, 59
Monk, Thelonius 142
Montenegro, Hugo 15, 19
Monterey Jazz Festival: 40 Legendary Years (doc.) 142
Moonraker 37
Moore, Roger 128
Moore, Terry xxvii
Moreau, Jeanne 96
Morgan, Susan 172, 220
Moriarty, Michael 35–36, 226
Morricone, Ennio 7, 10, 14–15, 19, 21–22, 24, 28, 83, 91, 195, 206

Morris, Frank Lee 174–177, 187, 222
Morris, Jeff 64, 218, 221
Morsella, Fulvio 8
Moua, Doua 211, 235
Mulock, Al 12, 216
Murdock, James xxvi
Murphy, Audie 50
Murphy, Eddie 69
Murphy, Warren B. 173
Murray, Alan Robert 207
My Bloody Valentine 76
Mystic River xvi, 135, 152–155, 209, 212, 214, 232

Naked Runner, The 49
Narr, Boone 127
Navy Log (TV) xxv
Neeson, Liam 75–76, 226
Neithardt, Guy 172
Nelson, Ed xxix
Nelson, Willy 84
Never Say Goodbye xx, 215
Newman, Paul 49
Nicholson, Jack 42
Niehaus, Lennie 37, 40, 71, 74, 78, 84, 112, 141–142, 146, 149, 154, 160, 179, 183, 185, 201, 206, 211
Ninomiya, Kazunari 203, 234
Niven, Kip 56, 220
Nixon, President Richard 178–179
Norris, Chuck 69
North by Northwest 63
Norton, Alex 143, 228
*NSYNC 151

O'Connell, William 32, 95, 119, 127, 217, 219, 221, 222, 223
O'Connor, Carroll 194, 218
O'Connor, Donald xix
O'Hara, Maureen 96
Oates, Warren xxx
Oliansky, Joel 139
Olin, Lena 109
Olivier, Sir Laurence xiv
Once Upon a Time in America 16, 54, 83
Once Upon a Time in the West 16, 37
Operation Moon 89
Orrison, George 144, 222, 223, 224, 225, 226, 227, 228, 229, 230
Outlaw Josey Wales, The xiv, xvi, 14, 31–35, **33**, 39, 41, 58, 59, 66, 89, 98, 112, 119, 122, 136, 165, 186, 211, 212, 214, 221
Ox-Bow Incident, The 19, 138, 154

Pacino, Al 42, 153
Page, Geraldine 95–96, 218
Paget, Debra xxix
Paint Your Wagon 32, 59, 64, 91–95, **93**, **197**, 217
Palance, Jack 37, 127
Pale Rider 32, 35–38, 39, 75, 138, 186, 200, 202, 226
Parallax View, The 167
Parfrey, Woodrow 32, 50, 122, 219, 221, 223
Parker, Charlie 'Yardbird' 138–143, 227
Parker, Eleanor 96
Parker, Isaac Charles 18
Parks, Michael 35
Parton, Dolly 129–130
Pasolini, Pier Paolo 89
Pearson, Durk 75
Pecheur, Sierra 121, 223
Peck, Gregory 16
Peck, Lieutenant Colonel Fred 201
Peckinpah, Sam 18, 26, 117
Peeping Tom 77
Penn, Christopher 35–36, 226
Penn, Sean 152–155, 232
Penny, Sydney 36, 226
Pepper, Art 64, 142
Pepper, Barry 205, 233
Perfect World, A 83–85, 147, 229
Perkins, Bill 146
Perry, Felton 53, 56
Peters, Bernadette 129, 227
Petersen, Wolfgang 79, 82, 83, 179, 229
Pevney, Joseph xx, 215
Phantom of the Opera 46
Philbin, Tom 79, 239
Phillippe, Ryan 203, 205, 233
Pierce, Charles B. 66
Pink Cadillac 129–130, 143, 227
Pissarro, Camille 171
Pistilli, Luigi 12, 215, 216
Pit and the Pendulum 102
Pitt, Ingrid 191, 217
Play Misty for Me xiii, xvi, 8, 27, 49, 57, 96, 101–105, **103**, 107, 108, 127, 157, 212, 213, 214, 218
Player, The 153
Plaza, Fuensanta 130
Poe, Edgar Allen 85, 99, 101, 102, 103
Point Blank 45, 175
Poore, Vern 142
Popwell, Albert 48, 56, 58, 61, 66, 217, 219, 220, 221, 224
Porter, Cole 74
Post, Ted 16, **17**, 53, 55, 216, 220

Potaux-Razel, David 160
Powers, Ron 203
Practice, The (TV) 81
Prescott, Simon 15
Presnell, Harve 94, 217, 233
Previn, Andre 92
Price, Ray 136, 224
Prince 139
Prince, Billy 141, 227
Prince, William 62, 122, 221, 223
Prior, Richard 139
Prisoner, The (TV) 175
Profumo di Donna 42
Psycho 105
Public Enemy, The 45, 73

Quade, John 32, 119, 127, 219, 221, 222, 223

Rabbitt, Eddie 120
Rackin, Martin 22
Rains, Steve xxvi
Rape Squad 68
Raven, The 102
Rawhide (TV) xiv, xvii, xxvi–xxxi,
    xxviii, 4, 5, 6, 8, 15, 16, 18, 19, 26, 31, 32,
    35, 91, 117, 122, 138, 148
Rawhide episodes:
'Incident at Alabaster Plain' xxvii
'Incident of the Black Sheep' xxix, 4, 26
'Incident of the Day of the Dead'
    xxviii–xxix
'Incident of the Garden of Eden' xxviii,
    xxix
'Incident of the Prophesy' xxx
'Incident of the Reluctant Bridegroom' xxix
'Incident of the Running Man' xxix, 15
'Incident of the Tumbleweed Wagon' xxvii
'Piney' xxx–xxxi
'The Backshooter' 15
'The Enormous Fist' xxx
'The Race' xxx
Reader's Digest (TV) xxv
Reagan, Ronald 69, 83
Red River xxvi
Redford, Robert 178
Reed, Rex 30, 35, 38, 62, 94, 105, 121, 147,
    170, 178, 193
Reeves, Jacelyn 205
Reeves, Scott (aka Scott Eastwood) 205, 211,
    233, 235
Reflection of Fear 32
Reisner, Dean 28, 35, 45, 50, 58, 102
Repulsion 105
Return of Josey Wales, The 35

Revenge of the Creature xix, 215
Reynolds, Burt xxi, xxxi, 42, 69, 72, **73**, 74,
    117, 128, 225
Rich, Charlie 120, 222
Richards, Emil 146
Richards, Keith xxii
Richardson, Chan 139, 141–142, 227
Richman, Mark xxvii
Rickles, Don 194, 218
Ride Lonesome 21
Ride the High Country 26
Rifleman, The (TV) xxxi
Rigg, Diana 92
Rijker, Lucia 156, 158, 233
Rio Bravo 3, 26, 36
Riot in Cell Block 11 174
Rivers, James 110, 142, 230
Road House 79
Robbins, Marty 84, 136, 224
Robbins, Tim 152–153, 155, 232
Roberts, Bruce 74
Robinson, Andy 49–50, 218
Rock, Phillip 52
Rocky 120, 158
Rodman, Howard 45
Rodney, Red 139, 141–142, 227
Rodriguez, Paul 185, 232
Rogers, Ginger xxi, xxii
Rojo, Antonio Molino 12, 215, 216
Ronzio, Frank 175, 222
Rookie, The 78–79, 222, 228
Rose, W. Axl 76
Rosenthal, Joe 203, 233
Rossi, Franco 89
Rossum, Emmy 152, 232
Rough Cut 144
Round Midnight 142
Roundtree, Richard 72, 74, 225
Rubinek, Saul 39, 229
Ruddy, Albert S. 155, 157, 233
Russell, John 32, 35–36, 221, 224, 226
Russo, Rene 80–81, 229
Ryan, Mitchell 53, 56, 219, 220

S.O.B 72
Sager, Carole Bayer 183
Samouraï, Le 171
Sampson, Will 31–32, 221
Sands of Iwo Jima 191
Santoni, Rene 49, 218
Savalas, Telly 194, 218
Saxon, John 25–27, 219
Scent of a Woman 42
Schenk, Nick 211

Schickel, Richard 138, 148
Schiff, Stephen 181
Schifrin, Donna 52
Schifrin, Lalo 26, 45, 51–52, 57, 59, 69, 100, 195
Schurr, S.W. 58
Schwarzenegger, Arnold xiv, 63
Scott, Brenda xxx
Scott, Charles 172
Searchers, The 3, 34, 122
Seberg, Jean 91–94, **93**, 217
Serna, Pepe 79, 228
Shadow of Chikara, The 66
Shaft 28, 74
Shanan, Rocky xxvi
Shane 35, 36, 37, 38, 127
Shank, Bud 142
Shaw Judson, Sylvia 148
Shaw, Sandy 75
Shawshank Redemption, The 153, 158
Sheen, Charlie 78–79, 228
Shenandoah 32, 66, 98
Sherman, Dan xxv
Sherman, Sanford 125, 128
Shootist, The 211
Shore, Dinah 206
Shryack, Dennis 35, 63
Siegel, Don 21–22, 25, 45–50, 52, 54, 57, 62, 95–96, 99–102, 105, 121, 144, 174–177, 211, 216, 217, 218, 222
Silliphant, Sterling 58
Silva, Henry 3
Silvani, Al 120, 222
Silvestre, Armando 24, 217
Simi, Carlo 5, 9, 14, 215
Sinatra, Frank 49, 152
Skaggs, Jimmie F. 130, 227
Slade, Mark xxx
Slash 76
Slattery, Desmond xxii
Slattery, John 203, 233
Slezak, Victor 108, 110, 230
Smith, Earl E. 66
Smith, William 125, 127, 233
Smokey and the Bandit 117
Smokey and the Bandit II 120
Snodgress, Carrie 36, 226
Soble, Ron 28, 219
Sophie's Choice 109
Soul, David 56, 220
Southern Pacific 130
Space Cowboys 130, 135, 149–152, 153, 183, 212, 231
Spacey, Kevin 147–149, 230
Spall, Timothy 144, 228

Spencer: For Hire (TV) 56
Spiegel, Sam 144
Spiegel, Scott 79
Spielberg, Steven 66, 109
Spy Who Loved Me, The 37
St Jacques, Raymond xxvii
St John, Marco 70, 225
Stafford, Jim 128, 223
Stagecoach xiv
Stallone, Sylvester xiv, 63
Stanley, Frank 56, 106, 166
Stanton, Harry Dean xxx
Stanwyck, Barbara 65
Star in the Dust xx–xxi, 215
Star Wars 117, 198
Starsky and Hutch (TV) 56
Sterling, Tisha 45, 48, 216
Stern, Tom 153, 158, 185, 205, 209, 211
Stevens, Cat 167
Stevens, Inger 17–18, 216
Stevens, Michael 160, 206, 211, 212
Stevens, Sally 52
Stewart, James 3, 136
Sting, The 72
Stinson, Joseph 66, 200, 202
Stoker, J.W. 122
Straczynski, J. Michael 209
Stradlin, Izzy 76
Straight No Chaser (doc.) 142
Streep, Meryl 109–12, **110**, 157, 230
Streets of San Francisco (TV) 52
Streisand, Barbra 65
Stroud, Don 25–26, 45–46, 48, 216, 219
Sturges, John 25, 219
Sudden Impact xvi, 36, 65–69, **67**, 75, 76, 77, 185, 212, 224
Sugarfoot (TV) xxxi
Superman: The Movie 121
Surtees, Bruce 26, 34, 36, 51, 71, 100, 137, 178
Sutherland, Donald 150, 194, 196, 218, 231
Svenson, Bo 200, 226
Swank, Hilary 156–158, **157**, 160, 210, 233
SWAT (TV) 56
Swimfan 205
Szarabajka, Keith 84, 229

Tales of Wells Fargo (TV) xxxi
Tall T, The 21, 26
Tarantula xx, 48, 67, 78, 130, 215
Tavernier, Bertrand 142
Taylor, Dub 168, 220
Taylor, Elizabeth 21
Tenth Victim, The 89
Terror of Tiny Town, The 27

Terror, The 102
Tessari, Duccio 4
Texan, The (TV) xxxi
Texas Opera Company 128
Them! xx
Thibeau, Jack 174, 222, 223, 224
This is Spinal Tap 181
Thomas, Craig 196, 198
Thompkins, William 'Bill' xxx, 6, 215
Thomson, Anna 38–39, 139, 229
Thomson, Linda 183
*Three Burials of Melquiades Estrada,
    The* 205
Thunderbolt and Lightfoot 96, 139,
    165–170, **166**, **169**, 186, 187, 212, 220
Tidyman, Ernest 28
Tiegs, Cheryl 117
Tightrope 36, 69–72, 141, 185, 212, 225
Tillis, Mel 120, 128, 222
Time After Time 77
Tiomkin, Dimitri xxvi
Tonight with Jay Leno (TV) 151
Toole, F.X. 155–156, 159–160
Torn, Rip 72, 74, 225
Toro, Efrain 146
Traverse, Claude 96
Trevanian 170, 173
True Crime 151, 165, 180–183, 187, 231
True Grit 18, 34
Trueman, Paula 31–32, 95, 217, 221
Tuggle, Richard 70, 175, 225
Tully, Tom 45, 217
Tunis, Roxanne 18, 180, 216
Two Mules for Sister Sara xxi, 21–25, **23**,
    24, 26, 85, 194, 196, 217
Two-Lane Blacktop 168

Undefeated, The 21
Unforgiven xiii, xiv, xvi, 14, 38–42, **40**, 79,
    83, 153, 158, 160, 179, 180, 186, 211, 212,
    214, 228
Untouchables, The 76
Ure, Mary 191, 217
Urich, Robert 56, 220
Usual Suspects, The 148

Vadis, Dan 27, 64, 119, 121–122, 127, 219,
    222, 223
Valdes, David 70, 225
Valee, Rudy 74
Van Cleef, Lee xxx–xxxi, **4**, 8–10, 12, 15, 36,
    215, 216
Van Doren, Mamie xxi
Van Horn, Wayne 'Buddy' 22, 30, 36, 48, 78,
    128–129, 218, 219, 223, 226, 227

Van Peebles, Mario 202, 226
Vang, Bee 210, 211, 235
Vanishing Point 168
Vanzi, Luigi 7
Vaughn, William xxii
Vega$ (TV) 56
Venora, Diane 139, 142, 182, 227, 231
Venus, Brenda 172, 220
Vera Cruz 21
Vernon, John 31–32, 218, 221
Vertigo 105
Viertel, Peter 143–144
Vincenzoni, Luciano 8, 12
Virginian, The (TV) xxxi
Visconti, Luchino 89, 100
Volonte, Gian Maria 5, 8, 10, 215

Wagon Train (TV) xxv, xxxi, 136
Wagoner, Porter 136, 224
Wainwright, James 25, 219
Wake Up and Kill 89
Walcott, Gregory xxix, 25–26, 118, 167, 171,
    219, 220, 222
Walker, Dreama 211, 235
Walker, Scott 28, 219
Wallach, Eli 10, 12, 15–16, 32, 153, 216, 233
Waller, Robert James 108–109
Walsh, Dylan 185, 232
Walston, Ray 92, 94, 217
Walter, Jessica 101, **103**, 103–104, 125, 157,
    218
Wanted: Dead or Alive (TV) xxxi
Ward, Fred 174, 222
Warren, Charles Marquis xxvi
Warwick, Richard 144, 228
Washington, Dinah 112
Washington, Isaiah 181, 231
Washington, Ned xxvi
Watanabe, Ken 203, 234
Watson, David xxvii
Wayne, John xiv, xxvi, 18, 26, 30, 42, 49, 69,
    191, 201, 211
Weaver, Dennis 49
Webb Peoples, David 38
Welch, Raquel 117
Wellman, William xxii, 215
West Point (TV) xxv
Westerfield, James 18, 216
Weston, Bill 144
When a Man Sees Red 137
Where Eagles Dare xv, 21, 46, 91, 191–194,
    192, 196, 217
Where's Poppa? 118
Whitaker, Damon 139, 227
Whitaker, Forest 139–140, **140**, 142, 227

White Hunter Black Heart xvi, 130, 135, 143–147, **145**, 228
White, Pete 172
Whitford, Bradley 84, 229
Wild Bunch, The 92
Wilke, Robert xxix
Williams, Hank 130, 137, 196
Williams, Joe 74
Williams, Paul 167
Willis, Bruce 63
Wills, Bob 84, 224
Wills, Chill xix
Wilmington, Michael 147
Wilson, John 141, 227
Winnetou the Warrior 26
Winston, Archer 105
Witches, The 89–91, 216
Witherspoon, Reese 210
Wolff, Frank 7
Woods, James 182, 231
Wooley, Sheb xxvi, 32, 221

Woolvett, Jaimz 38–39, 229
Worden, Hank 122, 222, 223
Wright, Samuel E. 139, 227
Wright, Will xxix
Wyman, Karen 96

Yakin, Boaz 79
Yamashita, Iris 203
Yeats, W.B. 109, 159
Yojimbo 4, 5, 206
Yoshida, Tsuyuko 203
Yoshioka, Adele 56, 96, 220
Young Frankenstein 74
Young, Bill 78

Zane Gray Theatre (TV) xxxi
Zelniker, Michael 139, 227
Zodiac 52
Zodiac Killer, The 52
Zwerin, Charlotte 142